Everyman, I will go with thee,
and be thy guide

Pindar

THE ODES

AND SELECTED FRAGMENTS

Translated by
G. S. CONWAY AND
RICHARD STONEMAN
Edited by
RICHARD STONEMAN

EVERYMAN
J. M. DENT · LONDON
CHARLES E. TUTTLE
VERMONT

'Epinician Odes', translated by G. S. Conway, first
published in Everyman in 1972 in *The Odes*

Translation of 'Paeans', 'Dithyrambs', 'Partheneia' and
'Fragments' © Richard Stoneman 1997

Introduction and other critical material © J. M. Dent 1997

This edition first published in Everyman Paperbacks in 1997

J. M. Dent
Orion Publishing Group
Orion House, 5 Upper St Martin's Lane,
London WC2H 9EA
and
Charles E. Tuttle Co., Inc.
28 South Main Street,
Rutland, Vermont 05701, USA

Printed in Great Britain by
The Guernsey Press Co. Ltd, Guernsey, C. I.

British Library Cataloguing-in-Publication Data
is available upon request.

ISBN 0 460 87674 0

CONTENTS

NOTE ON THE AUTHOR AND EDITOR

PINDAR (C. 518–438 BC) is the greatest of the lyric poets of archaic Greece. Born in Boeotia, possibly of an aristocratic family, he quickly achieved recognition throughout the Greek world as a poet and musician. His compositions were divided into seventeen books by the Alexandrian scholars, and comprise, besides the four surviving books of epinician odes (odes for victors in the panhellenic games), some other works addressed to men but a much larger quantity of hymns, paeans and dithyrambs and other compositions for the gods: most of these are lost or preserved only in fragmentary form.

Pindar was commissioned by the leading aristocratic families of Greece, notably those of Aegina, as well as by the 'tyrants' (absolute rulers) of the Greek cities of Sicily. His complex metres and the problems of following the chain of argument in his odes have made him one of the most difficult, but also most rewarding, poets to interpret, and his influence on European poetry has been considerable.

RICHARD STONEMAN was born in Devon in 1951. He prepared his dissertation on Pindar at the universities of Oxford and Cologne. He is the author of many books about Greece and Greek culture, including *Land of Lost Gods: the Search for Classical Greece* (1987), *A Literary Companion to Travel in Greece* (1984, new edition 1994), and *A Luminous Land: Artists Discover Greece* (the J. Paul Getty Museum 1997). He has translated the *Greek Alexander Romance* for Penguin and, for Everyman, *Legends of Alexander the Great*.

ABBREVIATIONS

AJP	*American Journal of Philology.*
AR	Apollonius Rhodius.
B	Bacchylides.
Bernabé	A. Bernabé, *Poetae Epici Graeci* (Leipzig 1987).
Bgk	T. Bergk, *Poetae Lyrici Graeci* (6th edn; Leipzig 1923).
BICS	*Bulletin of the Institute of Classical Studies.*
Bundy	E. L. Bundy, *Studia Pindarica* (Berkeley 1986).
Burkert	W. Burkert, *Homo Necans* (1972; English trans. Oxford 1983).
CQ	*Classical Quarterly.*
Davies	M. Davies, *Poetae Melici Graeci* (Berlin 1987).
DK	H. Diels and W. Kranz (eds), *Fragmente der Vorsokratiker* (Berlin 1968).
Ep.	*Epistle*
Farnell	L. R. Farnell, *Cults of the Greek States* vols I–IV (Oxford 1896–1909).
FGrH	F. Jacoby (ed.), *Fragmente der Griechischen Historiker* (Leiden 1957).
fl	flourished
GRBS	*Greek, Roman and Byzantine Studies.*
HSCP	*Harvard Studies in Classical Philology.*
JHS	*Journal of Hellenic Studies.*
Kinkel	I. Kinkel, *Poetarum Epicorum Graecorum Fragmenta* (Leipzig 1877).
LP	E. Lobel and D. Page (eds), *Poetarum Lesbiorum Fragmenta* (Oxford 1955).
Mus. Helv.	*Museum Helveticum.*
MW	R. Merkelbach and M. L. West (eds), *Fragmenta Hesiodea* (Oxford 1967).
Parke	H. W. Parke, *Festivals of the Athenians* (London 1977).
Paus.	Pausanias (an accessible translation is that of Peter Levi, two vols [Harmondsworth 1971]).
PMG	D. L. Page (ed.), *Poetae Melici Graeci* (Oxford 1962).

POxy	*Papyri Oxyrhynchenses.*
Privitera	A. Privitera, *Pindaro: Le Istmiche* (Milan 1980).
QUCC	*Quaderni Urbinati della Cultura Classica.*
SEG	*Supplementum Epigraphicum Graecum.*
SLG	D. L. Page (ed.), *Supplementum Lyricis Graecis* (Oxford 1974).
Σ	scholiast.
TAPA	*Transactions of the American Philological Association.*
West	M. L. West (ed.), *Iambi et Elegi Graeci*, vols I–II (Oxford 1971–2).
Wilamowitz	Ulrich von Wilamowitz-Moellendorff, *Pindaros* (Berlin 1922).
ZPE	*Zeitschrift für Papyrologie und Epigraphik.*

Pindar's works are abbreviated as follows:
Dith: Dithyrambs
I: Isthmians
N: Nemeans
O: Olympians
P: Pythians
Pa: Paeans.

Note: All dates are BC., except in the bibliography.

CHRONOLOGY

Date	Olympiad/ Pythiad	Pindar: Life and Works	Literary and Historical Events
518		Birth of Pindar	
499			Ionian Revolt
498	P–22	P 10	
497/6			Dithyramb victory in Athens
496	O–71		Birth of Sophocles
491			Gelon tyrant of Gela (to 485)
490	P–24	P 12, P 6; Pa. 6?	Battle of Marathon
488	O–73	O 14	Theron tyrant of Acragas (to 472); Gelon's Olympic victory
487		N 5	War of Athens/Aegina; Bacchylides 13
486	P–25	P 7	
485		N 2?, N 7?	Aeschylus' first victory; birth of Euripides?; Gelon becomes tyrant of Syracuse; Hieron becomes ruler of Gela
484	O–74		Birth of Herodotus?
482	P–26	I 6	
480	O–75	I 5 (or 478); latest possible date for Pa. 6	Battles of Himera, Salamis (September)

Date	Olympiad/ Pythiad	Pindar: Life and Works	Literary and Historical Events
479			Battles of Plataea (August), Mycale
478	P–27	P 3, I 8; Pa. 2? (before 476)	Death of Gelon; Hieron tyrant of Syracuse; Delian League founded
477		I 3/4?	Simonides' dithyramb victory
476	O–76	O 1, O 2, O 3, O 10–11; N 1?	Deinomenes ruler of Aetna; Bacchylides 5
475		N 3?, P 2?	
474	P–28	P 9, P 11, N 9?, P 3?, N 4; dithyramb frags 76?, 77?	Battle of Cyme
472	O–77		Aeschylus, *Persae*; death of Theron; Hieron at war with Thrasydaeus of Acragas (to 470)
470	P–29	P 1, I 2?; dithyramb frags 75? (before 461)?; O 12 (or 466)?	Aeschylus *Aetnaeae*, B 3; Sophocles' first victory; death of Simonides; Battle of the Eurymedon?; Bacchylides 4
467			Death of Hieron; accession of Thrasybulus
466	P–30	O 12; O 9	Restoration of democracy at Syracuse
465		N 6?	
464	O–79	O 13, O 7; N 10?	
463		Pa. 9? (or 478)	
462	P–31	P 5, P 4	

Date	Olympiad/ Pythiad	Pindar: Life and Works	Literary and Historical Events
461			Ostracism of Cimon
460	O–8	O 8; O 5 (or 456)	Birth of Thucydides (460–455)
459		N 8?	
458	P–32	I 1?, Pa. 4?	Aeschylus, *Oresteia*; Athens conquers Aegina
457/6			Aegina enters Delian League
457			Battles of Tanagra (summer) and Oenophyta (autumn); conquest of Boeotia
456	O–81		Death of Aeschylus
455			Euripides first competes at Athens
454	P–33	I 7?	Delian League's treasury moved to Athens
452	O–82	O 4	Bacchylides 6 and 7
447			Battle of Coroneia – Athenian loss of Boeotia
446	P–35	P 8; N 11? (or later)	Thirty Years' Peace
441			First victory of Euripides
440	O–85		Revolt of Samos
438	P–37	Death of Pindar	Phidias' statue of Athena erected in Parthenon

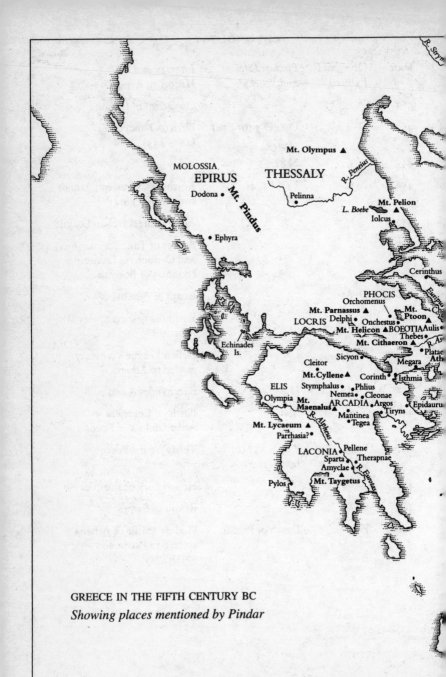

GREECE IN THE FIFTH CENTURY BC

Showing places mentioned by Pindar

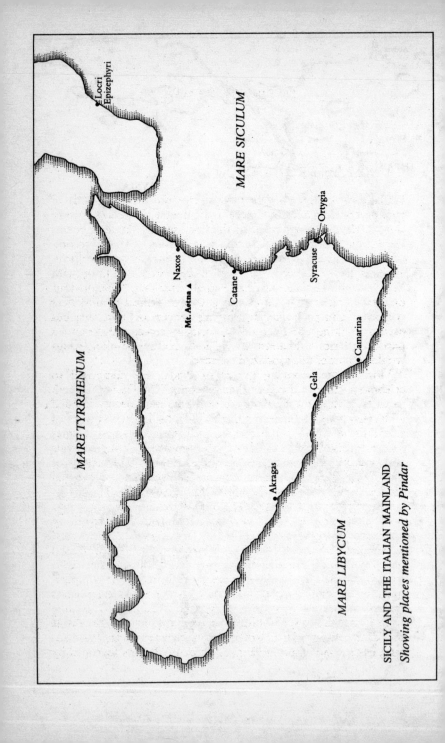

SICILY AND THE ITALIAN MAINLAND
Showing places mentioned by Pindar

INTRODUCTION

1.i *Pindar's life*

Pindar's work represents the most substantial surviving body of
lyric poetry from ancient Greece. Lyric poetry is, literally, poetry
sung to the accompaniment of the lyre, and all Pindar's poems
were composed for choral or solo performance to music accompanied by dance. There were many occasions for such performances in ancient Greece, and most of them were bound up with
ritual events which often had a religious character. Most obvious
of these are the festivals of the gods, for whom hymns were
composed and performed by singing dancers or marchers; but
even a drinking party would be formally structured around a
particular series of libations to the gods, and the drinking songs
would be part of this sanctified context.[1]

Most of the surviving poems of Pindar are composed to
celebrate victors in the Panhellenic Games. The Games, though
to us they appear a secular type of event, were deeply imbued
with religion and represented one of the most honoured ways of
celebrating the gods and heroes; in the pre-classical past, Games
had probably grown out of the custom of celebrating funerals
with athletic performances, and the endurance and victory of
the athlete were symbols of human achievement and a ritual
sacrificial substitute for the life of the dead man.[2] The art of
lyric poetry was a development of the archaic age (sixth and
early fifth centuries) and was associated with the growth of
interstate aristocratic culture in the Greek world. Aristocrats,
who in an earlier age had, like Alcaeus on Lesbos, composed
their own songs, came to act as patrons of trained poets who
would provide them with increasingly elaborate lyric compositions for ceremonial occasions. The earliest of the lyric poets is
the seventh-century Spartan poet Alcman (who may have come
from Lydia, the most sophisticated region known to Greeks at
that date). His surviving Partheneia (maiden songs) are fragmentary, enchanting and tantalizingly obscure. He was followed by

the sixth-century poet Stesichorus, whose strength lay in long narrative compositions in lyric verse, but sharing something of the style of the epic poetry associated with Homer. Substantial parts of his work have been recovered since 1970, enabling us to form a much better impression of his work than was possible for previous generations.

In the later sixth century things changed with the emergence of wandering poets, of whom the first known to us is Simonides of Ceos (556–468), who is credited in the ancient tradition as being the first poet to accept fees for his work. This gave him a reputation in ancient lore as a greedy man, but the reality is that he was fulfilling commissions entrusted to him by wealthy patrons for poems to celebrate their victories in the Games and other important events.[3] He also wrote elegiac poetry and epigrams. His nephew Bacchylides (fifth century) was a younger contemporary of Pindar, and his surviving works include epinicians, dithyrambs and other religious poetry.[4]

Lyric poetry continued to flourish into the fourth century, but as the centre of cultural gravity moved to democratic Athens, the celebratory genres were less in demand. (Even in the sixth century at Athens, Solon had forbidden the composition of formal lyric dirges, as part of a drive to reduce aristocratic ostentation.) Lyric became an integral part of Attic tragedy, and dithyramb and hyporcheme became more like concert pieces than religious celebrations. Pindar thus represents the last and greatest flowering of this distinctively aristocratic art form.

Pindar was born in Cynoscephalae in Boeotia in 518 BC and lived for most of his life in Thebes, the chief city of Boeotia. He apparently belonged to the Theban clan of the Aegeidae, to which he refers in Pythian 9.72–6.

Such biographical data as we have are contained in two brief *Lives*, the first prefixed to the Ambrosian MS containing Olympians 1–12, the second the work of the Byzantine scholar Thomas Magister (late thirteenth–early fourteenth century). The Ambrosian Life cannot be dated but is probably no earlier than the fifth century AD. Besides these lives there is a preface to a lost commentary to Pindar's work by the twelfth-century bishop of Thessaloniki, Eustathius; an entry in the Byzantine lexicon known as the Suda; and a metrical Life of the fifth century AD or later. All these lives derived their data from two earlier writers: the Peripatetic scholar Chamaeleon of Heraclea Pontica (c. 350–after 281), and the historian Ister, a pupil of Callimachus. A scholar named Aristodemus of Thebes (c. 150/30 BC: *FGrH* 383) wrote a work *On Pindar* in at least three books which is quoted a few times by ancient scholars. In addition, part of a life was discovered on a papyrus (*POxy.* 2438) which contains some criticism of theories presented in other Lives, and which may possibly be the work of the formidable Alexandrian scholar Didymus (80–10 BC).[5] From this it may plainly be seen that we have nothing like a primary source for the life and career of Pindar.

Furthermore, the authors of ancient lives, like Nature, abhorred a vacuum, and if they had no information about an author they would invent it, or make deductions from references in the author's works.[6] Thus, the tradition tells us that Pindar's father was Pagondas or Daiphantus; but the name Pagondas is simply lifted from the Second Partheneion where it is the name of one of the family for whom the poem was written.

The Ambrosian Life goes on to tell us: 'When Pindar was a boy, according to Chamaeleon and Ister, he went hunting on Mount Helicon and fell asleep from exhaustion. As he slept a bee landed on his mouth and built a honeycomb there. Others say that he had a dream in which his mouth was full of honey and wax, and that he then decided to write poetry.' This charming piece of nonsense is typical of the rest of the Life, and indeed of the ancient biographical tradition generally. The lesson to be drawn is that little credence can be attached to ancient statements about Pindar's life.

The only armature on which we can build a chronology of the poet's work is the dating of the poems themselves. The four surviving books of epinician odes were written to celebrate victors in the Panhellenic Games. Ancient scholars who wrote commentaries on Pindar's odes had access to the list of victors at the Olympic and Pythian Games (but not the Nemean and Isthmian), and were thus able to affirm that particular addressees had won their victories on particular occasions. The survival of part of an ancient list of Olympic victors enables modern scholars to check that the work of their ancient predecessors was, on the whole, accurate. But no such data are available for the other Games, still less for Pindar's surviving poems in other genres. The result is that, to construct any sort of chronology, recourse must be had to deductions from evidence in the poems themselves. But the problem of what shall count as evidence is acute. Ancient scholars, and many of their modern successors, were inclined to interpret freely any apparently personal passage, or any obscure statement, as having an autobiographical or direct historical reference. A supposed rivalry with Simonides and Bacchylides was a particularly popular resort for explaining difficult passages.[7] At other times it has been supposed that Pindar is apologizing for offences caused or for political tensions involving Thebes, which did in fact support the Persian side in the Persian War against Greece.[8] In recent years the pendulum has swung violently away from any such interpretation, seeking instead to interpret Pindar's work primarily in terms of rhetorical structures, so that many statements which seemed to be historical allusions have simply evaporated.

In brief we can be fairly sure of the following outline of his career. After training as a musician in his youth (according to the Ambrosian Life his teacher was his uncle, Scopelinus), he composed his first epinician ode (Pythian 10) in 498 BC at the age of twenty for Hippocleas of Thessaly. His talent is already mature in this poem, and he had probably learnt his craft in writing poems for local patrons and festivals, perhaps including the Partheneia for Theban families. At some stage he acquired a connection with Delphi, perhaps through a hereditary priesthood (certainly his descendants held such a priesthood, though Pindar could have been the first to hold it). This was the impetus for the considerable number of paeans composed on behalf of various states to honour Apollo at Delphi. His fame spread, no doubt initially through the interstate network of aristocratic family allegiances, and by the mid 480s he was writing odes for members of the Aeginetan aristocracy, notably the family of Lampon. His work also became known to the powerful rulers ('tyrants') of the Greek cities of Sicily, and in 476 he composed his most famous poem, Olympian 1, to celebrate the horse-race victory of Hieron of Syracuse at Olympia. His Sicilian period ended in 470 or soon after with the deaths of Theron (472) and Hieron (468). Few later poems can be dated with certainty, though the melancholy Pythian 8 is firmly fixed in 446, six years before Pindar's death at the age of eighty. (The round number of his age at death is itself suspicious, as are the exact dates given for his birth and death by the ancient tradition; but they will be approximately true.)

1.ii *The genres of Pindar's poetry*

Pindar's works were already collected in antiquity (Olympian 7 was inscribed in letters of gold in the temple of Athena at Lindos), and the first scholarly edition was that of the Alexandrian scholar Aristophanes of Byzantium (c. 257–180 BC). This may have been preceded by an earlier edition, referred to in the scholia to Olympian 5 as the *edaphia*, a word meaning 'foundations'. Aristophanes arranged the poems in seventeen books, the last four consisting of the surviving books of epinicians in the order Olympians, Pythians, Isthmians and Nemeans. The books were arranged with the religious ones preceding the secular ones: hymns, paeans (addressed to Apollo), dithyrambs (addressed to Dionysus; 2), prosodia or processional songs (2), partheneia or maiden songs (2), hyporchemata or songs with dancing (2), encomia, laments, epinicia.

It must be remembered that the generic divisions of ancient Greek lyric poetry were the creation of Alexandrian scholarship, and so these terms may not always represent distinctions that were apparent to Pindar.[9] In particular, epinician partakes of many of the same topics of praise as encomium (and even lament), with the addition of details of the victory in question; and the term hyporcheme could, theoretically, be applied to any of these types of poem since all were sung and most were accompanied by dance. There were certainly musical differences between some of the genres (the hyporcheme was regarded as having a Creten character, in either mode or rhythm), but these are hard for us to recover today.

The major perceptible difference is between odes with a religious theme and those written for a human addressee. In broad terms, all the former might be called 'hymns' (though Pindar sometimes uses the word even when he is writing for a human addressee, and all the latter might be called 'encomia'. Epinician and lament are both a type of encomium, as are such slighter pieces as the love-song frag. 123 which the Alexandrians probably classified under the name 'encomium'. Contemporaries might have called this last a *skolion* or drinking song, as from its content it is well suited to a symposiac context. Many of the epinicia also build on the symposiac character of lyric for their larger-scale celebrations. In the end it is not helpful to try to make too precise distinctions between different types of the poems for human addressees.

However, the religious genres deserve some further consideration. The major portion of Pindar's work which we have outside the epinicia is in a religious genre: the paean.

Paean

The paean is in origin a cry or appeal to Apollo as Healer (the word Paian means 'healer') and from this developed a particular kind of hymnic address to the god. The term shares an etymology with the name of a particular metrical rhythm, the paeon, but paeans known to us are not in paeonic rhythms. No paeans are preserved from the period previous to Pindar, and the few that survive from the Hellenistic period are fairly brief and perfunctory, containing the basic elements of appeal to the god, some honorifics, and little else. Pindar's paeans are, as far as we know, unique in their elaboration. They have interesting similarities to, as well as differences from, the epinicians. Like the latter, they generally contain a mythic narrative (relating to Apollo) as well as details of the city and festival for which they were composed. Though the language is complex and the style allusive as in the epinicians, the moral content, if one may put it that way, is much less. There is, of course, none of the concentration on the nature of human achievement that we find in the epinicians. But I believe it is possible to find an intensity and sense of the presence of the gods in their dwellings on earth which shines through the verse. Their prime purpose is to bring the god or gods in question into relation with the men and the city who have commissioned the paean.

Dithyramb

The first reference to the dithyramb in Greek literature (Archilochus frag. 120) shows it to be a choral song for Dionysus. Like the paean, the name is perhaps originally a ritual title or invocation of the god; Pindar (Olympian 13.19) is our witness for the alleged origin of the genre in Corinth, where Arion (originally from Lesbos c. 625–585) is said to have 'invented' it. Herodotus (1.23), and also the Byzantine lexicon known as the Suda, say that Arion first established a definite routine movement for the chorus and provided words to sing, on a subject from which it took its title. It was often accompanied by pipes rather than lyres, and the music was in the Phrygian mode.

In Pindar's day the dithyramb (like the tragic drama) was a piece with a title, consisting predominantly of a mythical narrative, and at Athens the subject of a competition like those for tragedy and comedy. Simonides in the previous generation is said to have won fifty-six dithyrambic victories, but no certain fragment of his dithyrambs survives. Several dithyrambs of Bacchylides seem to reflect this pattern very well; but from the scanty remains we have of Pindar's dithyrambs, it would seem that they focused more closely on the religious occasion and the worship of Dionysus, though it is impossible to establish how extensive the narratives may have been in the lost portions. Furthermore, at least one of Bacchylides' dithyrambs (no. 23, *Cassandra*) was classified in antiquity as a paean, because of the occurrence in it of the ritual cry *ié*. It may be that in fact paeans were just as susceptible of containing extensive mythical narratives: Bacchylides 17 (*Theseus*) may be an example. Likewise, some poems classified among the paeans in the papyrus of Pindar's poetry may actually be prosodia (processional poems) as Rutherford has argued,[10] and have been classified as paeans because of the occurrence of this same refrain.

In the century after Pindar the dithyramb became a virtuoso set-piece performance, in the hands of poets such as Melanippides, Philoxenus, Timotheus, probably Pratinas, and others.

Partheneion

A partheneion is a song sung by a chorus of maidens.[11] It was regarded in late antiquity as an example of a 'mixed' genre, partly sacred and partly secular. A maiden song could be performed on any occasion, though it seems often to have been as part of the initiation rites of adolescent girls: extant partheneia concentrate very much on the personalities of the girls participating in the performance, as well as on the god celebrated; one result of the extensive incidence of personalia is that they are very hard for us to interpret. Partheneia share with epinician this emphasis on people, but also recurring topoi and moral apophthegms, as well as mythical sections.

The earliest partheneia we have are those of the Spartan poet Alcman (seventh century), and such characteristics are as apparent in these poems as they are in the exiguous remains of Pindar's partheneia. We have no other partheneia from antiquity. Pindar's second partheneion is in fact stated by the ancient scribe to be a *daphnephorikon*, a particular type of song for Apollo; so it seems to be the female composition of the chorus rather than the occasion that calls out the particular features noted above.

Hyporcheme

As noted above, this name simply means a song accompanied by dance, which would apply to most of these genres. The implication is that in this genre the dance is the dominant feature of the performance. We have too few fragments of Pindar's hyporchemes (and none of anybody else's) to enable us to determine its characteristics. When Pindar refers at Pythian 2.69 to a Kastoreion (actually a war-dance, a specific kind of danced song), he may be referring to the hyporcheme composed for Hieron (frags 105–6); but there is no way of telling what that poem was about.

Encomium and epinician

An *enkomion* is a song sung in a *komos* or celebratory rout. Pindar several times refers to his epinicia as encomia (Nemean 1.7, Olympian 2.52, 10.77, 13.29) and once as an *enkomios hymnos* (Pythian 10.53). The fact that a large number of Pindar's encomia were for victors in the Games led to the creation in antiquity of the special term *epinikoi* '(hymns) for victories' or epinicia. The epinicia do not differ in generic requirements from the other encomia or the laments. At the beginning of Olympian 9 Pindar refers to the simple form of celebration that greeted Olympic victors in the days of Archilochus, a threefold acclamation as *kallinikos*, 'glorious victor', rather like 'hip-hip-hooray'. The epinician develops from that fundamental 'ritual' act in the same way as the literary paeans develop from the ritual cry to the god, or as the lament develops from the Linus-song (frag. 128c, Lament 3).

The epinician is the most complex achievement of Pindar's poetry, as far as we can judge, and the most profound in its meditation on the nature of human achievement and man's delicately balanced relations with the gods who give success but can also take it away. It is on the epinician that the following discussion of the mechanisms of Pindar's poetry will mainly be based.

2.i *The interpretation of Pindar's poetry*

Pindar's poetry has commonly been regarded as obscure, not just because of the difficulty of his Greek, but because the train of thought within a poem is often difficult to trace. Abraham Cowley prefaced his own translation of Olympian 2 (1668) with an essay which begins, 'If a man should undertake to translate Pindar word for word, it would be thought that one madman had translated another.' Voltaire accused Pindar of 'parler beaucoup sans rien dire'. Scholars whose profession it is to understand Greek poetry have often been no kinder. The ancient scholars, such as Aristarchus, Didymus and Aristophanes of Byzantium, whose commentaries survive in excerpts in the *scholia* to Pindar, pepper their explanations of the poems with such terms as 'he says in riddling terms', 'he hints darkly at', and the like. They frequently describe the mythic portions of the odes as 'digressions'; and when they are at a loss to understand something they will hypothesize an historical allusion to explain it.

To the perceived problem of obscurity has been added in modern times the anxious search for 'unity' and 'relevance'.[12] Modern scholarship on Pindar began with August Boeckh's edition, completed by Ludolph Dissen and published in 1821. Boeckh and Dissen believed that each poem could be explained by a single *Grundgedanke* or 'fundamental idea' which determined the whole of its content: Pythian 1 could thus be treated as a rhapsody on the theme of 'advice to Hieron to patronize the arts'. A variant of this approach found the unifying theme in some event or circumstance quite external to the poem and not mentioned in it: so that Pythian 9 became a 'historical allegory' focused on Telesicrates' impending marriage.

Both these styles of interpretation went though many variants in the hands of successive scholars. The most extreme proponent of the search for dominating ideas in the odes was Gilbert Norwood, who sought the unity of the odes in particular symbolic ideas, such as a bee, a beacon-fire or a horse. This kind of approach was taken up by J. H. Finley, who decided that the heroes were 'symbols' in Pindar's poetry; and to a lesser degree by J. B. Bury, who pointed to such phenomena as the mention of bronze in every triad of Nemean 10; but it is impossible to see such phenomena as in any sense 'explaining' what these poems are about.

The other approach, of seeking explanations for the content of the odes in events outside the odes, was taken to its extreme by the great German scholar Ulrich von Wilamowitz-Moellendorff,[13] whose publications at the beginning of this century overturned practically every received idea in classical scholarship and presented the ancient Greek world as a living presence. The trouble was, as David C. Young has mordantly remarked,[14] that Wilamowitz never quite realized that Pindar was dead. Wilamowitz's aim was to construct a biography of Pindar by using the odes as straightforward historical evidence, in conjunction with other evidence drawn from Wilamowitz's vast learning. Wilamowitz seemed to believe that he had entered Pindar's world and could interpret it as an insider. The poems were secondary to that imaginative goal. Wilamowitz's work became enormously influential and the literal and historical acceptance of Pindar's every word, and Wilamowitz's interpretations, is basic to the major study of C. M. Bowra,[15] which somehow fails to explain anything about Pindar at all.

In recent years there has been a pronounced reaction to this historicizing approach, taking its impetus no doubt in part from the 'New Criticism' of Cleanth Brooks and others, with its insistence that everything necessary for the interpretation of a poem is contained within the poem. The danger of this approach is that it will loose the poems entirely from their historical setting; but its benefits have been shown in the acceptance of the general principles formulated by Elroy L. Bundy in his *Studia Pindarica* (he died before the series of his studies could be completed).[16]

Bundy looked at the epinicians from the point of view of function. Their purpose is 'to praise the victor'. Everything in the poem serves this end – myth, gnomic utterance, personal statements, advice, complaints, lists of victories. Though Bundy does not mention it, it is possible to support this view of archaic poetry from a sociological point of view: praise and blame are deeply lodged in archaic society and sensibility, and the complex of cognate words *ainos* (story, fable), *parainesis* (advice) and *epainos* (praise) shows how closely these types of discourse are linked in archaic culture.[17] The social function of the poems is supported by a sophisticated and programmatic mode of presentation. Unknown to Bundy, this rhetoric-based approach had been in some degree anticipated by Erasmus Schmid in his edition of Pindar published in Wittenberg in 1616. Schmid divides the odes into very elaborately interwoven sets of rhetorical topoi, which are analysed in terms of their movement towards celebration of the addressee.

Bundy's approach is made less penetrable by the technical vocabulary he invented, using such words as 'vaunt' and 'foil'; but once understood, these illuminate the rhetorical structure of the odes very precisely. 'Foil' in particular is characteristic of an archaic way of thinking and writing which Geoffrey Lloyd has called 'polarity and analogy'.[18] Every statement may, by way of emphasis, call forth a corollary or polar opposite, so that praise evokes the danger of blame. Priamel is another form of foil. (See section 2.ii below.) Bundy sometimes seems to imply that foil has purely an abstract, structural function, and I think it important to emphasize that even 'foil' statements have their own meaning in the context of an ode.

The approach is best demonstrated in the analysis of an individual ode, and Bundy chooses Olympian 11 as his example. Olympian 4 (for Psaumis), being short, also encapsulates nicely the way this method of interpretation works. An opening invocation of a god (openings must be showy) introduces the statement of the poet's duty to praise. A gnomic statement, 'When friends have won success . . .' gives a reason for that duty. Pindar turns again to Zeus and prays him to accept the song he will offer. He then names the event at which Psaumis has won his victory, and utters words of congratulation as well as praising Psaumis' good citizenship. The praise thus achieved, Pindar must protect his utterance against possible imputations of inadequacy; so he insists that his words are true, introducing himself into the poem as a worthy praiser of the victor. The ode concludes with a short myth which explicitly amplifies the victor's achievement and does not so much compare him to Erginus as set Psaumis in a context of the world of the shining heroes and their achievements canonized in legend.

An element of the poem's content which Bundy does not treat is what Wolfgang Schadewaldt called the *Programm*:[19] in every ode there are certain topics that must be covered. These include the name and background of the victor, his city, the event at which he has won. Usually there also occur references to the setting – symposiastic or religious – the poet's relations with the victor, the dangers of not getting praise right, and of course a

myth. Bundy's approach has often been criticized for allowing
no scope for the myth; but those who have developed his
insights have been able to show that the myth also has its
position in the rhetorical structure of climaxes, as well as any
possible thematic links with the victor. I expand on these aspects
below. The important thing is to recognize that much in the
poems falls into place if one keeps one's eye on the victor and
his requirements of appropriate, specific and luminous praise.

The same insights can be adapted for the poems which do not
praise athletic victors, for example the paeans, which are
commissioned by particular states for performance at Delphi,
and have to focus on the god Apollo and his relations with the
state in question. The fragmentary state of most of these poems
naturally makes interpretation harder; and there remain stum-
bling blocks and obscure passages, as there do also in the
epinicians. Pindar is not an easy poet; but he is not, as Cowley
feared, a madman. Where we cannot understand him the fault
is likely to be ours not his. We lack information that was known
to his audiences, and we can never recover that. The important
thing is that we should not, as the historicist critics have done,
try to invent it.

2.ii *Rhetoric and structure*

To read Pindar's poetry with understanding requires some
familiarity with the rhetorical structures and the characteristic
connections of thought that articulate his discourse. In many
ways his structures can be seen as a kind of rhetoric before
rhetoric: he uses the topoi and forms of thought that characterize
later rhetoric as it was codified by theorists, but he does it in a
more instinctive way, and hence is often more 'irregular' than
later theorists would have permitted. But even the ancient
theorists concentrated more on the topoi – the elements of what
Schadewaldt called the *Programm*: family of the victor, his
homeland, the nature of the victory, and so on – than on the
connections of thought. At the risk of giving an over-mechanical
guide to what is always an organically arranged development in
the poems, I should like to draw attention to some of these
forms of connection.

Foil

It was Gildersleeve's insight that 'much in Pindar is foil' on which Bundy built to form his theory of the single purpose of Pindar's odes. But what is important to recognize is that even foil adds meaning to its context; it is not simply there to make the main point visible.

An approachable form of foil is the priamel, also called the tricolon crescendo. A well-known example is the opening of Olympian 1, but it may be better to approach it through a simpler example, frag. 221:

> Some take pleasure in the prizes and garlands
> of storm-footed horses,
> others in treasure-chambers full of gold;
> yet others enjoy embarking on the waves of the sea
> in a swift ship.

The passage will have gone on to focus on the subject Pindar actually wishes to adorn with his prize, as did the rather similar lines of Sappho:

> Some say that the most beautiful thing on the black earth
> is an army of horsemen;
> others, an army of foot soldiers;
> others, a fleet of ships;
> but I say, it is whoever one is in love with.

In Sappho's lines, there is no obvious similarity of category between the items in the priamel and the climax; in the Pindar fragment, we do not know what the climax was; but in the opening of Olympian 1 the two terms of water, and of gold, which is itself compared with fire, offer two opposing types of elemental perfection. The climactic term, the Games, introduces the third term of the crescendo, the sun, which then focuses on a refinement of the climactic term, the Olympic Games: so the three terms of the crescendo emphasize the idea of brightness (and the gold that is associated with divinity in Greek thought) which is one of the key images of Pindar's poetry and give a context of divine radiance to his subject. The tricolon is not mechanical, but is imbued with a symbolic significance as well.

(Attentive readers will have noticed that this paragraph on the priamel is structured as a tricolon crescendo, in the hope that it will thus be persuasive: priamel is, in a sense, a form of inductive argument.)

A less natural form of foil for us to understand is the following foil, where a statement or assertion of a value is immediately offset by its polar opposite.[20] This is a very characteristic pattern of archaic thought, found for example in some of the pre-Socratic philosophers who were wont to analyse the substance of the universe in terms of opposites: light and dark, wet and dry, and so on. Often in archaic poetry such polar expressions are used to modify very positive statements which may call down the jealousy of the gods. The trope is common in Theognis as well as Pindar. The reason is made clear in a well-known story. When Croesus asked Solon whether he was not the happiest of all men, Solon counselled him to 'call no man happy until he is dead'; life's mutability – what the Renaissance called the Wheel of Fortune – may bring down even the greatest. One does well not to forget that nothing mortal endures except by the grace of the gods. Some of the most surprising instances of this form of thought occur at the end of odes, where a climactic statement of praise for the victor's achievement is offset by a warning. A good example is the end of Isthmian 1: the Muses are asked to raise the addressee's name high, and to do so again in future; but the poet goes on:

> Now should a man
> Store hidden wealth within his halls,
> And upon others fall with mocking laughter,
> Little thinks he his soul shall fare to Hades
> With not a shred of glory.

Other examples of the trope are at the end of Olympians 5 and 7, and Nemean 11. In all these cases the positive statement of praise calls forth the cautionary thought; but the thought is linked to the purpose of epinician in that it reminds the achiever that the achievement is not his alone, but only because a god allows it. To us it seems strange to conclude praise with sober warning; but the polarity expresses a religious position that it is no less profound and firm for not being openly articulated.

Satiety and envy

A third form of foil takes us to the heart of the epinician philosophy. (I do not call it 'Pindar's thought' because the

complex of ideas is not unique to Pindar and because it is fully
functional in the odes, not something extraneous inserted by
Pindar to indulge his own putative vanity of wisdom.) This foil
consists of the various obstacles to praise which the poet has to
overcome. Before he can embark on a clear statement of the
victor's glory, he must discount or set aside the twin dangers of
excess of praise, which will induce satiety and resentment in the
listener, and of envy which is commonly felt by the humbler sort
for those who achieve great things. (As Plutarch wrote, in *On
Envy and Hatred*, 'we tend to hate those who lean more towards
wickedness, but envy is aroused rather by those who seem to
tend to virtue.')[21] These two dangers are not always sharply
distinguished: envy may be aroused either by the achievement or
by the praise of it. A clear expression of the idea is at Olympian
6.74, where a resounding statement of the glory of Iamus'
descendants is followed by the statement:

> Calumny
> But from the hearts of others' envy, threatens
> Those who came first, driving the twelve-lap course,
>   On whom the divine grace of Beauty
> Has shed the dewdrops of her fame most fair.
> Truth tells, Agesias . . .

and the poet goes on to build to a new climax of praise by
stating that the gods have forwarded Agesias' victory. If we hold
to this understanding of the role of envy in the odes it will
enable us to negotiate more obscure passages such as Nemean
1.24 where the translation is problematic, or those passages
where historicist critics have assumed that envy is directed at
the poet and not the victor (Olympian 2.86–8, for example).

The danger that resentment will be aroused by an excess of
praise raises not only the question of common people's attitudes
to athletic success, but also that of the criticism of the discerning
directed at a poet who does not praise competently. Excess
creates boredom or distaste (Olympian 2.95) and can be avoided
by the poet's judicious exercise of *kairos*, a word which is often
translated 'opportunity' but really means 'the right amount' (of
time or of anything else). Brevity is one of the laws of epinician:
Nemean 4.32 ff., 'Long is the story,/To tell the whole my
Music's rule forbids/And Time pressing apace.' The late rhetorician Menander (338.28ff. Spengel) shows an awareness of this

issue though he is willing to indulge poets more than prose orators: 'In [the poet's] case the licence to speak at leisure and wrap up the subject in poetical ornament and elaboration produces no satiety or disgust – though I am not unaware that some of the poets themselves introduce untimely expansions of their themes – whereas prose-writers and orators have very little licence.'

Break-off

This last form of foil, the statement of the need for brevity, commonly moves into another characteristic link-element of the Pindaric ode, the inelegantly named 'break-off formula' (a translation of Schadewaldt's *Abbruchsformel*). The passage of Nemean 4 just quoted is a very characteristic type of break-off. The continuation of that passage is one of the more difficult interpretative cruces in Pindar, but a simpler example may be found at Olympian 13.43–9:

> . . . your triumphs . . .
> I would defy a host of men to match;
> As easy would it be for me to number
>   The pebbles of the ocean.
>
> But for all things there is a measure set:
> To know the due time, therein lies true skill.
> Now I . . .

and the poet goes on to a new wave of praise, deepening the renown of Corinth for his victor.

The break-off always functions to end a passage where the praise is becoming dangerous by being overlong, or over-arrogant, and leads to a new approach to correct praise. (An unusual case is where it functions as following foil, and concludes an ode, at Olympian 3.43–5.) The break-off has an important function in concluding or introducing mythic narrative, too. Very frequently a mention of Heracles will be quickly followed by a break-off (e.g. Nemean 10.19, Pythian 9.89). Heracles, the hero who became a god, represents the acme of human achievement in epinician ideology; yet he also represents precisely that to which a mortal may not aspire. A human, however heroic, may not become a god; to wish to do so calls down the wrath of gods as well as the envy of men. (Pythian 3.61, 'Pray for no life immortal, soul of mine,/But draw in full

depth on the skills of which/You can be master.') The end of
Pythian 1 makes plain what is the highest reasonable ambition
for mortals:

> First in life's contest is to win good fortune,
> Next is to hold an honourable name;
>   He who can find
> And grasp both these, has gained the highest crown.

Break-offs are also found commonly in myths that are not about
Heracles, where sometimes they not merely call a halt to a
narrative that has gone on long enough, but are used to avoid
dilating on a part of the story that is unedifying or unsuitable
for praise. For example, Nemean 5.14–18

> Of a dread act, a deed maybe
> Unrightly dared, my heart forebodes to tell,
> Wherefore these warriors left this famous isle,
> What fate of heaven drove them from Oenone.
>   Be still my tongue: here profits not
> To tell the whole truth with clear face unveiled.
> Often is man's best wisdom to be silent.
>
> But if of fortune's wealth my praise is due . . .

The heroes have been mentioned and have given depth to the
victor's achievement; but to go on with the story would not
conduce to glory; so the story is abandoned and a new wave of
praise begins instantly.

Another example of such a break-off is preserved as frag. 180,
where Clement, who quotes it, plainly thought it was of value
as an independent moral statement: so it may be, but in Pindar
the moral thought is always subordinate to the purpose of
praise.

Similar break-offs from embarrassing or shocking stories
occur at Olympian 9.35, for example, and the famous instance
in Olympian 1.52, where Pindar 'rejects' the traditional tale that
the gods ate of the stew Tantalus had made of his own son to
test their percipience. This passage may lead us naturally to
consideration of the function of the myths in the rhetorical
structure of the odes.

Myth

Menander Rhetor, in the sentence following the passage quoted above, says:

> Myths, nakedly set out, pain and distress the hearer very much; they should therefore be as brief as possible. Antidotes need to be applied, for the sake of brevity and charm; e.g. not introducing every detail in a direct form, but omitting some points, conceding some, introducing some by combination, sometimes claiming to give explanations, or not committing oneself to belief or disbelief.

Most of these stratagems can be found in Pindar. Myth was a key element of the epinician programme; but how does it fit in? Often the ancient scholiasts were bewildered and could find no relevance for a particular myth; they (and Erasmus Schmid after them) often classified myths as 'digressions'. Commentators have often fallen into a counsel of despair, like Erich Thummer whose view is that all the myths in the odes are merely 'decorative', or C. M. Bowra for whom they become 'a panorama of irrelevant observations on topical questions'.[22] Yet the myths have two functions in the odes, one ideological and one rhetorical.

The ideological role is the one well expressed by Anne Pippin Burnett in her book on Bacchylides:[23]

> The spectator saw dancers whom he knew, wearing costumes that he had perhaps seen before; they were a part of his life, but he heard them describe themselves and their performance with the same music that described matters from another world and another time, and meanwhile in the dance these neighbours were instantaneously heroes or monsters or even gods. Such a spectator watched while his own familiar and tangible present became indistinguishable from a world that was strange and timeless. . . . All of which meant that the spectator at such a performance became a kind of communicant who celebrated the real presence of daimonic power as it inhabited the mythic past.

The rhetorical role of myth is not just that of deepening the context of the victory praised, but also of delaying praise to make the climax more intense. A myth may thus very often be introduced precisely as an outgrowth of a break-off formula, or of one of the gnomic statements which can also act as 'joints' of the epinician ode.

The ideological role of myth is perhaps most clearly expressed in a case like Pythian 9 where Pindar asserts a wish to praise a Pythian victory, and then launches straight into a myth as a way of building up to praise. The structural function of myth is illustrated in Pythian 9.78–81 which runs:

> ... great themes briefly to embroider
>   Wins the ear of the wise; yet, above all, true timing
>   Achieves the furthest goal. This precept
>   Iolaus long ago was seen to honour ...

A story about Iolaus ensues. (I believe that Conway's translation here is incorrect – see note – but the point that the myth is introduced by break-off will stand.)

A similar movement is found in Pythian 11, where the first part of the myth about Agamemnon is broken off with a gnomic statement about envy attending the great, and is then resumed in a form more appropriate to the poet's purpose of praise. At Nemean 3.26ff. the myth of Heracles is abandoned as 'irrelevant' (as Pindar archly expresses it): it has achieved its purpose of introducing the idea of extreme excellence, and Pindar now focuses on a myth appropriate to Aegina which will fulfil his aim, 'the flower of truth, which bids "Praise noble men"'.

It is true that not all myths are easy to tie to their odes in a thematic sense (the myth of Heracles in Nemean 1 is one over which commentators have broken their heads), but even in these cases their structural role can be explained along these lines.

The predominant function of the myths as praise – or introduction to praise, or, sometimes, substitute for praise[24] – can explain also why Pindar sometimes alters his myths, or rejects traditional versions. The agenda is not primarily a theological one, nor is it one of novelty for its own sake as Pindar pretends at Paean 7b. 10 ff., for example; the aim is to attune the expression of the story to the purpose of the ode: praise of the victor. This point can be understood by a consideration of the relationship of Paean 6 and Nemean 7: see the introductions to those odes. Köhnken's analysis of the myth in Olympian 1 is also very much to the point here: again, see the introduction to that ode.

Praise and fame

We have said much about the structure of the climaxes to praise and the delaying of the achievement of the praise. In what, then, does the praise itself consist? What are the climactic terms in which Pindar glorifies his addressees? Perhaps a programmatic statement may be found at Pythian 8.95–7:

> Creatures of a day! What is a man?
> What is he not? A dream of a shadow
> Is our mortal being. But when there comes to men
>   A gleam of splendour given of Heaven,
>   Then rests on them a light of glory
>   And blessèd are their days.

The radiance of achievement comes from the gods. It is by putting the victor in a relationship to the gods that Pindar validates his achievement and gives it an imperishable significance. This explains the frequency of prayers in many of the odes (Pythian 1 alone contains seven prayers).[25] The gods are enlisted in the victor's cause.

Aristotle says (*Nicomachean Ethics* 1101b 12–18) that we do not praise men for what they can take no credit for (physique, good looks, etc.) but only for the use of those gifts for some good and serious purpose.

> Ever are natural gifts the best,
>   But many a man struggles to win renown
>   By skills learnt from a teacher.
>   But each deed that a man may try
> Without heaven's help, is best buried in silence.
> (Olympian 9.100–4)

The attitude of the victor is thus important: he must recognize the grace given him and not be puffed up.

> If a man
> Makes of his wealth a stream
> Of healthful purpose, and of his possessions
> Lacks not a bounteous store,
> And adds thereto repute's good name,
> Then let him not seek to become a god.
> (Olympian 5.22–3)

On the other hand, he must not hide what gives him his chance of immortality, he must make it permanent by having a poet celebrate it in lasting words. Renown is no good unless it is apparent and permanent. The statement at the beginning of

Nemean 5 that words are more lasting even than statues is a
commonplace of ancient Greek thought, and the danger of not
spending to ensure lasting fame is vividly expressed in Isthmian
1.67–8:

> Now should a man
> Store hidden wealth within his halls,
> And upon others fall with mocking laughter,
> Little thinks he his soul shall fare to Hades
> With not a shred of glory.

Right use of achievement, right attitude to success, is crucial.
Wealth itself may be praised, but like natural gifts it must be
rightly used. Not least, it must be used to commission a suitable
ode which will immortalize the achievement in appropriate
terms and avoid the shame of oblivion. As Stephen Instone has
put it (apropos Pythian 11.54–8), 'athletic success, though the
crowning achievement, requires a successful life afterwards, a
life free from hybris; if you can achieve all that, then you will
not meet a dark death, i.e. oblivion, the fate of the unsuccessful;
rather, the successful and peaceable victor even when dead
provides honour to future members of his family.'[26]

The poet's authority

That being the case, the relationship of poet and addressee is
crucial to adequate praise. There is an epinician etiquette, which
requires that the poet prove himself adequate to the task of
illuminating the victor's achievement. In doing this the poet lays
claim not so much to divine inspiration (though the Muses are
invoked as guarantors for the 'facts' he purveys) as to 'the right
to be trusted' (the Greek word is axiopistia, and it is very
important in forensic rhetoric). This is the reason for the very
frequent first-person statements in the odes, which are introduced not simply as a sphragis, a seal, an assertion of authorship. Authorship, as Nagy has gracefully put it, implies
authority;[27] and the poet must establish his authority to praise.
This is relatively easily done in the odes for aristocrats, where
Pindar can speak as equal to equal, and may sometimes set up
relationships of proxeny (Nemean 7) or kinship (Pythian 5) to
emphasize the link. It is much harder in the poems for autocrats,
the Sicilian 'tyrants': the special means by which Pindar sets
himself up as adequate to the task of praising such great men

have been explored by me in my article 'The Ideal Courtier'.[28] The poet must in all cases show himself adaptable to requirements; and in many cases praise may take the form of advice:[29] since 'ought' implies 'can', to advise someone to do a noble act is tantamount to asserting that they have the capacity of nobility in them. A close parallel from another context is to be found in Xenophon's fictional dialogue *Hiero*, in which his interlocutor Simonides concludes by advising him (11.14–15):

> Take heart then, Hiero, enrich your friends, for so you will enrich yourself. Exalt the state, for so you will deck yourself with power ... And try to surpass all ... in deeds of kindness. For if you outdo your friends in kindness, it is certain that your enemies will not be able to resist you.

> And if you do all these things, rest assured that you will be possessed of the fairest and most blessed possession in the world; for none will be jealous of your happiness.

2.iii *The imagery of praise*

Praise is not simply a matter of a successful organization of conventional topoi. The centrality of athletic success to the self-image of aristocratic society (and also to the poleis of the nobility) is rooted in tradition and has profoundly religious connotations. I discuss some ways in which this extraordinary significance of athletics may have arisen in the next section. For the moment, it is enough to observe that Pindar's poetry is full of gods: they are not there as adornment, but because epinician is part of a religious ritual. There is a 'theology of epinician' which is probably as individual to Pindar as Aeschylus' theodicy in the *Oresteia* is to him; but it shares common features with the epinician poetry of Bacchylides and what we can recover of the other praise genres of other poets. Furthermore, the theology of the epinicians seems to differ from the ideas expressed in Pindar's other better-preserved poems, mainly the paeans, which do set out to justify the ways of gods to men (and heroes: see e.g. frag. 169), but have no reason to consider the position of outstanding human achievement in the divine order of things.

First, the successful athlete. His achievement is by the grace of god, and divinity is always expressed by Pindar in terms of light. So achievement is radiance: the 'gleam of splendour' of

Pythian 8.97, the 'far-flung light' of Nemean 3.64. The Olympic Games themselves are compared to the sun, brightest of stars, at Olympian 1.6–8. How shall the poet convey this radiance?

He will begin by invoking the gods for his own part. The goddesses of poetry are the Muses, who provide the matter of song and on whom poets must rely for accurate information. Homer invoked the Muse as his informant for the tales of Achilles and Odysseus. Hesiod knew that the Muses may sometimes lie, and Pindar is aware of the danger of false tales, false traditions; but he insists (Olympian 10.54) 'I can celebrate genuine fame.'

However, at least as important to Pindar's 'theory of poetry' as the Muses are the Graces, the Charites. Worshipped as goddesses in their own right at Orchomenus (Olympian 14), the Graces also have a symbolic role to play as guarantors of the beauty of poetry and of celebration: not so much Alexander Pope's 'grace beyond the reach of art' as Winckelmann's 'vernünftig gefällige', 'rationally pleasing'.

> ... in your gift are all our mortal joys,
>   And every sweet thing, be it wisdom, beauty
>   Or glory, that makes rich the soul of man.
>   (Olympian 14.5–7: the word translated 'glory' is
>   literally 'brightness'.)

The Graces are the rulers of the poet's technique, and as such are invoked at the beginning of Pythian 9. Compare Bacchylides' invocation at the beginning of his ninth ode, 'Graces of the golden distaff, may ye grant the charm that wins mortal ears; for the inspired prophet of the violet-eyed Muses is ready to sing ...'

But the Graces shed lustre not only on the poet's work but on the victor himself:

> Comes to you too, by favour of the Graces
> And of the sons of Tyndareus, no less,
>   The glory of the contests won ...
>
>   (Nemean 10.37–8)

and

> by Castalia's fountain
> As evening fell, his glory
> Flamed with the Graces' song.
>
>   (Nemean 6.36–8)

In this second passage, the Graces are bound up with the 'radiance' that characterizes the victor – not the fact of victory but the brightness of it. The beauty they give is what makes the victory far-seen.

The Graces are also involved with a second complex of imagery, that drawn from the processes of Nature.

> the dewdrops of the Graces
> They shower in gleaming beauty
> On the Psaluchid clan . . .
>
> (Isthmian 6.63–4)

These metaphors of watering, of vegetable growth, and of plucking and harvesting, are very common in Pindar. Not only are addressees frequently urged to 'pluck' the fruits of victory, but, more importantly, human achievement is seen as part of the organic processes of Nature. This is made particularly clear in the first eleven lines of Nemean 6, where the athletic successes of alternate generations are compared to the lying fallow of fields: cf. Nemean 11.37–43. Man is not a wild growth but a cultivated one. Central to this set of ideas is that of *phya*, the Doric equivalent of Attic *physis*, nature. *Phya* is what you are born with, and it cannot be altered; but it can and must be nurtured, cultivated, like a thoroughbred horse or a fine strain of rose. No amount of training will get exceptional results from an inferior raw material. It is Pindar's belief that such nature is the result of heredity: Nemean 6.15ff., 'Thus followed he the road / Where trod his grandfather Praxidamas, / True scion of this stock'. This is a message of a hereditary aristocracy.

Aristocratic culture lies at the root of another important complex of imagery, that drawn from the symposium. The poem is often described as a drink, or compared to one: Nemean 3.76ff., Olympian 7.1ff. The Graces are the special deities of the symposium, as their names indicate: Thalia (Festivity), Aglaia (Radiance) and Euphrosyna (good spirits). Nemean 9.48–55 pulls together many of these themes in a fine set-piece:

> Peace and the banquet like each other passing well; . . .
> And victory flowers anew
> In the sweet chant of song;
> While by the wine-bowl can the singer's voice
> Be more courageous yet. Then let the draught

> Be poured and mixed, that sweet and rich
> Proclaimer of the songs of revelry.

> And let the strong child of the vine be served
>   In silver goblets, which his steeds
> For Chromius won . . .
>   . . . Father Zeus, I pray thee,
>   May the song that I sing
>   To praise this deed of valour,
>   Be by the Graces blest . . .

Here the twin concerns of political peace and festal joy are linked together; gods and Graces are invoked to ensure the adequacy of the draught of song and praise, and (in the final lines, not quoted) the Muses are also invoked to ensure that the praise 'hits the mark' (Pindar drawing the metaphor of his own poetry, as often, from the events of the games he celebrates).[30]

The symposiac context is also important for the purpose of establishing a relationship between poet and addressee. The poem is presented as a gift, deserving a reward: e.g. Pythian 2.74. Athenaeus, in his long book on dining practices, *The Deipnosophists*, has many stories about poets who offered gifts to or claimed rewards from their hosts in a witty or cheeky way (e.g. 1.6, 1.11). It is in this context of gift-exchange that Simonides won his reputation for 'greed', perhaps simply for charging a fee rather than accepting a gift. But, as Sitta von Reden has argued,[31] there is a connection between charging a fee and being 'for hire'. The sophists of fifth-century Athens were attacked by Plato for charging fees for their teaching rather than simply associating with pupils of 'the right sort'. The rhetoric taught by the sophists was regarded by many as dishonest argument. A purchaser of a speech or poem can reasonably command the content of the address made to him. This explains the discussion in the opening of Isthmian 2 of the 'mercenary Muse'. Pindar deprecates any such commercial approach and claims always to be speaking the honest truth. Though his fees were no less high than Simonides', he does not offer 'praise for sale' but the inspired utterance of an honest man of high moral purpose. The ideal party companion.

3.i *The Games*

The ancient Greeks dated their history from the legendary foundation of the Olympic Games in 776 BC. They were celebrated every four years thereafter until their closure by the Christian emperor Theodosius in AD 393. As the occasion when the oft-warring Greek states set aside their differences and met as Hellenes to celebrate Zeus and the other gods and heroes with contests, sacrifices and other rituals, the Olympic Games had an enormous symbolic significance for all Greeks. The other Panhellenic Games, the four-yearly Pythian founded in 582 (dedicated to Apollo), and the two-yearly Isthmian (581: for Poseidon) and Nemean (573: for Zeus), had a significance almost as great. That much is easy to understand. What is less easy for us to grasp is the centrality of athletic contests to the worship of the gods. An anthropological perspective may help to shed light on this phenomenon.[32]

The first athletic contests described in Greek literature were those held by Achilles at the pyre of his dead comrade Patroclus. Such contests are an essential part of funeral rites or honours to a dead hero. They may be understood as a way of placating the dead by performing a mock-sacrifice in the form of an endurance test, in which the victor becomes the sacrificial victim and is, in a sense, offered for the life of the dead man. The fundamental insight into the centrality of sacrifice for Greek culture was developed by Walter Burkert in his book *Homo Necans*,[33] and its results were applied to the particular case of sport by David Sansone (see note 32), and to that of epinician poetry by Gregory Nagy.[34] All the major Panhellenic festivals, besides their dedication to a particular god, had a foundation legend which involved their first institution as the funeral celebrations for the death of a hero, and took place around the tomb of that hero: Pelops at Olympia, Neoptolemus at Delphi, Archemorus/Opheltes at Nemea, Melicertes/Palaemon at the Isthmus.

In historic times such ritual origins of the Games may have been as little understood as are, say, the origins of Orthodox church ritual in Byzantine court procedures among present-day churchgoers, or the origins of the Christmas tree in pagan Germanic practice; but, like these things, the origins gave an atavistic dimension to the celebrations and imbued the festivals with solemnity and depth. So athletic activity was a part of the worship of the gods and heroes.

However, it also became an expression of the intensely competitive spirit that characterized the ancient Greeks. Winning became important for its own sake. The ascetic hero Hippolytus in Euripides' play (1016–20), rejecting the life of the autocrat, says that his highest ambition would be to win in the Panhellenic Games, and second to that to live happily in his city with his fellows: athletic success is even more glorious than royal state. Beginning as a communal ritual, the Games soon became the occasion for a growing professionalism among performers and trainers. The concept of amateurism never existed in ancient Greece, despite some idealistic modern misconceptions,[35] and as early as the end of the sixth century the poet and philosopher Xenophanes of Colophon was attacking the excessive honours and rewards lavished on athletes (in his view his own thoughts were of much greater social value):

> But if a man wins a victory by speed of foot,
>   Or in the pentathlon, in the close of Zeus
> By Pisa's stream at Olympia, or in the wrestling,
>   Or by enduring the pains of the boxing match,
> Or the fearful trial which they call the pankration
>   He is honoured in the eyes of his fellow-townsmen
> With a seat of honour at Games and festivals
>   And maintenance at the public cost
> And a gift of treasure from the city.
>   Even for a horse victory he gets all that,
> Though he is not as deserving as I, for my wisdom
>   Is better than the strength of men and horses.
> From none of these . . .
> Will the city be better governed.

Though an aristocrat, Xenophanes' concern is with his city as a whole. Athletic achievement and its celebration, by contrast, benefited the clan to which the victor belonged. The erection of statues to victors began in the sixth century, as did the practice of commissioning odes to celebrate them. As mentioned above, the nobles might commission an ode for any great event, including a funeral; as a result of which, the Athenian lawgiver Solon attempted to limit the ostentation of the aristocracy by forbidding the performance of pre-composed laments at funerals. Solon is also said to have objected to athletes who 'incur huge costs while in training, do harm when successful, and are crowned for a victory over their country rather than over their rivals'.[36] Two centuries later, the Athenian thinker Isocrates (16.32ff.) could describe the Games as a contest of, above all, wealth: they were an occasion not for civic pride but for lavish and conspicuous expenditure.

Despite such rationalist protests, the prestige of the Games did not lessen. Aristocrats and even tyrants competed, in the latter case not in the physical events but only in the horse and chariot races, which required only the fielding of a good team and a driver. Many athletes acquired enormous prestige, notably Diagoras (the subject of Olympian 7). Other examples include the colossal Milo of Croton, and Theogenes of Thasos, who acquired the status of a hero, with a cult.[37]

3.ii *Events*

The first systematic treatise on the Olympic Games was written by Hippias of Elis (late fifth century), who compiled a list of all the victors, which lies at the basis of the ancient scholars' dating of the Olympian odes. A later work on the Olympic Games, in sixteen books, was the work of Phlegon of Tralles (mid second century AD). Both these works are lost. A papyrus fragment of an Olympic victor list (*POxy* 222) confirms a number of datings of the odes and in addition provides a list in order of the events, which is the same as that given by Pausanias (5.8) in the course of his long and thorough description of the site of Olympia (except that it places the equestrian events at the end, where Pausanias has them after the boxing; but Paus. 5.9.5 explains that they were subsequently moved to a later day of the festival). The order is:

Stadion (foot race)
Diaulos (double foot race)
Dolichos (long race)
Pentathlon
Wrestling
Boxing
Pankration
Boys' stadion

Boys' wrestling
Boys' boxing
Hoplite race (in armour)
Four-horse chariot race
Single-horse chariot race.[38]

Other festivals had a different combination of events:[39] for example, the Heraclea at Thebes we know to have incorporated Pankration, boxing, wrestling, tragic dancing, aulos-playing and cornet-playing.[40] Pythian 12 is for an aulos victory. The Panathenaea incorporated many musical competitions as well as athletics including the stade-race, pentathlon, wrestling and boxing for boys and youths; the same for men plus the diaulos, the dolichos, the mounted race and the race in armour.

Stadion
This was run over a single length of the stadium, approximately 200 metres. The diaulos was two lengths of the stadium: the contestants did not run in lanes, but turned around a single turning-post at the far end.

Dolichos
This was approximately 4,000 metres (20 or 24 lengths).

Pentathlon
This consisted of five events: discus, long jump, javelin, running and wrestling. The method of victory is not certain, but it is likely that if any contestant won the first three contests, he would be declared overall winner and the running and wrestling cancelled. The boys' pentathlon was introduced at Olympia in 628 but discontinued; it continued to take place at other venues (Nemean 7 is for a boy pentathlete). The weight of the discus seems to have varied considerably: see note on Olympian 10.72. This contest, like that of the javelin, was won by distance, but we know that the javelin also had to land within defined limits (Pythian 1.42-5) and that the thrower had not to overstep a mark in throwing (Nemean 7.70-4; H. M. Lee, 'The terma and the javelin in Pindar ... and Greek Athletics', JHS 96 (1976): 70-9). The long jump was a standing jump, and the jumper carried weights in his hands, by swinging which as he leapt he could increase the distance covered (cf. Nemean 5.19-20).

Wrestling

Tactics included controlling the opponent by seizing his wrists; headlock and necklock; the 'underhook' (holding under the shoulder), the waistlock, the leg-trip, and the shoulder-throw. The aim was to ground the opponent; but fighting might continue after the fall. Wrestlers, like all athletes, competed naked, their bodies anointed with olive oil.

Boxing

Boxers wrapped their hands and forearms with leather thongs, at first mainly as wrist protection, but from the fourth century the thongs became heavier and more damaging to the opponent. Boxing with extended thumbs meant there was a possibility of eye-gouging. Death was not unknown in both wrestling and boxing: see R. H. Brophy and D. Brophy, 'Death in the Panhellenic Games II' (*AJP* 106 [1985]: 171–98).

Pankration

This was a kind of no-holds-barred wrestling: see introduction to Nemean 2. The only tactics barred were biting and gouging. Finger-breaking, choking and limb-wrenching were commonly employed. The contest could take place on the ground as well as in the standing position of normal wrestling. The bout ended when a competitor signalled his submission.

Other events

Olympians 4 and 5 were composed for a victor in the mule-chariot race. This less dignified equestrian event did not feature in the official victor lists. It was discontinued at Olympia in 444.

RICHARD STONEMAN

References

1. See in general, B. Gentili, *Poetry and its Public in Ancient Greece* (Baltimore and London 1988); O. Murray (ed.), *Sympotica: A Symposium on the Symposion* (Oxford 1990); W. J. Slater (ed.), *Dining in a Classical Context* (Ann Arbor 1991).

2. D. Sansone, *Greek Athletics and the Genesis of Sport* (Berkeley 1988); M. B. Poliakoff, *Combat Sports in the Ancient World* (New Haven and London 1987); Gregory Nagy, *Pindar's Homer* (Baltimore 1990).

3. L. Woodbury, 'Pindar and the Mercenary Muse: *Isthm.* 2.1–13',

TAPA 99 (1968): 527–42; Sitta von Reden, 'Deceptive Readings: Poetry and its value reconsidered' *CQ* 45 (1995): 30–50. For a vivid recreation of the world of the epinician poets, see Mary Renault, *The Praise Singer* (London 1978). Pindar is said to have received 3,000 drachmas for N 5, 10,000 drachmas for his Athenian dithyramb – the equivalent of Protagoras' course fee for one student (Gentili, p. 162). Many cities in the Athenian Empire paid tribute of no more than 1,000 drachmas a year.

4. Edited and trans. R. C. Jebb (Cambridge 1905: repr. 1967).

5. Italo Gallo, *Una Nuova Biografia di Pindaro* (Salerno, 1968).

6. Mary Lefkowitz, *Lives of the Greek Poets* (London 1981).

7. O 2.86–8. Wilamowitz made this method of interpretation into a guiding principle.

8. See the notes on P 8 for political tensions; on N 7 for alleged offences.

9. The fundamental treatment is A. E. Harvey, 'The Classification of Greek Lyric Poetry', *CQ* 5 (1955): 157ff.

10. Ian Rutherford, *ZPE* 92 (1992): 59–72. See notes on Pa. 14.

11. A thorough modern treatment of Greek girl-choruses is Claude Calame, *Les Choeurs de jeunes filles en Grèce archaique* (Rome 1977).

12. D. C. Young, 'Pindaric Criticism' (see Further Reading) is the source of most of the examples that follow.

13. *Pindaros* (Berlin 1922).

14. Young, 'Pindaric Criticism', p. 55.

15. *Pindar* (Oxford 1964).

16. E. L. Bundy, *Studia Pindarica* (Berkeley 1986); originally published as articles in 1962.

17. Gentili, *Poetry and its Public*, pp. 107–14; G. Nagy, *The Best of the Achaeans* (Baltimore 1979), pp. 232–52.

18. G. E. R. Lloyd, *Polarity and Analogy* (Cambridge 1966).

19. W. Schadewaldt, *Der Aufbau des pindarischen Epinikion* (Tübingen 1996).

20. Cf. n. 18.

21. The ancient conception of envy has a good deal in common with the idea of the 'evil eye', the idea that praise without a prayer will bring misfortune. See P. Walcot, *Envy and the Greeks* (Warminster 1978); L. Di Stasi, *Mal Ochio: The Underside of Vision* (San Francisco 1981).

22. Both quoted by Adolf Köhnken, *Die Funktion des Mythos bei Pindar* (Berlin 1971), pp. 227ff. This book, and the same author's

various articles, are among the best studies of Pindar's myths and of his poetry generally.

23. A. P. Burnett, *The Art of Bacchylides* (Cambridge, Mass. 1985), pp. 8–9.

24. C. Carey, 'Three Myths in Pindar', *Eranos* 78 (1980): 143–62.

25. W. H. Race, *Style and Rhetoric in Pindar's Odes*, p. 136 and the whole chapter, pp. 119–40.

26. S. Instone, *CQ* 36 (1986): 93.

27. G. Nagy, *Pindar's Homer*.

28. *CQ* 34 (1984): 43–9. See also the important pages by D. C. Young, *Three Odes of Pindar* (see Further Reading), pp. 58–9, on 'first-person indefinite' and the way that the poet may speak for the addressee. Xenophon's dialogue *Hiero* is about the difference between a private citizen and a despot.

29. The words are cognate, as noted above, p. xxvi: Gregory Nagy, *Pindar's Homer*, Chapters 11–12.

30. Cf. I 4; P. A. Bernardini, *QUCC* 25 (1977): 13, n. 4.

31. Gentili, *Poetry and its Public*, p. 162; S. von Reden, 'Deceptive Readings'.

32. For what follows, see Sansone, *Greek Athletics*; Poliakoff, *Combat Sports*, appendix.

33. Berlin 1972; English translation, with the same title (Berkeley 1983).

34. Nagy, *Pindar's Homer*, Chapter 5.

35. D. C. Young, *The Olympic Myth of Greek Amateur Athletics* (Chicago 1984).

36. Diogenes Laertius, *Lives of the Philosophers*, 1.56.

37. There is a useful compendium of major Greek athletes in Poliakoff, *Combat Sports*, Chapter 7.

38. There is a survey of all the events of the Olympics in Judith Swaddling, *The Ancient Olympic Games* (London 1980), Chapter 6. For victor lists: L. Moretti, *Olympionikai, i vincitori negli antichi agoni olimpici* (Memorie dell' academia dei Lincei, classe di scienze . . . e filologia, ser. 8.viii.2 [Rome 1957]).

39. E. A. Gardiner, *Greek Athletic Sports and Festivals* (London 1910).

40. P. Roesch, 'Les Herakleia de Thebes', *ZPE* 17 (1975): 1–7.

FESTIVALS, VICTORS, EVENTS AND MYTHS

Festivals at which victories mentioned in the epinician odes were won

1. Panhellenic Games

Festival	City	Month	Prize
Olympia	Olympia	July/August	olive wreath
Pythia	Delphi	July/August	laurel wreath
Nemea	Nemea	July/August	parsley wreath
Isthmia	Isthmus	April/May	wild parsley

Greek history was dated by Olympiads, periods of four years (five by the Greek inclusive reckoning) beginning with the first celebration in June/July (= Month 1) 776 BC. The first Pythiad was almost certainly 582 BC. The series of the Panhellenic Games was as follows (the Greek year begins in midsummer):

Olympiad	Date	Month	Festival
75.1	480/79	July/August (month 1)	Olympia
75.2	479/8	July/August	Nemea
75.3	478/7	April/May (month 10)	Isthmia
		July/August	Pythia
75.4	477/6	July/August	Nemea
	476/5	April/May	Isthmia
76.1	476/5	July/August	Olympia

2. Local Games

Festival	City	Date/month	Prize	Reference
Adrasteia	Sicyon (or Sicyonian Pythia)		silver cups	N 9
Agriania (Demeter)	Argos	(March?)		frag. 70a

2. Local Games (*Cont.*)

Festival	City	Date/month	Prize	Reference
Aiaceia/ Delphinia	Aegina	new moon		N 5.44, O 7.83, P 8.66, Farnell vol. II, p. 466; vol. IV, p. 147
Alcathoia	Megara			O 7.83, N 5.45, N 3.84
Aleaia	Tegea			N 10.47
Asclepieia	Epidaurus	annual		N 3 (end), Paus. 2.26.7
Carneia	Sparta, Cyrene	July/August		P 5.90
Daphnephoria	Thebes	nine-yearly (probably in spring)		Farnell, vol. 4, p. 284
Delphinia – see Aiaceia				
Dia	Pellene		woollen cloak	N 10
Eleusinia	Eleusis	four-yearly, in second Olympic year		I 1.57
Ge and Nymphs	Athens	27 Boedromion		P 9.101
Hecatombaea (Hera)	Aegina	Panemos (June); uneven years BC		P 8.78ff.
Hecatombaea/ Heraea	Argos		bronze shield, myrtle wreath	O 7.83, N 10
Heliaea	Rhodes			

2. Local Games (*Cont.*)

Festival	City	Date/month	Prize	Reference
Hellotia (Athena)	Corinth			O 13.40
Heracleia/ Iolaeia	Thebes	annual, two days	bronze tripod, myrtle crown	O 7.83, N 4.20, I 4.61
Hydrophoria	Aegina	Delphinios		P 8.64, N 4.35, N 5.44
Koriasia/ Koreia (Athena)	Cleitor			O 7.153
Lycaea	Arcadia/ Parrhasia	winter	bronze armour	O 7.83, O 9.102, O 13.108, N 10.48, X *Anab* 1.2.10
Minyeia	Orchomenus			I 1.56
Olympia	Athens	19th Munychion		P 9.101
Panathenaea	Athens	28 Hecatombaeon = c. 17 July	jars of oil	O 13.38
Protesilaea	Phylake			I 1.59
Theoxenia	Pellene			O 9.98, N 10.44
Theoxenia	Acragas			O 3
Theoxenia	Delphi			Pa. 6.62
uncertain	Achaea		bronze vases	N 10.47
uncertain (Heracles?)	Marathon		silver cup	O 9.89, P 8.78; Parke, pp. 181ff.
uncertain	Euboea			I 1.57

Victors, events and myths

1. Olympian odes

Page	Ode	Victor	Event	Myth
3	1	Hieron of Syracuse	Horse race	Pelops
12	2	Theron of Acragas	Chariot race	Isles of the Blest
22	3	Theron of Acragas	Chariot race	Heracles' journey to Hyperboreans
29	4	Psaumis of Camarina	Chariot race with mules	Erginus at Lemnos
33	5	Psaumis of Camarina	Chariot race with mules	None
37	6	Hagesias of Syracuse	Chariot race with mules	Iamus
46	7	Diagoras of Rhodes	Boxing match	Tlepolemus and origin of Rhodes
55	8	Alcimedon of Aegina	Boys' wrestling match	Aeacus and walls of Troy
61	9	Epharmostus of Opous	Wrestling match	Deucalion and Pyrrha
69	10	Hagesidamus of Epizephyrian Locri	Boys' boxing match	None
77	11	Hagesidamus of Epizephyrian Locri	Boys' boxing match	Founding of Olympian Games
79	12	Ergoteles of Himera	Long foot race	None
82	13	Xenophon of Corinth	Short foot race and pentathlon	Bellerophon and Pegasus
92	14	Asopichus of Orchomenus	Boys' foot race	None

2. Pythian odes

Page	Ode	Victor	Event	Myth
95	1	Hieron of Aetna	Chariot race	Typhon and Mount Aetna
105	2	Hieron of Syracuse	Chariot race	Ixion
113	3	Hieron of Syracuse	Horse race	Asclepius

2. Pythian odes (*Cont.*)

Page	Ode	Victor	Event	Myth
123	4	Arcesilas of Cyrene	Chariot race	Medea and the Argonauts
144	5	Arcesilas of Cyrene	Chariot race	Battus
152	6	Xenocrates of Acragas	Chariot race	Antilochus and Nestor
156	7	Megacles of Athens	Chariot race	None
159	8	Aristomenes of Aegina	Wrestling match	Prophecy of Amphiaraus
166	9	Telesicrates of Cyrene	Foot race in armour	Apollo and Cyrene
175	10	Hippocleas of Thessaly	Boys' long foot race	Perseus and the Hyperboreans
180	11	Thrasydaeus of Thebes	Boys' short foot race	Orestes and Clytemnestra
187	12	Midas of Acragas	Flute-playing	Perseus and Medusa

3. Nemean odes

Page	Ode	Victor	Event	Myth
193	1	Chromius of Aetna	Chariot race	Infant Heracles and the Snakes
200	2	Timodemus of Acharnae	Pankration	None
203	3	Aristocleidas of Aegina	Pankration	Aeacids and Achilles
212	4	Timasarchus of Aegina	Boys' wrestling match	Aeacids, Peleus and Thetis
220	5	Pytheas of Aegina	Youths' pankration	Peleus, Hippolyta and Thetis
227	6	Alcimidas of Aegina	Boys' wrestling match	Aeacids, Achilles and Memnon
233	7	Sogenes of Aegina	Boys' pentathlon	Neoptolemus
245	8	Deinis of Aegina	Foot race	Death of Ajax
251	9	Chromius of Aetna	Chariot race	Seven against Thebes
257	10	Theaius of Argos	Wrestling match	Castor and Pollux
269	11	Aristagoras of Tenedos	Inauguration as Prytanis	None

4. Isthmian odes

NOTE ON THE TRANSLATION

G. S. Conway's verse translation of the epinicia was originally published in 1972. Since then there has been one other major verse translation of the epinicia by Frank J. Nisetich: *Pindar's Victory Songs* (Baltimore 1980). More modern in diction than Conway's, and with good introductory material, it lacks the detailed annotation that Conway provided. Conway's translation has many virtues, not least that it often functions as illuminating commentary on the original. On very many occasions the translation Conway offers represents an astute choice among difficulties and conflicting possibilities, or a sensitive response to the connotations of a Greek phrase. I give a few examples:

O 1.22 'victory's embrace' nicely conveys the erotic overtones of the word *emeixe* (literally, 'mixed him with victory').

O 2.7 'Upholder of his city' accurately conveys the verbal force of the first element in the adjective *orthopolis*.

O 7.44 'Reverence, Daughter of Forethought' is an imaginative way of conveying the sense of the difficult phrase *promatheos aidos*.

N 1.24 is a notorious crux in Pindaric interpretation. Conway has, I believe, got the sense right: see my 'The Niceties of Praise: Notes on Pindar's Nemeans', *QUCC* n.s. 2 (1979): 65–77.

N 8.48ff. In my view Conway has correctly interpreted the play on 'two' which has caused many commentators to flounder in assessing the number of victories in question.

N 10.42 'At Corinth in the Isthmus vale' correctly interprets Pindar's 'in the nooks of Corinth', where the scholiasts ask whether a victory at a Corinthian festival might be meant.

Naturally I do not always agree with Conway's interpretations. I have, however, not made any changes to his translation but have signalled differences of opinion in the notes.

I have found it necessary completely to rewrite his introductions to the odes to take account of advances in interpretation and method since the translation appeared. Occasionally I have been able to keep some of what Conway wrote, particularly on historical background on the Sicilian odes.

I have revised the notes to the translations very thoroughly and made many additions. Where Conway had found it necessary to provide the same note repeatedly to explain allusions (e.g. Hill of Cronos), I have left the note at its first appearance, but also included the information in the Glossary. If explanation of a reference is needed and is not in the notes, it will, I hope, always be found in the Glossary.

I have added to the book my own translations (prose divided into lines roughly corresponding to those of the original) of a large number of the fragments of Pindar. These include the paeans, dithyrambs and other named genres, except where the remains are too fragmentary to provide an intelligible translation; also all of the shorter fragments, even phrases, which seemed to me interesting in themselves or helpful in the understanding of Pindar's work. A complete translation of everything, including even the most fragmentary pieces, with facing Greek text, is available in the Loeb Classical Library, edited by W. H. Race.

In this Everyman edition I have indicated line numbers on the English translations as an aid to those who wish to use it alongside the Greek. Naturally, the English and Greek lines do not correspond exactly because of differences in Greek and English word order. The reader should be aware that line numbers in the notes refer to the *Greek* text and are occasionally two or three lines out from the English.

I hope that the reader will find this edition of Pindar an illuminating introduction to the work of this magnificent and difficult poet.

EPINICIAN ODES

For this it is gives to the path of song
Immortal life, if on the poet's tongue
    Fair praise is fairly set.

(Isthmian 4.57–8)

For Hieron of Syracuse

Winner of the Single-Horse Race (476)

In 476, when Hieron won this Olympic victory, he had been ruler of Syracuse for two years and was approaching the summit of his power, and controlled almost all of Sicily. His court was noted throughout the Greek world for its wealth and magnificence and for its patronage of the arts, in particular poetry and architecture.

This is one of four odes composed by Pindar for Hieron, the others being Pythian 3 (478), Pythian 1 (470) and Pythian 2 (uncertain date, perhaps 475). It celebrates a victory not in a horse race in the modern sense, but with a chariot drawn by a single horse (*keles*, as distinct from a *harma*, a four-horse chariot). Hieron also commissioned an ode from Bacchylides for the same event (B 5). The ode contains at the end a prayer that Hieron may achieve his ambition of a chariot victory at Olympia; he did indeed achieve this in 468, but the ode to celebrate was commissioned from Bacchylides (Ode 3) not Pindar.

The present ode begins with a tribute to the Olympian Games themselves, which induced the ancient scholars to place this in programmatic position as the first of the Olympian odes; apart from praise of Hieron and the horse Pherenikos, it is largely devoted to the myth of Tantalus and his son Pelops. The most convincing explanation of the relation of this myth to the subject of the ode is that proffered by Adolf Köhnken ('Pindar as Innovator: Poseidon Hippios and the relevance of the Pelops story in Olympian 1' *CQ* 24 [1974]: 199–206), who argues that the gift of swift horses provides the link: Hieron, like Pelops, is loved by the gods and gifted by them with winning steeds. For this reason the murderous deceit used by Pelops to win his race has to be omitted lest it insult Pindar's patron.

This is not the only change Pindar makes to the myths in this ode. The usual story about Tantalus, king of Sipylus in Asia Minor, was that he prepared a banquet at which the gods were to be guests, and in a fit of insane pride killed and cut up his young son Pelops to feed them. Clotho, one of the three Fates,

rescued Pelops from the cauldron and put his body together
again; but a part of his shoulder was missing as Demeter had
already bitten into it, and this was replaced by a piece of ivory.
Pindar dismisses this as a false tale invented by malicious
neighbours to explain his disappearance and replaces it with one
more honourable to the hero he celebrates: he had been seized
by Poseidon because of his beauty. Tantalus' punishment in
Hades is thus also given a different cause, namely his giving of
ambrosia and nectar, the food and drink of the gods, to his
mortal friends. Why does Pindar introduce the story at all?
Because his initial praise of Pelops–Hieron has entailed Pelops
being carried off to Olympus by the gods, and the story requires
that he be brought back to earth.

Though it is not unreasonable to see a theological motivation
in Pindar's stated desire to make the myths more creditable to
the gods and heroes, the main motive to be borne in mind is that
he must make his praise adequate to his subject: Hieron is a very
great ruler, and his victory must be presented as exceptionally
glittering, a successor and analogy to a glittering legendary past
where the only dark shadows are there as contrast to the hero's
achievement (Tantalus' doom), not an integral part of it (the
murder of Oenomaus).

str. 1   Best blessing of all is water,
    And gold like a fiery flame gleaming at night,
    Supreme amidst the pride of lordly wealth.
     But if you seek, beloved heart,
      To sing of the great Games,   5
    Then neither in the lonely firmament
    By day, look for another star more bright
    And gladdening than the sun, nor can we praise
    A greater contest than Olympia;
    Whence the bright arrows of renownéd song
     Play round the minds of poets,
      In hymns to honour   10
    The son of Cronos, as our steps approach
    The rich and blessed hearth of Hieron,

ant. 1   Who wields his rod of justice
    In Sicily, land of rich flocks, and culls
    Of all things excellent the noblest fruit;

Made glorious too by the fine flower
　　Of music's utterance –　　　　　　　　　　　15
Such strains as men will often blithely sing
Where we sit round the table of a friend.
Come, then, take from its peg the Dorian lyre,
If a sweet spell of thought's delight the grace
Of Pisa and of Pherenikos bred
　　Within your heart, when, speeding
　　　By Alpheus' bank,　　　　　　　　　　　20
His lovely limbs ungoaded on the course,
He brought his lord to victory's embrace,

ep. 1　　That master who delights in horsemanship
　　　King of great Syracuse;
And in the colony of Lydian Pelops,
That land of noble souls, his fame is bright;
　　Pelops, who stirred Poseidon's love,　　　25
The god of mighty strength, the earth-holder,
When Clotho drew him from the untainted bowl,
His shoulder shod with gleaming ivory.
True, there are many marvels; here or there
　　　Maybe the tongues of men
　　O'er-riding truth's sure word, deceive
With false-spun tales, the embroidery of lies.

str. 2　　For Beauty, goddess who fashions　　　30
All things that lovely are for mortal men,
Her shower of glory many a time enriched
　　That which deserves no firm belief
　　　To be a trusted tale.
But days to come will prove the surest witness.
Right is it a man speak well of the immortals,　　35
Less then will be his blame. Tantalus' son,
Unlike to bards of old, my tongue shall tell
How when your father gave the all-seemly banquet,
　　　On Sipylus that he loved,
　　　　To make return
Of hospitable gift to the immortals,
Then he of the Bright Trident seized upon you,　　40

ant. 2　　His heart mad with desire,
And brought you mounted in his glorious chariot

To the high hall of Zeus whom all men honour,
 Where later came Ganymede, too,
  For a like love, to Zeus.   45
But when you were thus vanished with no sign,
And the wide search of men had brought you not
Back to your mother, then quickly was heard
Some secret voice of envious neighbours, telling
That for the seething cauldron's fiery heat
  Your limbs with a knife's blade
   Were cut asunder,
And at each table, portioned to the guests,   50
The morsels of your flesh became their meal.

ep. 2 Senseless, I hold it, for a man to say
  The gods eat mortal flesh.
I spurn the thought. A slanderer's evil tongue
Often enough brings him to no good end.
 But if indeed any man ever
Won honour from Olympus' lords, that man
Was Tantalus. Yet could he not stomach   55
His high fortune, but earned for his excess
A doom o'erwhelming, when the Father poised
  A mighty stone above him,
  Which with its ever-threatening blow
To strike his head, robs all his days of joy.

str. 3 Thus bound within an endless
Prison of toil and tortured pain, his life
Is set, fourth penalty with other three,   60
  For that he stole from the immortals,
   And gave to his companions
In revelry, ambrosia and nectar,
Whereby the gods gave him undying life.
But if a man shall hope in aught he does
To escape the eyes of god, he makes an error.
Thence was it the gods sent his son down again 65
  To share the short-lived span
   Of mortal life.
But when the flower of rising youth shaded
His cheek with down, then for a speedy marriage

ant. 3   He counselled in his mind,
         From her father of Pisa to win the maid
         Hippodamia, of glorious fame. And coming   70
             Near to the salt sea's edge, alone
                 At night, he called aloud
         To the loud-roaring Wielder of the Trident,
         Who came, and stood before him. Then spoke Pelops,
         And said 'Lo, great Poseidon, if in your count
         The Cyprian goddess' gifts find aught of favour,   75
         Then shackle Oenomaus' brazen spear, and bring me
             On speeding chariot wheels
                 To the land of Elis,
         And grant me victory. For thirteen souls
         Now has he slain, her suitors, and holds back   80

ep. 3   The marriage of his daughter. Great danger
             Calls to no coward's heart;
         But for man, who must die, why should he nurse
         A nameless old age through, in vain, in darkness,
             And of all deeds that glorious are
         Have not a share? But for me shall this contest
         Lie for my challenge. Do thou but grant fair issue
         My heart's desire.' So he spoke, and his prayer   85
         Uttered no words that failed of their achievement.
             But for his glory's honour,
                 The god gave him a gleaming chariot,
         And steeds that flew unwearied upon wings.

str. 4   And mighty Oenomaus
         He slew, and took the maiden for his bride;
         Six sons she bore, chieftains leading the field
             In valorous deeds. By Alpheus' ford
                 He lies now, closely joined
         To the great feast of glorious sacrifice,   90
         His tomb oft visited, beside the altar
         Where many a stranger treads. And the great fame
         Of the Olympiad Games shines far afield,
         In the course known of Pelops, where are matched
             Rivals in speed of foot   95
                 And in brave feats

Of bodily strength. Thence, all his life, around him
The victor knows a sunlit day's delight,

ant. 4   Prize of the contest's struggle.
Yet for all men the blessing of each day
Is the best boon. My task is now to crown   100
   My hero in the horseman strain,
      And the Aeolian mode.
And well I know that of all living men
No host, both of more heart for noble ends
And more power to achieve them, shall by me
Be enriched in glorious harmonies of song.   105
Over your labours, Hieron, a god
   Keeps watch, bearing your cares
      Close to his thought;
And if he leave you not too soon, I trust
That a still sweeter glory I may proclaim,

ep. 4   Finding thereto a path ready for song
         To honour your swift chariot,   110
When I am come to Cronos' sunlit hill.
For I know well, my Muse in her array
   Nurses her strongest dart of all.
In various enterprise, various men
Ascend to greatness, but the highest crown
Is given to kings. Further seek not to glimpse.
Be it yours through all your life to tread the heights   115
      And mine no less to share
   Friendship with victors in the Games,
Through all Hellas pride of the poet's art.

Notes

1. **Best blessing of all is water**: this famous opening line, 'water is best'
(perhaps as far as many readers got with these difficult poems), is the
first term of a beautifully pure form of the priamel or climactic series:
water-gold-Games; and within Games, like a sun among stars – Olympia!

10. **son of Cronos**: Zeus, to whom the Olympic Games were sacred.
The conical Hill of Cronos is a prominent feature of the site at
Olympia, frequently mentioned by Pindar.

11. the blessed hearth of Hieron: this indicates that Pindar was present in Syracuse to take part in the performance of the ode.

17. the Dorian lyre: the reference is to the Dorian 'mode' or tuning of the lyre, hence a scale. This tuning was popular and widely used in the fifth century and earlier, and regarded as dignified, appropriate for ceremonial and solemn subjects: cf. Pindar frag. 67 'the Dorian scale is the most solemn'; Plato *Laches* 188d 'the true Hellenic mode, which is the Dorian'.

18. Pherenikos: the horse with which Hieron had won this race. Pherenikos had also won a race for Hieron at the Pythian Games of 478, and may also have won in 482, if the plural 'crowns' at P 3.73ff. can be pressed. At B 5.39 Bacchylides calls Pherenikos *polos*, 'a colt'. If he had won a race in 482 he must by now have been at least nine years old.

20. Alpheus' bank: the River Alpheus runs by Olympia.

20. lovely limbs: the few words devoted to Pherenikos' performance are unusual in Pindar, who, in contrast to Bacchylides, generally has nothing to say about the actual event.

24. Lydian Pelops: Pelops and his father Tantalus came from Sipylus in Lydia. The 'colony' is the district of Elis, in which Olympia lies. Pelops settled here and gave his name to the whole of the Peloponnese.

26. Clotho: one of the three Fates. Clotho is the spinner of the thread of life, Lachesis is the 'Apportioner' of destiny, and Atropos, 'who cannot be turned aside', snaps the thread at its close.

the untainted bowl: in place of the usual story of Pelops' rescue from the cauldron, Pindar substitutes this picture of his being washed as a new-born child in purifying water. The ivory shoulder is with him from birth, not a substitute for the piece eaten by Demeter.

30. Beauty: Greek 'Charis', Grace, signifying surface appeal as opposed to inner truth. Pindar rejects the specious appeal of traditional myths for something more in keeping with divine realities, and more worthy as praise of Pelops. Pausanias remarks (8.2.6; where he is talking of Lycaon but has also mentioned Tantalus): 'Those who have added so many constructions of lies to truthful foundations have made a lot of things that happened in the history of the world, things that happened in antiquity and things that still happen now, seem incredible to the majority of mankind.' Pindar's point is the opposite one, that people are too ready to believe what is invented, but both are concerned that original truth is damaged or devalued by alleged fictions.

33. days to come: for time as revealer of truth, cf. O 10.55

38. Sipylus: a Lydian mountain, modern Manisa Dagi.

40. he of the Bright Trident: Poseidon, god of the sea. In the usual version of the myth, it is Zeus, not Poseidon, who takes Pelops. Poseidon, however, takes Pelops not to his own realm, the sea, but to Olympus, associated primarily with Zeus. (See Köhnken, op.cit. in introduction.)

44. Ganymede: a beautiful youth carried off by Zeus as his boy-lover and cup-bearer. (His Latin name Catamitus is the origin of 'catamite'.) A terracotta statuette found at Olympia portrays Zeus' capture of Ganymede and is contemporary with this ode.

55. Tantalus: the punishment of Tantalus described here differs from those mentioned in Homer, *Odyssey* 1.582–92, where Tantalus is tormented by thirst, standing in a lake of water which retreats whenever he stoops to drink; and by hunger, as he stands beneath a fruit tree whose branches drift out of reach whenever he stretches to pluck the fruit. Pindar often seems to make a point of differing from the Ionian mythological tradition as represented by Homer.

60. fourth penalty: this may refer to his other punishments – the two Homeric torments, as well as eternal imprisonment – but the number is more easily referred to the other three sinners in Hades: Sisyphus, Tityus and Ixion.

65. his son: Pelops.

70. her father of Pisa: Oenomaus, ruler of Pisa.

75. 'Lo, great Poseidon': Pelops' prayer follows the regular pattern of Greek prayer, recalling the god's obligations incurred by former honours, and proceeding to a further request.

76. The Cyprian goddess: Aphrodite, goddess of love, whose traditional residence was at Paphos on Cyprus.

79. thirteen souls: Oenomaus promised the hand of his daughter to any suitor who could defeat him in a chariot race, for which his own chariot was equipped with invincible horses. Unsuccessful suitors were put to death. This is a common folktale motif (the *Turandot* theme).

83. nurse a nameless old age: literally 'chew, digest'; so 'wear out'. The digestive metaphor recalls that of line 55, Tantalus who could not 'digest' his good fortune (and indeed the polemic about the gods 'digesting' bits of Pelops).

86. steeds that flew . . . : Pindar suppresses the better-known version, represented in the east pediment of the Temple of Zeus at Olympia of 470–56, in which Pelops won his victory by bribing Oenomaus' groom Myrtilus to remove the lynch-pins from the axle of Oenomaus' chariot. Oenomaus crashed and died. Pelops then murdered Myrtilus to keep the secret safe, but the latter's dying curse on Pelops' family involved them in disaster for generations, from Pelops' sons Atreus and Thyestes onwards.

88. slew: the Greek says 'he seized his strength and his daughter', a euphemistic zeugma.

89. Six sons: Atreus, Thyestes, Plisthenes, Sciron, Pittheus (founder of Troezen), Alcathous (founder of Megara). In addition Pelops had an illegitimate son, Chrysippus, whose seduction by Laius was credited with bringing homosexual relations into the world. The list of sons varied somewhat, and a scholiast on Euripides, *Orestes* 4 manages to tot up fifteen sons for Pelops, in addition to Chrysippus.

90. sacrifice: literally, 'blood offerings'. Heroes were offered liquid libations, while gods received burnt sacrifice.

93. His tomb: the sanctuary of Pelops stood to the south of the Temple of Hera at Olympia; it contained his altar and a pit for sacrificial offerings, and has been made visible again by archaeology.

94. course: i.e. the stadium at Olympia.

98. the blessing of each day: this transitional *gnome* returns Pindar from his mythical theme to his particular subject by focusing on an aspect of significance in the story he has just told.

105. Harmonies: literally, 'folds of song'.

110. your swift chariot: Pindar expresses the hope that Hieron will win the most coveted of all victories, that with the four-horse chariot at Olympia. He did indeed win, in 468 BC; but it was Bacchylides who composed the ode for the occasion.

115. mine no less to share: the praise of Hieron is validated by Pindar's prayer to be his friend and equal, i.e. 'let me be great enough to praise you adequately' (cf. P 2.96).

For Theron of Acragas
Winner of the Chariot Race (476)

Theron became ruler of Acragas (modern Agrigento) about 488. He allied himself with his son-in-law Gelon of Gela, who in 485 made himself master of Syracuse and left the rule of Gela to his younger brother Hieron. Under these leaders the Greek forces inflicted a severe defeat on the Carthaginians at the Battle of Himera in 480. This victory brought Acragas and Theron to the summit of their wealth and power. When Gelon died in 478 he left the rule of Syracuse to Hieron, and the hand of his wife Damareta, the daughter of Theron, to another younger brother, Polyzelus. The harmony of relations between Hieron and Theron soon fell into disarray. Theron had married the daughter of Polyzelus, and Hieron a niece of Theron. Hieron fell out with Polyzelus, who joined forces with Theron's son Thrasydaeus, who had been installed as ruler of Himera. The people of Himera, discontented with the rule of Thrasydaeus, took sides with Hieron. By the year 476 there seemed every possibility that war would break out between Hieron and Theron, who between them were now rulers of virtually all of Sicily. This catastrophe was averted, largely it is said through the intervention of the poet Simonides, who acted as a negotiator between the two parties. (This last piece of information comes from the scholiasts, who may have derived it from the historian Timaeus.)

Lasting peace between the two rulers was restored in 470, and Polyzelus was pardoned. This probably took place in the early part of that year, since Theron's victory in the chariot race celebrated in the present ode, and Hieron's victory in the horse race, celebrated in Olympian I, both took place at the Olympic Games of 476. Both odes were written during Pindar's visit to Sicily in 476/5. Pindar's connection with the family of Theron was long-standing. In 490 he had composed Pythian 6 for the chariot victory of Theron's brother Xenocrates, whose young son Thrasybulus was the charioteer. A close friendship apparently sprang up between Thrasybulus and Pindar, who was at that time a man of twenty-eight, and the poem is a warm tribute to Thrasybulus. Pindar again wrote warmly of Thrasybulus in Isthmian 2, celebrating a victory won by Xenocrates in perhaps 476/5 (though it was composed a few years later).

Against this background of friendship with members of Theron's family, it is not surprising if this ode shows signs of concern about recent events. The 'many deeds ... done rightly or unrightly' of epode 1 are surely the recent political crisis in Sicily. Lines 86ff., also, have often been interpreted as hinting at unmentionable circumstances (but see note *ad loc*).

The ode is unusual in containing no myth in the proper sense, but a description of the life of the Blessed, who have been initiated in the Mysteries, in the Underworld. There are close resemblances between this passage and two fragments of Pindar's Laments (frags 129–30 and 131), both addressed to Theron. It seems inappropriate to interpret this circumstance as an outburst of morbidity on Pindar's part; rather, it seems likely that Theron, who commissioned these works, was a particular devotee of the Mysteries, which were a prominent feature of Sicilian religion, and requested allusions to his own beliefs in the odes.

The ode is dominated by two themes: the alternation of good and ill fortune in human life and the insecurity of man's lot under an inscrutable Fate. These themes are demonstrated through allusions to myths of the descendants of Cadmus (whom Theron also counted as an ancestor).

str. 1   Lords of the lyre, ye hymns, what god,
          What hero, what man shall we honour? Zeus
             Holds Pisa; the Olympiad feast
          Heracles founded, the first-fruits of war;
          Now for his four-horsed chariot victory
          Let Theron's name be praised, who to all strangers   5
             Shows the true face of justice,
          Of Acragas the staunch pillar,
             Upholder of his city,
          Of famous fathers the fine flower;

ant. 1   They after many a labour, took
          Beside this river bank their sacred dwelling,
             And were the eye of Sicily;

And an age sent of heaven attended them,   10
Bringing them wealth and honour, to crown their inborn
Merit. O son of Cronos, Rhea's child,
    Who rules Olympus' seat
  And the great Games by Alpheus' ford,
  Gladdened with songs, be gracious
  To grant this soil be still their homeland

ep. 1   For all their race to come. But of man's deeds   15
    Be they done rightly or unrightly,
    Not even Time, father of all,
      Can make accomplishment
Undone again. Yet if good fortune wills,
    Forgetfulness may come;
Quelled by the charm of noble joys, grief dies,
    Thrown to the ground again,   20

str. 2   When Fate brings from the hand of heaven
Happiness rich and wide. Such is the tale
    Told of the fair-throned maids of Cadmus,
Who suffered mightily, but heavy woe
Falls before greater good. With the immortals
Semele of the flowing locks lives still
    – Who died in the roar of thunder –   25
  And Pallas loves her ever, and Zeus
    No less, and dearly too
  The ivy-bearing god, her son.

ant. 2   The tale runs too, that in the ocean
With the sea-maidens, Nereus' daughters, Ino
    Was given undying life for ever.   30
Verily no term of death is set for mortals,
Who know not even if some peaceful day,
Child of the sun, shall bring us to its end
    'Midst happiness still unfailing.
  This way and that the currents run
    – Be they the tides of joy
  Or toil – that make the lot of man.

ep. 2   For as Fate, who accords our mortal race   35
    Their heritage of happy fortune,

To their heaven-sent prosperity
   Brings at another hour
An opposite load of ill, so, long ago,
   The fated son of Laius,
Slaying his father on the road, fulfilled
   Pytho's old oracle.   40

str. 3   This saw Erinys, fierce avenger,
And by their own hands slew that warrior race
   Of brothers. Polynices felled,
Was left Thersander, in new contests honoured
And in war's battles; this scion of the line
Stayed up the house of dead Adrastus' sons.   45
     Bred from that seed's descent,
     Right is it Ainesidamus' son
       Should win triumphant songs
     Of revel, and music of the lyre.

ant. 3   For he received Olympia's prize
And for his brother alike, the impartial Graces
   At Pytho and the Isthmus gave   50
His four-horsed chariot on the twelve-lap course
Their crown of flowers. Victory, for a man
Who braves the contest's struggle, sets at rest
     All discontent. Wealth too,
     Be it with noble deeds inwrought,
       Brings gifts of many a kind,
     Sustaining deep and troublous cares,

ep. 3   A shining star, light of sure trust for man,   55
     If but who holds it, knows what is
     To come – that straightway, when they die
       Hearts that were void of mercy
Pay the due penalty, and of this world's sins
     A judge below the earth
Holds trial, and of dread necessity
     Declares the word of doom.   60

str. 4   But the good, through the nights alike,
And through the days unendingly, beneath
   The sun's bright ray, tax not the soil

With the strength of their hands, nor the broad sea
For a poor living, but enjoy a life
That knows no toil; with men honoured of heaven,   65
    Who kept their sworn word gladly,
    Spending an age free from all tears.
      But the unjust endure
    Pain that no eye can bear to see.

ant. 4   But those who had good courage, three times
On either side of death, to keep their hearts
    Untarnished of all wrong, these travel
Along the road of Zeus to Cronos' tower.   70
There round the islands of the blest, the winds
Of ocean play, and golden blossoms burn,
    Some nursed upon the waters,
    Others on land on glorious trees;
      And woven on their hands
    Are wreaths enchained and flowering crowns,

ep. 4   Under the just decrees of Rhadamanthus,   75
    Who has his seat at the right hand
    Of the great father, Rhea's husband,
      Goddess who holds the throne
Highest of all. And Peleus and Cadmus
    Are of that number, and thither,
When her prayers on the heart of Zeus prevailed,
    His mother brought Achilles,   80

str. 5   He who felled Hector, Troy's pillar
Invincible, unyielding, and brought death
    To Cycnus, and the Ethiop son
Of Dawn. Many a swift arrow my quiver holds
Beneath my arm, speaking to men of wisdom,   85
But for the throng they need interpreters.
    Inborn of nature's wisdom
    The poet's truth; taught skills, rough-hewn,
      Gross-tongued, are like a pair
    Of ravens vainly chattering

ant. 5   Before the divine bird of Zeus.
Come, set your bow, my soul, upon its mark;

From a soft-spoken heart again,
On whom do we now launch our shafts of honour?   90
It shall be Acragas that holds my aim,
Telling on oath, no falsehood, that this city
    Not for a hundred years
Has bred a man, who for his friends
    Wrought goodness with more kind
A heart, and a more bounteous hand

ep. 5   Than Theron. Yet is high praise trampled down   95
    By envy, against all right confronted
    By madmen's hands, scheming in whispers
      To shroud in secret blame
Good deeds of noble men. Yet the sea-sands
    Are fled beyond all count,
And of the joys this man has given to others,
    Who could declare their number?   100

Notes

1. **Lords of the lyre**: The rhythms of Pindar's music, he implies, are determined by his words. For praise of the lyre cf. O 1.17. Aeschylus (*Suppliants* 697) speaks of 'reputation which loves the lyre'. The passage impressed Ezra Pound, who recalled it in Canto IV and quoted it in 'Hugh Selwyn Mauberley' III:

> O bright Apollo
> τιν ανδρα, τιν ηρωα, τινα θεον
> What god, man or hero
> Shall I place a tin wreath upon!

3. **Zeus holds Pisa**: Pisa, the chief city of Elis, stands as often for Olympia. Zeus was patron of the Olympic Festival.

4. **Heracles**: the story of Heracles' foundation of the Olympic Games is told in O 10.

7. **famous fathers**: Theron's ancestors were among early Greek colonists who founded Gela about 689 BC. A century later his family moved to found the neighbouring city of Acragas.

9. **this river bank**: the ancient city was founded in the angle of the

Rivers Hypsas and Acragas (now Fiume del Drago or di Sant'Anna and Fiume di San Biagio).

12. Son of Cronos: Zeus.

16. deeds ... done rightly or unrightly: in form the expression is a polar one: the mention of good achievements brings forth, like the sun its shadow, the mention of bad ones. There may be an allusion to the political trials of Sicily in recent years, particularly as Pindar hopes for forgetfulness of things unpleasant. But the passage may simply look forward to the theme of the myth, the wiping out of suffering by the joys of the afterlife.

23. maids of Cadmus: Semele and Ino, daughters of Cadmus the legendary founder of Thebes, from whom Theron claimed descent. Both are rewarded after death for their suffering, like the initiates in the Mysteries whose fortune Pindar describes below.

26. Semele: Semele was loved by Zeus and asked him to come to her in his true form so that she could be certain of his identity. He came in the form of a thunderbolt, and she was consumed by fire. At the time she was already pregnant by Zeus, and the god preserved the infant in his own thigh until the time of his birth; when born, the child became the god Dionysus, 'the ivy-bearing god'. Later he went down to the Underworld to rescue Semele, and gave her immortal life in heaven.

30. Ino: Semele's sister, who incurred the wrath of Hera for several reasons. Because Ino had nursed the infant Dionysus, Hera drove her mad so that she threw herself into the sea. She was preserved however to live an immortal life with the Nereids (the sea-nymphs, daughters of Nereus).

31. no term of death is set: for the sentiment cf. N 6.6–8.

38. son of Laius: Oedipus, who, brought up by King Polybus of Corinth to remove from him any opportunity of killing his father as an oracle had predicted he would, did not recognize his true father Laius, king of Thebes, when he met him in the road, and killed him. He then compounded his unwitting crime by marrying Laius' wife Jocasta, his own mother, and had by her two sons, Eteocles and Polynices, as well as two daughters, Antigone and Ismene. The myth is the subject of Sophocles' *Oedipus the King*.

41. Erinys: the goddess of vengeance. Usually occurring in the plural, the Erinyes were the avenging spirits who plagued men who had committed grave crimes and drove them mad.

43. Polynices: after Oedipus left Thebes, his sons Eteocles and Polynices shared the rule of the city. They quarrelled and Polynices was banished. With the help of Adrastus king of Argos, Polynices took part in the unsuccessful expedition of the 'Seven against Thebes', during which he and Eteocles were killed in single combat with each other.

43. Thersander: the son of Polynices. He was the sole survivor of the line of Oedipus. The passage is a reference to the second, successful expedition against Thebes by the 'Epigoni' (Successors) led by Thersander and his generation. During the first expedition the warriors halted at Nemea and instituted the new athletic contest, the Nemean Games, at the grave of the child Opheltes. The implication is that Thersander, in the next generation, was honoured in a re-enactment of the First Games.

45. Adrastus: king of Argos, later of Sicyon, and one of the Seven against Thebes. He alone survived the expedition, and ten years later accompanied the new expedition of the Epigoni. His son Aigialeus died in the battle, but his line was kept alive because Thersander was the son, by Polynices, of Adrastus' daughter.

46. Aenesidamus' son: Theron.

49. his brother: Xenocrates, who won the chariot race at the Pythian Games in 490 and at the Isthmian Games in perhaps 476/5: see P 6 and I.7.

50. the impartial Graces: Euphrosyne, Thalia and Aglaia. See further the notes on O 14. The Graces are givers of all that enhances the life of man, both of the charm of poetry and of the lustre of victory.

53. discontent: For the sentiment cf. Solon 13.69–70; West, 'One who tries to do well may fall unwittingly into dire and deep misfortune, while to him who does mischief god gives blessed fortune, a release from disturbance of mind.' (The word for 'disturbance of mind' is a cognate of 'discontent'.) Bacchylides (3.87) states that 'gold is contentment'. The words lead in to the passage about the afterlife: wealth adorned with noble deeds is an assurance of a happy life after death. Wealth is often used as a metaphor of the 'treasure in heaven' of initiates in the Mysteries: see B 3.10ff. for the association of wealth, light and mystic knowledge, and Empedocles frag. 132 DK, 'happy is he who has obtained the riches of a holy heart'.

56. knows what is to come: cf. Homeric Hymn to Demeter 480–2; B 3.10 ff.; Pindar frag. 137.

59. A judge below the earth: Rhadamanthys was the judge of the dead.

61. But the good . . .: There is a similar description of the life of the Blessed in frag. 129.

68. three times: For this doctrine of reincarnation cf. frag. 133. The idea was adopted by Plato in the myth of the Republic. The ancient commentator Aristarchus pointed out the full, odd implication of these lines, that the dead pay for the sins they committed while alive, and conversely the living pay for the sins they committed in the Underworld.

70. Cronos' tower: the centre of the home of the Blessed. See Hesiod, *Works and Days* 16–73a: 'Zeus son of Cronos sent them to dwell apart from men on the borders of the earth, far from the immortals; and Cronos is their king; and they live there with untroubled hearts in the Islands of the Blest by the deep stream of Ocean: blessed heroes, for whom the fertile earth brings forth scented fruits three times a year.'

76. the great father: Cronos.

Rhea: wife and sister of Cronos, mother of the Olympian gods.

77. Peleus: one of Pindar's favourite heroes, son of Aeacus and king of Aegina. The sea-nymph Thetis, who was fated to bear a son stronger than his father, was married to him by Zeus, and she gave birth to Achilles. Peleus is not usually counted among the select band of heroes permitted to pass eternity in the Islands of the Blest.

78. Cadmus: the founder of Thebes, he married Harmonia the daughter of Ares. Usually, he is said to have been turned into a snake and buried in Illyria; but see Euripides, *Bacchae* 1338–9, where he and Harmonia are despatched to the Islands of the Blest.

79. Achilles: Some sources say that Achilles spent his afterlife on the White Island in the Black Sea, as husband of Helen (Hesiod, *Works and Days* 166 – possibly an interpolation; the information is not in Homer).

83. Memnon: the leader of the Ethiopians in the Trojan War, and son of Eos (the Dawn) and Tithonus, a half-brother of Priam. See N 3.62–3.

Many a swift arrow: i.e. Pindar has many ways to praise his addressee including a plentiful repertoire of myths.

86. The poet's truth: Conway's is a mistranslation. Pindar says 'wise is he who knows much by nature'. The expression is praise of Theron for his inborn aristocratic ability. That ability includes both athletic skill and the ability to understand Pindar's poetry. Those who can only learn by rote attack the victor with the shafts of their malice, like ravens. Previous commentators, from the scholiasts onwards, took the ravens to be rival poets of Pindar, perhaps Bacchylides and Simonides, and took the general statement as an assertion of Pindar's poetic credo. But this is a misreading of the passage. The eagle in Pindar invariably represents the victor and not the poet: see Stoneman, 'The Theban Eagle'. For well-taken criticisms of my view, see I. L. Pfeijffer, 'The Image of the Eagle in Pindar and Bacchylides', *Classical Philology* (1994): 305–17.

89. On whom do we now launch . . .?: the form of the phrase echoes that of line 2 as the poem comes full circle with its theme of praise.

95. envy: more correctly, 'satiety'; i.e. people get sick of hearing the praises of the good.

95. whispers: the Greek word actually means 'to bawl aloud', i.e. to try to drown praise by heckling.

OLYMPIAN 3

For Theron of Acragas
Winner of the Chariot Race (476)

This ode celebrates the same victory as the second Olympian, but whereas that ode was probably performed at Theron's palace, the present one was composed for performance at the festival of the Theoxenia in Acragas. The Theoxenia was a religious festival found in many cities of Greece, which took the form of a banquet at which the gods were supposed guests. The Dioscuri, Castor and Polydeuces, were among the more common dedicatees of these festivals, and were popular in Sicily. See also N 10.49.

In this ode Heracles, the legendary founder of the Olympic Games, is represented as coming to take charge of the ceremony and to act as host to the divine guests ('To rule this feast', line 34). The short invocation at the opening of the ode is addressed to these twin deities and their sister Helen: they were the offspring of Leda by Zeus (who came to her as a swan but their human father was Tyndareus, king of Sparta.

The structure of the ode is straightforward. It begins with praise of the Dioscuri, and celebrates the athletic victory by a myth of the origin of the Olympic Games: this concerns the bringing by Heracles of the olive tree from the Hyperboreans (the people beyond the North Wind) for Olympia; this leads into the explanation of why he was in the Land of the Hyperboreans, namely in pursuit of the Golden Hind, one of the canonical Twelve Labours (see further note on 33). The narrative is constructed in ring-composition, as often, leaping back in time to fill in the background of the key event and returning through the narrative to its original starting point.

The third triad returns to the feast of the Theoxenia, where Heracles attends the feast with the Dioscuri; the link of the festival with the victory is made by the claim that Heracles has appointed the two athlete-gods presidents of the Games, a claim not otherwise known. The final focus on the victor states that he has achieved the summit of human ambition, and

both he and the poet must here stop short before overdoing
things.

str. 1   Great sons of Tyndareus, dear to your guests,
        And Helen of the lovely tresses,
    I pray your pleasure, when my voice rings out
    To honour famous Acragas, and raise
        On high the name of Theron,
    And his Olympian victory, in proud song
    To match the steps of his untiring steeds.
        And the Muse, surely, stood beside me
    Unveiling new and sparkling paths of music,
        In Dorian cadence linked,   5

ant. 1   To voice the songs of our triumphant revel.
        For the wreaths bound upon our locks
    Command me to the task divinely given,
    Worthily for Aenesidamus' son
        To join in harmony
    The sweet strains of the richly-varied lyre
    With the notes of the flute, and the due setting
        Of words; and Pisa too enjoins
    My speech, for from her bidding come to men
        The songs inspired of heaven,   10

ep. 1   For every man on whom the unswerving eye
        Of the Hellenic judge,
        Man of Aetolian breed,
    Who guards the rites long years ago established
    By Heracles, sets on his brow aloft
    That shining glory, wreathed upon his hair,
        Of the green olive leaf; which once
        From Ister's shady streams
    Amphitryon's son brought hither, to be
    The fairest emblem of Olympia's Games.   15

str. 2   For the Hyperborean folk, Apollo's servants,
        He so persuaded with fair words,
    When, for the all-hospitable grove of Zeus,
    His loyal heart begged for the tree, to make
        Shade for all men to share,

And for brave deeds of valorous spirits, a crown.
For he had seen long since his father's altars
      Sanctified, and the light of evening
Smiling at mid-month to the golden car
      Of the full-orbéd moon;   20

ant. 2   And of the great Games had set up the contest
               And sacred judgment, with the rites
         Of the four-yearly feast, on the high banks
         Of Alpheus' holy river. But the land
               Of Pelops, and the vales
         By Cronos' hill nourished no lovely trees,
         And his eyes saw a garden spread defenceless
               Beneath the fierce rays of the sun.
         Then at length did his heart bid him be one,
               To journey to the land   25

ep. 2   Of Istria, where, long since, Leto's daughter,
               Lover of horsemanship,
               Received him. For he came
         From Arcady's high peaks and winding glens,
         By constraint of his father, to perform
         The bidding of Eurystheus, and bring back
               The Hind of golden horns, which once
                     Taygeta had vowed
               To Orthosia, a sacred gift,
         And on it wrote the sign of consecration.   30

str. 3   And in that search he saw, too, the famed land
               That lay behind cold Boreas
         Of bleak and frozen breath; and standing there
         Marvelled to see the trees. And in his heart
               A dear resolve was born,
         To set them planted there, where ends the course
         Twelve times encircled by the racing steeds.
               So comes he now with kind intent
         To rule this feast, with the twin sons divine
               Of Leda's generous breast.   35

ant. 3   For to these he gave charge, when he departed
               To high Olympus, to preside

Over that glorious contest, where are matched
The prowess of brave hearts, and the swift-wheeling
    Race of the charioteers.
Thus, then, my heart bids me declare this glory
Was given of Tyndareus' sons, those famous horsemen,
    To Theron and the Emmenid clan,
Who of all mortals give them greatest welcome
      With tables richly spread,   40

ep. 3   And guard with reverent loyalty the rites
      Of the blest gods of heaven.
      Is water best of all,
And gold of man's possessions the most worthy?
Yet for his valorous deeds Theron treads now
The highest peak, touching from hence the far
    Pillars of Heracles. Beyond
      Is pathless, for the wise
    Or the unwise. That road shall I
Never pursue; name me a madman else.   45

Notes

1. **sons of Tyndareus**: the king of Sparta and husband of Leda, who gave birth to the Dioscuri and Helen. Though all were born from eggs, only Polydeuces was normally regarded as a divine being; Castor was his human twin. See further N. 10.55 ff. and note.

2. **Helen**: Helen takes part with her brothers in the Theoxenia: see Euripides, *Helen* 1666–9: (the Dioscuri are speaking) 'when you reach the end of your path of life, you will be called a god and will share the libations to the Dioscuri and take part in the hospitality festivals which men will offer to us.'

5 **In Dorian cadence linked**: literally 'joining my voice to the Dorian sandal (i.e. rhythm)': the rhythm of the dance is marked by the raising and lowering of the foot.

6. **the wreaths bound upon our locks**: participants in religious rites, such as the Theoxenia, as well as guests at banquets, wore wreaths in their hair.

8. **the lyre ... the flute**: the 'flute' is strictly a reed pipe, not a flute at all: see O 12. The combination of lyre and pipe is fairly common in the

odes (O 7.12, 10.94, P 10.39, N 9.8); but Pindar may be saying that he has invented a tune particularly appropriate to the Dioscuri. Compare Alcman frag. 24, which reports 'Alcman was once mixing Dorian lyre with Lydian songs while bringing songs to Zeus Lycaeus at Sparta; he did not reach Sparta before he had greeted both that city and the Dioscuri.'

9. Aenesidamus' son: Theron.

12. the Hellenic judge: the judges at the Olympic Games were known as Hellanodikai, 'judges of the Hellenes'. Only Greeks, Hellenes, were allowed to compete at the Games.

Man of Aetolian breed: The Eleans claimed to be descended from the Aetolians of Northern Greece and thus to predate the Dorian invasion of the Peloponnese.

13. olive leaf: the prize for victors in the Olympic Games was a wreath of olive leaves.

14. Ister: the Danube. A strange place to find an olive tree.

15. Amphitryon's son: i.e. Heracles, son of Alcmena by Zeus; Alcmena's husband was Amphitryon, king of Thebes.

16. the Hyperborean folk: No earlier author refers to a visit of Heracles to the Hyperboreans, the people who live 'beyond the North Wind'. Pausanias (5.7.7.) makes clear that this was a local tradition of Olympia, explaining the origin of the prize of the olive wreath. The Hyperboreans were regarded as loyal servants of Apollo, who spent six months of each year with them (cf. P 10.30ff.). Gifts came to Olympia from the northern lands along the amber route, which made this legendary region a suitable origin for divine gifts.

17. the grove of Zeus: the precinct of Olympia, 'all-hospitable' because of the crowds which flocked there to attend the festival and the Games.

19. his father's altars: the altars of Zeus, set up by Heracles when he founded the festival.

22. high banks of Alpheus: 'crags', an odd word for the low banks of the Alpheus.

23. the land of Pelops: the kingdom of Elis, in which Olympia lay. Pelops became king of Elis after overthrowing Oenomaus, as related in O 1.

26. Leto's daughter: the goddess Artemis, sister of Apollo; as a huntress she is also associated with horses.

28. By constraint of his father: the Twelve Labours imposed on Heracles by Eurystheus were a result of the enmity of Hera: Zeus had had to give his consent to these trials. He made it a condition that when they were completed Heracles should become an immortal. By making them a fulfilment of the will of Zeus himself Pindar sanctifies Heracles' deeds.

29. The Hind of golden horns: the pursuit of the hind was normally localized in Arcadia, not as far north as this. It is possible that this represents an older version of the myth, or even that the Hind is a recollection of the reindeer, the only species of the deer family in which the female has antlers. The golden antlers may be a recollection of the practice of wrapping a beast's antlers with gold foil before sacrifice.

29. Taygeta: according to the scholiast, a nymph who was turned by Artemis into a stag to save her from pursuit by Zeus. When she returned to human form, she dedicated the Hind to Artemis in gratitude.

30. Orthosia: a cult title of Artemis, 'she who makes upright': cf. her Spartan title of Orthia.

33. A dear resolve was born: did Heracles go a second time to fetch the tree? (as argued by E. Robbins, *Phoenix* 36 [1982]: 295–305). It seems more natural to suppose that he took it on the same occasion as he pursued the Hind. The ring-composition of the narrative returns here to the point it had reached in line 13; the intervening passage has filled in the background, added depth to the action of installing the olive.

34. To rule this feast: Heracles' attendance at the Theoxenia reintroduces the Dioscuri, the gods of the feast.

36. he gave charge: The Dioscuri are not elsewhere regarded as having any part in running the Olympic Games. They did, however, have altars at Olympia, and as athlete gods are suitable in a general way for an athletic role. But Pindar's claim here has the sole purpose of putting them into relations with Heracles.

38. Emmenid clan: cf. P 6.4.

41. rites of the blest gods: the phraseology seems to refer to the Mysteries which are so prominent in O 2.

42. Is water best of all: a deliberate self-quotation, recalling the opening of O 1.

44. the pillars of Heracles: the straits of Gibraltar. This, the western-most limit of Heracles' journeying, represented for the Greeks the limit of the known world. They are an emblem, in Pindar and elsewhere, of the extreme of human achievement.

44. Beyond is pathless: An elegant suggestion that Theron can go no further, and that Pindar's poem too must go no further than this. Praise is achieved.

For Psaumis of Camarina
Winner of the Mule-Cart Race (460 or 456; or 452)

The small town of Camarina was founded by emigrants from Syracuse in 599, and was destroyed following a revolt in 553. Rebuilt in 492 by Hippocrates, tyrant of Gela, it was destroyed again by his son Gelon in 484, and again reoccupied by the people of Gela in 461/0.

Psaumis was recorded as the victor in the horse-chariot race at Olympia in 452. However, mule-cart races were not included in the victor lists, and this is not the same event as the victory of 452. It is reasonable to suppose that, if Psaumis had won a chariot race when this ode was composed, Pindar would have mentioned it. Therefore the ode must precede 452. Olympian 5 is also described as composed for a mule-cart victory, presumably the same one, though there is no way of telling why the victory was honoured with two odes. These difficulties have led some scholars to suppose that one of the odes, Olympian 5, is not by Pindar; or alternatively that Olympian 4 is in fact for the chariot victory of 452 and Olympian 5 for the mule victory of 456 (D. Gerber, *QUCC* n.s. 25 [1987]: 7–24; M. Fernandez-Galiano, *Emerita* 10 [1942]: 112–48). The ancient editor's labelling of Olympian 4 as for a mule-chariot victory would thus be assumed to be an error, perhaps a transference from Olympian 5, which is explicitly said by the poet (line 3) to be for a mule-chariot victory.

If Olympian 4 is not for the Olympian victory of 452, it may be dated to 456 or to 460. The reference in Olympian 5.8 to Camarina as a 'new-built city-seat' might fit better in 460 than 456.

The mule-cart race ceased to be an Olympic event in 444.

Psaumis was a wealthy private citizen of Camarina who had helped make possible the rebuilding of the city. It is remarkable that a private citizen should have the wealth to do this and to compete in two other expensive events at the Games; Psaumis may have been the object of some envy in his native city.

This beautifully simple ode is an excellent example of the genre, in which all the main generic elements are on display and clearly articulated.

str. 1   Great Zeus, the thunder's charioteer
        On its unwearied path
    In the height of heaven, hear me. For thine
        The swiftly circling seasons
        Have sent me now with song,
    And the lyre's rich embroidery,
    To be the herald of the Games,
        Greatest contest of all.
        When friends have won success
    A generous heart is quick with praise
        To greet the happy tidings.   5
    O son of Cronos, lord of Aetna,
        That windswept mount where Typhon
        The monster hundred-headed
    Is held in thrall, receive, I pray thee,
    For the Olympian victor's honour,
        And for the Graces' favour,
        This my triumphant song,

ant. 1   Bringing a light will long endure   10
        On famous deeds of strength.
    For Psaumis' chariot shall I sing,
        Who at Pisa has won
        The crown of olive, and now
    Burns to raise high the glorious name
    Of Camarina. May the hand
        Of heaven give gracious issue
        To all his further prayers.
    Mine now to praise his ready skill
        Nursing his gallant steeds,
    And that with hospitable joy   15
        He welcomes many a guest;
        And with a heart unsullied
    Labours for Peace, the city's friend.
    No strain of falsehood will my songs
        Admit. Trial by deed
        Gives proof to all mankind.

ep. 1   As when the son of Clymenus,
             Facing the Lemnian women,   20
             Staved off dishonour's threat;
         When he had won the race for men
             In full bronze armour clad.
         Thus spoke he to Hypsipylia
         As he stepped forth to take the crown;
             'Such then, for speed, am I,
         In strength of hand and heart no less;
         Even on men whose years are few,   25
             White hairs do often grow,
             Despite of flowering youth
                 Its natural season.'

Notes

1. **Zeus:** Zeus is always mentioned at some point in every Olympian ode. He is referred to below as 'lord of Aetna', which was his main cult title in Sicily.

5. **To greet the happing tidings:** the verb is that used of a dog greeting its master.

7. **Typhon:** the mythical monster who attacked Zeus and the Olympian gods, and in punishment was imprisoned underneath Mt Etna. For the myth see P 1.15ff. The windswept mount is Etna.

13. **May the hand of heaven:** this prayer for Psaumis' further success, coupled with the phrase 'nursing his gallant steeds' in the lines which follow, could be taken to indicate that Psaumis was hoping to enter for the horse-chariot race at some later Olympic Games. This seems preferable to taking it as a reference to the present victory as won in the horse-chariot race.

17. **No strain of falsehood:** the gnomic remark is the pivot to the short myth.

19. **As when the son of Clymenus:** a story about Erginus the son of Clymenus is told by Pindar at the end of Pa. 8. Here he identifies him with another Erginus, son of Orchomenus, who was one of the Argonauts who sailed to Colchis to bring back the Golden Fleece. Breaking their voyage on the island of Lemnos, they took part in the funeral games organized by Queen Hypsipyle in honour of her father

Thoas. Erginus won, defeating amongst others the sons of Boreas, the North Wind, who were supposed to be the fastest of all creatures. Pindar is our only source for the detail that Erginus had prematurely grey hair: Libanius, who refers to the fact (Ep. 303) presumably had got it from Pindar. The relevance of the story is presumably that Psaumis was also grey-haired.

For Psaumis of Camarina
Winner of the Mule-Cart Race (460 or 456)

This ode was composed for a mule-cart victory, and according to the ancient editors for the same victory as Olympian 4. But see the introduction to that ode. The year 460 is a slightly more likely date than 456 for Olympian 5.

The scholiasts tell us that the ode is not found *en tois edaphiois*, whatever exactly that means: perhaps 'not in the earliest collections of Pindar's odes'. It may be therefore that it is not by Pindar (see C. M. Bowra, *Pindar*, pp. 414–20 – who dates it to 448). This would help to explain why there should be two odes for the same victory (if indeed they are), something not elsewhere exampled in Pindar's work; for Psaumis must have commissioned odes from two separate poets. The style and metre of the ode are simpler than is usual in Pindar, and there is no myth.

str. 1   Daughter of Ocean, pray you
  Accept with a glad heart this song, the sweet
   And choice reward for brave exploits
   Of lofty spirits, and for the crowns
    Won at Olympia,
   The gifts of Psaumis and his team
    On their untiring course.

ant. 1   He has raised up your city
  Camarina, the mother of his people,
   Honouring in splendid festivals
   The six twin altars of the gods,   5
    With oxen sacrifice,
   And in the five-day games and contests,
    In well-matched rivalry

ep. 1   Of four-horsed chariots and the race
  Of the mules' car, and in the contest

Of single horsemen. To you
His victory brought the peerless grace of fame,
And for his father Acron
And for his new-built city-seat,
Has bidden the herald's voice proclaim their honour.

str. 2   Leaving that lovely land,
Where Oenomaus and Pelops dwelt of old,
His song honours your sacred precinct,   10
Pallas, protectress of his city,
And Oanis your river
And the lake of his country's name;
The holy channels too

ant. 2   Of Hipparis whose streams
Give water to his people. And he builds
Well-founded mansions, grown with speed
Like to a forest's lofty branches,
Bringing his city's folk
From the harsh bonds of their distress
Into the light of day.

ep. 2   Toil and expense, for deeds of courage,   15
Must ever be the cost of valour's
Accomplishment, hidden
Within the veil of danger. But to those
Who win the victory,
Even amidst their citizens
Comes the reward of wisdom's reputation.

str. 3   O guardian Zeus, who dwellest
In the high clouds of heaven, and on the hill
Of Cronos, honouring the stream
Of Alpheus and the holy cave
Of Ida's name, to thee
With song and the flute's Lydian strain
I bring a suppliant's prayer,

ant. 3   Begging thee to enrich   20
This city with the glory of brave spirits;
And you, Olympia's victor, may

A long life and a happy heart,
    Rejoicing in your steeds,
The gift of great Poseidon, bring you
    Blessings through all your days,

ep. 3   And may you see your sons, Psaumis,
               Standing beside you. If a man
                   Makes of his wealth a stream
           Of healthful purpose, and of his possessions
                   Lacks not a bounteous store,
               And adds thereto repute's good name,
           Then let him not seek to become a god.   24

Notes

1. **Daughter of Ocean:** The nymph Camarina is represented on coins of the city as an Oceanid.

3. **his team:** the Greek word used here is the one regularly applied to a chariot drawn by mules.

5. **in splendid festivals:** the religious rites, including the sacrifice of oxen, which took place before the athletic contests began, and to which Psaumis evidently made a notable contribution.

twin altars: the altars of the twelve gods at Olympia are referred to by Pausanias in his description of Olympia, 5.14.4–10, but have not been found. They were dedicated to Zeus–Poseidon, Hera–Athene, Hermes–Aphrodite, the Graces–Dionysus, Artemis–Alpheus, Cronos–Rhea.

8. **new-built city seat:** Camarina was refounded in 461: see introduction to O 4.

9. **that lovely land:** Elis, the land of Olympia, where Pelops became king after ousting Oenomaus (see O 1).

10. **Pallas:** Pallas Athena, guardian goddess of Camarina.

11. **Oanis, Hipparis:** the two rivers of Camarina. The correct spelling of the former is Oanos.

The lake: Lake Camarina.

13. **he builds:** Psaumis had made generous use of his wealth in rebuilding the city.

15. **Toil and expense:** Psaumis' lavish expenditure in entering three events at Olympia and contributing to the sacrifices, as well as his building contributions at home, are envisaged as arousing the envy or malice of his fellow-citizens; but the successful conclusion of the competition should quench such malice. One would normally expect a pivotal gnome of this kind to lead to a myth; but instead the ode begins its conclusion with a new prayer.

18. **the ... cave of Ida's name:** the well-known cave of Mt Ida is on the mountain of that name in Crete, where Zeus was nursed by Amalthea and suckled by goats; the scholiasts quote Demetrius of Scepsis, the second-century BC geographer, for the information that there was a cave of the same name in Elis. This is otherwise unknown and may be speculation based on this passage.

19. **the flute's Lydian strain:** the 'flute' is a double-reed pipe: see note on P 12 (introduction). On the Lydian mode see note on O 14.17.

21. **The gift of great Poseidon:** horses were associated with and sacred to Poseidon, the 'earth-shaker'; he is credited with the institution of horse-racing.

24. **let him not seek to become a god:** the downbeat warning note of the conclusion is a commonplace of Greek thinking, but it is relatively unusual to find it as the climax of a celebratory ode. Cf. N 11, I 1, O 7.

OLYMPIAN 6

For Hagesias of Syracuse
Winner of the Mule-Cart Race (468)

Hagesias was a citizen of Syracuse and also of Stymphalus in Arcadia. He was a member of the clan of the legendary seer Iamus. This family was in the first rank of the priesthood at Olympia and held as a hereditary right the oracular service at the Olympian altar of Zeus. The principal theme of this ode is praise of this family, and the myth concerns the birth of Iamus and his appointment to Zeus' service at Olympia.

Hagesias (this form of the name is more likely in Doric dialect than Conway's preferred Agesias) was one of the lieutenants of Hieron, the ruler of Syracuse, who died in 467. Though the Olympic victor lists do not include mule-cart victories, so that there is no firm date for this ode, 468 is likely. The troubled times of the end of Hieron's reign and the imminent fall of the Deinomenids seem to be reflected in the hope expressed at the end of antistrophe 5 that 'the tides of time' will not 'cast aside (Hieron's) days of good fortune'; and a similar anxiety for Hagesias is found in the final epode, in the lines recommending that a ship should rely on two anchors 'in the winter's storm, at night'. The two anchors are Hagesias' two cities of Syracuse and Stymphalus. They were not enough to save him, for, according to the scholiasts (98), Hagesias was put to death after the fall of Hieron's dynasty.

Conway proposed that this ode was performed once in Stymphalus and a second time in Syracuse; the praises of Hieron suggest a Syracusan performance, but the assertion in epode 5 that Hagesias is now travelling from Stymphalus to his second home and being received by Zeus of Aetna would make no sense in a Stymphalian performance, and the inference is unfounded.

The ode's structure is straightforward: its brilliant opening takes the form not of an invocation but, as often, of a statement about poetry and its responsibilities. The myth is told in more linear fashion than usual, and the ode is notable for its mention of both the charioteer Phintis and the chorus-trainer Aeneas.

str. 1   Pillars of gold, as for a stately palace,
Let us upraise, to build a strong-walled forecourt
    Fronting the chamber of our song.
For to a growing work we needs must set
A rich entablature, seen from afar.
    But he who won Olympia's crown,
Steward appointed to the prophetic altar
Of Zeus in Pisa, who shares the ancient fame   5
    Of glorious Syracuse' foundation,
For such a man, what hymns shall not encompass
His path, unenvied of his citizens,
    In strains of long-desiréd song?

ant. 1   Then let this son of Sostratus know well
This path of glory where his sandals' tread
    Is given of heaven. Noble deeds
Untried of danger, be it upon land
Or ships at sea, no honour win. But widespread   10
    The records of a valorous act
Sternly encountered. Fitting for you that praise,
Agesias, which from Adrastus' tongue
    In days of old most justly sprang,
Crying aloud to Oikleus' son, the prophet
Amphiaraus, when the split earth engulfed him,
    His chariot and gleaming steeds.

ep. 1   For when on seven burning pyres were laid   15
Their warrior dead, then spoke at Thebes, in sorrow,
    The son of Talaus this word,
    Saying 'Woe is me for the eye
Of all my host, at once a mighty prophet
And alike matchless in the fray of spears.'
Thus, too, behoves this man of Syracuse
And master of this revel, a like praise.
    I am no man of strife, nor prone
    To envy's quarrels, but on oath
    Due sworn, my voice to this his honour   20
Shall clearly witness, and the honey-sweet
Song of the Muses shall affirm the word.

str. 2   Come then, Phintis, yoke for me now the power
Of your strong mules, that we may ride our car

With all speed on the clear-lit road,
To bring me to the source at last, where sprang
This race of men. Better than other steeds
    They know well where to lead me   25
Along this road, who at Olympia
Have won the crowns of victory. Fitly
    Must we now open wide for them
The gateway of our songs. Today must we
Begone beside Eurotas' stream, to journey –
    Timely the hour – to Pitane.

ant. 2   She, so they tell, was loved of great Poseidon,
          Son of Cronos, and bore the babe Evadne,   30
              Child of the crown of violet tresses,
          Hiding the pains of maiden motherhood
          Beneath her robe. But when the month was come
              Of labour's term, she sent her handmaids
          And bade them give the child for watch and ward
          To Eilatus' hero son at Phaisana,
              Who ruled in Arcady, and dwelt
          By Alpheus' stream. There was the young babe nursed
          And grown, and by Apollo's love first knew   35
              The touch of Aphrodite's joy.

ep. 2   Yet could she not from Aepytus keep hidden
         Through all her time the divine seed she bore.
             And he, struggling in bitter strain
             To hold within his heart a wrath
         Unbearable, to Pytho straight departed,
         To seek a ruling of the oracle
         For this most grievous woe. But she laid by
         Beneath a thicket's shade her silvered urn,   40
             And she let fall her crimson girdle
             And bore a son, inspired of heaven.
             And to serve at her side Apollo,
         God of the golden locks, sent Eleithuia
         The kindly goddess, and the Fates divine.

str. 3   And from her body's travail and the pains
          That were but sweet delight, was born Iamus,
              Sped forth to the bright light of day.

And she in her soul's anguish left the babe
There on the ground. But by the will of heaven   45
   There came to him two snakes grey-eyed,
And gave to nourish him, with gentle care,
The sweet and harmless venom of the bees.
   Then came the king, riding in haste
From rocky Pytho, and from all the household
Demanded of the child Evadne bore,
   Saying he was the son begotten

ant. 3   Of Phoebus, and should be beyond all others
A peerless prophet for the race of man,   50
   And that his seed should last for ever.
So he declared it to them. But all vowed
They had not heard nor seen aught of the babe,
   The five days of his infant being.
For in a deep brake had he lain concealed,
A pathless waste, and o'er his tender limbs
   Flowers of gold and purple splendour,
Iris and Pansy shed their rays upon him;   55
Thence was it his mother for all time proclaimed
   That he be called of men Iamus,

ep. 3   This his immortal name. And when he won
Youth's joyous fruit, fair Hebe's gleaming crown,
   He went to the midwaters down
   Of Alpheus' stream, and called aloud
To the god of far-spreading might, Poseidon
His ancestor, and to the archer god
Ruler of heaven-built Delos, and this prayer
He spoke, at night, beneath the starlit sky:
   That on his brow be laid the honour   60
   To be the shepherd of his people.
   Brief and clear called his father's voice,
Answering 'Rise my son, hence to the place
Where all men meet, bearing my bidden word.'

str. 4   And they came to the lofty rock, where rules
The high-throned son of Cronos. There he gave him   65
   Of the seer's art this twofold treasure;
First that he hear the voice that knows no lie;

And when that Heracles, brave heart and hand,
   Revered son of Alcides' seed,
Should come to establish to his father's name
The feast where many a countless foot shall tread,
   With the ordinance of games and contests
Greatest of all, then shall the second honour,
His oracle, high on the supreme altar
    Of Zeus be set. Thus he ordained.   70

ant. 4   Thenceforth for all the sons of Iamus' seed
Through all Hellas their race holds high renown;
   And fortune's day attended them;
To deeds of noble grace paying due honour
They tread their way of light. Witness shall be
   Their each achievement. Calumny
But from the hearts of others' envy, threatens
Those who came first, driving the twelve-lap course,   75
   On whom the divine grace of Beauty
Has shed the dewdrops of her fame most fair.
Truth tells, Agesias, that your mother's kin,
   Dwelling beneath Kyllene's height,

ep. 4   Often and yet again the sanctities
Of prayer and sacrifices rich presented
   To Hermes, herald of the gods,
   Who of the Games is president,
And shares the contests' glory, honouring
That land of noble souls, Arcadia.   80
Then surely, son of Sostratus, it is
That god, who with his father, lord of thunder,
   Decrees you now your glad success.
   Methinks a whetstone on my tongue,
   Clear-sounding, brings me, nothing loth,
A sweet-flown breath of song. From Stymphalus
My mother's mother came, that maid of flowers,

str. 5   Metope, who bore Thebe, famous rider   85
Of horse. Her lovely waters shall I drink
   Weaving the rich refrains of song
To honour famous men of arms. Come then,
Aeneas, rouse the chorus of your singers

First to praise Hera, the fair Maid,
Then to know well whether in very truth
We make of no account that sorry taunt,
    The old-worn slight 'Boeotian swine'.   90
For you give to my words their true report,
Unerring tally of the fair-tressed Muses,
    A rich-filled bowl of sounding song.

ant. 5   Bid them not spare to tell of Syracuse
And of Ortygia, where Hieron
    Rules with his rod of justice. Wise
And clear the counsels of his mind, who worships
The red-strewn carpet where Demeter treads,   95
    And the feast of her daughter, goddess
Of the white horses, and the lofty power
Of Zeus of Aetna. Him the sweet-sung notes
    Of lyre and voices know full well.
And may the tides of time not cast aside
His days of fortune, but with happy welcome
    And friendly heart may he receive

ep. 5   This triumph of Agesias, as he rides
From home to second home, leaving the walls
    Of Stymphalus his motherland,
    And the rich flocks of Arcady.   100
Well is it in the winter's storm, at night,
Two anchors to make fast to the ship's prow.
To the men then of his race, or here or there,
May friendly heaven bestow a path of glory.
    A straight-run sail free from all toil
    Grant him I beg, great god of ocean,
    Husband of Amphitrite, goddess   105
Of the gold spindle, and to the air on high
Raise up the joyful blossom of my songs.

Notes

5. Steward: the history of the Iamids is told by Herodotus 9.33, and
Pausanias 6.2.4. The importance of Iamus as a clan ancestor is
emphasized by his inclusion in the pediment of the temple of Zeus at
Olympia which represents the beginning of Pelops' chariot race.

9. Noble deeds: Hagesias, whose father was Sostratus, probably had fought in some of Hieron's campaigns.

13. Adrastus: the legendary king of Argos, son of Talaus, who led the expedition of the Seven against Thebes.

13. Amphiaraus: the seer of Argos who participated in the expedition. On the defeat of the Seven, Amphiaraus fled from the battlefield in his chariot, and was struck in the back by a spear thrown by Periclymenus. Zeus then opened up the earth and Amphiaraus and his chariot disappeared from view. The hero re-emerged at Oropus in Attica, where a healing shrine developed around the spot. Parts of his story are also told at P 8.41, N 9.13, I 7.33

16. 'Woe is me...: The passage looks like an adaptation of some hexameter verses and may be a close quotation from the epic *Thebais* which told the story of the Seven against Thebes: see the scholiast 26 and *Thebais* frag. 7 Bernabé.

19. envy's quarrels: cf. line 74.

20. this his honour: that he is worthy of the same praise as Amphiaraus both as warrior and as prophet (by virtue of his Iamid descent).

22. Phintis: Hagesias' charioteer.

28. Pitane: a district of Sparta lying west or southwest of the Spartan acropolis (Paus. 3.14.6), to the east of which runs the River Eurotas. Pitane contained the graves of the Agiad kings of Sparta, and other sanctuaries. In this passage the locality becomes personified as its nymph. No other source records the myth that follows, and it may be a local tradition.

33. Eilatus' hero son: Aepytus, king of Arcadia.

Phaisana: unkown.

45. two snakes: snakes are generally associated with uncanny powers such as divination, as is honey; a contemporary legend told that Pindar himself had had honey placed on his lips by bees as he slept!

47. harmless venom: i.e. honey. The word for venom is *ion*, used for the pun on Iamus.

55. Iris and Pansy: the Greek is *ia*, meaning violas or pansies – again for the pun on Iamus. There is no mention in the Greek of irises.

58 called aloud . . . to Poseidon: this solemn scene recalls Pelops' prayer to Poseidon in O 1.

59. The archer god . . . of Delos: Apollo, born on the Aegean island of Delos.

63. the place where all men meet: Olympia.

64. the lofty rock: the hill of Cronos.

67. the voice that knows no lie: this seems to refer to the practice of divination from chance remarks overheard.

69. The feast: the festival and Games of Olympia, the highest ranking of the Panhellenic Games.

70. His oracle: the scholiast quotes Heraclides *On Oracles* for the information that the Iamids customarily prophesied from the pattern of the cuts in the skins of dead sacrificial animals.

74. Calumny: the danger of envy and malice being directed against those who make high claims or achieve great success is a regular theme of the epinician ode, and has already appeared at line 19. There is at this point no particular reason to see a reference to possible political enemies of Hagesias in Syracuse.

77. your mother's kin: this does not refer to Hagesias' descent from Evadne but to his maternal relatives who were worshippers of the Hermes of Arcadia. Kyllene is the most prominent mountain in Arcadia.

81. lord of thunder: Zeus.

82. a whetstone on my tongue: the tongue is whetted to bring forth a telling saying. The continuation of the metaphor, in which the whetted tongue brings forth clear music of breezes, is one of Pindar's most remarkable mixtures. See Stoneman, 'Ploughing a Garland'.

84. My mother's mother: Metope, wife of Asopus (the river), gave birth to the nymph Thebe. This neat genealogy has the function of bringing poet and addressee into a quasi-intimate relationship, as required for the duty of praise.

88. Aeneas: the chorus leader. Paus. 6.4 refers to an Iamid named Aeneas, who may be the same man or a relative. If so, Pindar is mentioning as many members of the Iamid clan as he can.

89. Hera, the fair Maid: this unusual epithet of Hera, usually goddess of marriage, is echoed in the cult mentioned by Pausanias (8.22.2) of Hera the child. Hera had cult at Stymphalus.

90. Boeotian swine: the people of Boeotia had a reputation, particularly among the quick-witted Athenians, for being slow and stupid, and this phrase was not uncommonly used by them. Pindar archly implies that his poetry disproves the adage. He refers to it again in his dithyramb for the Athenians, frags. 75, 83.

91. tally of the ... Muses: the reference is to the 'message stick', used for messages of which the contents needed to be kept secret. The message was written on a strip of paper wound round a stick; in order to read it, the recipient needed an exactly similar stick to wind it round again. Aeneas is thus the accurate transmitter of Pindar's words and music in the poet's absence.

95. The red-strewn carpet: the Greek literally refers to Demeter of the red feet, an unexplained epithet. Conway's translation is one possible interpretation. Hieron was holder of a hereditary priesthood of Demeter.

goddess of the white horses: Persephone, an important goddess in Sicily (cf. in general O 2 and notes).

101: Two anchors: Stymphalus and Syracuse. Ships generally had two anchors. For the metaphor cf. Euripides frag. 774 = *Phaethon* 123–5 Diggle; [Demosthenes] 56.44. The winter's storm may well refer to political unrest in Syracuse in Hieron's last years.

104. great god of ocean: Poseidon.

105. Amphitrite: the wife of Poseidon. Like other Nereids she was traditionally represented as carrying a golden spindle.

For Diagoras of Rhodes
Winner of the Boxing Match (464)

Diagoras was a member of one of the leading families in the island of Rhodes, the Eratidae, who in earlier times had ruled as kings in the city of Ialysus. The family remained pre-eminent. and Damagetus, the father of Diagoras, seems to have been *prytanis* or president of the ruling council of the island.

Diagoras, with his sons and grandsons, won unique distinction in the athletic field in boxing and the pankration. Diagoras, a man of exceptional stature, won victories at all four Panhellenic Games, including four at the Isthmian and two at the Nemean Games, as well as many at other local athletic contests, mentioned in the fifth strophe and antistrophe of this ode. His three sons won between them five victories at Olympia, and his two grandsons were successful at Olympia and Delphi. Pausanias, writing in the second century AD, records that statues of Diagoras and his sons and grandsons were to be seen at Olympia: Paus. 4.24.2, and especially 6.7.1–7. The bases of the statues still remain though the bronze statues are long gone.

This ode, composed in 464, was much admired and was set up in letters of gold in the temple of Athena at Lindos on Rhodes.

In 407 BC, when the Athenians were in the last stages of their long and disastrous war with Sparta, the eldest son of Diagoras, Dorieus (himself winner of three Olympic victories), was captured by the Athenians in a sea battle. Although prisoners were normally either ransomed or executed, the distinction of Dorieus' family was such that the Athenians did neither, but set him free immediately.

The splendid opening simile leads into an unusually rich and attractive poem. The mythical section is made up of three stories, with passing reference to a fourth, the legend of the birth of Athena. These stories illustrate three significant features of Rhodian life: the worship of the sun god Helios, their skilled craftsmanship and their Dorian ancestry. According to legend the Argives (who actually colonized Rhodes in historic times) had come under the leadership of Tlepolemus the son of Heracles.

The three myths are told in reverse chronological order, each leading to an earlier event which deepens the perspective on the island's present glory. The three myths also share a common feature, namely that each tells how wrongdoing or mischance led ultimately to a happy outcome. Tlepolemus' murder of Licymnius led to the colonization of Rhodes; the negligence of the sons of Helios in founding a sanctuary 'without holy fire' was nonetheless rewarded by Zeus' gift of craftsmanship; and Helios' unfortunate absence from the original distribution of the parts of the world among the gods led to the creation of an island especially for him – Rhodes.

The common theme of these stories must have been part of Pindar's conscious design, but it is not now possible to discern what external cause may have prompted him to write the ode in this way. It may be that Diagoras committed some technical fault during the contest but was victorious despite that. The downbeat ending, with its typically Greek warning of mutability of fortune, may also recall this theme of uncertainty and chance; but nothing is known of Diagoras' circumstances that would permit us to conjecture a connection.

In a powerful analysis of this ode, Carol Dougherty (*The Poetics of Colonization* [Oxford 1994], pp. 120–30) shows how the trials and purification of the founder-hero are a potent analogy for the sacred value to a city of the enduring athlete. 'By comparing Diagoras with Tlepolemus, Pindar suggests that a victorious athlete has similar powers to confer upon his city, and he thus deserves the reward of fame in return for the toils of victory in the boxing competition' (line 126). This goes a long way to explaining one of the three myths.

str. 1 As when a man raises a cup
   Brimmed with the sparkling dewdrops of the vine, and drinks
    Toast to a young bridegroom, wishing him joy
     From one home to another,
     And from his wealthy hand presents him
      The cup, of pure gold, pride of his possessions;   5
      To his kith and kin and to the banquet's grace
     Paying due honour, there amidst his thronging friends

He sets him envied, who has won
A marriage of true minds.

ant. 1   So I too, for the men who honour
The athletes' field, proffer this draught of flowing nectar,
The Muses' gift, the sweet fruit of the mind,
Paying my homage due
To those who at Olympia,   10
And at Pytho have won the victor's crown.
He has true wealth, whom good reports encompass.
Now on one, now to another, Beauty's refreshing grace
Shines with the rich notes of the lyre
And the far-echoing flute.

ep. 1   Thus then, set to this twofold strain, my sail rides in
Diagoras to honour, and to praise
The ocean maid, daughter of Aphrodite,
Bride of the Sun, this isle of Rhodes.
Here shall my songs bring sweet reward
To him whose giant limbs, striding the fray,
By Alpheus' stream and at Castalia   15
Won him the boxer's crown, and to his father
Damagetus, whom Justice loves to honour.
Three cities crown their island home, near to the tongue
Of wide-spread Asia,
Amidst their folk of Argive warrior breed.

str. 2   Gladly shall I tell o'er their race,   20
And point their ancient seed, sprung from Tlepolemus,
And from great Heracles' broad-shouldered stock
In common ancestry.
From Zeus their father's line can boast
Descent, and from Amyntor by their mother
Astydamia. Yet for the race of man
Ever about his struggling thought hangs there a net
Of countless riddles, whence indeed   25
Is it most hard to tell

ant. 2   What fortune shall be best, or now
Or in the final hour, for any man to win.
For did not once the founder of this land,

In Tiryns long ago,
With his staff of hard olive wood,
In anger strike Alcmene's bastard brother,
Licymnius, and slew him as he came
From Midea's chamber? Troubled thoughts confound

even 30

The wise. But he went to the god
To ask the oracle.

ep. 2   Then to him from his temple of sweet incense spoke
The god of golden hair, and bade him launch
From Lerna's shore, and sail his ships straight-run
To the land circled by the sea,
Where once the great king of the gods
Showered upon the city snowflakes of gold;
In the day when the skilled hand of Hephaestus   35
Wrought with his craft the axe, bronze-bladed, whence
From the cleft summit of her father's brow
Athene sprang aloft, and pealed to the broad sky
Her clarion cry of war.
And Heaven trembled to hear, and Mother Earth.

str. 3   Then was it too that the great god
Hyperion's son, giver of light to mortal men,
This task to his beloved sons enjoined   40
To ensure well hereafter:
That they first to the goddess build
A shining altar, and founding holy rites
Of sacrifice, make glad the heart of Zeus,
And the maid of the sounding spear. Now Reverence,
Daughter of Forethought, gives to men
Virtue and valour's joy.

ant. 3   And yet comes too, on stealthy wing, that   45
Cloud of forgetfulness, drawing our baffled minds
Off from the straight road of their acts' intent.
For they mounted aloft,
But carried in their hands no seed
Of burning flame, but on the city's height
Founded a precinct without holy fire.

Yet for these men Zeus brought the saffron cloud, and
                                   rained 50
    A flood of gold, and the grey-eyed
    Goddess herself endowed them

ep. 3   The gift of skill, that of all men on earth, their hands
    In craft excelling have the mastery.
      And the roads carried their worked images
        Of life and movement, and widespread
        Was their renown. To men of knowledge
    Wisdom grows freely, innocent of guile.
    Now on the tongues of men are told the stories
    Of ancient days, that when Zeus and the immortals 55
    Made a division of the lands of earth,
Not yet to see was Rhodes, shining upon the waves
      Of ocean, but the isle
      Lay hidden deep within the salt sea's folds.

str. 4   But for the Sun no lot was drawn;
For he was absent, and they left him of broad earth
    No heritage, that holy god. And when   60
      He made known his mischance,
    Zeus was in mind to portion out
    The lots again; but he allowed him not,
    For he said that beneath the surge of ocean
His eyes had seen a land growing from out the depths,
      Blessed with rich nourishment for men
      And happy with teeming flocks.

ant. 4   And straightway then the god commanded
Lachesis of the golden fillet to raise aloft
    Her hands, and swear, not on her lips alone,   65
      The great oath of the gods,
    Promising with the son of Cronos
    This land once risen to the light of heaven
    Should be thenceforth as for a crown of honour
His own awarded title. The great words spoken, fell
      In truth's rich furrow. And there grew
      Up from the watery wave

ep. 4   This island, and great Helios who begets the fierce
          Rays of the sun, holds her in his dominion,   70
          That ruler of the horses breathing fire.
            There long ago he lay with Rhodes
            And begot seven sons, endowed
          Beyond all men of old with genius
          Of thoughtful mind. And of these one begot
          His eldest Ialysus, and Camirus
          And Lindus; and in three parts they divided
Their father's land, and of three citadels the brothers
            Held each his separate share,   75
          And by their three names are the cities called.

str. 5   Here then, to make him rich amends
      For piteous misfortune, for Tlepolemus,
          That ancient leader of the men of Tiryns,
            Are set, as for a god,
            These flocks, a rich-fed sacrifice,   80
          And the high seat of judgment of the Games.
          Whence have their flowers twice crowned Diagoras;
And the famed Isthmus saw him four times victorious,
          Nemea once and again, crowned too
            In Athens' rock-built city.

ant. 5   And in Argos he knew the prize
      Of bronze, and in Arcadia won their awards,
          And in Thebes too, and in the Games which honour
            Men of Boeotian breed.   85
            At Pellene and in Aegina
          Six times he won; at Megara the pillar
          Of stone inscribes a like tale. Ah, great Zeus,
Dwelling on Atabyrios's broad shoulder, I pray thee
          Honour my song, which sings the rite
            Due to Olympia's victor;

ep. 5   And to Diagoras, whose boxing skill proclaims him
          A man to valour born, grant him the joy
          Of honour in the hearts of his own people,   90
            And strangers too. Straight is the road
            He treads, to insolent pride sparing
          No mercy. Well he knows the part bequeathed him

> Of upright minds from noble ancestry;
> Whose seed, forget not, stems from Callianax.
> Then in rich honour for the Eratid clan
> Small wonder that the city festals ring. And yet,
>   In one brief breath of time,
> Or here or there the changing breezes blow.   95

Notes

1. **As when a man . . .:** it would appear that the ode was to be performed at the banquet in Rhodes held to celebrate Diagoras' victory. Pindar's statement at line 7, 'I . . . proffer this draught', may suggest that he went to Rhodes himself to perform the ode; but the Greek actually says 'I . . . *send*' the ode, which has an opposite implication.

12. **flute:** actually 'pipe'. See on P 12

15. **By Alpheus' stream:** at Olympia.

18. **Three cities:** Camirus, Ialysus and Lindus, the three main cities of the island of Rhodes.

the tongue of wide-spread Asia: the Bozburun peninsula.

19. **Argive warrior breed:** in legend, Rhodes was colonized by Argives under the leadership of Tlepolemus. History records the colonization of the island from Rhodes in later times.

20. **Tlepolemus:** the son of Heracles by Astydamia, the daughter of Amyntor, king of Ormenium near Mt Pelion. According to the *Iliad* (2.653–70) he led nine ships to Troy, and was killed by Sarpedon (5.627–69).

23. **From Zeus:** Zeus was father of Heracles by Alcmene.

30. **the founder of this land:** Tlepolemus.

27. **Alcmene:** daughter of Electryon, king of Mycenae, and sister of Licymnius; mother of Heracles and hence grandmother of Tlepolemus.

29. **Licymnius:** the usual view was that Licymnius died as the result of an accident: Tlepolemus was beating a slave over the head with a cudgel, and the elderly half-blind Licymnius stumbled between them and was killed. Pindar has changed this to a deliberate murder in anger (unexplained).

29. Midea's chamber: Midea is the name both of Licymnius' mother, who bore him illegitimately to Electryon, and of a town in the Argolid. What was Licymnius doing in her chamber?

31. the god: i.e. Apollo at Delphi.

33. From Lerna's shore: the killing of a man must normally be punished by exile. The story reflects the traditional role of the Delphic oracle in the sending out of colonies, also in historic times; the story corresponds to that told at *Iliad* 2.653–70. (But Apollo's role in the tale is the focus of Pindar's attention: Dougherty, *The Poetics of Colonization* [Oxford 1994], p. 124.)

34. snowflakes of gold: this metaphor of the wealth of Rhodes reflects Zeus' propensity for sending showers of gold, as he did to Danaë when she conceived Perseus, or as he did to Alcmene, according to I 7.5, when she conceived Heracles.

35–8. The story of the birth of Athena was well known; it is told in Homeric Hymn 28, and in Stesichorus frag. 233, *PMG*; and was portrayed on the east pediment of the Parthenon. See N. O. Brown, 'The Birth of Athena', *TAPA* 83 (1952): 130–43.

39. Hyperion's son: Helios, the Sun god.

41. his beloved sons: the earlier inhabitants of Rhodes, before the incursion of the Argives, were known as the Heliadae.

42. the goddess: Athena, the leading deity of the island, represented as a warrior with a spear.

48. no seed of burning flame: this accidental omission became a regular and unusual feature of Rhodian sacrifice: see Diodorus Siculus 5.56.5–7.

51. grey-eyed: a Homeric epithet of Athena, better to be interpreted 'owl-faced', because the owl is her bird. (Cf. 'ox-faced Hera'.)

53. innocent of guile: the legendary inhabitants of Rhodes, before the Heliadae, were the Telchines, who were renowned for craftsmanship and cunning wizardry. (They built walking tables, for example.) Pindar is emphasizing that the art of the Heliadae contained no element of trickery.

63. rich nourishment for men: the fertility of Rhodes is exceptional among the often barren Aegean islands.

64. Lachesis: one of the three Fates, the apportioner. Lachesis derives from a Greek word meaning 'to receive by lot', and it is therefore appropriate for her to be called upon in reference to the allotment of Rhodes to Helios.

77. rich amends: the flocks for sacrifice are a reward for former trials. In the Games, success – and its celebration – is the reward of effort.

80. the high seat of judgment of the Games: Tlepolemus is represented as the tutelary hero of the Rhodian games, which were dedicated to the Sun god. (The scholiasts think the reference should be to the Halieia, which was the major festival in their own time; but in Pindar's day this was an insignificant festival: P. A. Bernardini, *Stadion* 3 [1977]: 1–3.)

83. Arcadia: at the Lycaea. **Thebes:** at the Iolaeia. **Aegina:** at the Aiaceia or Delphinia (cf. N 5.44).

Megara: at the Alcathoia.

87. Atabyrios: the highest mountain of Rhodes, sacred to Zeus. This spelling is preferable to Conway's Ataburion.

93. Callianax: an ancestor of Diagoras; it is also the name of his son-in-law, as Pausanias tells us.

the Eratid clan: Eratus is the eponymous ancestor of Diagoras' family.

For Alcimedon of Aegina
Winner of the Boys' Wrestling Match (460)

Despite the opening invocation of Olympia, it seems clear that the ode, as was customary, was performed in the victor's home city of Aegina after his return from the Games. The date is given by the scholiasts on the basis of the victor lists.

Like other odes for Aeginetan victors, this one includes a myth relating to the family of Aeacus, the first legendary king of Aegina; in this case the building of the walls of Troy by Apollo and Poseidon, helped by Aeacus. The theme it emphasizes is that of co-operation, a dominant motif of the ode. Repeatedly the praise of the victor is shared with others (Timosthenes, line 15; Zeus, 16; the city, 21–30; Aiakos, 31–52; and the trainer 54–66). Finally he receives solo praise at lines 67–9. W. H. Race elegantly sums up the unity of this ode which reflects on the three things an athlete needs: divine assistance, natural gifts and training.

> From beginning to end it provides a meditation on the nature of success – how its foundations are laid by gods, furthered by family predecessors who may not live to share directly in the victories of their offspring (Aiakos, Iphion, Kallimachos), aided by expert teaching, and finally realized in deed. . . . All of these factors and considerations lie behind this boy's victory at Olympia, the queen of truth.
>
> (*Style and Rhetoric in Pindar's Odes* [Atlanta 1990] p. 163)

The concluding prayer for the continuing prosperity of Aegina may reflect the threats posed to Aegina's independence by the increasing power of Athens, which finally overcame Aegina, after two years' attrition, in 457.

str. 1   O mother of the gleaming crowns of contest,
        Olympia, queen of truth,
      Where men of prophets' power, proven consultants
      Of sacrificial fires, their questioned answer

Demand of Zeus, lord of the lightning flash,
    Whether for men who thirst   5
To win the highest guerdon of true valour,
There be a word to grant their hearts' desire,
    And respite from their toils.

ant. 1   For to the grace of reverent minds is given
              The answer to men's prayers.
          Then look with favour, Pisa's tree-clad precinct
          By Alpheus' stream, on this our song of triumph
          And crowned procession. Great fame has he for ever   10
              Who wins your honoured prize.
          To one man hence, and to another thence
          Are blessings given; many the roads that lead
              With heaven's help to good fortune.

ep. 1   For you, Timosthenes, destiny has   15
          Decreed that Zeus be guardian of your race,
          Who at Nemea made your name renowned,
              And by the hill of Cronos
          Gave to Alcimedon Olympia's crown.
          Fair was he to behold, and in his deeds
              Belied not beauty's form;
          King of the wrestlers' ring, he has proclaimed
          Aegina his country, land of long-oared galleons,   20
          Where Saviour Themis, throned beside great Zeus
              God of the host and guest,

str. 2   Is given abundant worship. For in matters
              Of many a purport, veering
          On every wind that blows, fitly to make
          Due disposition with an upright mind
          Is hard indeed. Yet have the immortals ruled
              This sea-girt land shall be   25
          For strangers of all race a god-sent pillar
          Of true justice; and may the rolling years
              Uphold them in this task.

ant. 2   Their isle is by a Dorian people governed,
              The stock of Aeacus,   30
          Whom long ago the son of Leto summoned

With wide-ruling Poseidon, to join with them
To build a crown of walls for Ilium.
   For it was so ordained,
That in the surge of war and battles, wrecking   35
The pride of cities, then from Troy should pour
   Billows of angry smoke.

ep. 2   And when the work was newly built, three serpents
Of fierce grey eyes leapt up to mount the wall,
And two fell back and in a stupor stunned,
   Breathed out their spirit's life.
But one sprang over with a mighty cry.   40
Straightway Apollo pondering on the sign
   Spoke and proclaimed it thus:
'Where your hands, hero Aeacus, have laboured
There shall this city Pergamos be taken,
So tells this portent sent by Cronos' son,
   Zeus the loud thunderer.

str. 3   'And not without your seed, but to the first   45
   And the fourth generation
The city's rule shall yield.' So spake the god,
A word most clear, and sped away to Xanthus,
Driving to meet the Amazons richly horsed,
   And to the streams of Ister.
Poseidon with his golden mares bore Aeacus   50
Home to this isle, and drove his flying chariot
   To the Isthmus overseas,

ant. 3   Visiting the hills of Corinth, where are offered
   The festals in his honour.
Now one joy cannot please all men alike,
And if I for Melesias raise high
My songs of praise for his young pupil's deeds,
   May no sharp stone of envy   55
Be flung at me. For at Nemea he too
Won a like prize, and again in the struggles
   Where grown men match their limbs

ep. 3   In the Pankration. The teacher's skill
Must be of knowledge bred; foolish indeed

Who has not well and truly learnt; a mind   60
    Is but a poor lightweight
Lacking the proof of trial. But here stands one
Who, best of all men, from his own achievements
    Can point the forward way
Whence from the sacred games a man may win
That prize the most desired of all. And now
To him Alcimedon's honour has given   65
    His thirtieth victory.

str. 4   For this young boy by favour of kind heaven
              And his own manly prowess,
          Has on four vanquished rivals shed the fear
          Of mocking tongues, and a return most hateful,
          Flitting in secret through the back-door home;
              And on his father's father   70
          Has breathed a vigour to make naught of age;
          For in good fortune a man may forget
              Thoughts of the world to come.

ant. 4   But I must wake old memories and tell
              The flowers of victory
          Won by the strong hands of the Blepsiad clan;   75
          Whose brows have now with six crowns been adorned
          At the Games where the woven wreath is prized.
              Those too who are no more,
          Of offerings duly paid them take their share,
          And the dust of the grave cannot keep hidden
              Their kinsmen's honoured grace.   80

ep. 4   From Hermes' daughter, the maid Messenger,
          Iphion shall hear and to Callimachus
          Tell the rich lustre of Olympia's glory,
              That Zeus has now bestowed
          Unto their race; and may he favour them
          With honour upon honour, and ward off   85
              The bitter pains of sickness.
          I pray that to their share of noble fortunes
          He send no Nemesis of jealous will,
          But in prosperity and free from ills,
              Exalt them and their city.

Notes

2. men of prophets' power: the descendants of Iamus, whose story is told in O 6, held the hereditary rights of divination at Olympia. These lines suggest that Alcimedon had consulted the oracle about his chances before entering the contest. The divination was made from the cuts and marks on the skin of the sacrificed animals.

12. To one man hence: these lines are by way of consolation to Alcimedon's elder brother Timosthenes, who had won only a Nemean victory while his younger brother had won the greater prestige of an Olympian one. Timosthenes may have been the commissioner of the ode, since their father Iphion was no longer alive (line 81).

16. Zeus: the presiding deity of both the Olympic and the Nemean Games.

God of the host and guest: Zeus was protector of the laws of hospitality. These lines are a tribute to Aegina's reputation for just dealing, to which Pindar often refers. Owing to her success in maritime commerce, traders from many parts of Greece and the Mediterranean were constant visitors to the island.

30. a Dorian people: Greece was divided into three ethnic groups: Dorians (most of the Peloponnese and some islands), Ionians (including Athens, and many islands) and Aeolians (northerly parts of the mainland and islands). The Dorians traced their ancestry to Heracles and were regarded as having arrived in Greece in the 'return of the sons of Heracles', a movement which used to be referred to by scholars as the 'Dorian invasion', constituting the resettlement of Greece after the Dark Ages which followed the Mycenaean period. Aegina, lying close to the Peloponnese, was Dorian while its close neighbour Athens was Ionian. The three ethnic divisions were unmistakable because of the differing dialects they used.

the son of Leto: Apollo. As a punishment for their taking part in the revolt of the gods against himself, Zeus assigned Apollo and Poseidon to be labourers for Laomedon, king of Troy (Ilium), who gave them the task of building the city's walls. The two gods, knowing that the walls would be impregnable if built entirely by divine hands, called in the mortal Aeacus to help in the work. See *Iliad* 7.446, 21.443.

37. three serpents: the two which fall at the walls represent Achilles and Ajax, grandsons of Aeacus, who died in the Trojan War; the third

which overleaps them is Achilles' son Neoptolemus, the fourth generation (counting inclusively in the Greek manner) from Aeacus. But the
first generation must then refer to Telamon's participation in the first
Trojan War with Heracles – depicted on the later of the two pediments
of the temple of Zeus on Aegina. By Pindar's reckoning Telamon
should actually be the second generation, Aeacus being the first.

47. Xanthus: in southern Asia Minor, and one of Apollo's favourite
haunts. But it is nowhere either the River Ister (Danube) or the land of
the Amazons, normally located beyond the Thermodon in northeastern
Asia Minor.

54. Melesias: Alcimedon's trainer. He was, according to the scholiast
on N 4.155a (but not the scholiasts on this ode), an Athenian, and a
trainer of high reputation. He may be the Melesias who was father of
the well-known Athenian politician Thucydides (not the historian). He
is also mentioned in N 4 and 6. Pindar's allusion to the danger of envy
in praising him may have something to do with the growing political
tension between Athens and Aegina. Melesias had clearly been an
athlete himself, and had won a similar victory to Alcimedon's in his
youth at Nemea, and as an adult in the pankration. Alcimedon's victory
was the thirtieth gained by a pupil of Melesias (line 66).

66. four vanquished rivals: the wrestling contest was apparently a
knock-out competition, in which Alcimedon had had to overcome four
other competitors. The gloating allusion to the ignominy of the
defeated, skulking home by back ways, casts a most vivid light on the
Greek passion for competitive success: cf. P 8.83–7.

70. father's father: name unknown.

75. the Blepsiad clan: the family to which Alcimedon belonged. We do
not know who the other victors were.

81. Iphion, Callimachus: probably the father and uncle respectively of
Alcimedon; both were no longer alive. In these cases it is regular for
there to be an allusion to the son's fame reaching the Underworld: cf.
e.g. O 14.

85. bitter pains of sickness: apparently there had been illness in the
family.

86. Nemesis: the goddess of vengeance.

For Epharmostus of Opous
Winner of the Wrestling Match (466)

Epharmostus was a citizen of Opous, a city of Eastern Locris in central Greece. It is probably to be identified with the site at Palaikastro, east of Atalante. He had won wrestling victories at all four Panhellenic Games as well as many other local festivals. This ode, though included among the Olympians, celebrates both his Olympic victory of 468 and his Pythian victory of 466 (line 12). The ode was commissioned by Lampromachus, the proxenos ('consul') of Opous at Thebes, to celebrate both victories as well as Lampromachus' own victories at the Isthmus and elsewhere.

The myth of Deucalion and Pyrrha is chosen for its local appropriateness, since they, the only survivors of the Flood, were the legendary founders of Opous. A dominant theme of the ode is the superiority of natural talent over acquired gifts, and the need of divine support in order to achieve anything grand. This is illustrated by the deeds of Heracles.

str. 1   Voices that chanted at Olympia
        The melody of Archilochus, ringing
        With its threefold refrain the victor's praise,
        Gave a fit lead to the triumphant march
        Of Epharmostus and his loyal friends
            Beside the hill of Cronos.
          But now with a far-ranging flight
          Of arrows from the Muses' bow,
        Let us enfold Zeus, lord of the red lightning,   5
          And with a like aim shower
          The headland of revered Elis,
        Which Lydian hero Pelops long ago
        Chose for Hippodamia, a splendid dower.   10

ant. 1   And let an arrow wing its joyful way
        To Pytho too. No word of ours shall fall

Spiritless to the ground, while the lyre's notes
Throb through the air to enrich a wrestler's glory,
A man from famous Opous, and to honour
    The city and her son.
   For Themis and her noble daughter,   15
   Eunomia the preserver, hold
This city a bright jewel in their crown.
    Castalia knows well
   Her flowers of valour, and Alpheus' stream,
Whose crowns, most prized of all, raise to high fame
This tree-clad city, mother of Locrian men.   20

ep. 1   Now with the glowing fires of song
Shall I exalt the name of this dear city;
   And swifter than a well-bred steed,
   Or a ship's wingéd sails,
My message shall go speeding far and wide,   25
If Fate's decree grants that my hand may till
The precious beauty of the Graces' garden.
   For of their gift is every joy,
    And from a divine power
Are noble and wise hearts endowed to man.

str. 2   How was it else the hands of Heracles
Could wield his club against the Trident's power,   30
When by the walls of Pylos stood Poseidon
And pressed him hard; and with his silver bow
Phoebus Apollo menaced him close in battle;
   And Hades too spared not
   To ply him with that sceptred staff,
   Which takes our mortal bodies down
Along the buried road to the dead world.   35
    Away, away this story!
   Let no such tale fall from my lips!
For to insult the gods is a fool's wisdom,
A craft most damnéd, and unmeasured boasting

ant. 2   Is music for mad minds. Let no voice babble   40
Such follies: keep far from the immortal gods
All war and battle. Let Protogenia's city
Play on your tongue, where by decree of Zeus,

God of the lightning's quivering flash, there came
    Deucalion and Pyrrha,
    Down from Parnassus' height, and first
    Made them their home, then without wedlock
Founded a people of one origin,
    A race made out of stone;   45
    And from a stone they took their name.
For them raise high your chant of song. Old wine
Praise if you will, but for the flowers of song

ep. 2   Fresh blooms are best. Now the tale runs
That earth's dark soil was flooded by the waters,   50
    But by the arts of Zeus, their strength
      Suddenly ebbed again.
And of that race were sprung your ancestors,
Bearers of brazen shields, sons of the maids
Of the stock of Iapetus, and from
    The sublime sons of great Cronos.   55
      And ever, since those days,
Have they ruled, kings of this their native land.

str. 3   Until it fell that the lord of Olympus
From the Epeians' land bore off the daughter
Of Opous, and the glades of Maenalus
Witnessed their happy union. Then he took her
To Locrus, lest his old age leave him childless.   60
    But his bride held within her
    The mighty seed, and he rejoiced
    To see a son so given, and named him
By the same name his mother's father bore.
    And he grew up to manhood,
    In beauty and alike in deeds   65
Beyond all praise. And Locrus gave to him
The city and its people for his rule.

ant. 3   And many a stranger joined him there, from Argos
From Thebes and from Arcadia and from Pisa.
But chief of all newcomers he bestowed
Honour upon Menoetius, the child
Of Aegina and Actor. His son it was   70
    Came with the sons of Atreus

To the broad plain of Teuthras. There
He with Achilles stood his ground
Alone of all, when Telephus cast back
    The warrior Danai
Down on their ships. Well might be seen
By a wise eye the brave heart of Patroclus.   75
Thereafter, midst the fray of murderous battle,

ep. 3   The son of Thetis bade him never
Take post save by his own all-conquering spear.
    Now may invention grant my tongue,   80
        Riding the Muses' car,
Fit words to tell my tale, and a bold mind
Endow me with wide-ranging power to frame
This song of mine. For I am come to pay
    Due homage to Lampromachus,
        First, for his Proxeny,
Then for the Isthmian crowns that proved his valour,

str. 4   When he and Epharmostus on one day   85
Both won the victor's place. And twice again
By the sea gates of Corinth, triumph blessed them.
And Epharmostus in Nemea's valley
And at Argos amongst men won glory,
    And amongst boys at Athens.
    And barely freed from beardless years,
    Finely he matched with older men
At Marathon for the silver prize. His swift   90
    And deftly-balanced craft,
    Unthrown himself, felled all his rivals.
How mighty a shout hailed the parading victor,
For youth and beauty and fine deeds achieved.

ant. 4   Amongst the people of Parrhasia too   95
At the feast of Lycaeon Zeus, they marvelled
To see his skill, and at Pellene also
When he bore off the cloak, that warm protection
From the chill breeze. The tomb of Iolaus
    Witnessed his glories too,
    And the city Eleusis by the sea.
    Ever are natural gifts the best,   100

But many a man struggles to win renown
  By skills learnt from a teacher.
  But each deed that a man may try
Without heaven's help, is best buried in silence.
Some paths there are may find a further goal

ep. 4   Than may some others, but no single   105
Study will nurse all men alike to skill.
    True art is a steep road to climb.
      But treating of this prize
He has now won, be bold with a clear voice
To tell abroad that by the gift of heaven
This man was born strong-handed, nimble-limbed   110
    And in his eyes the light of valour,
      And at the feast of Oileus
Has set his victor's crown on Ajax' altar.

Notes

1. **The melody of Archilochus:** the cry of *tenella kallinike*, like 'hip-hip-hooray', which, as the scholiast tells us, had been enshrined as a brief song, addressed to Heracles, by Archilochus (frag. 324, West). *Kallinikos* – 'beautiful in victory' – was a title of Heracles. *Tenella* mimics the sound of an arpeggio on the lyre – like e.g. 'tarantara' in English. Pindar is saying that all Epharmostus got for his victory at Olympia two years before was three cheers; now he is getting a proper ode.

7. **headland of Elis:** i.e. Olympia. 'Pinnacle' might be a better translation of *akroterion*.

9. **Lydian . . . Pelops:** Pelops was the son of Tantalus, king of Sipylus in Asia Minor: see O 1 and notes for the story of his winning of Hippodameia by defeating her father Oenomaus in a chariot race at Olympia, after which he became ruler of Elis.

12. **Pytho:** Delphi, the scene of Epharmostus' Pythian victory of 466.

26. **the Graces' garden:** this metaphor of Pindar as the gardener of the Graces fits with a complex of Pindaric imagery in which the poem, and the victor's achievement, are blossoms on a plant, and the poem is an ornament provided by the Graces.

30. **How was it else . . .?:** Heracles did not fight all three opponents at

once. His fight with Poseidon (armed with his trident) took place when Heracles attacked the Minyans of Pylos (scholiast on *Iliad* 11.690, who says that Hera and Hades also took part in the fight); however, the description of this event at *Iliad* 5.382–404 refers only to Hera and Hades (cf. Panyassis frags. 6 and 20 Kinkel, with Matthews' commentary 52–7). The fight with Hades may be this same occasion, or it may refer to Heracles' visit to Hades to bring back the hound Cerberus; however, *Iliad* 5.397 does say that the fight with the three gods also took place 'among the dead'. The fight with Apollo took place when Heracles stole the Delphic tripod, a motif popular in vase-painting. The specific reference here may be that Epharmostus, as is stated in lines 88–90, had competed with athletes in a higher age-class. The praise of Heracles as able to fight even the gods is quickly dismissed as impiety, and Heracles becomes an example of the danger of 'going too far'; the topic makes a break-off formula to lead into the myth.

41. Protogenia: there were two Protogenias. The first was a daughter of Deucalion and Pyrrha. She married a king of Elis and had a son called Opous. His daughter was the second Protogenia who was carried off by Zeus as related in strophe 3, and became the wife of Locrus, king of Locris. See below on line 48.

43. Deucalion and Pyrrha: their story is the Greek equivalent of the Hebrew legend of Noah. Like Noah, Deucalion and Pyrrha built an ark, which came to rest, when the waters subsided, on Mt Parnassus. They descended the north side of the mountain and founded the city later called Opous, and on the orders of Zeus created a new human race out of stones. From this race, Pindar claims, came the Locrians.

46. And from a stone they took their name: the Greek word for 'people' is *laos* and for 'stone' *laas*. Though the words are unconnected etymologically, the tag was popular, appearing also in Hesiod (frag. 234), Callimachus (frag. 496) and Epicharmus (frag. 122, Kinkel) as well as others.

47. Old wine ... fresh blooms: The scholiasts say that this is a stab at the older epinician poet Simonides, who in frag. 97 (*PMG* 602) stated: 'New wine never outclasses the gift of yesterday's vine; ... and tales are empty-headed ...' [the rest is corrupt]. The statement seems to be a warning that Pindar is about to introduce one of his new versions of a myth: here, it seems, he has doubled the generations in order to make Zeus the direct ancestor of the Opountines, as follows:

DEUCALION
(grandson of Iapetus) and PYRRHA
|
PROTOGENIA
|
OPOUS
|
PROTOGENIA = ZEUS (son of Cronos)
|
OPOUS (adopted by Locrus)

57. lord of Olympus: i.e. Zeus.

58. Epeians: inhabitants of Elis. Opous is a place-name in Elis also, here envisaged as a man, father of Protogenia (2).

63. his mother's father: i.e. Opous.

70. Menoetius: the brother of Peleus and father of Patroclus, who went with the sons of Atreus to the plains of Teuthras (i.e. Mysia in Asia Minor, then ruled by Teuthras' son Telephus): this prelude to the Trojan War was told in the epic *Cypria*.

76. the son of Thetis: Achilles, who according to *Iliad* 16.89–90 would not allow Patroclus to fight without Achilles by his side to protect him – a motif which probably first occurred in the *Cypria*, as it is only alluded to fleetingly in the *Iliad*. When Patroclus did go off to fight without Achilles, as told in the *Iliad*, he was killed by Hector. The mythical moment may be intended as a parallel to the competition of Epharmostus and Lampromachus side by side (lines 84–5).

80–1. invention: not now the myth, but the praises to come.

84. Lampromachus: now we discover that the ode is to celebrate a victory of Lampromachus as well – at the Isthmian Games alongside Epharmostus. A proxenos had a function equivalent to that of a consul, a post which Lampromachus held at Thebes. It was probably he who commissioned the ode from Pindar.

86. the sea gates of Corinth: i.e. at the Isthmus.

89. freed from beardless years: the Greek says 'wrenched'. Epharmostus was of an age to compete with youths, but the judges insisted he compete with men (perhaps because of exceptional physical maturity) – and yet he still won! – like Heracles defeating the gods.

at Marathon: the games at Marathon were dedicated to Heracles and silver cups were the prize.

95. Parrhasia: i.e. Arcadia, whose people celebrated the Lycaea near the temple of Zeus on Mt Lycaeon, in winter. (Cf. O 13. 108, N 10.48.)

96. Pellene: a city in Achaea in the northern Peloponnese, where the prize in the local Games was a woollen cloak.

98. The tomb of Iolaus: the festival of the Iolaeia at Thebes; Iolaus was Heracles' charioteer. See note on N 4.20.

99. Eleusis: the games were part of the Eleusinian festival which included the Mysteries.

100. Ever are natural gifts the best: a recollection of the sentiment of line 27, virtue comes from the gods and inadequate spirits can never improve themselves by teaching. This shibboleth of aristocratic culture led directly to Socrates' question, 'Can virtue be taught?' Here, the point is that Epharmostus needed divine help to win, as did Heracles against the gods, and as Patroclus needed the support of the greater Achilles.

103. buried in silence: cf. I 4.30: 'Who does not put to proof his worth, remains forgotten and unsung.'

108. this prize he has now won: the Pythian victory.

112. Ajax' altar: Ajax the Less, son of Oileus of Locris – not the son of Telamon. The ode must have been performed at a festival of Ajax.

For Hagesidamus of Epizephyrian Locris
Winner of the Boys' Boxing Match (474?)

This ode has been seen by commentators since the scholiasts as the fulfilment of a promise made in the briefer Ode 11 for the victory of 476; but Bundy has shown that Olympian 11 is a self-sufficient ode in its own terms and there is no need for this assumption. It does however celebrate the same victory: no other Olympic victory of Hagesidamus is known. Pindar was unusually busy in 476 with the three great Sicilian odes (Olympians 1–3). The repetition of the motif of a debt and late delivery in this ode may however suggest that Pindar is conscious that the victory celebrated is already some time in the past; but the poet's debt (lines 3, 9, 34) is also a conventional topos of epinician poetry, so this cannot be regarded as a firm argument. The theme of time and truth is a leitmotif of the poem, appearing at lines 6, 55, 85 (time) and lines 4–6, 36, 54 (truth).

str. 1 Olympian victor, son of Archestratus,
   Where on my heart is writ that name?
    Read it me now.
  For a poem I owed to him, a pleasant song,
  And I forgot. Ah Muse, I beg you, and Truth
  Daughter of Zeus, with your right hand upraised
  Shield me from this reproach of a pledge broken,   5
   And a friend's dues dishonoured.

ant. 1 For time, eating up the days from long ago,
   Has shamed me for my heavy debt;
    Yet of this blame
  Payment with interest can heal the wound.
  Look then, so surely as the surging wave
  Sweeps down the rolling pebble, so my song   10
  Honouring you and yours, shall the debt render
   And grace the bond of friendship.

ep. 1   For in Locri of the West, Integrity
              Has honour. In Music's art
        And in brazen War their pride is high. To Cycnus   15
              Yielded the day
        Even mighty Heracles. Let Agesidamus,
        Victorious in Olympia's boxing contest,
              A due tribute
        To Ilas render, as of old Patroclus
              Gave honour to Achilles.
        For he who tempers fine the spirit's blade   20
        In a man to valour born, may with god's help
              Bring him to high renown.

str. 2 Few without toil can win the joy that lights
              This life for each deed truly done.
                    The laws prescribed
        Of Zeus now bid me sing the matchless contest,
        Founded beside the ancient tomb of Pelops
        By Heracles, who set six altars there,   25
        After that he had slain Poseidon's son,
              The warrior Cteatus,

ant. 2 And Eurytus too he slew, so to exact
              From Augeas, that proud despot,
                    Rewards for service
        He would not deign to pay: under Cleonae,   30
        Hiding in ambush on the road, he felled
        Those haughty Moliones, and avenged
        The day they lay in Elis vale, and ravaged
              The host he led from Tiryns.

ep. 2   Nor waited long that lord of the Epeians,   35
              King Augeas, who broke
        Faith with his guest, till that he saw his homeland
              And all his wealth
        In the fell strokes of iron-handed war
        Wasted beneath the breath of stubborn flame,
              And his own city
        Sunk in the pit of doom. Strife with the mighty
              Is hard to set aside.   40
        And he in his unwisdom last of all

Fallen into captive chains, could not escape
   The headlong sword of death.

str. 3   Then gathering all the host and his rich spoils,
      The valiant son of Zeus in Pisa
         Measured and founded
    In his great father's name a holy precinct,   45
    And fenced and marked out on clear ground the Altis,
    And the encircling plain he ruled should be
    For rest and feasting, to honour Alpheus' river
      With the twelve kings divine.

ant. 3   And he named the Hill of Cronos, for long years   50
      While Oenomaus ruled, a hill
         Nameless and showered
    With winter's snow. Now in that birthday hour
    The Fates stood by, this new-established rite
    To consecrate, and Time, whose proof at last
    Stands the sole judge of Truth that shall abide.   55
      And now the rolling years

ep. 3   Make plain the tale, how from the gifts of war
      He set aside the first-fruits,
    And after sacrifice founded a feast
      For each fourth year,
    The first Olympiad and its victors' honours.
    Say then, who won the new-appointed crown   60
      For strength of arm,
    For speed of foot, or in the chariot's course,
     His prayer for victory's glory
    Burning within his soul, and thence the crown
    Won by his body's act? In the foot race,
      The stadium's straight course,

str. 4   Licymnius' son Oeonus won the day,   65
      Who from Midea led his host.
        In the wrestlers' match
    Echemus brought glory to Tegea.
    Next Doryclus who dwelt in Tiryns city
    Carried the boxer's prize, and in the race

Of four-horsed chariots, Halirothius' son   70
    Samos of Mantinea.

ant. 4   Then Phrastor with the javelin hit the mark,
    And Niceus with his circling arm
      Won the long throw,
Past all his rivals hurling the disc of stone.
Then from the warrior company flashed forth
A cheer of thundering praise, while to the hour
Of evening's beauty the unclouded moon   75
    Distilled her lovely light;

ep. 4   And all the precinct rang with festal song
    In triumph's mode of revel.
Now in this ancient pattern shall my songs,
    To grace the name
Of victory's proud spirit, sound the praise
Of thunder and the fire-wrought bolt of Zeus,   80
    Lord of the tumult,
And the almighty symbol of his power,
    The lightning's burning stroke.
Then shall the graceful melodies of song
With the flute's note enchant the air, those strains
    Promised so long ago

str. 5   From famous Dirke. As when a man, whose years   85
    Have past the surging tides of youth,
      Receives with joy
The dear son of his marriage, and his heart
Warms with a father's love – for if the wealth
Of his own house must fall to foreign hands
And strangers' tillage, spells thence a bitter thought,
    Bane to his death-bed hour –   90

ant. 5   Or if a man takes down to Hades' gate
    Brave deeds unheralded in song,
      Then all in vain
His labour's breath, and brief his span of joy.
But you, Agesidamus, the lyre's rich notes
And the sweet pipe shower with their joyful honour,

And the Pierides, the maids of Zeus,
    Make widespread your renown.   95

ep. 5   With these are linked my songs eager to spread
      Their wings o'er Locri's fame,
    And on her glorious manhood shed a grace
      Sweeter than honey.
    Praise have I given to Archestratus' son,
    That comely youth, whose strength of arm I saw   100
      That far-off day,
    Victorious beside Olympia's altar.
      Lovely his body's grace,
    That spring-tide hour of beauty, which long since
    Freed Ganymede – so willed the Cyprian queen –   105
      From death's relentless power.

Notes

4–6. Pindar's prayer to Truth to keep him from falsehood is paralleled at frag. 205; he also deprecates the reproach of offending a xenos.

9. **Payment with interest:** does this imply that the ode will be longer than the patron asked for? Seneca (*Ep.*6.7) says to his addressee 'I owe you a little extra, so here is an anecdote . . .' The scholiasts assumed that the ode was the interest due on O 11. But the asyndeton at 'Look then' indicates that what follows is the fulfilment of the debt just stated. Pebbles were used in working out accounts, so there may be a double point to the metaphor: the poem will cancel the debt as the sea washes over the pebbles.

13. **Integrity:** if the Epizephyrian Locrians had a particular reputation for scrupulousness in their business affairs – as according to Demosthenes *Against Timarchus* 744 they had since ancient times – this would provide a motive for the complex of financial imagery in the poem. The legendary Locrian lawgiver Zaleukos was particularly emphatic on matters of property and contract.

15. **Cycnus:** a son of Ares the war god (just mentioned), whose custom it was to behead travellers, who fought Heracles in Phthiotis. See Hesiod, *Shield of Heracles* 72–4. The story was also told by Stesichorus in his *Cycnus*. Heracles nearly pursued his father Ares, too; hence the proverb: 'not even Heracles against two'.

17. Ilas: the trainer of Hagesidamus. The trainer is usually mentioned in odes addressed to boys.

19. Patroclus: a native hero of Locris, supported in battle by the greater hero Achilles; cf. on O 9.75ff.

24. The laws prescribed of Zeus: the procedures of the Olympic Games.

the ... tomb of Pelops: a central feature of the precinct at Olympia: its remains have been uncovered in modern times.

25. six altars: see note on O 5.5.

Heracles: The fifth labour of Heracles was the cleansing of the stables of Augeas, king of Elis. Augeas agreed to pay Heracles a tithe of cattle for this task, but on its completion refused to keep his side of the bargain. Later Heracles collected an army from Tiryns and marched into Elis to take his revenge. Cteatus and Eurytus, the 'Moliones', sons of Molione by Poseidon, allied themselves with Augeas and defeated the army of Heracles in Elis while he was sick. Later Heracles ambushed these two brothers and killed them while they were travelling through Cleonae. Heracles raised another army, invaded Elis, sacked the capital city and threw Augeas into prison, where he died. The story of Augeas is told by Pausanias 5.1.9–5.2.2.

In the *Iliad* (2.750) the Molione are sons of Actor, not Poseidon. The meaning of their name is uncertain. Later authors (e.g. Ibycus frag. 285, Davies) regarded them as Siamese twins. Their story was told by Pherecydes and was portrayed on the throne of Apollo at Amyclae (Paus. 3.18.5); their tomb at Cleonae was mentioned by Pausanias (2.15.1).

35. Nor waited long: the time theme again.

Epeians: the people of Elis, named after king Epeius, son of Endymion; his brothers Aetolus and Paeon became eponyms of the northern Greeks. Pisa was subject to the Epeians under Oenomaus but became independent under Pelops according to Paus. 5.1.7–9. Aetolus became king after Epeius, was exiled, and Endymion's grandson Eleius became king. Eleius' son was Augeas. In historical times, the Eleans conquered Olympia in 571 BC and became presidents of the Games.

broke faith with his guest: another sounding of the note of honest dealing.

39-40. Strife with the mighty: Augeas had to yield to Heracles, as Heracles yielded to Cycnus above.

44. The valiant son of Zeus: Heracles. Paus. 5.8.3 describes Heracles' celebration of the Games.

45. the Altis: the enclosure surrounding the sacred precinct of Olympia.

46-9. the twelve kings divine: actually 'gods'. See note on O 5.5.; and line 25 above.

54. Time . . . judge of Truth: cf. 4-6; Simonides frag. 175 Bgk.

6off. Say then, who won . . .? this account of Heracles' celebration of the Games probably follows local traditions.

65. Licymnius: brother of Alcmene, the mother of Heracles. His death, perhaps accidental, at the hands of Tlepolemus who subsequently colonized Rhodes, is told in O 7.

Oeonus: according to the scholiasts, another story told that Oeonus had been torn apart as a child by the dogs of Hippocoon.

Midea: a town in the Argolid, home of Licymnius.

Echemus: the ruler of Tegea and Arcadia, and a noted friend of the gods. Hesiod, frags. 23a31 and 176 MW, tells us that he married Timandra but she left him for a worse man. Later he fought a single combat with Hyllus, the son of Heracles, who was invading the Peloponnese from the north (the 'return of the sons of Heracles', later known as the Dorian invasion). Hyllus' condition was that if successful he should be given the throne of Mycenae, but if defeated the invaders would postpone the invasion for fifty years. Hyllus was killed by Echemus and the invasion postponed.

Doryclus, Phrastor, Niceus: nothing is known of these contestants.

72. disc of stone: of twenty surviving discuses, most are bronze, a few marble, one of lead. Their average weight is 2.5 kg, though individual weights range from 1.5 to 6.5 kg. A modern discus weighs 2 kg. In *Iliad* 22 (the funeral games of Patroclus) the throwing contest is performed with a circular iron ingot.

80. the fire-wrought bolt: the thunderbolt was represented on the coins of Epizephyrian Locri, and also on coins of Elis.

84. flute: actually a reed pipe: see on P 12.

85. strains promised so long ago: the summation of the promise of praise in time.

86. As when a man . . .: There are two similes here. First, the heir is related to the old father as the ode is related to the victor: an heir keeps the wealth in the family as the ode preserves the victor's fame, so that the ode is linked again to the theme of the payment of debts. Secondly, an old man may die without his deeds being celebrated in song; but Hagesidamus *has* got a song to pay for his deeds and keep his fame alive.

96. Pierides: another name for the Muses.

105. Ganymede: the beautiful youth stolen away by Zeus to be his cup-bearer on Olympus: see on O 1.44.

the Cyprian queen: Aphrodite, goddess of love.

Freed . . . From death's relentless power: song combined with youthful beauty makes the ultimate payment of saving from death and fulfils the debt of the poet.

For Hagesidamus of Epizephyrian Locri
Winner of the Boys' Boxing Match (476)

This ode and Olympian 10 were both written for the same
victory of Hagesidamus at the Olympic Games of 476. The
scholiasts differ as between 484 and 476, but the victor list,
POxy 222 = *FGrH* 415, confirms 476. As the preserved part of
the victor list only begins in 480, it is theoretically possible that
Hagesidamus won in 484 as well; but he could not have been a
boy on both occasions.

Olympian 11 has generally been read as a promise of a further
ode to come – arguing from the future tenses in lines 14, 16 and
18; and the reference in Olympian 10.9 to a debt has been taken
to refer to the promise made in Olympian 11. However, W. J.
Slater ('Futures in Pindar', *CQ* 19, 1969: 86–94) showed that
future tenses normally refer to the fulfilment of intentions within
the ode in question; and E. L. Bundy, who chose Olympian 11
as the programmatic subject of his revolutionary approach to
Pindar's poetry (*Studia Pindarica* 1962/86), shows that the ode
is entirely self-sufficient as a statement of praise.

str. 1   Often man's need is for the wind's breath blowing,
       Often he prays from heaven the showering rain,
          Child of the cloud. But if success
       Wins him the hard-fought crown, then for rich choirs
       Of sweet-flown song the debt is entered, prelude
       To age-long story for his deeds of valour,   5
          A pledge that will not fail.

ant. 1   Ample this store of praise and gladly given
       For Olympia's victors: here my Muse shall tend
          Her flock. Yet only of god's giving
       In a poet's heart is born the flower of song.   10
       Thus for your boxing skill, Agesidamus,
       Son of Archestratus, a poem I pledge you,
          Music to herald a rich

ep. 1   Blazon of glory for your crown of olive,
          And to bring honour to your race in Locri
                Under the western sky.   15
          There join me, Muses, in the songs of triumph;
          No grudging hosts I promise shall await you,
               But a folk that have dared noble deeds,
          Scaling the heights in poetry and in battle.
                Well I know
          Nor russet fox nor roaring lions can change   20
                Their inborn nature.

Notes

1. **Often man's need . . . :** an unusually pure and elegant form of the priamel, comparable in structure with the opening of O 1.

12. **I pledge you:** literally, 'I shall sing.' Conway's translation assumes the interpretation of this ode as a promise of O 10. In fact the statement 'I shall sing' refers to the fulfilment of the need of praise in *this* ode (lines 16–21: see Bundy, p. 22).

13. **your crown of olive:** Pindar's Greek calls the olive 'golden', a common metaphor in the odes.

16. **There join me:** i.e. in the victor's home town. Locri Epizephyrii was a colony on the coast of southern Italy, founded by the Locrians of Opous on the Greek mainland.

20. **Nor russet fox nor roaring lions:** representatives of cunning and valour respectively, ideal qualities for a boxer.

For Ergoteles of Himera
Winner of the Long Foot Race (probably 466)

Pausanias, who saw the dedicatory statue of Ergoteles at Olympia, writes:

> Ergoteles son of Philanor won the long-distance running twice at Olympia, and twice at Delphi and once each at the Isthmus and Nemea; he was not originally fron Himera as the inscription says he was, but they say he was a Cretan from Knossos; he was expelled from Knossos by a revolution, and went to Himera where he was made a citizen and received all kinds of honours; probably because he was going to have himself proclaimed a Himeraean in the Games.

> (Paus. 6.4.11)

A metrical inscription from the actual dedication was found in 1953 (*SEG* xi. 1223a) and confirms the number of victories. In this ode Pindar refers to two Pythian victories, one each at Olympia and Isthmia, and no Nemean victory.

The long foot race was probably run over a distance of 4,000 metres.

The poem is intimately bound up with political events in Sicily, which can be summarized as follows. Terillos, the ruler of Himera, was expelled by Theron of Acragas in the late 480s. Terillos appealed to Carthage and the Carthaginians invaded Sicily in 480, defeating Theron and Gelon at the Battle of Himera. In 476/5 Theron installed his son Thrasydaeus as ruler of Himera; the Himeraeans appealed to Hieron for help, but Hieron informed Theron of the appeal and the latter suppressed the revolution with numerous executions and then resettled the city, which remained under Syracusan domination until 466.

It is likely that Ergoteles was one of the many new citizens admitted in the period after 476. One of his two Olympic victories is firmly dated by the victor list (*POxy* 222: *FGrH* 415) to 472, and the other was probably in 464 (as one of the scholiasts also states). One Pythian victory was in 470 and the

other probably in 466, as argued by W. S. Barrett, 'Pindar's
Twelfth Olympian and the Fall of the Deinomenidai', *JHS* 93
(1973): 23–35. (Previous scholarship had placed the other
Pythian victory in 474, thus leaving a gap of six years between
the victories of 470 and 464.) If that is the case, the ode was
composed soon after the victory of 466. (The Nemean and
Isthmian victories are of course undateable as there are no victor
lists.)

   This date fits the historical circumstances well, as Hieron's
son Thrasybulus, who succeeded him as ruler of Syracuse in
467/6, was overthrown by midsummer 466, and democracy was
restored with the result that Himera was freed from Syracusan
domination. Diodorus (11.72.2) informs us that a colossal statue
of Zeus the Liberator (Zeus Eleutherius) was erected in Syracuse
on this occasion. Pindar's opening invocation would be directed
at this new dedication.

str. 1   Daughter of Zeus, who holds the gift of Freedom,
                Fortune our saviour goddess,
          I pray your guardian care for Himera,
          And prosper her city's strength. For your hand steers
          The ships of ocean on their flying course,
          And rules on land the march of savage wars,
          And the assemblies of wise counsellors.   5
                And yet the hopes of man
             Now ride on high, now are sunk low,
          Cleaving their way through seas of false illusion.

ant. 1   For no man born of earth has ever yet
                Found a trustworthy sign
          From heaven above, what future days may bring.
          Blind are the eyes of our imagination
          Of times to come. How often is man's thought
          Thwarted by the event, now disappointing   10
          Expected joy, now when a man has met
                The surge of sorrow's pain,
             In a brief hour of time changing
          His bitter grief to profound happiness.

ep. 1   For you, son of Philanor,
          Well may we see that like a fighting cock,

Whose skill only his homely hearth may know,
   The glory of your racing feet
Had fallen like the fleeting leaves of autumn   15
      Unhonoured to the ground,
Had not revolt, man against man, denied you
Knossos, your own homeland. Now, as it falls,
Winning Olympia's crown, Ergoteles,
Twice victor, too, at Pytho and the Isthmus,
You have brought glory to the Nymphs' warm springs,   19
Here in this land which is your new-found home.

Notes

1. **Zeus, who holds the gift of Freedom:** the cult title is unusual, but is found in various parts of Greece and is always linked to a specific historical liberation. The allusion to the end of tyrannical rule in Himera and Syracuse is unmistakable: see introduction, and the article by Barrett cited there.

13. **son of Philanor:** Ergoteles.

14. **a fighting cock:** coins of Himera carried the image of a cock.

18. **Twice victor ... at Pytho:** i.e. in 470 and 466. Though it was classed by the ancient scholars as an Olympian ode, the most recent victory celebrated in this ode (on either dating) is in fact a Pythian.

19. **the Nymphs' warm springs:** the hot springs of Himera still flow: the place is now called Termini Imerese. Tetradrachms of Himera show a nymph pouring a libation on an altar, and a figure at the side *reaches into* the fountain, perhaps the action described by Pindar as *bastazeis*, 'you touch or handle', and vaguely translated by Conway (no doubt in puzzlement) as 'you have brought glory to': see R. Hamilton, *Phoenix* 38 (1984): 261–4.

For Xenophon of Corinth

Winner of the Short Foot Race and the Pentathlon (464)

Xenophon's double victory took place in 464 BC; the date given by the scholiasts is confirmed by Pausanias (4.24.5), Diodorus (11.70) and Dionysius of Halicarnassus (9.61). This ode, in addition to celebrating Xenophon's unusual feat, is a panegyric of the innumerable athletic victories won by members of Xenophon's clan, the Oligaethidae, as well as of the city of Corinth itself.

The genealogy of the various family members mentioned in the ode, with further information, is given by the scholiasts on this ode. In an ingenious article, W. S. Barrett ('The Oligaethidae and their Victories', in *Dionysiaca: studies presented to Sir Denys Page* [1978]: 1–20) has argued that this genealogy was constructed by them from information in this ode itself, supplemented by another epinician ode, part of which has now been discovered on *POxy* 2623: it is possibly by Simonides and probably composed for Autolykos for an unknown, probably Pythian, victory. Correction from the papyrus results in an alteration of Eritimos' place in the tree as indicated.

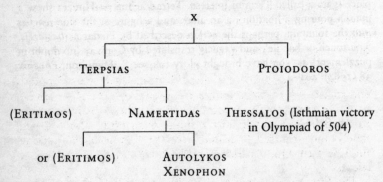

The structure of the ode is simple. The first triad sings the glories of Corinth; the second those of Xenophon for his present successes at Olympia, and for his previous victories at the Isthmian and Nemean Games, and commemorates victories won by his father and other near relatives. The third triad turns again to Corinth, and tells of her notable legendary figures, including Glaucus, the Lycian leader in the Trojan War (*Iliad* 6.152–211) and grandson of Bellerophon of Corinth.

The mention of Glaucus leads into the story of Bellerophon and the winged horse Pegasus. Bellerophon went to King Proetus of Argos to be purified after an accidental murder. Proetus' wife Anteia (Homer) or Stheneboea (Euripides) fell in love with him and, being rebuffed, falsely accused him of trying to seduce her. Proetus, to get rid of Bellerophon without committing the sacrilege of killing a suppliant, sent Bellerophon to his wife's father, Iobates, king of Lycia, with a secret note asking him to destroy Bellerophon. Iobates, likewise unwilling to murder his guest, asked Bellerophon to do him the service of destroying the Chimaera, a fire-breathing monster with the head of a goat, the body of a lion, and a snake for a tail, which lived in the nearby mountains (the volcanic Mt Chimaera in southern Turkey). Bellerophon consulted the seer Polyidus, and was advised to catch the winged horse Pegasus. His capture of the horse, with the help of Athena, by the fountain Pirene at Corinth, is the subject of the central stanzas of the ode. Bellerophon killed the Chimaera by flying above it and shooting it with arrows.

Iobates then asked him to defeat his enemies the Solymi, and their allies the Amazons, the race of female warriors; a mission in which Bellerophon was again successful. Eventually Iobates was persuaded that Bellerophon was innocent of the offence against Anteia, gave him another daughter in marriage and made him heir to the Lycian throne. Bellerophon however, at the height of his good fortune, was presumptuous enough to try to fly up to heaven on Pegasus. Zeus sent a gadfly to sting Pegasus, who bucked and threw Bellerophon to earth. Bellerophon fell into a thorn bush and – lame, blind, lonely and accursed – drifted over the 'Plains of Wandering' until he died. Quite a lesson for those who pride themselves on success.

The fifth triad returns to the athletic feats of other members of the Oligaethid clan, and the ode ends with a short prayer to Zeus for the family's continued good fortune.

str. 1   Three times victorious at Olympia
    Is the house that I praise; the trusted friend
    Of fellow-citizens, and to her guests
        A generous host. Herein is mirrored
    Corinth the happy city, the proud portal
    Of Isthmian Poseidon, and the nurse   5
        Of glorious youth. Here dwells
    Eunomia and that unsullied fountain
    Justice, her sister, sure support of cities;
    And Peace of the same kin, who are the stewards
        Of wealth for all mankind –
    Three glorious daughters of wise-counselled Themis.

ant. 1   Far from their path they hold proud Insolence,   10
    Fierce-hearted mother of full-fed Disdain.
    Fair words have I to say, and a bold heart
        Calls to my tongue to speak them frankly;
    No man can hide what nature breeds within him.
    But to you, sons of Aletes, how often
        The Hours, decked in their wreaths,
    Have given the glory of the victor's triumph
    For supreme valour in the sacred Games,   15
    All rivals far surpassing, and how often
        For men of your own kin,
    Have they implanted in their hearts the skills

ep. 1   Of ancient times? The inventor's craft
            Makes every work of man.
            Whence came the graceful dithyramb
        Of Dionysus with its prize of oxen?
        Who first with harness tamed the horse's power?   20
            Or on the temples of the gods
        First set the double image of the eagle?
        The sweet breath of the Muse adorns your city,
        And your young warriors with their dreaded spears
            To Ares pay full honour.

str. 2   O sovereign lord, who rules Olympia,
    Grant, father Zeus, your blessing for all time   25
    Upon my songs, and let no mischief touch
        This people; and for Xenophon

Grant to his lot the fair breeze of good fortune.
And pray accept for him this chant of triumph
    For the crowns that he brings
From Pisa's plain, where first he won the prize
In the Pentathlon contest, then again   30
Crowned victor in the foot race of the stade.
    Never before this day
Has one man thus achieved this double glory.

ant. 2   Twice too the wreath of parsley on his brow
Declared him victor at the Isthmian Games,
Nor can Nemea tell a different story.
    And by the banks of Alpheus' river,
The lightning speed of foot of Thessalus,   35
His father, is inscribed in glory's roll.
    In the foot race at Pytho,
Both for the single and the double stade,
In one brief day he took the prize of honour;
And the same month in Athens rock-built city
    A day of sparkling feet
Set on his locks three times the crown of splendour.

ep. 2   Seven crowns Hellotia's feast presented;   40
    And where Poseidon guards
Between two seas the rules of contest,
Too long 'twould be to sing of Ptoiodorus,
His grandfather, or tell of Terpsias
    And Eritimus. And your triumphs
On Delphi's field, or on the Lion's plain,
I would defy a host of men to match;   45
As easy would it be for me to number
    The pebbles of the ocean.

str. 3   But for all things there is a measure set:
To know the due time, therein lies true skill.
Now I, one man charged with a common purpose,
    Whether I sing the ancient wisdom,
Or of the wars and the heroic valour   50
Of Corinth and her ancestors, no falsehood
    Shall dwell upon my tongue –
Sisyphus, with a craftsman's hand of genius

Like to a god: Medea who defied
Her father's word, and took of her own will
    The husband of her choice,
And saved the Argo and her warrior crew:

ant. 3   Or again in the heroic strife of old   55
    Beneath the walls of Troy, your valiant sons
    Were deemed to sway the battle on either side,
        Some faithful to the sons of Atreus,
    Striving to rescue Helen, others resisting
    With all their warrior might. For when there came
          Glaucus from Lycia,   60
    The Danaans' hearts were chill with deadly fear,
    Hearing him boast that in Peirene's city
    His own forebear once held the sovereign power,
        And the great heritage
    Of kingly palace and wide patrimony:

ep. 3   That grandsire who once strove in vain
        Beside Peirene's spring,
      And suffered much, seeking to yoke
    The snake-head Gorgon's offspring, Pegasus.
    Till Pallas, goddess maid, brought him the bridle   65
        And golden headband, and behold
    A dream was truth. 'Sleep not, Aeolid king,'
    Said she, 'but take this charm of steeds, and offer
    The Horse-Tamer, your sire, a snow-white bull,
        And show to him this bridle.'

str. 4   Such words, as he lay slumbering in the dark,   70
    It seemed the maiden of the shadowy aegis
    Spoke unto him, and he leapt to his feet
        And seized the magic bit, that lay
    Beside him on the ground; and went with joy
    To find the prophet of his country's people
        The son of Koiranus.   75
    And he made known to him the whole issue
    Of this strange matter – how that he had lain
    The whole night through upon the goddess' altar,
        As the seer had foretold him,
    And how the child of Zeus, whose sword is lightning,

ant. 4   In her own hands brought him the golden charm
        That tames the savage spirit. And the prophet
        Bade him obey at once the magic vision,   80
           And to Poseidon, the earth-holder,
        To sacrifice the strong-limbed bull. Then too
        That he should build an altar with all speed
           To Athene, queen of steeds.
        Yet the gods' power can lightly bring to pass
        Such things as will deny both the sworn word
        And all the hopes of men. Thus with all zeal
           Mighty Bellerophon
        Seized the winged steed, setting between his jaws   85

ep. 4   The soothing charm, and mounting him,
           In his bronze panoply
          Played him in sport, to try his pace.
        And once, with him, he smote the Amazons,
        From the chill bosom of the lonely air,
          That archered host of women-kind;
        And felled Chimaera breathing fire, and slew   90
        The Solymi. His fate – 'twere best unspoken.
        But Pegasus dwells in the ancient stalls
          Of Zeus upon Olympus.

str. 5   But for my words, like whirring javelins
        Sped on their course, let not my eager strength
        Launch such a shower of darts wide of the mark.   95
           For I come with intent to honour
        The Muses on their glorious thrones, and pay
        Like service to the Oligaethidae.
           No more than a brief word
        Must tell their thronging triumphs at the Isthmus,
        And at Nemea; but the trusty herald,
        Chanting his welcome cry at either contest
           Attests with me the truth   100
        Of sixty victories won by this clan.

ant. 5   And of their prizes at Olympia
        My song has told already. If more shall come,
        Then should I ring their praises loud and clear.
           Now I must hope; yet will the issue

Lie in the hands of heaven. But if the genius
Of their inheritance plays its true part,   105
    Then shall we trust in this
To Zeus and Ares for the accomplishment.
Six crowns they won beneath Parnassus' brow,
More at Argos and Thebes; in Arcady,
    There will the sovereign altar
Of Zeus Lycaeus testify their deeds.

ep. 5   Pellene too, and Sicyon
                And Megara saw them victors,
                And the Aeacid strong-built precinct;
             Eleusis too and Marathon's fair plain,   110
             And the rich cities by the soaring height
                Of Aetna; from Euboea and all
             Hellas, a search would find more than the eye
             Could see. Now on light feet, we say farewell.
             Zeus, who brings all to pass, pray grant them honour,
                And fortune's dearest joys.   115

Notes

1. **Three times:** the two victories of Xenophon won on the same day, which this ode celebrates, and one gained forty years previously by Xenophon's father Thessalus, referred to in line 35.

4. **portal of ... Poseidon:** because Corinth stands right at the southern end of the Isthmus of Corinth.

8. **Themis:** the goddess of Right. Her three daughters are similarly linked in a prayer to the Fates (*PMG* frag. lyr. adesp. 1018): 'send us red-breasted [*sic*] Eunomia (Lawfulness), and her shining-throned sisters Justice and Peace bearing crowns, and help this city to forget gloomy events.'

10. **Insolence ... mother of full-fed Disdain:** the genealogy is usually the other way around: Koros, 'satiety', breeds hybris, insolent pride: so Solon 6.3, Theognis 153–4. But Herodotus (8.77) quotes an oracle of Bakis in which Koros is son of Hybris, as here. The idea is not perspicuous.

13. **what nature breeds:** the superiority of the products of inborn,

aristocratic nature to anything that can be achieved by mere learning is a leitmotif of Pindar's thought.

14. Aletes: according to the scholiasts, a great grandson of Heracles, one of the leaders of the 'return of the sons of Heracles', otherwise known as the Dorian invasion, which in legend resulted in the Dorian settlement of southern Greece.

17. The inventor's craft: it is a characteristic of Greek thought that all the gifts of civilization are attributed to a 'first discoverer'. Corinth turns out to be peculiarly rich in such discoverers.

19. dithyramb: the dithyramb was a form of choral dance and song associated especially with festive occasions and with the god Dionysus. It was traditionally said to have been invented by Arion of Corinth c. 600 BC. According to the scholiasts, Pindar elsewhere attributed its invention to Naxos (frag. 115) and to Thebes (frag. 71).

19. with its prize of oxen: literally, 'the bull-driving dithyramb'. The reference may be to a prize, or more probably to the driving of a bull in a procession for Dionysus.

20. harness: no other authorities refer to any special role of the Corinthians in the invention of harness, apart from Bellerophon's introduction of the bit, described later in this ode.

21. the double image of the eagle: probably a reference to the use of eagles as *akroteria* or finials on either end of a temple.

35. Thessalus: his father's victory of 504 which may have been celebrated by Simonides (see the article by Barrett cited in the introduction).

38. Athens: at the Panathenaea, celebrated in the month of Hecatombaeon (June/July).

40. Hellotia's feast: the Hellotia was a Corinthian festival in honour of Athena.

40. Between two seas: at the Isthmian Games, sacred to Poseidon.

42. Terpsias, Eritimus: two members of Xenophon's family: see the family tree in the introduction.

43. your triumphs: i.e. of your clan.

44. the Lion's plain: the Nemean Games. The word translated 'plain' actually means 'pasture'; cf. N 6.42 for this image of the Nemean lion grazing.

48. To know the due time: this 'break-off formula' is characteristic of Pindar's technique; praise should not be overdone, and it is time to deepen the focus by turning to the mythic glories of Corinth.

52. Sisyphus: the legendary founder of Corinth. He was noted as a trickster, for example by his secret marking of the undersides of the hoofs of his cattle to aid identification when stolen. Pindar presents his cunning in favourable terms here, and makes no allusion to his fate in Hades as one of the great sinners condemned eternally to push a rock up a hill.

53. hedea: the daughter of Aeetes, king of Colchis on the Black Sea. She helped Jason and the Argonauts to recover the Golden Fleece, fell in love with Jason, and accompanied him as his bride back to Greece. She was subsequently rejected by Jason when he married Glauce the daughter of the king of Corinth, and took a terrible revenge (described in Euripides' *Medea*). Like Sisyphus', Medea's Corinthian credentials seem decidedly ambiguous.

55. your valiant sons: According to Herodotus (1.173), the Lycians traced their origins to the Corinthian immigrant Sarpedon, who lived for three generations and thus became contemporary with the much younger Glaucus, grandson (Pindar calls him the son) of Bellerophon: Sarpedon and Glaucus were the leaders of the Lycian troops in the Trojan War (*Iliad* 6.152–211). It is rather unusual to find Pindar following so closely a myth in its Homeric version.

61. Peirene's city: Corinth. Peirene was the name of a fountain on Acrocorinth, the rock citadel of Corinth.

62. his own forebear: Bellerophon.

64. Pegasus: the winged horse, offspring of Poseidon and Medusa before she was transformed into the snake-headed Gorgon. (Sometimes art depicts Pegasus and her human son Chrysaor being born from the bleeding stump of her neck.)

67. 'Sleep not, Aeolid king': Bellerophon slept in the temple of Athena to receive a visitation which would guide his actions. Bellerophon was a descendant of Aeolus, the father of Sisyphus.

69. The Horse-Tamer, your sire: the Horse-Tamer is Poseidon, reputed father of Aeolus. 'Sire' thus means 'ancestor'.

70. the shadowy aegis: the aegis was a magical shield consisting of a goatskin edged with the Gorgon's snaky locks.

75. The son of Koiranus: Polyidus the seer from Argos.

81. the earth-holder: a regular title of Poseidon.

82. queen of steeds: the cult title Athena Hippia is attested at Tegea and Olympia, but her association with horses is not generally prominent.

83. the gods' power: cf. P 2.49; frag. 108: a common thought in Pindar.

87–90. the Amazons . . . Chimaera . . . Solymi: see introduction to the ode.

91. His fate: another Corinthian myth with a sour ending, like those of Sisyphus and Medea. Pindar breaks off and emphasizes the good fortune of the horse.

105. their inheritance: a recollection of the sentiment of line 13.

108. Zeus Lycaeus: Parrhasia is another name for Arcadia. Its major festival was that held at the Sanctuary of Zeus on Mt Lycaion.

109. The Aeacid . . . precinct: the island of Aegina.

114. on light feet: a compliment to the racing feet of Xenophon.

For Asopichus of Orchomenus
Winner of the Boys' Foot Race (488?)

According to the scholiast this victory took place in 488 BC, the seventy-third Olympiad. There is no independent evidence of the date. The ode is an accomplished and lovely piece, which evokes the Graces, the ancient deities of Orchomenus, close to Thebes, and sets the victory of the boy in their radiance while at the same time suggesting that Olympic victory can outweigh even the sad death of his father and make the line immortal.

str. 1   Whose haunts are by Kephissus' river,
       You queens beloved of poets' song,
    Ruling Orchomenus, that sunlit city
       And land of lovely steeds,
    Watch and ward of the ancient Minyan race,
       Hear now my prayer, you Graces three.   5
    For in your gift are all our mortal joys,
    And every sweet thing, be it wisdom, beauty
    Or glory, that makes rich the soul of man.
       Nor even can the immortal gods
    Order at their behest the dance and festals,
       Lacking the Graces' aid;
    Who are the stewards of all rites of heaven,   10
       Whose thrones are set at Pytho
    Beside Apollo of the golden bow,
       And who with everlasting honour
    Worship the Father, lord of great Olympus.

str. 2   Euphrosyne, lover of song,
       And Aglaia revered, daughters
    Of Zeus the all-highest, hearken, and with Thalia,   15
       Darling of harmony,
    Look on our songs of revel, on light feet
       Stepping to grace this happy hour.
    For in this Lydian measure, harvested

From the rich fruits of mind, I come to praise
Asopichus, whose Minyan house, Thalia,
　　Now of your favour wears the pride　　　　　20
Of the Olympian victor. Then let Echo
　　　Speed to Persephone's
Dark-walled dwelling, to his father Cleodemus
　　　Bearing the glorious tidings,
That his young son, matched in the famous games
　　Of Pisa's far-renownéd vale,
Has set the wingéd garland on his brow.　　　　24

Notes

1. **Kephissus' river:** the river which runs by Orchomenus.

4. **Minyan race:** the prehistoric inhabitants of Orchomenus (*Iliad* 2.511)
and Thessaly. The city was founded, according to legend, by their
eponym Minyas. His 'treasury', now to be seen at Orchomenus, is a
Mycenaean beehive tomb. Heinrich Schliemann excavated Orchomenus
and christened the characteristic grey slip pottery 'Minyan ware'.

5. **Graces three:** the Graces are central to Pindar's artistic theology: the
Muses provide the theme; the Graces adorn it. Equally, they shed lustre
on the victor himself. At Orchomenus the Graces were worshipped in
the form of three aniconic stones, perhaps meteorites. In myth they
have the names Euphrosyne, Thalia and Aglaia (Cheerfulness, Festivity
and Radiance): cf. Hesiod, *Theogony* 909. There was a night festival of
the Graces at Orchomenus, the Charitesia, which included musical
competitions.

10. **Whose thrones are set at Pytho:** no other authority mentions such
a group at Delphi, though a statue of Apollo on Delos held the Graces
in its right hand (Paus. 9.35.3).

17. **this Lydian measure:** the Lydian 'mode' was a form of tuning of the
lyre – perhaps a high one – hence a scale. Theorists refer to various
forms of the Lydian mode. Plato regarded it as a 'slack' mode, soft and
suitable for symposia. Pindar imagines it being performed at Niobe's
wedding, and seems to employ it especially in odes for young athletes.

21. **Echo:** Echo, the messenger of the gods, is summoned to take the
news of Asopichus' victory to his dead father in the Underworld.

24. Wingéd garland: literally, 'has crowned his brow with wings'. The victor's wreath is also called 'wings' in P 9.125. The reference may be to the waving ribbons that bound it on; or to the wings of the goddess Victory.

For Hieron of Aetna
Winner of the Chariot Race (470)

In 470 Hieron had reached the summit of power, and Pindar makes of this poem not merely an epinician ode but a panegyric of Hieron, almost a portrait of the ideal sovereign.

The victory over the Carthaginians at Himera in 480 BC, in which Hieron took part – his elder brother Gelon was in charge of the Greek forces – and the naval victory of the Syracusan fleet over the Syracusans in 474 off Cumae in southern Italy had staved off if not finally removed these external threats to the Greek cities of the west. Hieron succeeded to the rule of Syracuse in 478, and had been steadily building up his power. In 472 Theron, the powerful ruler of Acragas, died and was succeeded by his son Thrasydaeus who was foolish enough to quarrel with Hieron. He was completely defeated and fled overseas. The city of Acragas was leniently treated, and under a new government was unlikely to cause Hieron further trouble. Such, in brief, was the political situation when this ode was written, and it makes reference to several of the recent events.

Not long after 480 Hieron had turned out the inhabitants of Catana and Naxos on the east coast of Sicily, who seem to have been potential sources of opposition to him, and founded in their place a new city of Aetna. He peopled it with five thousand immigrants from the Peloponnese and five thousand from Syracuse, and established in it a 'Dorian', that is to say aristocratic or oligarchic administration, the type of government for which Pindar frequently, as in this ode, expresses his approbation. It is clear that Hieron took great interest and pride in the city of Aetna, not only because it gave him the prestige which in Greek eyes attended the founder of a new city, but because he intended it to be the future home of his family. The rule of Syracuse, which he had inherited from his elder brother Gelon, was due to pass on his death to his younger brother Polyzelus. Deinomenes, Hieron's young son, was therefore designated as the ruler of Aetna, as this ode makes clear. An indication of Hieron's pride in his new city is that he had the Pythian victory here celebrated proclaimed as that of 'Hieron of Aetna', and described as such in the ode.

The succession of three myths – Typhon, Philoctetes, and the Dorians – all focus on the addressee and his affairs – respectively celebrating Sicily, Hieron and Aetna. The vivid description of Mount Aetna in eruption must be based on Pindar's own experience, presumably when he visited Sicily in 476/5. There is no evidence to show that he visited Sicily for the performance of this ode at Aetna.

Pindar's reference to Philoctetes in the third triad alludes to the fact that Hieron, for a good many years before his death in 467, suffered from an illness: he is said to have been carried to his campaigns on a litter. Like Philoctetes, Hieron is an ailing saviour of his people. In the fourth antistrophe and epode Pindar refers to the Battles of Salamis (480) and Plataea (479), at which the Greeks drove back the Persian invaders. Alongside these two mainland victories, he mentions the Battle of Himera (480) and that of Cyme (Latin Cumae: 474), with the implication that Hieron's contributions to Greek freedom are as great as those of the mainland Greeks.

The final triad contains words of advice, which should be interpreted in the light of the common rhetorical trope by which 'ought' implies 'can': to advise a course of action is to state that the addressee has the capacity to carry it out. Thus advice functions as praise, of a ruler whose capacity for right action is undoubted.

str. 1   O glorious lyre, joint treasure of Apollo,
        And of the Muses violet-tressed,
      Your notes the dancers' step obeys, leading
        The festal's joyous glory;
        And the singers heed your bidding,
    When on the vibrant air your prelude strikes,
    To guide the harmonies of choral song.
      Your power subdues the lightning's sword   5
      Of everlasting flame. On the sceptre
      Of Zeus, his swift wings folded on his side,
        The eagle sleeps, the king of birds,

ant. 1   When o'er his arching head your melodies
        Have thrown a mist of shadowy dark,

A gentle seal upon his eyes. And he slumbers,
   His smooth and supple back
   Rising and falling, held
By your flowing tones in thrall. And strong-armed Ares 10
Lays far aside his harshly-pointed spears
  And soothes his soul in mellow dream;
And on the immortals' hearts your shafts instil
A charméd spell – by grace of Leto's son
   And the low-girdled Muses' skill.

ep. 1   All things that Zeus loves not fall riven down
Before the voice of the Pierides,
Whether on land or on the restless sea;
He too, that enemy of the gods, who lies
     In fearsome Tartarus,   15
Typhon the hundred-headed, who long since
Was bred in the far-famed Cilician cave.
Today the cliffs that bar the sea o'er Cumae
  And Sicily's isle, press heavy on
His shaggy breast, and that tall pillar rising
To the height of heaven, contains him close – Aetna
     The white-clad summit,
Nursing through all the year her frozen snows.   20

str. 2   From the dark depths below she flings aloft
   Fountains of purest fire, that no
Foot can approach. In the broad light of day
   Rivers of glowing smoke
   Pour forth a lurid stream,
And in the dark a red and rolling flood   25
Tumbles down boulders to the deep sea's plain
  In riotous clatter. These dread flames
That creeping monster sends aloft, a marvel
To look on, and a wondrous tale even
  To hear, from those whose eyes have seen it.

ant. 2 Such is the being bound between the peaks
   Of Aetna in her blackened leaves
And the flat plain, while all his back is torn
   And scarred by the rough couch
   On which he lies outstretched.

O Zeus, grant us thy grace, lord of this mountain
Fronting a fruitful land, the peak whose name   30
   Her famous founder has bestowed
To be the glory of its neighbour city:
Whose name the herald spoke at Pytho's games,
   Proclaiming in the chariot race

ep. 2   Hieron the victor. Men who sail the sea
Ask first the blessing of a kindly breeze
To set their voyage forth: better then their hope
For prosperous return to mark its end.   35
     So let us reckon now
From this success, hereafter shall this city
Win glorious honour for her victors' crowns
And racing steeds, and in the banquet-songs
   Win wide renown. O Lycian Phoebus,
Ruler of Delos, lover of the fountain
Castalia by Parnassus, may this prayer
      Live in your heart,
And make this land a mother of brave men.   40

str. 3   For from the gods comes every skilled endeavour
   Of mortal quality, be it
Wisdom, or strength of arm, or eloquence.
   So when the praise I purpose
   Of this great man, let not
My song fall like a bronze-tipped javelin
Flung from the hand astray outside the line,
   But may a lengthy throw outstrip   45
Its every rival. May future days, as now,
Keep safe his wealth and great possessions, and grant him
   Forgetfulness of times of toil.

ant. 3   Well might he call to mind the wars and battles
   Which he endured with steadfast soul,
When there was won, under god's hand, such honour
   As no man in all Hellas
   Has reaped e'er now, a proud
And lordly crown of wealth. Like Philoctetes   50
Has he today taken the path of war:
   And when their bitter need constrained them

Proud hearts have fawned on him to win his friendship.
To Lemnos once, they tell, there came those heroes
   Of godlike fame, to bear away

ep. 3   The archer son of Poias, who lay wasted
With lingering wounds; who destroyed Priam's city,
To end the long toils of the Danai.
Feeble his step and sick his body's form,   55
    But thus had Fate ordained.
So too may a god's hand be near to guide
Hieron's path through all the years to come,
And grant fulfilment of his heart's desires.
   For Deinomenes too, sing, Muse
This praise of the four-horsed car. His father's crown
Can be no alien joy to him. Come then,
      For Aetna's king
Let us unfold a song to charm his soul.   60

str. 4   For him has Hieron founded this fair city
   In freedom built of heaven's will,
Within the pattern of the laws of Hyllus;
    For sons of Pamphylus,
    Yes, of great Heracles,
Who dwell beneath Taygetus' height, love ever
To abide under Aigimius' laws of Doris.   65
   Coming from Pindus' distant mount
They held Amyclae's city in wealth and fame,
Neighbours of the white-horsed Tyndaridae:
   And great the glory of their spears.

ant. 4   Zeus, who brings all to pass, grant to this city
   Beside the banks of Amenas,
That such fair fortune men's report may ever,
    In words of truth, assign
    To her citizens alike,
And to her kings. With thy aid may her prince,
Charging likewise his son, honour her people   70
   And bring them harmony and peace.
I pray thee, Cronos' son, let no Phoenician
Or Tuscan war-cry stir from home, who saw
   Their pride of ships wrecked before Cumae –

ep. 4   That ruin laid upon them by the leader
        Of Syracusan warriors, who hurled
    Their flower of youth from their swift ships of war
    Down to the ocean wave, and saved Hellas   75
        From grievous slavery.
    From Salamis, in thanks from men of Athens,
    I shall seek my reward; in Sparta's city
    Tell of Kithaeron's battle, where disaster
        Came to the Medes with curving bows.
    But by the fertile shores of Himera
    The sons of Deinomenes fill the song,
        Which for their valour
    They won amidst the downfall of their foes.   80

str. 5   To tell a timely tale, weaving a pattern
        Of many threads in brief compass,
    Wins less reproach of men; for dull surfeit
        Blunts eager expectation,
        And to recount the praise
    Of other men burdens a citizen's heart
    With hidden anger. Yet since envious eyes   85
        Hurt less than looks of pity, renounce
    No good design. With justice at the helm
    Govern your people's course, and on the anvil
        Of truth let all your words be forged;

ant. 5   Should but a trivial spark flash from your tongue,
        From you 'twill seem a light inspired;
    You are the steward of many, and many can bear
        True witness to your deeds,
        Be they or this or that.
    Guard well the fair flower of your spirits' temper;
    Would you have sweet praise ever in your ear.   90
        Let not your purse-strings tire of spending,
    But like a pilot spread to the winds your sail;
    Nor be deceived, my friend, by tempting gains.
        Only in chronicle and song

ep. 5   Is known beyond the grave the sounding glory
    Of how they fared in life who are no more.
    The generous heart of Croesus cannot die;

But for his burnings in the brazen bull,   95
    Phalaris' ruthless soul
Earns hate and infamy from all mankind;
Not for him sounds the blended harmony,
Under the roof-trees echoing to the lyre,
    Of children's lips in soft refrain.
First in life's contest is to win good fortune,
Next is to hold an honourable name;
      He who can find
And grasp both these, has gained the highest crown.   100

Notes

1. **glorious lyre:** literally, 'golden phorminx'; golden because divine. The phorminx is the smaller lyre, usually constructed with a tortoise shell as a sound-box, rather than the square-boxed kithara. The Homeric Hymn to Apollo, 188–206, describes how all the gods are charmed by Apollo's playing of the lyre.

6. **sceptre of Zeus:** the eagle accompanied Zeus in Phidias' chryselephantine statue of the god at Olympia: Paus. 5.11.1.

12. **your shafts:** the word is usually used of arrows, rather than of something beneficent.

low-girdled: perhaps, 'deep-bosomed', a standard epithet of the Muses. The female costume of a loose shift gathered over a low girdle emphasized the depth of the bosom.

13. **All things that Zeus loves not . . .:** the hostility of lower creatures to music is a frequent belief in Greece: Aelian (*On the Nature of Animals* 10.28), for example, states that the ass has a hatred of music. The monster Typhon's loathing of music is nicely paralleled by Grendel's rage at the sound of the harp in *Beowulf* 86ff.

16. **Typhon:** this mythical monster was the son of Earth and Tartarus. As well as having a hundred heads, he consisted from the legs down of coils of serpents and instead of hands had hundreds of serpent heads. He attacked Zeus and the other gods and almost overcame them, but was eventually overcome by the thunderbolt of Zeus, who then hurled Mount Aetna on top of him. See Hesiod, *Theogony* 820–69; Aeschylus, *Prometheus Bound* 367–71. Pindar described his fate in another poem too: frags 92–3. This, the first myth of the ode, takes the form of a natural description celebrating Sicilian topography.

17. Cilician cave: Typhon's birthplace in Asia Minor.

18. Cumae: (Greek: Cyme) on the west coast of Sicily, site of the sea battle where the Carthaginians had been defeated in 474. Typhon is envisaged as sprawled underneath the whole island.

20. all the year her frozen snows: contrary to the assertions of some commentators, snow persists on the summit of Aetna even in mid August. This wonderful passage is one of many in Pindar which give the lie to the view sometimes expressed that the Greeks had no feeling for the natural world and landscape.

30. lord of this mountain: i.e. of Aetna, and thus also of the city of Aetna.

grant us thy grace: the prayer effects the transition to the city and the victor. The naming of the 'victor' in line 33 is the only reference in this ode to the chariot victory, the nominal occasion of the ode.

35. prosperous return: P. von der Muhll (*Mus. Helv.* 25 [1968]: 229) showed that *nostos* here as elsewhere means not 'return home' but 'conclusion of voyage'; i.e. the prayer is for the successful arrival at the outward destination.

39. Lycian Phoebus: the epithet is usually taken as referring to Apollo's association with Lycia in Asia Minor; it may, however, alternatively be linked with *lykos*, 'wolf', or with the Indo-European root *luk-*, 'light'. Delos was Apollo's birthplace. The prayer marks a new transition, to concern with the city.

44. like a bronze-tipped javelin: the javelin was not thrown at a target, but the winner was he who threw furthest; however, the javelin had to land within the boundary lines. Pindar is saying that the praise he offers will not be excessive.

46. future days: time is the only guarantee of settled renown, as often: cf. O 2.15ff.

50. Philoctetes: the legend of Philoctetes, son of Poias, tells that he was left on the island of Lemnos by the Greek army on their way to the Trojan War, because he was suffering from a poisoned wound, the smell of which was insupportable to the troops. Ten years later, when Troy was still untaken, an oracle declared the city could not be captured without the help of the arrows of Heracles, which the latter had given to Philoctetes. The Greeks therefore sent two of their leaders, Odysseus and Diomedes, to Lemnos to bring Philoctetes to Troy. He killed Prince Paris with his arrows and the city was soon taken. The story is the basis of Sophocles' *Philoctetes*. There was a statue of Philoctetes in Syracuse: Pliny, *Natural History* 34.59. The parallelism with Hieron, taking the field in a state of ill-health, is clear: it may refer either to his campaigns in general, or – in view of the phrase 'proud hearts have fawned on him' – to his campaign against Thrasydaeus in 470, in which the latter was 'humbled' (Diodorus Siculus 11.53.5).

58. Deinomenes: Hieron's young son, nominally king of Aetna.

Muse: the third invocation of a god in the ode leads into the third myth, that of the Dorian ancestry of the city.

62. the laws of Hyllus: i.e. Dorian customs. Hyllus was the son of Heracles and married the daughter of Aegimius of Doris. The three tribes of the Dorians were named Hylleis, Dumanes and Pamphyloi after Hyllus and the sons of Aegimius.

63. Yes, of great Heracles: a mistranslation. Pamphylus was not a son of Heracles. Translate rather 'Yes, and . . .'. The 'sons of Heracles' was the normal term for the Dorian ancestors.

64. Taygetus: the highest mountain of the Peloponnese, which overlooks Sparta, regarded as the Dorian state *par excellence*.

66. Pindus ... Amyclae: Mount Pindus in northwest Greece, and Amyclae, south of Sparta, represent the northern and southern limits of Dorian settlement.

Tyndaridae: the Dioscuri, Castor and Polydeuces, who were worshipped at Amyclae. See N 10.

67. Zeus: the fourth divine invocation in the ode. The prayer is repeated at line 71.

Amenas: a stream near Aetna.

71. Phoenician: Carthage, on the north coast of Africa, was a colony of the Phoenicians who originated from the east coast of the Mediterranean. The reference is to their defeat at Himera in 480.

Tuscan: the Etruscans, defeated at Cumae in 474.

75. saved Hellas: a slight exaggeration: Hieron's victories had saved Sicily but hardly the whole of Greece.

76. Salamis: the Battle of Salamis, September 480.

Kithaeron's battle: the Battle of Plataea 479.

78 the Medes: the normal Greek name for the Persians. Media was conquered by the Persian king Cyrus II in 550 BC; but the people continued to be known to the Greeks collectively as the Medes.

81. To tell a timely tale: Pindar dilates on the duty of the poet to get praise right, neither too much nor too little. The advice which follows functions as praise of Hieron who is presumed to be in a position to act according to these principles of virtue.

85. envious eyes: a common Greek opinion: cf. Herodotus 3.52.5. Also Marlowe, *The Jew of Malta* (prologue by Machiavelli).

94. Croesus: the sixth-century BC ruler of Lydia in Asia Minor, whose enormous wealth was a byword. The mention of the proverbial Croesus has almost the function of a fourth myth in deepening the moral. Perhaps Hieron was interested in Croesus: he is the subject of the main myth in Bacchylides' Ode 3, also for Hieron.

96. Phalaris: tyrant of Acragas c. 570/65–554/49 BC. His cruelty was legendary: he was said to have roasted his enemies alive inside a bronze bull – perhaps a recollection of Carthaginian sacrifices to Moloch in a time of Carthaginian influence in Sicily.

Earns hate: literally, 'ill reputation holds him down': the same verb as is used of Aetna pressing down on Typhon. Hieron's kingship is as far from Phalaris' cruelty as is Zeus' rule from the evil of Typhon.

For Hieron of Syracuse
Winner of the Chariot Race (475?)

This ode, though placed by ancient editors among the Pythians, was not composed to celebrate a victory at the Pythian or any other Panhellenic festival. None is mentioned in the ode. It would appear that the victory took place in some local games at Syracuse (line 6), or maybe at Thebes (line 3).

Even more than Pythian 1, this is a poem about kingship, its glories and responsibilities, and also about the duties and qualifications of the poet who would celebrate a king adequately. Earlier commentators have seen it as a plea to Hieron not to listen to Pindar's enemies who slander him at Hieron's court, perhaps soon after his return from Sicily; but I have argued (*CQ* 34 [1984]: 43–9) that no such reference need be intended and that the passages apparently concerning Pindar are really part of his celebration of Hieron. A central theme is gratitude, its opposite being illustrated in the myth of Ixion.

It is not possible to date the ode, though it clearly belongs to the period after Pindar and Hieron had become personally acquainted in 476/5, and that it was written after Pindar's return to Greece is clear from line 68 which states that Pindar is sending the ode to Hieron across the sea. It is sometimes suggested that the ode belongs to 468 and is written in reaction to the disappointment of Bacchylides being commissioned to celebrate Hieron's Olympic victory of 468. But besides the dubious legitimacy of the form of argument, the reference to Hieron's assistance to Zephyrian Locri at line 18, which was given in 478 BC, might seem rather out of date, as much as ten years afterwards.

str. 1 Great city of Syracuse, precinct of Ares
   The god of surging war, you divine nurse
   Of men and horses in their armoured pride,
    Now in your honour am I come
     From sunlit Thebes,
    Bringing this music to proclaim

The four-horsed team, striding the trembling earth
Which has given victory to Hieron,   5
    Lord of the chariot's speed.
With wreaths of shining glory has he crowned
Ortygia, seat of the river-goddess
    Artemis, by whose aid
   The light touch of a gentle hand
Restrained those fillies with their spangled reins.

ant. 1   For the goddess, archer maid, lends of both hands
With Hermes, god of contests, to set ready   10
His gleaming harness, when to the polished car
    And wheels tense to the bridle's bidding,
     He firmly yokes
His horses' strength, and breathes a prayer
To the great god of might, the trident-wielder.
Various men in various ways can fashion,
    Each for his lord and king,
A sounding harmony of song, his tribute
To deeds of valour. How often does the voice
    Of Cypriot men resound
   With praise of Kinyras, who won   15
The happy love of golden-haired Apollo,

ep. 1   And was the cherished priest
    Of Aphrodite; a friendly deed
Will ever stir the grace of reverent praise.
   Thus for you, son of Deinomenes,
Locris Zephyria, the maiden city,
    Saved by your power
From her despairing toils with enemy hands,
Sings at her door and lifts her eyes to freedom.   20
But by the gods' command, so the tale runs, Ixion
   Rolling full circle on his wingéd wheel
    Speaks thus to mortals: –
'See that your onward path fails not to pay
Your benefactor fair return of kindness.'

str. 2   Well had he learnt. For given a life of joy   25
By goodwill of the sons of Heaven, such bliss
He could not compass, but in frenzied madness

His passion sought the bed of Hera
    Whose wedded joys
Are for the right of Zeus alone.
But pride and insolence drove him to this
Outrageous folly, nor was he slow to suffer,
    As such a man well might,
Anguish unutterable. Two sins were his   30
That brought him to his pain; one that this warrior
    Had been the first who brought
    Into the world of men the shedding
Of kinsman's blood, and that with treachery;

ant. 2   Then, that in the profound and secret depths
Of her own bridal chamber, he assailed
The wife of Zeus. Well is it for a man
    To take the measure of each deed
    By his own stature.
    Unto the full deep tides of woe   35
Loves which transgress the law cast a man down,
Who sets foot there. For with a cloud he lay,
    Pursuing a sweet falsehood,
That man of folly. In semblance like the all-high
Sovereign daughter of Cronos son of Heaven,
    This phantom came, this guile
Proffered him by the hands of Zeus,
A beauteous bane. Thus on the four-spoked wheel   40

ep. 2   He gave his limbs to bondage,
    His own destruction. Fallen in chains
From whence is no escape, he heard the message
    That he must spread to all the world.
Far were the Graces when the mother bore –
    Ne'er such a mother,
Never such son – her babe of monstrous breed,
Who had no honour amongst men nor in
The laws of Heaven. She reared him up and named him
Centaur,
And the Magnetian mares knew him as mate   45
    By Pelion's ridges;
And that strange race was born, like to both parents,
Their mother's form below, above their sire's.

str. 3 God achieves all his purpose and fulfils
 His every hope, god who can overtake   50
 The wingéd eagle, or upon the sea
  Outstrip the dolphin; and he bends
   The arrogant heart
 Of many a man, but gives to others
Eternal glory that will never fade.
Now for me is it needful that I shun
  The fierce and biting tooth
Of slanderous words. For from old have I seen
Sharp-tongued Archilochus in want and struggling, 55
  Grown fat on the harsh words
  Of hate. The best that fate can bring
Is wealth joined with the happy gift of wisdom.

ant. 3 This gift is yours and with a liberal heart
 You clearly show it, you prince and lord of many
 A battlemented street and host of men.
  If there be anyone to say
   That in all Hellas
  A man was born e'er now more blessed 60
 In great possessions and in glory's honour,
His vain wit struggles with a fruitless aim.
  Decked with fair flowers shall be
 The ship that brings my song, to speak the praise
Of your brave spirit. The brunt of savage wars
  In your young heart bred courage;
  From whence also shall I affirm
That you have found an infinite renown,

ep. 3. Wielding your sword now 'midst 65
  The horsemen's ranks, now upon foot.
In elder years the wisdom of your counsel
  Allows me, free from any fear,
To spread your praises to the furthest height
   That tongue can tell.
Farewell. Like to Phoenician merchandise
This song is sent across the foaming seas;
But for the song of Castor in Aeolian strains,
 Pray you, in honour of the seven-stringed lyre 70
   Greet it with favour.

Be what you are, the man whose worth you have heard.
In the eyes of a child an ape is lovely,

str. 4   Always lovely. But the best blessing came
To Rhadamanthus, who was given the fruit
Of mind that knows no wrong, who takes no pleasure
    Within his heart in false deceits,
        Such words as ever
    Are partners to the deeds of men   75
Who whisper in the ear. Secret purveyors
Of slander are an evil without cure,
    Alike to those who speak it
And those who hear – like a fox is its temper.
Yet, as for gain, where does it prove of profit?
    For I, while all the nets
    And gear ply deep below the sea,
Float, like the cork, undrenched upon the water.   80

ant. 4   No man of guile can utter from his lips
A word compelling to a good man's ear;
Yet fawning upon all he weaves around them
    His fateful ills. No share have I
        In his bold craft:
    Let it be mine to love my friend,
But as a foeman to my foes, like to a wolf
Shall I pursue them stealthily, now here
        Now there setting my tracks   85
In winding ways. But he whose tongue speaks truth,
Comes to the fore, whosoe'er makes the law,
    Be it a tyrant, be it
    The milling crowd, be it wise men
Who rule the state. But must we never strive

ep. 4   Against god, who upholds
    Today the power of these, tomorrow
To others gives high glory. But the souls
    Of envious men not even this thought
Can soothe; but like a man who drags too far
    His measuring line,   90
They pierce their own hearts with a grievous wound,
Ere they can win that which their dreams devise.

Lightly to bear upon our neck the yoke that we
Have taken up, is wisdom's way. To kick
   Against the pricks   95
Leads to the path of doom. May it be mine
To dwell amongst good men and earn their praise.

Notes

4. I come: i.e. the poem comes; not the poet himself (cf. line 68).

6. Ortygia: the small island which was part of the city of Syracuse and joined to it by a causeway. There was a cult of Artemis on the island. According to the scholiast, Hieron's stables were on the island.

8. fillies: races with mares were not introduced into the Panhellenic Games until a later date. This is further evidence that this victory was won at some minor local games.

9. archer maid: Artemis, the huntress-goddess.

12. the trident-wielder: Poseidon, god not only of the sea but of horses.

15. Kinyras: a legendary king of Cyprus, renowned for his prosperity and generosity, who was also a priest of Aphrodite and a favourite of Apollo. The choice of mythical parallel for Hieron is odd. The scholiast guessed that Hieron was of Cypriot descent (unlikely) or that the family of Deinomenes were priests of Demeter and Kore. But the comparison is more general. Hieron, not part of the hereditary aristocracy of Greece, must perforce be compared with a king (as he is with Croesus in P 1), and Greek legend had not many extant kingly families to choose from. However, it may also be relevant that Kinyras was said to have introduced temple prostitution in Paphos on Cyprus (Clement of Alexandria, *Protrepticus* 2.13; L. Woodbury, op. cit. in n. on 19, 291, n.18). This allusion would then lead into the reference to Locri: the Cypriots praise Kinyras for his action, the Locrians praise Hieron for preventing the same. See note on line 19.

17. a friendly deed ... reverent praise: here, and in the last two lines of this epode, Pindar announces the main theme of this ode.

18. son of Deinomenes: Hieron.

19. Locris Zephyria: the city of Locri-in-the-west was an independent Greek colony on the coast of southern Italy. In 478 Hieron prevented its annexation by the tyrant Anaxilas of Rhegium and his son Leophron, and married the daughter of Anaxilas (died 476). The Locrians, according to Justin 21.3, vowed to prostitute their young women in the temple of Venus (Aphrodite) if they were successful in the war against Leophron: the young women are grateful that Hieron's intervention has made such an action unnecessary, and this is the point of the comparison with Kinyras. The grateful young women were, in Pindar's expression, already outside their houses and on their way to the temple: normally it would be unthinkable for a Greek maiden to be seen in public. See Leonard Woodbury, 'The Gratitude of the Locrian Maidens', *TAPA* 108 (1978): 285–99.

21. Ixion: Ixion was a proverbial example, with Tantalus and Sisyphus, of the dire punishment inflicted by the immortals for sacrilege. Ixion had murdered his father-in-law by pushing him into a pit of fire, but Zeus pardoned him and gave him a place in heaven. Here, however, he further disgraced himself by attempting to rape Hera, but she deceived him by sending a cloud in her own shape. The cloud in due course gave birth to the first Centaur (Kent-auros, prick-air). Ixion's punishment was to be tied for eternity to a revolving wheel in Hades.

49. God achieves all his purpose . . . : the moral Pindar draws from the tale of Ixion's ingratitude is that the praise-poet must avoid all kinds of malicious words which would make him as punishable as Ixion. God would not let him escape.

55. Archilochus: a seventh-century poet of Paros, best remembered in antiquity for his savage and scurrilous invectives, mainly against one Lycambes. But his poems (some of which survive in fragmentary form) range more widely than this and include humorous and erotic themes also.

56. Grown fat: i.e. enjoying himself (cf. Aeschylus *Agamemnon* 276).

wealth . . . wisdom: it is better to be a wise and truthful poet like Pindar, and prosper, than to suffer the fate of Archilochus The mention of wealth alludes to Hieron's presumably generous patronage of Pindar.

67. praise of your brave spirit: there being nothing to say about the chariot victory, Pindar concentrates on Hieron as king and general.

69. the song of Castor: a kind of war-dance, perhaps here a metonymy for the hyporcheme composed for Hieron (frags 105–6). Other commentators take it to refer to the present ode.

72. Be what you are: the human ideal of 'to thine own self be true' is a nice way to praise a king: his nature is already great and in his actions he is to realize that greatness. But advice, to be accepted as an honour, must come from a worthy source; so in the next lines Pindar goes on to characterize himself as a worthy equal of Hieron, a courtier not a flatterer or slanderer.

an ape is lovely: the function of this proverbial expression here has received many interpretations. In my view (see my 'The Ideal Courtier') the ape represents the flatterer, whose imitative tendencies make him ape-like (Plutarch, *On Flatterers* 52b): but the good king Rhadaman-thys is not deceived by such performances, and no more will Hieron be: he can appreciate an honest courtier.

79–80. nets and gear: the scholiast interpreted this as Pindar's assertion that he will not be sunk by the attacks of those who slander him at Hieron's court – or of his rivals – or of Greek aristocrats who were angry at his praises of princes. But, as a scholiast on I 7.40 expresses it, 'I' here means 'you': Pindar is identifying himself with his addressees ('we are both in this together'), and it is Hieron who is untouched, because of his goodness, by the attacks of detractors (cf. the similar passage at N 1.24).

83. No share have I: the topic of slander surmounted, that of Pindar's reliability supervenes. He recommends the adaptability praised often by Theognis: equals must fit in with each other, and make common cause against the enemy.

90. envious men: the detractors of Hieron are mentioned yet again. They pull at the plumbline to alter its position, but it springs back and their purpose is frustrated. In a further metaphor (line 94) they are described as 'kicking against the pricks', making a truculent stand against the obvious greatness of the king.

96. May it be mine: the final confident assertion that Pindar is an honest and worthy poet, fit to praise a king. As the Tswana praise-poet of southern Africa writes:

> I shall keep on telling about you,
> my voice is now used to you;
> I now want to make you my friend,
> Hail to you, son of a fine person!

(I. Schapera, *Praise Poems of Tswana Chiefs* [Oxford 1965], p. 245.)

For Hieron of Syracuse (474?)

Although written in the form of an epinician ode, this poem does not celebrate a specific Pythian victory, but is rather a letter of consolation, its main theme the illness from which Hieron suffered for many years before his death in 467. There is mention in the fourth strophe of victories won by Hieron at the Pythian Games 'in times past' or 'long since', and it is for this reason that the ancient editors assigned the ode a place among the Pythians.

The ode is one of Pindar's more transparent compositions and its structure and train of thought unusually satisfying. The ode begins with a wish that Pindar could bring back to earth again the mythical Centaur, Chiron, and his pupil the healer Asclepius. The story of the birth and death of Asclepius takes us to the third strophe, where Pindar briefly points the moral of the story, that to attempt to obtain good things beyond the normal lot of humankind is to court disaster. The succeeding stanzas explain the relevance of this narrative to Hieron's condition and incorporate motifs of praise as well. In the fourth antistrophe Pindar expresses a prayer to the Great Mother which explains why he cannot come to Syracuse and is sending an ode instead; the introduction of the poet's persona gives the opportunity for a passage of advice on the topic of the changeability of human fortune, exemplified by the stories of Peleus and Cadmus. The conclusion of the poem presents Pindar's oft-repeated conviction that immortality is only to be won through poetry.

The date of the ode cannot be fixed with certainty. The Pythian victories referred to in line 74 were won in 482 and 478. It does not mention the Olympic victory of 476, nor the Pythian of 470, but it does mention Aetna which was founded in 476. The argument of the poem makes it plain that Pindar is already acquainted with Hieron and is writing after his return from his visit to Sicily of 476/5. Wilamowitz thought that the ode was a consolation for a failure to win a Pythian victory in 474, as well as for ill-health, since the impossibility of bringing health and a Pythian crown are referred to together in line 73; though uncertain, it is the best piece of evidence we have for a date. The contrast of tone with Pythian 2 (perhaps 475) is remarkable, but it is not possible to base any arguments thereon.

str. 1   Would that Chiron, the son of Philyra –
                If so be that my lips the prayer must utter
                    That lives in every heart –
                Would that he might regain the life he left long since,
            That man of widespread power, the son of Cronos son of
                                                                Heaven,
                    And that wild creature of the woods,
                        That lover of mankind,
                    Were lord of Pelion's valleys still;
                    Such as he was when long ago he nursed   5
            Gentle Asclepius, that craftsman of new health
                For weary limbs and banisher of pain,
                The godlike healer of all mortal sickness.

ant. 1   His mother, daughter of Phlegyas the horseman,
                Ere with the help of Eleithuia, the nurse
                    Of childbirth, she could bring
                Her babe to the light of day, was in her chamber stricken
            By the golden shafts of Artemis, and to the hall of
                                                                Death   10
                    Went down. For so Apollo willed.
                        Not lightly falls the wrath
                        Of the children of Zeus. For she
                In the madness of her heart had spurned the god,
            And unknown to her father took another lover,
                Even though her maiden bed she had already
                Shared with Apollo of the flowing hair,

ep. 1   And bore within her the god's holy seed.   15
                She waited not to see the marriage feast,
                        Nor stayed to hear
                    The sound of swelling bridal hymns,
                Such notes as maiden friends of a like age are wont
            To spread in soothing songs upon the evening air.
                        But no! her heart

Longed for things far off, things unknown, as many
                                                  another   20
        Has longed ere now. For in the race of men
    There is a throng whose minds are utmost vanity, who
    Disdaining that which lies to hand, peer ever forward,
        Hunting for folly's phantom, feeding on hopes
            Never to be fulfilled.

str. 2   Such the all-powerful, ill-fated madness
            That held the proud heart of fair-robed Coronis;   25
                For with a stranger, come
    From Arcady, she lay in love's embrace. Yet failed not
    A watching eye to see; for at Pytho, amidst the lambs
            Of sacrifice, the temple's king
                Loxias stood; yet saw;
            Seeking advice from none, save that
        Most true consultant, his all-knowing mind.
    For all things that are false he touches not, nor can
        A god, nor can a man deceive him, whether
        In aught they do or aught the will may purpose.   30

ant. 2   Thus now, he saw that son of Eilatus,
            Ischys, the stranger, share her bed of love,
                That impious treachery;
        And sent his sister storming in resistless anger
    To Lakereia, where by the high banks of Boibias
            The maiden had her home. And fate
                Of a far other kind
            Turned to her ruin and smote her down: 35
            And many a neighbour, too, suffered alike
    And was destroyed beside her; as when on the mountain
        From one small spark a raging fire leaps up,
        And lays in ruin all the widespread forest.

ep. 2   But when upon the high wood pyre her kinsmen
            Had set the maid, and the flames of Hephaestus
                Shot their bright tongues
            Around her, then cried out Apollo: 40
    'No longer shall my soul endure that my own son
    Here with his mother in her death most pitiable
            Should perish thus,

In sorry grief.' So spoke he and in one stride was there,
   And seized the babe from the dead maid; and round him
The blazing flames opened a pathway. Then he took
The child to the Magnetian Centaur, that he teach
                                    him   45
   To be a healer for mankind of all
     Their maladies and ills.

str. 3   All then who came to him, some plagued with sores
    Of festering growths, some wounded by the strokes
      Of weapons of bright bronze,
Or by the slinger's shot of stone, others with limbs
Ravaged by summer's fiery heat or by the winter's cold, 50
   To each for every various ill
     He made the remedy,
    And gave deliverance from pain,
  Some with the gentle songs of incantation
Others he cured with soothing draughts of medicines,
  Or wrapped their limbs around with doctored salves,
  And some he made whole with the surgeon's knife.

ant. 3   And yet to profit even the skills of wisdom
    Yield themselves captive. For a lordly bribe,   55
      Gold flashing in the hand,
Even this man was tempted to bring back to life
One whom the jaws of death had seized already. With
                                fierce hands
   Swiftly the son of Cronos loosed
    His anger on these two;
   His blazing bolt stripped from them both
  Their breath of life, and hurled them to their fate.
A man must seek from heaven only that which is fitting
  For mortal minds, perceiving well the path
  Before his feet, the lot that is our portion.   60

ep. 3   Pray for no life immortal, soul of mine,
But draw in full depth on the skills of which
     You can be master.
    Now if Chiron the wise dwelt still
Within his cave, and if some spell to charm his soul

Lay in the honeyed sweetness of my songs, then
                                          might I   65
            Surely persuade him
For men of noble mind to grant them a physician
    Of feverish ills, some son born of Apollo,
Or even the son of Zeus himself. Then might my ships,
Cleaving the waves of the Ionian sea, have brought me
        To Arethusa's fountain and the home
            Of my good host of Aetna,

str. 4   The king of Syracuse, who rules his people   70
            With a mild hand, jealous of no good man,
                And to his guests a friend
Most fatherly. Had I then touched upon his shores
Bringing a double blessing, first the gift of golden health,
            Then this triumphant song, to throw
                Its bright ray on the crowns
            That graced him at the Games of Pytho,
When Pherenikus led the field long since
At Kirrha – then my sail had seemed for him, I doubt not,
        Crossing the deep seas, a more glorious   75
        And radiant light than any star of heaven.

ant. 4   But now is it my wish to voice a prayer
            To the great Mother, the revered goddess
                To whom, and to great Pan
Young maids before my door at nightfall often sing
Their praise. But if, Hieron, your mind perceives the deeper
                                          truth   80
            Of spoken words, then have you learnt
                From men of old this teaching:
            'For every good bestowed to man
    The immortals give two evils.' To receive
Such truth, however, with an ordered temper, fools
        Cannot endure, but only noble minds
        Turning the good side outwards to the eye.

ep. 4   Yours is a destiny of happy fortune;
            In you, if any man, all-powerful fate
                Beholds a leader
            And sovereign monarch of a people.   85

Yet a life free from care came neither to Peleus,
Aeacus' son, nor to Cadmus that godlike king;
    Though they of all men
Won, so men say, the highest bliss, who heard the Muses
  In golden diadems chanting their songs   90
Upon the mountain and within the seven gates
Of Thebes, when one took for his bride Harmonia,
    The dark-eyed maid, the other glorious Thetis,
    Daughter of wise Nereus.

str. 5   And the gods shared with both their marriage feasts,
    And seated upon golden thrones beside them
      They saw the royal children
Of Cronos, and received from them their wedding-gifts:
And by the grace of Zeus were from their former toils
                             uplifted, 95
    And peace was in their hearts established.
      Yet at another time
      One of them by the bitter woes
Of his three daughters saw himself stripped bare
  Of all his happiness, what though to one, Thyone
    The white-armed maiden, Zeus the almighty father
    Came down to her to share her lovely bed.

ant. 5   And Peleus' son, that one son whom the immortal 100
    Thetis in Phthia bore, gave up his life
      In the forefront of war,
To the sharp arrow's point, and o'er him as his body
Burnt on the funeral pyre, the Danai raised up on high
    Their grievous cry of woe. And yet
      If any mortal man
      Holds in his heart the way of truth,
Then must he seek only from heaven to find
Good fortune's gifts. Now here, now there blow the
                             high-flung 105
    Winds of the sky. Man's wealth lasts not for long,
    When it comes in full richness of good measure.

ep. 5   Humble 'midst humble men, great 'midst the great
    Shall be the path I tread. But the will of heaven
      That each new day

Endows my spirit, this shall I practise
And serve with all my skill. But though a god shall bring
me   110
The joys of wealth, it is my hope to win high fame
Through the days to come.
Nestor and Lycian Sarpedon, those heroes
Of far renown, we know them from old story
In the rich harmonies built by the poets' craft.
In glorious songs brave spirits and brave deeds can live
Long down the years, but only to the few
Is this achievement easy.   115

Notes

1. **Philyra:** daughter of Ocean and Tethys; Cronos mated with her in the form of a stallion and she bore the centaur Chiron, whose parentage thus differs from that of all other Centaurs, the result of the mating of Ixion with a cloud shaped like Hera (P 2.21 and note).

4. **wild creature:** the Greek word *phèr* is the Homeric term for the centaurs.

8. **His mother:** Coronis by name. See P 9 for her story. Phlegyas was the eponym of the Phlegyans of Orchomenas (Paus. 2.26.6).

10. **shafts of Artemis:** the origin of illnesses, especially infectious illnesses, was attributed in legend to arrows shot from the bow of Artemis, or of her twin brother Apollo. The story is told by a series of explanations, looping back in time, in a particularly lucid piece of ring-composition.

20. **her heart longed for things far off:** a leitmotif of the ode, this is a prime example of what mortals must not do, in Pindar's philosophy. The scholiasts quote a parallel passage from Hesiod (frag. 61 MW); the same enthusiasm for remote fulfilments is expressed by the fictional figure of this same Hieron in conversation with Simonides in Xenophon's dialogue, *Hiero* 1:30.

25. **a stranger:** Ischys, named at line 31.

29. **his all-knowing mind:** the usual version of the myth has Apollo receive the news from a crow. Crows were at this time white; Apollo, in his rage, turned the bird black. The interview with the crow is

portrayed on a beautiful contemporary kylix (plate) from Delphi. See further, Callimachus, *Hecale*, frag. 260.56ff.

32. his sister: Artemis (cf. line 10).

34. Boibias: a large lake, still called by this name, in Eastern Thessaly near Mt Pelion.

38. high wood pyre: literally, 'wall of wood'. Cf. Bacchylides 3.49 where a pyre is called a 'house of wood'. Is Pindar 'capping' Bacchylides' phrase?

40. Hephaestus: god of the forge, and of fire.

45. Magnetian: this epithet derives from the Magnetes, a tribe of Eastern Thessaly. This reference to the Centaur completes the ring-composition and brings the story full circle to its starting point in line 5.

51. incantation: for the use of music in healing, cf. *Odyssey* 19.547.

53. wrapped ... with doctored salves: the word for salves, *pharmaka*, is more likely to have here its primary meaning of 'amulets' – which are 'tied on'.

57. on these two: Asclepius and the man whom he resuscitated.

60. the lot that is our portion: the son falls into the same unwisdom as the mother (line 20), with the same dire results.

63. if Chiron the wise . . .: the prayer resumes that of the opening line.

67. some son born of Apollo: i.e. a man as skilled in medicine as was Asclepius. Apollo as god of disease was also god of healing.

the son of Zeus: i.e. Apollo.

69. Arethusa's fountain: the spring on Ortygia, the small island joined to Syracuse by a causeway. Hieron's stables were on Ortygia. See also note on N 1.1–2.

Aetna: Hieron had refounded the town of Catana on the east coast of Sicily under the new name of Aetna in 476. Pythian 1 is addressed to him as 'Hieron of Aetna': see note there. This allusion dates Pythian 3 later than 476.

73f. crowns ... Pherenikus: the racehorse which won the chariot race for Hieron at the Pythian Games of 478 and probably also 482. The doubt arises because Bacchylides in Ode 5.39, for Hieron's Olympic victory of 476, calls Pherenikus a *polos*, 'foal', and a horse cannot remain a foal for six years: a five-year-old horse is already a *hippos teleios*. The 'crowns' may refer to a single victory only. See R. C. Jebb, *Bacchylides* (London 1905), p. 198 and n. 2.

78. the great Mother: this goddess was commonly identified with the goddess Rhea, but her origin is in Asia Minor where she is known as Cybele. According to Paus. 9.25.3, Pindar's house stood close to a shrine of the Mother: 'across the Dirke are the ruins of Pindar's house and a sanctuary of Mother Dindymene, with a statue by Aristomedes and Sokrates of Thebes that he dedicated'. Pindar celebrates the Mother in his second dithyramb and in his Hymn to Pan (frags 95–9). It may be that his composition of this hymn for a certain festival was what prevented him travelling to Syracuse on this occasion.

81. 'for every good ... two evils': though the detail is different, the idea recalls that of *Iliad* 24.527, where Zeus is said to have two jars, one of good and one of evil, from which he apportions men's fortune.

83. Turning the good side outwards: a proverbial saying, like the English 'looking on the bright side'.

87. Peleus: see Glossary. His wedding feast was arranged by Chiron on Mt Pelion, and was attended by all the gods. Cf. N 4.65–8.

92. Nereus: the Old Man of the Sea, father of the fifty Nereids or sea-nymphs, of whom Thetis was one.

94. children of Cronos: the Olympian gods Hestia, Demeter, Hera, Hades, Poseidon and Zeus.

97. One of them: Cadmus. The tragic stories of the daughters of Cadmus were well-known legends. Semele (here referred to by her other name, Thyone) became the mother of Dionysus by Zeus, but through the devices of the jealous Hera was destroyed by a thunderbolt. Dionysus later brought her up from Hades to live with the immortals. Her sister Ino took the infant Dionysus to look after him, in anger at which Hera drove her mad; she jumped into the sea with her infant son, but became an immortal sea-nymph. A third daughter, Agave, was the mother of Pentheus whom she killed in Bacchic frenzy, as described in Euripides' *Bacchae*.

100. Peleus' son: Achilles, killed in the Trojan War by an arrow which pierced his heel, his only vulnerable point. Phthia in Thessaly was Achilles' homeland.

111. It is my hope: Pindar presents himself as one skilled in praise, and indicates his expectation of reward for the praise. The last lines exemplify the power of song to immortalize, as Homer immortalized the heroes at Troy.

112. Nestor: king of Pylos in the southwest Peloponnese. He was the oldest of the Greek leaders in the Trojan War.

Sarpedon: leader of the Lycians, allies of the Trojans. He was killed by Patroclus in the fight which led to the latter's death at the hands of Hector.

For Arcesilas of Cyrene

Winner of the Chariot Race (462)

Arcesilas IV was the king of Cyrene, the wealthy Greek colony in Libya. His Pythian victory was won in 462. Arcesilas was the descendant – in the eighth generation according to this ode – of the Greek leader Battus, of the Aegean island of Thera (Santorini). (Parts of his story are also told in Pythian 5.) Battus led the Greek colonists from Thera who established themselves in Libya in about 630. Their expedition was prompted, according to the story, by the oracle of Delphi, which frequently plays a role in the legitimation of colonizing expeditions. Battus, who suffered from a stutter, consulted the oracle at Delphi for a cure; the answer given was that he was destined to lead this expedition and establish a colony in Libya. Thus the line of Battiad rulers of Cyrene was established. There is a parallel narrative in Herodotus 4.147–58; the decree relating to the foundation of the colony is preserved, *SEG* ix.3.

Battus was the reputed descendant of Euphemus, one of the Argonauts who sailed with Jason to Colchis in quest of the Golden Fleece. The story of this expedition occupies the greater part of the ode. The story of Argo was old in Homer's day; it is alluded to by Hesiod, *Theogony* 922–1002, and was the subject of several epics. The only full narrative surviving today is that of the Hellenistic poet Apollonius of Rhodes, whose *Argonautica* shows the influence of earlier treatments including the present one. The corresponding passages are AR 4.1551ff., 1751ff. The story probably recalls early trading expeditions to the eastern end of the Black Sea. See D. Braund, *Georgia in Antiquity* (Oxford 1994), pp. 14–18.

Jason's expedition was the result of his being sent by Pelias his uncle and usurper of his father's throne, to fetch the Golden Fleece from Colchis. Here he was helped by Medea, the daughter of the local king, Aeetes, and a sorceress and prophetess, to accomplish the tasks set for Jason. After they had won the fleece, Medea, who had fallen in love with Jason, accompanied the heroes back to Greece.

The ode is exceptionally long and the narrative parts are told
in a more straightforward linear style than is customary in most
of Pindar's odes. This style is indebted to the form of 'lyric epic'
which was perfected by the early-sixth-century poet Stesichorus.
It plainly cannot have been performed by a chorus of dancers
and must have been given as a solo recitation.

In the twelfth stanza Pindar turns to an entirely different
subject, namely an appeal to Arcesilas to grant a pardon to
Damophilus, a nobleman of Cyrene who had been involved in
some aristocratic dissensions with Arcesilas and subsequently
exiled. At least part of his exile was spent at Thebes where he
had become acquainted with Pindar. Clearly it would have been
impolitic to include such an appeal in an ode for public
performance unless a favourable response was already assured,
and it seems likely that the ode is the spectacular culmination of
some extended diplomacy; it is very probable that the ode was
in fact commissioned by Damophilus. Arcesilas' brother-in-iaw
Carrhotus, who acted as his charioteer at Delphi, may well have
been the intermediary. The presentation of the interview
between Jason and Pelias emphasizes the desirability of agree-
ments reached by peaceful discussion rather than force, and this
parallel to Damophilus' situation may be seen as the moral core
of the long narrative glorifying Cyrene's past.

str. 1   Come Muse, today I bid you stand beside
           A man well-loved, Cyrene's king, that city
           Of noble steeds, and in his hour of triumph
                 Honour Arcesilas,
              Raising on high a gale of song,
           Hymns due to Leto's children and to Pytho.
           There long ago the priestess on her throne
           Beside the birds of Zeus, the golden eagles,
           Foretold – nor was Apollo far away –   5
           That in the fruitful land of Libya,
           Leaving his holy isle in days to come,
                 Battus should found
           A city famous for her chariots
                 On a white-breasted hill:

ant. 1   And thus Medea's word, spoken in Thera,
           In the seventeenth generation he should fulfil: 10

That word which long since the princess of Colchis,
　　The inspired child of Aietes,
　Breathed forth upon her deathless tongue;
When to those demi-gods, the sailor comrades
Of warrior Jason, thus she spoke: 'Hearken,
Ye sons of dauntless mortals and of gods,
This I proclaim, that from this sea-girt isle
There shall be born in days to come a root
That shall in Epaphus' daughter's land engender　　15
　　Cities far-famed
To mortal hearing, founded in the soil
　　Sacred to Zeus of Ammon.

ep. 1　No more the short-finned dolphins shall escort them,
　　But racing steeds shall carry them;
　Reins they shall ply instead of oars, and drive
Chariots swift as wind. A sign there was
　　To tell that Thera
　Shall prove the mother of great cities,　　20
When, leaping from the prow where Lake Tritonis
Pours to the sea, Euphemus took the gift,
Token of a host's friendship, from a god
In mortal guise who gave a clod of earth;
　　And from aloft, to mark the sign,
　　A peal of thunder
Sounded from Zeus the father, son of Cronos.

str. 2　This so befell, as on our ship we hung
The bronze-fluked anchor, the bridle of our swift Argo, 25
When for twelve days we had carried from the Ocean
　　Over earth's desert backs
　Our good ship's hull, when we had beached
And drawn her to the shore by my designs.
Then came to us this deity, all alone,
Clad in the noble semblance of a man
Of reverent bearing, and with friendly speech
Made to address us with a kindly greeting –
Such words with which a man of good intent　　30
　　Speaks to invite
The strangers newly come to share his table,
　　And bids them a first welcome.

ant. 2   Yet did the dear plea of our homeward voyage
          Call to us and forbade our stay. His name
          He gave, Eurypylus, saying he was
                 The son of the immortal
              Holder of Earth, Ennosides;
          He saw our haste to be away, and straightway
          He stopped and seized a clod beside his foot   35
          And in his right hand proffered the gift of friendship.
          And, for he felt no misbelief, Euphemus
          Leapt to the shore and grasped his outstretched hand,
          And took the earth, that sign of heaven's will.
                 But now I learn
          That it is lost, washed down as evening fell
              From the ship's deck, to wander

ep. 2   On ocean's dark smooth tide, with the sea spray.   40
                 Many a time, indeed, did I
          Charge to the serving-men who ease our toil
          To watch it well; but they forgot. Thus now
                 The deathless seed
              Of Libya's far-spreading plains
          Is spilt upon this isle, e'er the due time.
          For had that prince, son of the horseman's god
          Poseidon – whom Europa, Tityus' daughter   45
          Bore by Kephissus' banks – had he, Euphemus
                 Come home to holy Taenarus
                    And cast that seed
          Where cleft earth opens to the mouth of hell,

str. 3   Then had his sons in the fourth generation
          Seized with the Danai this broad mainland.
          For then from mighty Sparta and Argos' gulf
                 And from Mycenae the peoples
              Shall rise and move from their abode.
          But now Euphemus, taking from a breed
          Of foreign women one to be his bride,   50
          Shall found a chosen race. And they shall come,
          Paying due honour to the gods, unto
          This island, where they shall beget a man
          Born to be lord of those dark-misted plains.
                 And on a day

In time to come, this man shall tread the path
    Down to the shrine of Pytho,

ant. 3   And Phoebus from his golden-treasured hall   55
Shall speak to him his oracle, proclaiming
That he shall bring a mighty host in ships
    To the rich land of Nile
  The precinct of the son of Cronos,
So rang Medea's rhythmic utterance.
Bowed down in silent wonder, motionless
The godlike heroes heard her potent wisdom.
O son of Polymnestus, richly blessed,
Your path it was the prophecy made plain,   60
The inspired prediction of the Delphic Bee;
    For thrice she named you
Fortune's predestined king, who shall raise high
    The glory of Cyrene,

ep. 3   When you rode down to ask of heaven's will
    Some remedy for your laboured speech.
Yes, verily now, even in these after-days,
As in the prime of purple-flowering spring,
    Arcesilas   65
  Born of this stock, eighth in descent,
Prospers no less. Apollo and Pytho's field
Granted him fame amidst the neighbouring peoples
For his racing steeds; and I the Muses' gift
Shall dower him, of the golden fleece recounting
    The tale. For when the Minyae
      Sailed on that quest,
Glory from heaven was planted in their race.

str. 4   What then begot their sea-borne journey forth?   70
What peril bound their spirits to the task
With adamantine bonds? It was foretold
    That Pelias should die
  Or by the hands or by the untiring
Designs of the proud sons of Aeolus;
And in its icy grip a prophecy
Held the depths of his soul, that word spoken
From tree-clad mother-earth's deep navel-stone;
That above all he should keep watch and ward,

If one should come wearing a single sandal,   75
    From a high home
On mountain steeps, unto the sunlit land
    Of glorious Iolcus,

ant. 4   Whether he be stranger or citizen.
    And lo, after due time there came a man
    Of wondrous strength. Two spears he carried
        And wore a twofold vesture,
      A garment of the countrymen
    Of the Magnetes' race covering close   80
    His splendid limbs, and slung upon his shoulder
    A leopard-skin to shield the hissing rain.
    And locks of glorious hair fell rippling down
    In gleaming streams unshorn upon his back.
    And swiftly coming, as if in trial to prove
        His dauntless spirit,
    He took his station in the market-place
        Amidst the surging crowd.   85

ep. 4   They knew him not; and looked on him in wonder;
        And one amongst them spoke, and said:
    'This man is not Apollo, surely, nor
    The god of the bronze chariot, the lord
        Of Aphrodite?
      Iphimedeia's sons, they say,
    In gleaming Naxos died, Otus and you
    King Ephialtes the daring. And indeed
    Tityus by Artemis was hunted down   90
    With darts from her unconquerable quiver
      Suddenly sped, so that a man
        May learn to touch
    Only those loves that are within his power.'

str. 5   Thus were the folk their idle tales exchanging
    One to another's ear, when suddenly,
    Driving his team of mules in headlong haste,
        Pelias came riding by
      Mounted upon his polished car.
    And terror seized him when his glancing eye   95
    Fell on the clear sign of the single sandal
    On the man's right foot. But he concealed the fear

Within his heart, and spoke to him; 'What country,
Tell me, stranger, you boast your own? What woman
Of earth-born mortals bore you from a belly
    Hoary with age?
Tell me your birth and see you sully it
    With no unlovely lies.'   100

ant. 5 But he, with a bold heart and gentle words
Answered him thus: 'Chiron my teacher was,
This shall I prove. From Chariclo, I say,
    And Philyra's cave I come,
  Where the chaste daughters of the Centaur
Nursed my young days. Through all my twenty years
I gave them no rough word or hasty deed;
And now I tread my homeward path, to claim   105
The ancient honours of my father. Here
A kingship is installed, not by the right
Derived of heaven, which the hand of Zeus
    Long since assigned
To chieftain Aeolus and to his children,
    To hold a throne of honour;

ep. 5 But, so I learn, yielding in godless trust
    To the cold thoughts of envy's evil,
Pelias by force has stolen the dominion
My parents held of old. For they, when first   110
    I saw the light,
  Fearing that leader's overweening
And cruel pride, laid forth within the house
Dark robes of mourning, as though their babe were dead;
And amidst wailing women sent me forth
Secretly, wrapped in purple swaddling clothes,
    That only the dark of night might know
      My path, and gave me
To Chiron, Cronos' son, to be my guardian.   115

str. 6 But of this story the main part you know.
But show me clear, grave citizens, the house
Of my forefathers, riders of white steeds.
    For I, the son of Aeson
  Born of this soil, let me not come
To find my home a foreign land of strangers.

My name that godlike creature gave to me
And called me Jason.' So he spoke, and coming
Into his house, his father's eyes failed not   120
Straightway to know him, and his ageing lids
Poured forth a flood of tears, for he rejoiced
        Through all his soul
To see his son a man most excellent,
        Fairest of all mankind.

ant. 6   And both his brothers came and stood before them,
         Hearing the famed report of his arrival,
         First Pheres from his nearby home beside   125
             The spring of Hypereis,
           And Amythaon from Messene;
         And quickly came Admetus and Melampus
         To give him kindly greetings. And a banquet
         Was spread for all, and Jason welcomed them
         With gracious words. And he made ready for them
         The due gifts of a hospitable house,
         And served them all the joys of mirth and gladness,
                 And for five nights   130
         And five long days they culled the blessed fruit
             And flower of happy living.

ep. 6   But the sixth day Jason in grave discourse
             Told to his kinsmen all the story
         From its first hour. And all were of one mind
         To follow him. And he rose from his seat
                 Straightway, and they
         Likewise; and to the palace doors
         Of Pelias they flocked with surging steps
         And took their stance within. And he, that son   135
         Of Tyro, maiden of the lovely hair,
         Heard, and himself came forth to meet them there.
             But Jason with soft-flowing speech
                 And gentle voice,
         A sure foundation laid of words of wisdom,

str. 7   Saying: 'Son of Poseidon of the Rock,
         Too prone are mortal minds, against all right,   140
         To choose a treacherous gain, howe'er it be

Their footsteps onward roll
To a disastrous reckoning.
But you and I must with a sacred pledge
Contain our wrath, and for the future weave
A happier fortune. This, which you know, I tell:
One mother's womb bore Cretheus and bold-hearted
Salmoneus; and we now, their grandsons bred,
Look on the golden sun's broad ray. But if
Enmity breeds
Twixt men of the same race, to hide the shame   145
Even the Fates veil their eyes.

ant. 7   It ill befits us two with bronze-edged swords
Or javelins to quarrel the division
Of our fathers' great honours. No, for I
Give you the flocks of sheep
And herds of tawny cattle, and all
The fields whence, though you robbed them of my parents,
You tend their culture and make fat your living.   150
Nor do I take amiss that these furnish
Your house with wealth beyond all measure. But
Both for the royal sceptre and the throne
On which long since the son of Cretheus sat
Dispensing justice
To his horsemen folk, these with no wrath between us
Release to me again,

ep. 7   Lest out of these some further ill should rear   155
Its ugly head.' So did he speak.
And Pelias answered softly: 'As you have willed
So shall I be. But now the elder portion
Of a man's years
Holds me already in its toils;
But for you the full flower of blossoming youth
Burgeons apace. You have it in your strength
To undo the vengeful anger of the powers
Of earth below. To bring his spirit again
Phrixus commands us journey to
Aietes' hall,   160
And fetch from thence the thick fleece of the ram,

str. 8   Which saved him from the ocean long ago,
And from the impious darts of his step-mother.
This bidding a wondrous dream declared to me;
     And I sent to consult
    Castalia's oracle, if any
Quest should be made. They bade me with all speed
Make ready a sea-borne mission. Now, do you   165
With goodwill take this challenge and complete it,
And I, I swear to grant to you the crown
And kingdom for your rule. To this great oath
May he who is our common ancestor,
      Zeus, be the witness.'
And on these terms they were agreed, and parted.
     Jason, losing no moment,

ant. 8   Himself sent heralds far and wide, proclaiming   170
The voyage now to be. And the three sons,
Tireless in battle, of Zeus the son of Cronos,
     Came with all haste, the child
    Born of the dancing-eyed Alcmene,
And Leda's twin sons; and that pair of heroes
Of the high-crested locks, sons of Poseidon
The earth-shaker, those men of no less honour
Than of valour, from Pylos and the steeps
Of Taenarus; wide fame they won, Euphemus   175
And Periclymenus that man of strength;
      And from Apollo,
That master of the lyre of happy fame,
     Orpheus, father of song.

ep. 8   And Hermes of the golden wand sent forth
    His two sons to the stubborn toil,
Eurytus and Echion, happy souls
Of joyful youth; and swift came two who dwelt
     Beneath the strong
    Foundations of Pangaeum's height;   180
For gladly with a joyful heart their father
Boreas, sovereign of the winds, commanded
Zetes and Calais to the task, those heroes
Whose backs on either side bear fluttering wings
     Of purple. In these demi-gods

The goddess Hera
Kindled the all-persuading sweet desire

str. 9   For the ship Argo, that not one should stay   185
Left at his mother's side to nurse a lifetime
Free from danger, but each, even at the risk
        Of death, amidst companions
    Of a like age should win that fair
And potent spell that should redound his valour.
And when this flower of sailor-men had come
To Iolcus city, Jason mustered them
And gave thanks to them all. And at his side
Mopsus, the seer, studied the will of heaven   190
By flight of birds and drawing of sacred lots,
        And right gladly
He gave the signal for the host to embark.
        When they had raised the anchor

ant. 9   And slung it high upon the ship's bowsprit,
Then their commander, standing on the stern,
Took in his hands a golden cup and called
        To Zeus whose spear is lightning,
    The father of the sons of heaven,
To the swift-running tides of wave and wind,   195
To the nights and to the highways of the ocean,
To days propitious and the friendly hand
Of Fate that grants return. Then from the clouds
Answered the fateful thunder's voice, and far-flung
Broke the bright flashes of the lightning's ray.
        And the heroes
Took breath of courage, trusting in these signs
        From heaven. Then the seer   200

ep. 9   Rang out his bidding to lay on the oars
    And spoke them words of cheerful hope,
And on they sped with swiftly-swinging blades
In tireless rhythm. The South Wind's breezes blew
        To send them onwards,
    And when they came before the mouth
Of the inhospitable sea, they founded
A holy place, a precinct of Poseidon

God of the Ocean, where was a red herd
Of Thracian bulls, and an altar new built   205
   Of hollowed stone. Then driving onwards
     Into deep peril,
They offered prayer to the great Lord of Ships

str. 10 That of the Clashing Rocks they might escape
The devastating onset – two pillars
Alive, that rolled with hurtling speed more swiftly
   Than the embattled ranks
     Of the loud-roaring gales. But now   210
That voyage of the heroes ended their mischief.
They came then to the Phasis, where they joined
In bitter conflict with the swarthy-faced
Men of the land of Colchis, in the kingdom
Of Aietes himself. Then from Olympus
The queen of swift arrows, the Cyprian goddess,
     Sent down the wryneck,
Its dappled feathers spread and firmly tied
   To the four spokes of a wheel,   215

ant. 10 That bird of passion's frenzy, never before
Seen amongst men. And the goddess made plain
To Aeson's son the lore of prayers, and spells
   Of magic incantation,
    That he might rob Medea's heart
Of reverence for her parents, and a dear
Desire for Hellas light in her mind a flame,
Driving her with Persuasion's lash. And soon
She showed him all the tests he should accomplish   220
Set by her father's hand. And she distilled
Medicines with olive oil, and gave to him
     Ointments to allay
The pains of burning; and they vowed to join
   In sweet wedlock together.

ep. 10 But when Aietes set within their midst
    The ploughshare hard as adamant,
And oxen breathing flames of burning fire   225
From nostrils tawny-red battered the ground
    With brazen hooves,
    Pawing the soil this side and that,

Single-handed Aietes brought them in
And threw the yoke upon them. And he marked out
And ploughed straight furrows, cutting the earth's back
   Two cubits depth; and said 'O king,
     Whoe'er you be,   230
Who rules this ship, this task complete for me,

str. 11 Then take the imperishable coverlet,
The fleece with fringe of gleaming gold.' He spoke,
And Jason threw aside his saffron cloak,
    And putting his trust in heaven
    Set to the task. Nor could the flames
Give pause to his brave spirit, thanks to the counsels
Of the stranger maid, mistress of pharmacy.
And he dragged forth the plough, and on the oxen   235
Thrust the compelling yoke to bind their necks,
And in their strong-ribbed frames unceasingly
Plunging the goad, this man of might toiled through
     The allotted measure.
Aietes, speechless, groaned aloud in woe,
    Aghast to see his strength.

ant. 11 But his comrades stretched out their hands to greet
Their mighty leader, crowned him with green garlands 240
And welcomed him with words of dear rejoicing.
    Straightway Aietes spoke,
   That wondrous son of Helios,
And told where Phrixus' knife had laid outstretched
The shining fleece; yet in his heart he hoped
That Jason might even so this further labour
Fail to accomplish. For the fleece was laid
In a deep thicket, held within the fierce
Jaws of a ravenous dragon, far surpassing
    In length and breadth   245
A ship of fifty oars, welded and built
    By many a hammer's blow.

ep. 11 Long were my path upon the beaten high-road,
    And time presses apace. I know
A shorter way; to many another man
Can I be leader in the poet's craft.

      With cunning hands –
       Well known the tale, Arcesilas –   250
He slew that dragon of the glaring eyes
And speckled back, and with her own aid stole
Medea, who brought death to Pelias.
Then to the Ocean main and the Red Sea,
    And to the race of Lemnian women
      Who slew their menfolk,
Where for a garment's prize they showed their prowess

str. 12 In contests of strong limbs; and with those women
They mated. Yes, there in a foreign soil   255
Some fated day, maybe, or the night watches
    Witnessed that seed implanted,
    From which should spring the glorious light
Of your high fortune. There Euphemus' line
Was bred, to last forever; then, mingling
With men of Lacedaemon blood and custom,
They brought their home in due time to the land
Once named the Fairest Isle; thence to your race
The son of Leto granted Libya's plain,
      To make it rich
Under god's honour, and give government   260
      To the divine city

ant. 12 Of golden-throned Cyrene, there devising
The rule of wisdom and of righteous counsel.
Now let your thought, I pray, rival the wisdom
      Of Oedipus. For if
    With his sharp-bladed axe a man
Strips off the branches from a mighty oak,
And brings to shame its lovely form, yet still
Though reft of its fair fruit it may give witness   265
Of its true being, whether it comes at last
To feed the fires of winter, or bear the load
On rising columns of its master's palace,
      Serving a drear
And lonely task, and amidst alien walls
    Knows its own place no more.

ep. 12 You are a doctor prompt to the moment's hour;   270
    Paean pays honour to your name;

To heal a festering wound there needs the touch
Of gentle hands. To cast a city in ruins
   Easy enough
   Even for men of meanly stature;
Once more to raise it to its high estate
Is hard indeed, so be it no deity
Comes suddenly to take the helm, and steer
The rulers' course. For you the heavens are weaving   275
   Of such blest gifts a lasting pattern.
     Be bold to seek
With all your spirit Cyrene's happy fortune.

str. 13   Take too, and ponder in your heart, the word
   That Homer spoke: 'By a good messenger
   Is brought' said he 'to every matter spoken
     The highest honour.' So too
    The Muse by a true-made report
   Wins the more praise. Well has Cyrene's city
   And Battus' hall, that palace of renown,   280
   Seen in Demophilus a man of just
   And righteous mind. Bred here, a boy 'midst boys,
   His counsel drawn as from a hundred years
   Of elder wisdom's fruit, he brings to naught
     The far-flung boasting
   Of evil tongues, knowing well to hate the man
     Whose deeds are insolence.

ant. 13   He quarrels with no good men, nor brooks delay   285
   To end a task. For fit occasion grants
   But a brief hour to men. This he knows well,
     And waits on the due moment
    As a good servant and no slave.
   Of all pains this, they say, cuts the most sore,
   If one who knows good fortune finds his footstep
   Shut from the door by harsh constraint. Does not
   Even now great Atlas struggle to bear up   290
   The weight of heaven, far from his fathers' land
   And his possessions? But almighty Zeus
     Set free the Titans.
   For as time passes and the breeze abates,
     The sails are set anew.

ep. 13   But now it is his prayer, when this drear cup
              Of grievous ill is drained at last,
          To see his home, and by Apollo's fountain
          Joining the banquet's throng, to spend his soul
                  Oft and again   295
              In youthful joys, 'midst citizens
          Lovers of skill, playing his rich-wrought lyre,
          And to find peace, bringing harm to no man,
          And from his townsfolk suffering naught himself;
          And to you would he tell, Arcesilas,
              How that he found a glorious spring
                  Of heavenly songs,
          When of late times he was a guest at Thebes.

Notes

1. **I bid you stand**: the phrase implies a performance as a *stasimon*, with the performer(s) standing still rather than dancing. It seems to me likely that this ode was performed by a single singer. Cf. O 6.22-8, where the chorus leader is bidden to 'come' to Pitana.

2. **city of noble steeds**: horses are a pre-eminent indicator of a powerful aristocracy – and of course relevant to the particular occasion, a chariot victory.

7. **his holy isle**: Thera (modern Santorini).

8. **white-breasted hill**: the hill on which Cyrene was founded is, like many hills, breast-shaped. The epithet 'white' seems to be provoked by the thought of the breast rather than of the hill, which tends rather to green or brown.

10. **seventeenth generation**: the arithmetic is hardly worth trying to calculate, but a good attempt to reconcile the various sources is made by L. Malten, *Kyrene* (Berlin 1911), pp. 191-3, with a complex genealogical table.

15. **Epaphus' daughter's land**: Epaphus, son of Zeus and Io, was a legendary king of Egypt. His daughter Libya gave her name to the neighbouring region.

16. **Zeus of Ammon**: Conway's expression is not correct: the god is Ammon, identified with Zeus. His oracle and shrine were at Siwa, 500 km southeast of Cyrene. The location is sometimes considered part of

Egypt. Pindar wrote his Hymn to Ammon (frag. 36) for the 'Ammonians in Libya' and dedicated a statue of Ammon at Thebes (Paus. 9.16.1). In the sixth century there was a temple of Ammon at Cyrene.

20. Lake Tritonis: this mythical Libyan lake is conceived in legendary geography as having an outlet into the Mediterranean. In the usual version of the story, the Argonauts had returned via the River Phasis in Colchis to Ocean and thence into the Red Sea, whence they carried their ship overland across the desert to this lake. But Pindar (line 252) makes them return by the same route as they sailed out, through the Aegean – a route inconsistent with an entry to Lake Tritonis!

22. Euphemus: the present of a clod of earth was a sign that this soil should be the hero's home. But, as is narrated at lines 40ff., Euphemus let the clod slip overboard and it was later washed ashore on Thera, so that his descendants made their home there: if only he had cast it on the Peloponnese, his descendants would have been settled there and would have been able to partake in the 'Dorian Invasion', four generations later (line 48), and colonize Cyrene at that early date, instead of several centuries later.

26. earth's desert backs: the phrase recurs at line 226, where Jason ploughs 'earth's back'.

33. Eurypylus: the son of Poseidon and brother of Triton, as the scholiast points out (*FGrH* 469F1). Cf. AR 4.1561. The usual story was that Triton himself presented Euphemus with the clod. 'Ennosides' means 'earth-shaker'; the term is used by Stesichorus *SLG* 143.4; cf. Pindar Pa. 4.41, frag. 60ab.

44. Taenarus: the cape on the central promontory of the Peloponnese, now Cape Matapan. There is a large cave here which was reputed to be an entrance to the Underworld.

46. Europa: in Hesiod (frag. 253.1–2, MW) Euphemus is the son of Mekionike of Hyrie, a daughter of Eurotas. By altering the ancestry, Pindar makes Euphemus a genuine Minyan, as in Herodotus 4.150.2

50. his bride: a woman of Lemnos named Malache.

51. they shall come ... unto this island, where they shall beget: the descendants of Euphemus will come from the Peloponnese to Thera, and beget Battus.

53. dark-misted plains: of Libya.

56. Nile: the Nile is not normally reckoned to be in Libya, but it sounds grand.

59. son of Polymnestus: Battus.

60. the Delphic Bee: the priestess of Apollo at Delphi; cf. note on Pa. 8.

63. your laboured speech: Battus suffered from a stutter. See introduction.

66. Apollo and Pytho's field: possibly the briefest passage of praise of the victory in any of the odes.

69. the Minyae: Minyas was an early king of Orchomenos in Boeotia; his descendants are the people of central Greece, Boeotia and Iolcus. The Argonauts are often described simply as Minyans.

71. Pelias: he has usurped the throne of Iolcus from his half-brother Aeson, who was Jason's father.

72. Sons of Aeolus: the full genealogy is as follows:

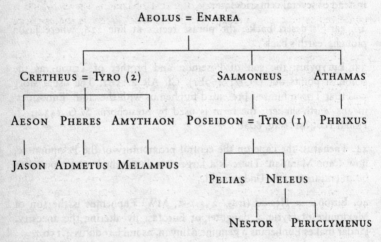

74. deep navel-stone: the oracle at Delphi.

76. a high home: Jason was brought up on Mt Pelion by the centaur Chiron.

80. Magnetes: a tribe living around Mt Pelion.

87. god of the bronze chariot: Ares, the god of war.

89. Otus, Ephialtes: two giants, sons of Poseidon and Iphimedeia, who tried to make a stairway to heaven by piling Mt Pelion on Mt Ossa. They put Ares into chains and were destroyed by Apollo.

90. Tityus: another big man. He has already been referred to at line 46 as an ancestor of Euphemus.

98. Hoary with age: some commentators have seen Pelias' address to Jason as one of studied insolence: but the term may be a baroque way of implying 'venerable'.

99. no unlovely lies: cf. *Iliad* 4.404; but the expression seems here to be simply litotes. The line inspired the passage of A. E. Housman's *Fragment of a Greek Tragedy*: 'Nor did he shame his mouth with hateful lies'.

102. Chariclo: the wife of Chiron: Philyra is his mother (P 3.1).

109. cold thoughts: literally, 'white heart', the antithesis of Homer's 'black mind' which has not, as in English, a moral connotation. Black is the proper colour of the *phren*, the seat of consciousness, which is conceived as an organ, perhaps the liver. Pelias' 'mind' is the opposite of what it should be.

138. Poseidon of the Rock: a Thessalian title of the god, who was supposed to have opened up the valley of Tempe between Mt Olympus and Mt Ossa. See the scholiast; Herodotus 7.129.4., Bacchylides 14.19–20 alludes to a victory at this place, Petraea.

152. Son of Cretheus: Aeson.

159–60. Phrixus: the son of Athamas, king of Boeotia. When Athamas was on the point of sacrificing him, due to the machinations of his stepmother Ino, the gods sent a golden-winged ram which carried him away with his sister Helle. Helle fell into the sea which is now called the Hellespont (Dardanelles); Phrixus was brought to Colchis where he sacrificed the ram to Ares in gratitude. Its golden fleece was hung in a sacred grove guarded by a dragon.

No other author refers to the need to bring back Phrixus' soul as well as the fleece. Two scholiasts suggest that this may be a second best if they cannot find his bones to bring back (the collection of relics had become quite common in the fifth century), or that it gives a more dignified motivation to the voyage. A third quotes *Odyssey* 9.64, where

Odysseus says that he did not sail away from the land where his comrades had died before calling out their names three times. None of these explanations really solves the puzzle.

171. three sons ... of Zeus: Heracles, son of Alcmene, and Castor and Pollux, twin sons of Leda.

173. sons of Poseidon: Euphemus from Taenarus, Periclymenus from Pylos. The full list of Argonauts generally ran to about fifty names.

180. Pangaeum: a mountain in eastern Thrace.

203. inhospitable sea: the Black Sea, also called the Euxine, 'Hospitable' as an apotropaic euphemism for its true nature.

206. an altar: an earlier altar had been raised by the sons of Phrixus; the Argonauts rededicated it to Zeus (Timosthenes of Rhodes, frag. 28; Herodorus of Heracleia, *FGrH* 31F47).

208. Clashing Rocks: the Clashing or Wandering Rocks, the Symplegades, which crushed ships between them. Jason sent a dove through ahead; the rocks closed, and as they drew apart again, the ship slipped through. They never moved again.

211. Phasis: the modern River Rioni and its tributary the Qvirila.

214. the wryneck: this bird was used as a love-charm, tied to the spokes of a wheel, with suitable incantations.

220. all the tests: the main task was to plough the Field of Ares with a pair of fire-breathing oxen. Pindar omits the second task, that he should sow the field with dragon's teeth. From these teeth armed warriors sprang up; Jason induced them to fight each other instead of against himself, and thus escaped.

250. brought death to Pelias: Medea persuaded Pelias' daughters to chop him up and put him in a cauldron for rejuvenation. She had previously made this trick work with an old sheep, but this time she ensured that it failed.

252. Lemnian women: in the usual version of the myth, the Argonauts called at Lemnos on their outward journey; here, Pindar makes the visit the climax of the expedition, because Euphemus married a Lemnian woman (line 50). The Lemnian women had killed their husbands because the latter had left them to seek other wives on the mainland, on the grounds that the Lemnian women smelt awful.

253. contests: the games in which the Argonauts competed were organized by Hypsipyle, the queen of Lemnos. (Cf. O 4.19–27.) The scholiast quotes a passage of Simonides (= *PMG* 527) about this contest for a garment.

255. your high fortune: i.e. of Arcesilas.

258. Fairest Isle: Kalliste, another name for Thera.

259. son of Leto: the story of Apollo's abduction of the nymph Cyrene is told in P 9.

263ff. if with his . . . axe: this parable of the oak tree is the beginning of the plea for Damophilus, the lopped branch.

270. Paean: Apollo in his character as god of healing.

281. a boy 'midst boys: for the phrase, cf. N 3.72–4.

289. Atlas: the leader of his brother Titans in their war against Zeus. When defeated, he became Mt Atlas in northwest Africa and was condemned to carry the sky on his shoulders for ever.

291. almighty Zeus set free the Titans: no other writer says so; the usual implication is that they were imprisoned for eternity, though three of them, Cronos, Rhea and Prometheus, were released later. However, Aeschylus' *Prometheus Bound* has a chorus of Titans who are evidently not imprisoned. Pindar frag. 35 says they were released by Zeus. Hesiod, *Works and Days* 173b, which says that they were released, seems to have been inserted to reconcile contradictory statements in the preceding lines.

294. Apollo's fountain: a fountain in Cyrene.

299. a glorious spring of heavenly songs: i.e. Pindar himself. Pindar introduces himself in the last line as a *sphragis* or seal on the poem.

For Arcesilas of Cyrene (462/1)

This ode, like Pythian 4, celebrates the victory won by Arcesilas, king of Cyrene, at the Pythian Games of 462. While Pythian 4 was written as a personal presentation for Arcesilas at his palace, this ode was intended to celebrate the return of the winning team to Cyrene after their success at Delphi. The mention of the festival of Carneian Apollo at lines 79–80 indicates that the ode was performed at that event. Apollo was the dominant god of all Dorian peoples, and Cyrene was supposed to originate from the offspring of the nymph Cyrene and the god Apollo: see Pythian 9.

Pindar gives unusual prominence in lines 29–54 to Carrhotus, the brother-in-law of Arcesilas who had also acted as his charioteer. The ancient scholar Didymus offered an elaborate explanation based on his historical reading about Cyrene: another friend of Arcesilas, Euphemus, had been given the task not only of competing in the chariot races at the Games but also of raising money for an army in Greece; Euphemus had won his victories and settled colonists at the Hesperidae (near modern Benghazi) but had then died and Carrhotus had taken over the leadership of the colony. This may be true, but it is hard to see its relevance to the ode, which mentions none of these matters, which can hardly constitute an explanation for the praise of Carrhotus. In fact charioteers often receive special praise precisely because they have given as much effort as the nominal victor: e.g. Thrasybulus in Pythian 6, Phintis in Olympian 6 (see M. R. Lefkowitz, 'Pindar's Pythian 5', in *First-Person Fictions* [Oxford 1991], pp. 169–90; first published in *Pindare*, Entretiens de la Fondation Hardt 31 [Geneva 1985], pp. 33–58).

The bulk of the ode is dedicated to the celebration of Cyrene as a Dorian city, and to the cementing of ties between it and Pindar the Dorian poet as its appropriate celebrant (see note on line 75). The centrepiece of this is the legend of Battus, the ancestor of Arcesilas, who, as described in Pythian 4, was proclaimed by the Delphic oracle as the man who was to lead a

company of Greeks from Thera to colonize Libya and make
Cyrene their capital. The usual story of how Battus was freed
from his stutter (in some versions he is pictured as being actually
dumb) was that after arriving in Libya he met a lion, and the
fright restored his powers of speech. In Pindar's more interesting
version the shock to the lion seems to have been greater than to
Battus. Pythian 4 tells that Battus went to Delphi to ask for a
cure for his stutter, but does not record that the oracle which
promised him the kingship of Libya made any mention of a
cure; here, lines 57–62 imply that the promise of a cure was
part of the response.

str. 1   Wide is the power of wealth,
           Whenever a mortal man brings home,
      Linked with untarnished honour, this gift of destiny,
        A follower that shall win him many a friend.
      Arcesilas, favoured of heaven, this to achieve,   5
          Joined with fair fame,
      Has been your journey's goal, since first your footsteps
                            mounted
        The firm foundation of your life's renown,
        By the kind grace of Castor of the golden chariot,
        Who after wintry storms sheds on your happy
                       homestead 10
        Serene and sunlit days.

ant. 1   Wise men can better bear
          The power bestowed on them by heaven;
      And for you, as your travel on your road of justice,
        Abundant is the fortune that enfolds you.
      Firstly, for that you are a king of mighty cities,   15
          The genius bred
      Of your inheritance sees this majestic honour
        Here allied to the wisdom of your mind.
      Next that now too, upon the famous field of Pytho,   20
      You have won glory with your steeds, and this triumphant
        Chorus of manly voices,

ep. 1   Wherein Apollo takes delight. Therefore forget not,
     While at Cyrene in Aphrodite's pleasant garden
        Your praise is sung, to ascribe

This glory to none other but the hand of god.   25
   Nor fail to welcome first of your companions
      Carrhotus in true friendship,
Who to the palace of the sons of Battus,
Who rule by right divine, has not returned
      To bring with him Excuse
Daughter of late-contriving Afterthought;
But as a guest beside Castalia's fountain   30
      Has set upon your brow
The crown of honour of his racing chariot.

str. 2   For with unbroken reins
       He drove his flying-footed team
The twelve laps of the sacred course. Of his strong chariot
   He broke no single piece of gear, but all
That skilful workmanship of craftsmen's hands he
                          brought   35
      Past Krisa's hill
To the god's deep valley; there it hangs now, consecrated
   Within the shrine of cypress wood, hard by
That statue shaped from one tree's native growth, which
                          once   40
The Cretan bowmen dedicated in their chapel
      Beneath Parnassus' height.

ant. 2   Forth then, to welcome him
       With true goodwill, who served us well.
Alexibiades, your name shines with the glory   45
   Lit by the Graces of the lovely hair.
Blest is your lot indeed, who after mighty toil
      Win for your name
A lasting monument of noble words. For you
   When forty drivers fell, with dauntless courage   50
Brought through your chariot unscathed, and now are come
Back from the glorious Games to Libya's plain, and to
      The city of your fathers.

ep. 2   No man is spared his lot of ill, nor ever shall be.
Yet does the happy fortune given of old to Battus   55
      Still ride its course, faring
Or high or low – a towering fortress for the city,

Shedding a radiant light to every stranger.
 Battus it was, from whom
The roaring lions fled away in terror,
When spoken words fell from his tongue, made free
 By powers across the sea.
For Apollo, founder and leader of his venture, 60
Struck the fierce creatures with that deadly fear,
 That for Cyrene's master
His oracle might not be found to fail.

str. 3   To Apollo, too, we owe
 The cures he gives to man and woman
For sore disease. He it was bestowed the lyre, and
        grants 65
 The Poet's gift to those for whom he wills it.
He sets within man's heart the love of lawful living
 And peaceful concord,
And rules the secret shrine where breed his oracles;
 Whence for the valiant sons of Heracles
And of Aegimius he made their home in Sparta,
In Argos and holy Pylos. Mine to sing the lovely 70
 Glory that came from Sparta,

ant. 3   For thence were bred the sons
 Of Aegeus' seed, my ancestors, 75
Who came to Thera, not without the gods' goodwill,
 But destiny decreed their path. Thence came
Our heritage of the banquet, rich in sacrifice,
 Where we pay honour
In the Carneian festival to your name Apollo, 80
 And to the fair-built city of Cyrene,
Where once the bronze-armed Trojans dwelt, sons of
        Antenor,
Who came with Helen, when they saw their home in ashes,
 Burnt in the flames of war.

ep. 3 And that proud horsemen's race receives a gracious
        greeting, 85
Since with rich gifts and sacrifice those warriors met them,
 Whom in their ships of war
Aristoteles led, driving an open pathway

Through the deep seas. And honouring the gods
    He founded greater precincts,
And for processions in Apollo's worship,   90
Sureties of mortal safety, he ordained
    That there be made a road
To run straight-cut across the level plain,
Stone-paved, resounding to the horses' tread.
    There in his grave, where ends
The market-place, he lies apart in death.

str. 4   Blest was his life 'mongst men.
    Thereafter have his people worshipped   95
His hero's grave. And other sacred kings who trod
    The road of death are laid before the palace
In tombs apart. Maybe to souls below the earth
    Great deeds are known,
Sparkling in the soft dew of flowing songs of triumph, 100
    A wealth of joy for them and glorious honour
Shared with their son, Arcesilas – his due tribute.
With young men's voices must he now give praise to Phoebus,
    God of the golden sword,

ant. 4   For he has won from Pytho,   105
    Due reward for his rich endeavour,
The gracious song that hails the victor. Such a man
    Wins the praise of the wise. On all men's tongues
These words I hear: that in the wisdom of his mind
    And of his speech   110
He far surpasses all men of his age: in courage
    A broad-winged eagle amongst birds; in combat
A tower of strength: to share the Muses' gift, he soared
Even from his mother's arms aloft: in racing chariots
    His skill is now revealed.   115

ep. 4   All roads that lead to fame in his own countryside
He has been bold to tread. Now does the hand of heaven
    Gladly ensure his power;
Grant him in times to come, oh blessed sons of Cronos,
    A like success in action and in counsel.
    And may no cruel breath   120
Of wintry winds that waste the fruits of autumn,

> Strike to make havoc of his years hereafter.
> > The mighty mind of Zeus,
> As all know well, governs the destiny
> Of men he loves. I pray him now to grant
> > That at Olympia
> A like renown falls to the race of Battus.

Notes

10. Castor: the scholiasts state that there was a temple of the Dioscuri at Cyrene; this is quite likely in a Dorian city with traditions resembling those of Sparta.

after wintry storms: commentators, from the scholiasts onwards, say that this alludes to recent political upheavals in Cyrene which had prevented Arcesilas from leaving the city, so that he had to entrust his chariot to another driver. The political use of weather metaphors is common, but there is no external evidence for political troubles at Cyrene (though they may well have existed; Arcesilas fell from power some years after this and a democracy was established), and the chariot would normally be driven by someone else for its owner. The allusion is passing and has mainly the function of a polar expression, foil to the brightness of success.

24. Aphrodite's ... garden: presumably a shrine of Aphrodite which the procession would pass. (There was a garden shrine of Aphrodite in Athens – Paus. 1.19.3 – and Sappho's poems to Aphrodite also envisage worship in gardens.)

26. Carrhotus: Arcesilas' brother-in-law, and his charioteer.

34. broke no ... piece of gear: chariots were often wrecked in the course of a race: the fictitious Pythian chariot race described in Sophocles' *Electra* resulted in the destruction of nine of the ten chariots. According to line 49 below, forty drivers crashed during the event at which Carrhotus was victorious.

37. Krisa's hill: Krisa, also known as Kirrha, lay some miles down the valley from Delphi, and until the year 450 the events of the Pythian Games were held at Krisa. After his victory, Carrhotus drove his chariot from Krisa up to Delphi and consecrated it there. Pausanias (10.15.4) records a Cyrenian dedication of a chariot which contained a statue of Cyrene as driver, accompanied by Battus, whom Libya is crowning with a wreath. The sculptor, Amphion of Knossos, probably worked about the year 400, rather later than this ode.

39–40. shrine of cypress wood: the beams of Apollo's temple were of cypress, not the whole structure.

40–2. That statue: many Greek temples contained an ancient wooden statue (*xoanon*) which in the classical period came to be replaced by a bronze or even gilt one. The Cretans, according to Homeric Hymn 3.538–41, provided the first priests of Apollo's temple on its foundation in legendary times.

45. Alexibiades: Carrhotus, son of Alexibius.

49. forty drivers: the race must have been run in heats as it would be impossible to have forty drivers abreast in any stadium.

55. Or high or low: another polar expression. Gnomic utterance, as often, provides the lead-in to the myth.

57. The roaring lions: the normal version of the myth had Battus restored by his fright at the first sight of a lion; here, the restored voice is heroic enough to scare the lions in their turn!

59. powers across the sea: i.e. Apollo's oracle at Delphi.

71. the valiant sons of Heracles and of Aegimius: the ancestors of the Dorian tribes. See Glossary.

75. Aegeus' seed: the Aegidae of Sparta, a distinguished Dorian clan, apparently had a branch in Thebes, from which Pindar claimed descent (cf. I 7.15). Theras, the Spartan colonist of Thera (Paus. 3.15.8), had a son, Oeolycus, whose son was Aegeus of Sparta. Thera also sent out a colony to Cyrene: so Pindar and the people of Cyrene are cousins, as it were. Herodotus' narrative of the foundation of Cyrene (4.147–9) includes the news that the Aegids of Sparta built a temple to Laius and Oedipus, which implies close links of the clan with Thebes. There is no need to assume, as the ancient commentators hinted, that the 'I' of line 72 is actually the chorus: here, as elsewhere in the epinicians, the first-person denotes the poet. (See Lefkowitz, op. cit., in introduction.) Pindar's linking of self and celebrand is his way of asserting his worthiness to offer adequate praise.

80. Carneian festival: the Carneia was a major festival in Sparta, held in the month Carneios (July/August). Its existence in Cyrene pays tribute to that city's Spartan ancestry, but we do not know at what season it was held in Cyrene. If it was at the same time of year the ode must have been composed very swiftly after the Pythian victory.

83. Trojans: refugees from Troy, after its destruction by the Greeks, were supposed to have settled on the site which afterwards became Cyrene. Helen was said to have gone with her husband Menelaus to Egypt: the story provides the plot of Euripides' *Helen*.

86. gracious greeting: Battus and his followers, on arriving at Cyrene, are said to have honoured the memory of these Trojans as tutelary deities of the city. 'This dim legend', as Farnell calls it, may have been drawn to Pindar's attention by the fact that the procession had to pass the graves of these sons of Antenor.

87. Aristoteles: another name for Battus.

93. a road ... stone-paved: this road has been uncovered by modern excavations, and the unusual position of the hero's grave confirmed. Pindar presumably got these details from informants in Greece, perhaps Damophilus, as there is no evidence that he visited Cyrene.

103. young men's voices: the choir performing the ode.

121. wintry winds: the weather metaphor recurs (cf. line 10), and may be another reference to political instability in Cyrene.

124. Olympia: this prayer of Pindar's was granted in 460 when Arcesilas won in the chariot race at the Olympic Games. But Arcesilas lost his throne some time in the twenty years following, and was killed in the revolt that ended the monarchy.

For Xenocrates of Acragas
Winner of the Chariot Race (490)

Xenocrates was the brother of Theron, who became ruler of Acragas in 488 and, with Hieron, was one of the two most powerful rulers in Greek Sicily. Pindar later wrote the second and third Olympian odes for Theron in 476.

While this ode is addressed to Xenocrates, it is written largely in honour of his son Thrasybulus, who was probably the charioteer on this occasion. It appears that he was a charming young man and that Pindar, now twenty-eight years old, struck up a warm friendship with him, which is reflected in the language and tone of the ode. The official epinician ode for the occasion was, according to the scholiasts, commissioned from Simonides, now aged sixty-six and more widely known than the young Pindar. The ode may perhaps have been offered as an informal tribute or a speculative composition without a formal commission; the later ode for Xenocrates, Isthmian 2, has been interpreted as containing a suggestion that payment for the present ode may now be overdue, but this is probably illegitimate: see the introduction to that ode. The erotic poem of which we have frag. 124 was also addressed by Pindar to Thrasybulus.

The ode is monostrophic and therefore probably processional: it seems to have been performed as a procession to the Temple of Apollo at Delphi, whereas the regular epinician would have been performed at home in Acragas.

The myth concerns Antilochus, treated as an example of a son's fidelity to his father, appropriate on an occasion when the son Thrasybulus had steered his father's chariot to victory. Thrasybulus' action obtained enduring life in song for his father, as Antilochus rescued his father's life.

str. 1   Listen, I plough the meadow
    Of Aphrodite of the glancing eyes, or of the Graces,
      While to the shrine and centre-stone of sounding earth
        We take our way. For here,

For the blest fortune of the Emmenidae,   5
For Acragas by her river, and for Xenocrates,
    To grace the crown he won at Pytho,
  A treasure-house of song is built and ready
    In Apollo's golden-gifted vale.

str. 2   This neither winter's rain,   10
The harsh invading host, born of the thunder-cloud,
Nor down to the deep sea-bed, flung with the rolling shingle
    Shall the gales bear away;
  But in unclouded light its front shall stand,
And for your father's honour, Thrasybulus, shared   15
    By all his race, it shall proclaim
  Your chariot victory in Krisa's dell
    Glorious on the tongues of men.

str. 3   On your right hand you set him,
And thus fulfil the charge, given of old they say,   20
By Chiron on his hill to Achilles, far from home,
    The strong-armed son of Peleus: –
  'To Cronos' son, first of all gods, I bid you
To deep-voiced Zeus, lord of the lightnings and the thunder,
    Your worship in full measure pay;   25
  Then to your parents while their life shall last,
    Like honour never fail to render.'

str. 4   In years of old this bidding
Mighty Antilochus obeyed full well, giving
His life to save his father. Firm he stood awaiting   30
    The Ethiop captain's might,
  Death-dealing Memnon, when the darts of Paris
Stayed Nestor's horse and chariot, and in hot pursuit
    On old Messene's king bore down   35
  Memnon's great spear. Shaken in terror's grip
    Then loudly he cried to his son.

str. 5   Nor to the empty air
Called he in vain. There stood, godlike, heroic courage,
And bought with his own death his father's life. This
                        deed   40
    Young men of old deemed glorious,

In pride of place for valour's debt to parents.
Those days are gone. Now Thrasybulus follows still
 This rule of a father's due, and kindles,
 Matching his uncle's honour, a flame of glory.
  Wisely he rules his wealth, and reaps   45

str. 6   The rich fruit of his youth
In due justice, nor with rough pride's intemperate ardour;
And in the Muses' vale his skill is known. On thee
  Poseidon, great earth-shaker,   50
 Proud monarch of the chariot's racing steeds,
He now attends with loyal gifts, well pleasing to you.
 Sweet is the temper of his heart,
 In friendship and friends' company more sweet
 Than the bees' storeyed honeycomb.

Notes

1. I plough the meadow: for the metaphor cf. N 6.33, N 10.26; Richard Stoneman, 'Ploughing a Garland: Metaphor and Metonymy in Pindar', *Maia* 23 (1981): 125–38.

Aphrodite ... the Graces: the same two deities are invoked at the beginning of Pa. 6, performed at Delphi at an unknown date. Wilamowitz surmised that both these odes were performed at the same Pythian festival, the paean first and then this one. The Graces and Aphrodite are nowhere else conjoined in Pindar's poetry. They would be appropriate in a context of erotic admiration of Thrasybulus, for whom Pindar also wrote the erotic encomium, frag. 124ab.

5. the Emmenidae: the family to which Theron and Xenocrates belonged.

7. A treasure-house of song: the sacred precinct at Delphi contained a number of treasuries, erected by individual cities, which contained the offerings sent by them to the god. Their remains can be seen, and the Treasury of the Athenians has been reconstructed. For the metaphor of the ode as a building see the opening of O 6.

The harsh invading host: the military metaphor is later picked up by the myth, lines 30ff. For the metaphor in reverse (war as weather) see I 5.50, I 7.27 and note.

20. On your right hand you set him: i.e. you keep constantly in mind the duty you owe to your father.

22. Chiron: Achilles, like some other legendary heroes, was sent as a boy to be educated by the centaur Chiron: see N 3.43 and note. A largely lost work attributed to Hesiod, *The Precepts of Chiron*, contained advice on the education of children (frag. 285, MW) and the present passage may be derived from that work.

far from home: Conway's translation muffles the point of the epithet 'orphaned': Achilles was sent to Chiron by his father Peleus after the boy's mother, the sea-nymph Thetis, had returned to her own element.

29 Antilochus: a hero of the Trojan War, who saved his father Nestor, usually regarded as king of Pylos but here called king of neighbouring Messene, at the cost of his own life. The story was probably in the *Aethiopis*, and was followed in that poem by Achilles' killing of Memnon. Cf. *Iliad* 8.130 when Nestor is in danger but is saved by Diomedes.

45. his uncle: Theron.

49. the Muses' vale: Thrasybulus was apparently a poet or musician.

51. Poseidon: Poseidon is particularly associated with horses.

For Megacles of Athens
Winner of the Chariot Race (486)

The Pythian victory of Megacles celebrated here was won in 486, but it is not quite clear from the list of victories whether this, or one of the Olympian or Isthmian victories credited to him and other members of his family, were the immediate occasion of the ode. Megacles was a member of the wealthy and aristocratic Athenian family the Alcmaeonidae. His ancestor Alcmaeon had offered hospitality to the messengers from Croesus of Lydia to Delphi, and as thanks had been invited to visit Croesus at Sardis. Croesus offered him as much gold as he could carry away from his treasury on his person. Alcmaeon thereupon dressed in extremely baggy clothes and wide boots, filled them with gold, poured gold-dust over his hair and put some more in his mouth. Croesus was so amused that he gave him gifts of the same value again, and Alcmaeon staggered home a wealthy man (Herodotus 6.125). Thus he and his descendants could easily afford the upkeep of racehorses. Megacles' grandfather Megacles had been responsible for the rebuilding of the temple of Apollo at Delphi after it was destroyed by fire in 548. Such wealth was not well-liked in the incipient democracy of Athens, and in 490 Megacles was ostracized on the grounds of collusion with the Persian invader, as mentioned in line 18.

The full family relations are as follows:

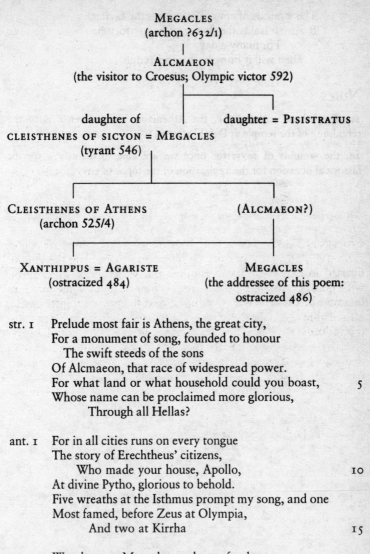

Megacles
(archon ?632/1)

|

Alcmaeon
(the visitor to Croesus; Olympic victor 592)

daughter of   daughter = Pisistratus
cleisthenes of sicyon = Megacles
(tyrant 546)

Cleisthenes of Athens   (Alcmaeon?)
(archon 525/4)

Xanthippus = Agariste   Megacles
(ostracized 484)   (the addressee of this poem:
                                ostracized 486)

str. 1   Prelude most fair is Athens, the great city,
         For a monument of song, founded to honour
             The swift steeds of the sons
         Of Alcmaeon, that race of widespread power.
         For what land or what household could you boast,   5
         Whose name can be proclaimed more glorious,
             Through all Hellas?

ant. 1   For in all cities runs on every tongue
         The story of Erechtheus' citizens,
             Who made your house, Apollo,   10
         At divine Pytho, glorious to behold.
         Five wreaths at the Isthmus prompt my song, and one
         Most famed, before Zeus at Olympia,
             And two at Kirrha   15

ep. 1   Won by you, Megacles, and your forebears.
             Now for your new success
           My heart rejoices, but I grieve
         That noble deeds find for their recompense

The wounds of envy. Yet so runs the saying,
If a man holds the flower of happy fortune   20
        For many a day,
    Then will it bring both good and ill.

Notes

10. **Erechtheus' citizens:** i.e. the Athenians. The reference is to the rebuilding of the temple at Delphi after 548.

18. **the wounds of envy:** for once we are able to identify a specific historical occasion for the application of the topos of envy.

For Aristomenes of Aegina
Winner of the Boys' Wrestling Contest (446)

The ode is dated by the statement of the scholiast to the year 446; it is therefore Pindar's last securely dated epinician. It is written throughout in an exceptionally serious tone, and editors, including Conway, have found this an unusual poem to celebrate the victory of a boy in an athletic contest. Explanations have been sought in the historical circumstances of Aegina at the time. The scholiasts give two incompatible reasons for the opening invocation of Peace at the beginning: the first is that Pindar is celebrating the conclusion of a period of civil strife in Aegina, the second is that the Persian Wars have just ended (!). Both reasons are plainly deductions by the scholiasts from Pindar's text and have no independent value (Lefkowitz, *First-Person Fictions*, p. 75). The former assumption receives some support from frag. 109, which again links Peace, good weather and the cessation of civil strife, and was cited by the historian Polybius (4.31) as an example of appeasement: it refers to the siding of Thebes with Persia in the Persian Wars. An alternative interpretation, that Peace is regarded as a symposiac virtue (M. Dickie in D. E. Gerber, *Greek Poetry and Philosophy*) seems to ignore this parallel.

There is no way of recovering the background to the alleged civil strife in Aegina at this time. It has been suggested that it resulted from attempts in Aegina to throw off the hegemony of Athens after the defeat of the latter by Thebes at Coronea in 447. The reference to the giants Porphyrion and Typhon in lines 12ff. may be an allusion to this humbling of Athenian power.

The sombre tones undoubtedly outweigh the celebratory elements in this ode, but they nonetheless belong to the epinician mode and contribute to the ultimate aim of praise of the victor and add depth to the experience of success.

str. 1   Peace, goddess of friendly intent,
    Daughter of Justice, you who make cities great,
    Holding the supreme keys of counsel and of wars –

For Aristomenes, I beg your welcome,   5
   For the honour of his victory at Pytho.
You understand well both to give and to receive
   Gifts from a gentle hand in due season.

ant. 1   But when a man breeds in his heart
   Pitiless wrath, then does your spirit fiercely
Rise up to face the enemies' power, and to throw down 10
   Insolence to the depths. Porphyrion
   Even he knew not your strength when he provoked you
Beyond all measure. Dearest of all good things to win
   Is from the house of one who gives it freely.

ep. 1   But violence brings to ruin even   15
   The boastful hard-heart soon or late.
Cilician Typhon of the hundred heads
   Could not escape his fate, nor could
   Even the great king of the Giants,
      But by the thunderbolt
   They were laid low, and by Apollo's shafts;
Who now has graciously welcomed Xenarkes' son
   From Kirrha, with the green wreath of Parnassus
   Crowning him, and the Dorian song of triumph.   20

str. 2   Near to their heart the Graces hold
   This island, queen of Justice, who knew well
The glorious valour of the sons of Aeacus;
   From the beginning perfect was her fame.
   In many a song her praise is told, the nurse   25
Of heroes of supreme renown, victors proclaimed
   On the athletes' field and in the surge of battle.

ant. 2   Glorious too, her breed of men.
   Time passes and allows me not to offer
To the lyre and softly-singing voices all the legend   30
   Of her renown – lest surfeit breed resentment.
   But for the task in hand, let me now pay
The debt to you, son, for this latest deed of glory,
   And by my art raise it on spreading wings.

ep. 2   For in the wrestler's ring your skill   35
   Put not to shame your mother's brothers,

Theognatus victor at Olympia,
   And hardy-limbed Cleitomachus,
  Matching his Isthmian victory.
     But raising high the glory
Of the Meidylid clan you bring to proof
That word of sooth which Oikleus' son long since foretold,
  When within seven-gated Thebes he saw
  Those sons stand firm in the sharp thrust of battle;   40

str. 3   When the Epigoni from Argos
   Marched on their second journey. Thus he spoke
As the battle raged: 'By nature's gift, father to son,
  Do noble souls excel. Clear is the vision   45
  My eyes behold – Alcman, a speckled dragon
Brandished upon his gleaming shield, foremost of all
  Sets foot within the gates of Cadmus' city.

ant. 3   'But he who in that first essay
   Suffered disastrous loss, hero Adrastus,   50
Is now upheld by tidings of a better omen:
  But for his house far otherwise shall it be,
  For he alone of all the Danaan host;
Shall gather up his son's dead bones, before he comes
  By the gods' fortune with his folk unscathed

ep. 3   To the broad streets of Abas.' Thus   55
   Amphiaraus' voice proclaimed.
  But I too with my own hands gladly set
   Garlands on Alcman's grave, and shower
   The dewdrops of my song upon him.
    For he is neighbour to me,
  And is the guardian of my possessions,
And when to the centre-stone of earth, that home of song,
  I made my way, he met me and proved the skills
  Of prophecy that all his race inherit.   60

str. 4   But thou, god of the far-shot arrows,
   Ruling the glorious temple in the glens
Of Pytho, where all find a welcome, thou hast given
  Aristomenes this greatest of all joys;
  And once in his own land you gave to him

The treasured prize of the Pentathlon, at the feast   65
    Of Leto's children. O king, now I pray thee

ant. 4   Look down with kind intent to hear
        My harmonies, where and for whomsoever
    My music brings its varied notes. Those mellow voices   70
    In songs of triumph have Justice at their side.
        For the fortunes of your house I beg, Xenarkes,
    The gods' unfailing favour. Many a man may think
        That he who wins success with no long labour

ep. 4   Is a wise man 'midst fools, arming   75
        His life with skills of prudent counsel.
    But success lies not in the power of men;
        It is a deity bestows it,
        Exalting one man now, another
            Crushing beneath strong hands.
    Forward then, but with measured step. Megara
And Marathon's plain gave you their prize; and your own
    country
    At Hera's contest, Aristomenes,
        Saw you indeed prevailing, thrice a victor.   80

str. 5   Now from on high on four young bodies
        You hurled your strength with fierce intent. For them
    No happy homecoming from Pytho was decreed,
        As that of yours, nor at their mother's side   85
        Could pleasant laughter ring a joyful greeting
    For their return. But shunning hostile eyes, they creep
        By quiet paths, o'erwhelmed by their ill-fortune.

ant. 5   But he to whom is given new glory
        In the rich sweetness of his youth, flies up
    Aloft, high hope fulfilled, on wings of soaring valour,   90
        In realms that brook no dullard cares of wealth.
        But man's delight flowers but for a brief moment,
    And no less swiftly falls to the ground again, shattered
        By destined will that may not be gainsaid.

ep. 5   Creatures of a day! What is a man?   95
        What is he not? A dream of a shadow

Is our mortal being. But when there comes to men
A gleam of splendour given of Heaven,
Then rests on them a light of glory
And bléssed are their days.
Aegina, mother beloved, grant that in freedom
This city's onward path be set, by the goodwill
Of Zeus and great king Aeacus, of Peleus
And noble Telamon and of Achilles.   100

Notes

1. **Peace:** see introduction to ode. Praised also at O 4.16.

8ff.: But when a man: political harmony is a strong defence against
aggression: the moral is the opposite of that drawn from Polybius
regarding frag. 109, an approval of appeasement.

12. Porphyrion: king of the Giants who took part in the struggle against
Zeus and the other Olympian gods. The view that Insolence (hybris)
was their downfall is the standard one: cf. B 15.57-63.

13. Dearest of all good things: the sentence emphasizes the greater
value of gifts given freely than possessions taken by force, i.e. the gifts
of Peace to her own citizens.

16. Typhon: another of the Giants, whose birthplace in legend was in
Cilicia. In P 1 Pindar pictures him confined beneath Mt Etna.

17. thunderbolt: the weapon of Zeus. Usually Zeus is said to have
defeated both, but Apollo is introduced as a transition to the subject of
the Pythian victory.

19. Xenarkes' son: Aristomenes.

20. green wreath: literally 'grass'; i.e. the laurel of which the victor's
wreath was made.

21. the Graces: as illuminators of athletic success.

22. queen of Justice: the island had a high reputation for fair dealing in
its trading ventures, but the reference here probably also includes its
political situation at the time.

33. son: i.e. Aristomenes.

35. your mother's brothers: nothing further is known of Cleitomachus.

Theognatus' name is retored in *POxy* 222.15 (a list of Olympic victors) as winner in the boys' wrestling at Olympia in 476. A statue was erected in his honour by Ptolichos of Aegina: see Paus. 6.9.1. An epigram attributed to Simonides (D. L. Page, *Further Greek Epigrams* [Cambridge 1981], p. 244) also celebrates this victory, but is probably a composition by a learned Alexandrian poet rather than a contemporary.

38. the Meidylid clan: to which Aristomenes belonged.

39. Oikleus' son: Amphiaraus, the seer who accompanied the Seven against Thebes under the leadership of Adrastus, king of Argos. The prophecy recounted here refers to the second expedition against Thebes, made a generation later (hence called the expedition of the Epigoni) and led by Alcmaeon (the Doric form is Alcman), the son of Amphiaraus. The occasion of Amphiaraus' prophecy is not made clear, but it may be based on the narrative somewhere in Stesichorus' *Eriphyle*, where frag. 148 runs: '. . . the hero Adrastus addressed [him] thus: "Alcmaeon, why have you risen up leaving the feasts and the fine singer?" The son of Amphiaraus, beloved of Ares, replied, "You may drink and delight your soul with festivity; but I . . ."' The legend of the Seven against Thebes was also the subject of Bacchylides' ninth ode. This is the only non-Aeginetan myth told in any of Pindar's Aeginetan odes.

44. By nature's gift: one of Pindar's favourite themes, the superiority of inherited talent, provides a point of contact between the successes of Aristomenes and the legend of Amphiaraus and his son.

52. far otherwise: although the second expedition was successful, Aegialeus, the son of Adrastus, was killed. Normally Adrastus was said to have died immediately of grief on hearing the news, and did not return to Argos.

55. streets of Abas: the city of Argos. Abas was a legendary early king of the city.

56. I too: the scholiasts explain this passage in various ways, by reference to a hero-shrine of Alcmaeon in Aegina, or near Pindar's house in Thebes, or by saying that Amphiaraus is Pindar's neighbour. Plainly they are guessing. The passage does seem to imply that Pindar lived close to a shrine of Alcmaeon and perhaps deposited his valuables there for safekeeping. The passage should be interpreted in the light of other poetic statements about meetings with divinities, like Hesiod's vision of the Muses at the beginning of the *Theogony*. Pindar may be suggesting that his vision of Alcmaeon included a prophecy of Aristomenes' victory; no doubt Aristomenes would have understood the point. Pindar's meeting with Alcmaeon is quickly echoed in Aristomenes' welcome from the gods: line 66.

65. feast of Leto's children: the Delphinia, an Aeginetan festival dedicated to Apollo and Artemis.

71. Justice at their side: Aristomenes' victory, and its praise, are well deserved; but the phrase has a deeper resonance, for Justice flourishes in cities where there is Peace, and the justice of Aegina was already alluded to in line 22.

72. Xenarkes: the father of Aristomenes. It is usual to include an address to the father in an ode for a boy victor.

78. with measured step: the word translated 'forward then' specifically means 'enter the games'. Pindar is advising the boy not to be a pothunter.

Megara and Marathon: the Alcathoia and an unidentified festival.

79. Hera: the Hecatombaea held in Aegina.

81. four young bodies: up to eight pairs might compete in the wrestling. A knockout competition would entail four bouts for the eventual victor.

85. no happy homecoming: this gloating over the defeat of the losers is unpleasant, but Pindar expresses the sorrow and pain of defeat as a foil to Aristomenes' glory.

92. man's delight: the topoi of victory are expressed through lament for man's ephemeral nature. For other downbeat endings to odes of praise, cf. O 5.24 and note; Introduction p. xxx.

95. dream of a shadow: a proverbial phrase, *onar skias*, facetiously altered by Aristophanes (*Acharnians* 686) to *onou skia*, 'shadow of a donkey'.

98. in freedom: the phrase picks up the emphasis on civil concord at the beginning of the ode.

100. Aeacus: the great heroes of Aegina make a belated appearance in the last line of the ode, as guarantors of his prayer.

For Telesicrates of Cyrene
Winner of the Race in Armour (474)

The city of Cyrene was a prosperous Greek colony in Libya. It was ruled by the Battiad monarchy until about 440 when the king was deposed and a democracy established. The ode launches with very little preamble into the beautifully told myth of the love of Apollo for the nymph Cyrene, and establishes the amatory theme which is prominent in the ode: cf. line 74 'fair women', lines 97–100 on the girls' admiration for the victorious Telesicrates, and the marriage story which concludes the ode. The erotic attractiveness of the victor is a common topic of praise in the epinicians, but the dominance of it here has led commentators to suppose that perhaps Telesicrates was about to be married. A more complex interpretation is offered by Leonard Woodbury, 'Cyrene and the *Teleuta* of Marriage in Pindar's Ninth Pythian Ode', *TAPA* 112 (1982): 245–58: he compares Apollo's gaze on the masculine but lovely Cyrene with the girls' gaze on Telesicrates, and emphasizes the congruence of erotic desirability with service to the polis. See further Anne Carson, 'Wedding at Noon in Pindar's Ninth Pythian', *GRBS* 23 (1982): 121–8, with further bibliography.

str. 1   The Pythian victory let me now proclaim,
        With the deep-girdled Graces' aid,
    Of Telesicrates, clad in his brazen armour,
        And cry aloud his happy name,
     Who brings a crown of glory to Cyrene,
        Famed for her charioteers:
   She it was whom once Apollo of the flowing hair   5
        Seized from the windswept vales of Pelion,
    And in his golden car bore off the huntress maid;
        And of a land, most richly blessed
     With flocks and fruits, made her the enthronéd queen,
    To find on this third root of earth's mainland
        A smiling and fertile home.

ant. 1   And Aphrodite of the silver feet
        Welcomed this guest from Delos, laying   10
    The touch of her light hand upon his god-built car,
       And o'er the sweet bliss of their bridal
      She spread love's shy and winsome modesty,
        Plighting in joint wedlock
    The god and maiden daughter of wide-ruling Hypseus.
      He was then king of the proud Lapithae,
    A hero of the seed of the great god of Ocean,
       Child of the second generation,
       Whom in the famous dells of Pindus once   15
      The Nymph, daughter of Earth, Creusa bore,
       Sharing the joys of love

ep. 1   With the river-god Peneius. And by Hypseus
    Was reared this maid, Cyrene of the lovely arms.
       But she loved not the pacing tread
       This way and that beside the loom,
       Nor the delights of merry feasts
    With her companions of the household. But the bronze –
                           tipped 20
      Javelin and the sword called her to combat
       And slay the wild beasts of the field;
       And in truth many a day she gave
      Of peaceful quiet to her father's cattle.
      But of sleep, sweet companion of her pillow,
      Little she spared to steal upon her eyes
       Towards the dawn of day.   25

str. 2   Once as she battled with a fearsome lion,
       Alone, without a spear, Apollo,
    Far-shooting god of the broad quiver, came upon her;
       And straightway called from out his dwelling
      Chiron and thus addressed him: 'Son of Philyra,
       Come from your holy cave,   30
    And marvel at a woman's spirit and mighty vigour;
      With what undaunted mind she wages battle,
    A young maid with a heart that rides o'er every labour,
       And a spirit that is never shaken
      By the cold storms of fear. What mortal father
      Begot this maid? And from what race of men
       Has she been reft, to dwell

ant. 2   'Within the dark dells of these clouded mountains?
                For her soul breeds a boundless wealth
        Of valour. Is it right to lay on her the touch
                Of an ennobling hand, or even   35
                To pluck the flower of love, sweeter than honey?'
                    Then spoke the inspired Centaur,
        Gentle laughter gleaming beneath his kindly brows
            And of his wisdom made straightway this answer:
        'Secret, great Phoebus, are the keys of wise Persuasion
                To love's true sanctities; both gods   40
            And men alike, in reverent modesty,
            Are loth to taste in the open light of day
                The first sweet fruits of love.

ep. 2   'Yet thou, for whom even to savour falsehood
        Is sacrilege, art led by thy desire's delight
                Thus to dissemble. Dost thou ask,
                O king, of what race is the maiden?
                Thou who knowest well the fated end   45
        Of all things, whither all roads shall lead, who know'st the
                                                          number
            Of leaves that earth puts forth to meet the spring,
                How many grains of sand the surge
                Of ocean, or the sweeping gales
            Send rolling down beside the river banks;
            Thou who see'st clearly what shall be, and whence
        It shall betide! Yet if I needs must rival
                My wisdom against thine,   50

str. 3   'Thus shall I speak: to this glade didst thou come
                To be a husband to this maid,
        With the intent to carry her far o'er the ocean,
                To a choice garden of great Zeus.
            There thou shalt set her to rule o'er a city,
                And gather an island folk
        To be her people, where a high hill crowns the plain.   55
            And soon shall Libya, queen of spreading meadows,
        Gladly welcome to her gold halls thy glorious bride;
                And forthwith will she freely give her,
            To be her own lawful domain, a portion
            Of land yielding all manner of rich fruits,
                And beasts for the hunter's chase.

ant. 3   'There shall she bear a son, whom glorious Hermes
                 Will take from his fond mother's breast,
            And carry to the enthronéd Hours and Mother Earth;   60
                 And they will gently nurse the babe
               Upon their knees, and on his lips distil
                     Ambrosia and nectar,
            And shall ordain him an immortal being, a Zeus
            Or holy Apollo, a joy to men who love him.
            And he shall ever be at hand to tend their flocks,
                 Agreus his name to some, to others
               Nomius, and some will call him Aristaeus.'   65
               So Chiron spoke and decreed for the god
                    His bridal's dear fulfilment.

ep. 3   Swift is the act, and short thereto the paths
            When gods make speed to achieve an eager end. That day,
                  That very day saw the decision,
                  And in a chamber of rich gold
                  In Libya they lay together.
            There she is guardian of a city rich in beauty,   70
               And glorious in the Games. For at holy Pytho
                  With the sweet flower of his success,
                  Carneades' son has dowered Cyrene,
            And by his victory proclaimed her glory.
            Gladly will she receive him, as he brings
            From Delphi to his country of fair women
                    The fame all men desire.   75

str. 4   Brave deeds, high merits are ever rich in story,
                 But great themes briefly to embroider
            Wins the ear of the wise; yet, above all, true timing
                 Achieves the furthest goal. This precept
               Iolaus long ago was seen to honour,
                  By Thebes of the seven gates.   80
            For when this hero had struck off Eurystheus' head
               With his sword's shining blade, the city laid him
            To rest beneath the earth within Amphitryon's tomb,
                 The charioteer, his father's father,
               Where that great guest of the Sparti was laid,
               Who came to dwell in the Cadmeans' city,
                    Those riders of white steeds.

ant. 4   Wife to Amphitryon, and bearing, too,
                 Within her womb the seed of Zeus,
        The wise Alcmene, in single pangs of labour, bore   85
                 Twin sons invincible in battle.
            Dumb is the man whose tongue never made play
                 With Heracles' great name,
        And has not ever in remembrance Dirke's stream,
            That nourished him and Iphicles. Now would I
        To both sing songs of triumph, who served me in good stead,
                 Answering my prayer; and may I never
            Lose the pure light of the sweet-singing Graces,   90
            For thrice at Aegina and by Nisus' hill
                 Have I sung this city's glory,

ep. 4   And thus escaped the blame of helpless silence.
        Wherefore let no man, whether he be friend or foe
                 Seek to conceal an act well done
                 For the good of all, thereby contemning
                 The rule which Nereus once proclaimed,
        The Old Man of the Sea: 'Even to an enemy   95
            If he is acting nobly, we should offer
                 Full-hearted praise and that most justly'.
            How many a crown, too, have you won
        At the season's feast of Pallas, where young maidens
        Watching, each breathed a silent prayer that one
        Like Telesicrates might be her well-loved
                 Husband or dearest son,   100

str. 5   Whether at the Olympian Games, or at the contests
                 In the vale of deep-breasted Earth
        And all the games of your own land. But while I seek
                 To slake my thirst for song, a voice
            Bids me requite a debt, and for your forbears
                 Revive their ancient glory,
        Telling the tale, how for a Libyan bride they rode   105
            To the city of Irasa, to seek the hand
        Of Antaeus' glorious daughter, maid of the lovely hair.
            Many a gallant chief of men
        Of her own kin, and many a stranger sought her
        To be his bride, for indeed was her beauty
                 Wonderful to behold.

ant. 5   And much they longed to cull the ripened fruit
        Of Youth's fair vision, golden-crowned.   110
    But planning for his child a yet more glorious marriage,
        Her father called to mind the story,
      How Danaus long ago achieved in Argos
        For eight and forty daughters,
Before the noon of day, the speediest of marriage.
      For he set all the gathered company
There at the finish of the race-course, and proclaimed
        That all the heroes who were come   115
      To be his daughter's suitors, must decide
      By trial of their speed of foot, which maid
        For each should be his bride.

ep. 5   So too the Libyan king, to a groom thus chosen
Offered his daughter's hand. And at the line he set her,
        Adorned in all her fair array
        To be the goal and final prize;
        And declared to them all: 'That man
Who first, leading the field, shall touch the maiden's
                    robes,   120
      Shall take her for his bride.' Then down the course
        Swiftest of all, Alexidamus
      Raced to his prize, the noble maid,
    And through the ranks of Nomad horsemen led her
    By hand, while they flung countless sprays and wreaths
    On him who many a time e'er this had worn
        The plumes of Victory.   125

Notes

4. Cyrene: city and nymph at once.

7. richly blessed with flocks and fruits: the land of Libya was noted for its fertility in classical times.

12. Hypseus: king of the Lapiths, who dwelt in the region around the mouth of the River Peneius; father of Cyrene, he is spoken of as a grandson of Poseidon because his father was the River Peneius, and all river-gods are sons of Poseidon. Cyrene's mother was Creusa, daughter of Ge (Earth).

25. sleep: the girl watched all night to guard the cattle and then rose very early to go hunting.

26. with a fearsome lion: this passage was imitated by Ronsard, Odes 1.3, ant. 1, where he states that Apollo fell in love with the nymph Florence when she was fighting a wolf on the banks of the Arno.

came upon her: this beautifully lucid and straightforward narrative takes a linear form unusual among Pindar's myths.

29. Chiron: the son of Philyra by Cronos: see P 3.1ff. and note. Surprised in the act of making love to Philyra by his wife Rhea, Cronos turned himself into a stallion, thus causing Philyra's child to be half-man. half-horse.

39. Persuasion: persuasion is regularly conceived of as having an erotic force in Greek.

55. an island folk: Cyrene was founded by colonists from Thera, as is described in P 4 and P 5.

65. Aristaeus: a deity of agricultural work, especially sheep-keeping, cheese-making and olive cultivation. He was regarded as the inventor of bee-keeping: see Virgil, *Georgics* 4.315ff. His name means 'harvester', while his titles of Agreus and Nomius mean respectively 'hunter' and 'shepherd'; the three titles are repeated by Apollonious Rhodius, 2.500ff. His story is retold by Diodorus Siculus, 4.81, on the basis of Pindar's account.

71. Carneades' son: Telesicrates.

74. country of fair women: possibly an allusion to an impending betrothal or marriage of Telesicrates.

76. Brave deeds: the actual praise of Telesicrates' victory is unusually brief, but the transition via Iolaus to Heracles puts Telesicrates in the same category as the greatest of athlete-heroes.

79. This precept: the sentence is difficult. Conway's translation is the usual one, but it may alternatively mean 'Thebes observed Iolaus honouring him [i.e. Telesicrates]'. That is, the sentence alludes to a victory of Telesicrates at the Iolaeia in Thebes: Bundy 17ff.

79. Iolaus: son of Iphicles and nephew of Heracles. When news reached him that Eurystheus, king of Mycenae, was planning to kill the children of Heracles, he prayed that he might be restored to his youthful strength in order to prevent this. His prayer was granted, Eurystheus slain, and the children saved by his timely action.

82. that great guest of the Sparti: Amphitryon's native city was Argos before he came to settle in Thebes. The Sparti are the Sown Men, who grew from the teeth of a dragon sown by Cadmus in the soil of Thebes.

86. Twin sons: Heracles and Iphicles.

88. in good stead: what favour is this? Possibly Pindar refers to a victory of Telesicrates at the Heracleia in Thebes, and speaks as if his interests and the victor's are identical (Bundy, p. 70). Several expressions in the prayer are conventional; cf. the phrases at Theognis 341ff.

90. thrice at Aegina: the list of victories continues with Aeginetan victories and one at the Alcathoia of Megara.

91. this city: such expressions always refer to the city of the laudandus (Bundy, p. 23, n.53). Some commentators have taken it to be a reference to Thebes and an apology by Pindar for some imagined dereliction of his patriotic duty. It looks forward to the reference to the citizens in line 93.

94. Nereus: the Old Man of the Sea. It is not known what Pindar's source is for the sentiment; perhaps there was a poem, 'Sayings of Nereus' or the like.

95. Even to an enemy: the expression is a polar one; the idea of friends calls forth that of enemies; it should not be taken as implying that Telesicrates has particular enemies.

98. feast of Pallas: this can only mean the Panathenaea. It would be very odd to refer to a local festival of Cyrene in these terms. It is surprising that Telesicrates should have competed *often* at the Panathenaea; and why would Athenian girls have been thinking of Telesicrates as a husband? But from the next lines it appears that Telesicrates had spent some time competing at Athens.

101. Olympian Games: women were not admitted to the Olympic Games. Furthermore, the word for Olympian here is neuter plural, and the Olympic Games would be described in the feminine singular. The reference must be to some other Olympian Games, perhaps those at Athens, which were held on the 19th Munichion (April/May). The main event was cavalry racing (Parke, p. 144).

102. deep-breasted Earth: probably the festival of Ge and the Nymphs at Athens, held on 27th Boedromion (September/October). ('In the vale' is not in the Greek.)

105. Antaeus: an ancestor of Telesicrates, through his daughter who married Alexidamus (line 121). No other source describes his bride-race, which is a common folklore motif.

112. Danaus: This is not the usual story of the fifty daughters of Danaus who murdered their husbands (except two), as alluded to in N 10.6 (see note), but refers to a second attempt to find husbands for the remaining forty-eight daughters (Hypermestra and Amymone were already spoken for).

> No one would marry them because they were criminals, so he announced he would give them away without a bride price to anyone who thought they were beautiful; some men did turn up though not many, so he held a race for them, and the first home had first choice and the second home had second choice and so on down to the last. The girls left over had to wait for more lovers to arrive and another race.
>
> (Paus. 3.12.2)

122. Nomad horsemen: the pastoralists of Libya. The word is used by Polybius as an equivalent for 'Numidian'.

For Hippocleas of Thessaly
Winner of the Boys' Double-Stade Foot Race (498)

This is the earliest of Pindar's odes that we possess, written when he was twenty years old. It is his only ode for a Thessalian patron. Hippocleas was a native of Pelinnaeon (or Pelinna) in western Thessaly.

The Aleuadae, 'sons of Aleuas', mentioned in the opening strophe were an aristocratic Thessalian family who claimed descent from Heracles and had an important place in the government of Thessaly. It was this family who commissioned this ode on behalf of Hippocleas. The head of the clan at the time was Thorax, to whom Pindar expresses his thanks in the fourth strophe; perhaps Pindar had prior family connections which secured him this early commission. Thorax and his brothers, Eurypylus and Thrasydaeus (69), took the side of the invading Persians, as did Thebes, in 480.

The myth in this ode concerns the Hyperboreans, the 'people who live beyond the North Wind'. They were especially loved by Apollo, which would be an appropriate reason for their employment in a Pythian ode. Perseus, the other subject of the myth, also had Thessalian connections as an ancestor of Heracles and thus of the Aleuadae. The scholiasts, however, castigated the myth in this ode as a 'pointless digression'; but see note on line 20.

str. 1   Happy is Sparta; blessed is Thessaly,
       For from one ancestor has each its king,
       Sprung from great Heracles valiant in battle.
          And is this boast untimely?
       No, for Pytho and Pelinnaeon call me
       And the sons of Aleuas, bidding me
       Bring for the honour of Hippocleas,   5
       This choir of men in glory's song of triumph

ant. 1   For he is tasting of the contests' joy,
       And the vale of Parnassus has declared him,

To all the neighbouring folk, first of the boys
    Who ran the double course.
Be it sped by heaven's will, sweet, O Apollo,   10
Is a man's success, its end and its beginning;
And this he owes first to your favour, then
To his heritage of skill, bred from his father,

ep. 1   Who won Olympia's prize
Twice in the race of men armoured for war;
And at the contest in the folded meadow
Beneath the rock of Kirrha, the fleet foot   15
    Of Phrikias once again
Gave him the victor's crown. May a kind fate
  Alike in days to come, grant them
Fresh blossoms to adorn their wealthy splendour.

str. 2   Of the dear joys that Hellas gives, they hold
No meagre share, and may they meet from heaven
No envious turning of the ways. Whose heart   20
    Knows naught of sorrow, let him
Be named a god. But happy, and well worthy
Of poets' song, is he whose valiant skill
Of hand or foot wins for his strength and daring
The highest prize of victory in the Games,

ant. 2 Or he who lives to see his youthful son   25
By fit decree of fate win Pytho's crowns.
Not for his feet the brazen vault of heaven;
    Yet of the fairest glories
That mortals may attain, to him is given
To sail to the furthest bound. Yet neither ship
Nor marching feet may find the wondrous way
To the gatherings of the Hyperborean people.   30

ep. 2   Yet was it with these that Perseus
The warrior chief once feasted, entering
Their homes, and chanced upon their sacrifices
Unto the god, those famous offerings
    Of hecatombs of asses;
For in their banquets and rich praise Apollo   35

Greatly delights, and laughs to see
The rampant lewdness of those brutish beasts.

str. 3　　Nor is the Muse a stranger to their life,
But on all sides the feet of maidens dancing,
The full tones of the lyre and pealing flutes
　　　Are all astir; with leaves
Of gleaming laurel bound upon their hair,　　　　40
They throng with happy hearts to join the revel.
Illness and wasting old age visit not
This hallowed race, but far from toil and battle

ant. 3　　They dwell secure from fate's remorseless vengeance.
There with the breath of courage in his heart,
Unto that gathering of happy men,
　　　By guidance of Athene,
Came long ago the son of Danaë,　　　　45
Perseus, who slew the Gorgon, and brought her head
Wreathed with its serpent locks to strike stony
Death to the islanders. But no marvel,

ep. 3　　　Be it wrought by the gods,
Can to me ever seem beyond belief.　　　　50
Hold now your oar, and quickly from the prow
Cast anchor to the deep sea-bed, to hold
　　　Our ship from the rocky reef.
For like a bee flitting from flower to flower,
　　The rich strain of my songs of triumph
Lights now on one tale now upon another.

str. 4　　But while the men of Ephyra pour forth　　　　55
My pleasant songs beside Peneius' bank,
I hope that for the crowns he won, my music
　　　May bring Hippocleas
Yet greater glory amongst his own age-fellows
And amongst elder folk, and tender maids
Cherish his image in their hearts. Who knows?
Or here or there the shafts of love may strike.　　　　60

ant. 4　　Let every man who strives, and wins his aim,
Grasp and hold firm today's eager desire;

What may betide a twelve-month hence, the mind
    Of no man can foresee.
In Thorax is my trust, my generous host,
Who labours for my pleasure, and has yoked
This four-horsed chariot of the Muse, in friendship   65
Given and returned, leading my willing steps.

ep. 4   As gold shows its true worth
When tried upon the touchstone, so too shines forth
An upright mind. Now shall my praises ring
In honour also of his noble brothers,
    For they make prosperous
And glorify the state of Thessaly.   70
    In good men's hands, born of true blood,
The pilotage of cities rests secure.

Notes

4. Pelinnaeon: Hippocleas' native city, perhaps better named Pelinna.

16. Phrikias: the father of Hippocleas.

20. from heaven no envious turning . . .: the gnomic passage about the level of happiness which mortals can expect looks forward to the contrasting state of the Hyperboreans who are blessed even though they are not gods. 'Fate's remorseless vengeance' (line 44), which they are spared, picks up the anxiety in this line about the gods' envy of success.

30. the wondrous way: the word for 'wondrous' is repeated at line 48, 'no marvel . . . wrought by the gods'.

31. Perseus: Pindar is the only writer to refer to this visit of Perseus to the Hyperboreans. Perseus fulfils in this ode the role that in most other odes is borne by Heracles, the exemplar of the extreme of human achievement, which none can surpass.

33. the god: Apollo, who spent a season of each year away from Delphi, feasting with the Hyperboreans: cf. O 3.16.

hecatombs of asses: a hecatomb is a sacrifice of a hundred beasts. The donkey sacrifices of the Hyperboreans are referred to also by Callimachus, frag. 186.8–10, 492. Donkeys were often sacrificed to ithyphallic deities in real life, and the ritual may have involved castration, which would give point to Pindar's reference to the animals' large erections. See W. Burkert, *Homo Necans* (1983) p. 69, who also notes that the Moi-Sedang of Vietnam habitually laugh during the castration of an animal.

45. Perseus: the story of Perseus and the Gorgon is told in P 12. Perseus brought the head of Medusa, which turned anyone who looked at it to stone, back to the island of Seriphos, where his mother Danaë was held captive by King Polydectes, and turned the king and his followers into stone.

51. Hold now your oar: Pindar addresses himself and breaks off his myth to make a new beginning.

55. men of Ephyra: his chorus. There is no known place called Ephyra in Thessaly, and the designation is puzzling. Pelinna is on the River Peneius.

62. today's eager desire: I prefer to translate 'attainable goals'.

65. chariot of the Muse: this ode, commissioned by Thorax. For the metaphor cf. O 9.81.

For Thrasydaeus of Thebes
Winner of the Boys' Foot Race (474 or 454)

The scholiasts tell us that the name Thrasydaeus appeared twice in the Pythian victor lists, once under the date 474 and once for 454. Two events were in question, the diaulos (double stadium) and the stadium. Though their expression is confused, the order in which the events are named suggests that the diaulos victory was the earlier. One scholiast stated that the ode was for the stadion victory, as does the heading in the manuscripts, not the diaulos, and this is what Pindar also says at line 49.

It seems unlikely that the same Thrasydaeus is in question on both occasions: one who was a boy in 474 would be in his mid thirties in 454 and unlikely to be on top running form in the men's class. The fact that much of the praise is devoted to the victor's father is evidence that the victor is, as the heading informs us, a boy.

The question of date is important because it reflects on the myth used in the ode, which concerns the murder of Agamemnon by Clytemnestra. It has seemed to many readers that Pindar's handling of the myth betrays a clear awareness of the treatment in Aeschylus' *Oresteia*, staged in Athens in 458. But other critics have thought that the comments about tyranny in line 53 best fit a period when Pindar had just returned from the Sicily of the tyrants, and was at pains to defend his reputation in aristocratic (and therefore anti-tyrannical) Thebes. Similar phrases occur at P 9.80–91 (of 474), but it is hard to know whether to attach any weight to such 'biographical' elements in the odes. For discussions of the issues see C. M. Bowra, *Pindar* (Oxford 1964), Appendix 1, pp. 402–5, and John Herington, 'Pindar's Eleventh Pythian Ode' in D. E. Gerber (ed.), *Greek Poetry and Philosophy: Studies ... in Honour of Leonard Woodbury* (Chico 1984), pp. 137–46.

The ode was apparently performed at the Ismenion in Thebes, the chief shrine of Apollo there, at nightfall (line 10). A fragmentary poem probably by Corinna (*Papiri della Società*

Italiana 1174) is entitled *Orestes*, and was performed somewhere in Thebes at moonrise. It is possible that poems on
Apolline themes (which the story of Orestes is) were felt
appropriate for festivals centred on the Ismenion. See D. L.
Page, *Corinna* (London 1963), pp. 27–8.

The myth as told by Pindar in lines 17ff. follows closely the
outlines known to us from Aeschylus' *Oresteia*. The myth was a
familiar one, already referred to in the *Odyssey* (11.404–34,
though with no reference to the sacrifice of Iphigeneia, and
3.193ff., 303–5, where Aegisthus is the chief culprit). It was
perhaps also in the epic *Nostoi* ('Returns of the Heroes').
Stesichorus (?632–566) made it the subject of one of his long
lyric narratives (*PMG* 215–19) and it became popular in Attic
red-figure vase-painting, perhaps as a result of the treatment by
Aeschylus. (For a summary of the literary tradition, see E.
Vermeule, 'The Boston Oresteia Krater', 70 [1966]: 1–22.). Stesichorus was probably the first to make Clytemnestra the chief
criminal in the case. It is possible that Pindar drew directly on
Stesichorus, but the unusual question form of the allusions in
lines 22ff. indicates (to some readers) a direct response to the
issues raised in dramatic form in Aeschylus' great drama.

str. 1   Daughter of Cadmus, Semele
       From your high place amidst the queens of heaven,
       And Ino Leucothea, you who dwell
       By the immortal sea-nymphs, Nereus' daughters,
       Come with the noble mother of Heracles
          To the shrine of Melia,
        To the treasure-house of golden tripods,
        The temple that above all others
          Apollo held in honour,   5

ant. 1   And he named it the Ismenion,
       The seat of prophecy that knows no lie.
       Daughters of Harmonia, the god now summons
       To assemble here that band of heroine women
       Who dwelt within this land, that you may sing
          In praise of holy Themis
        And Pytho, and the centre-stone
        Of earth, whose word is justice – here
          As evening's shadows fall.   10

ep. 1   Thebes will you honour, city of seven gates,
              And the contest of Kirrha,
          Where Thrasydaeus has once more enriched
          His father's house with a third victor's crown,
          Won in the rich domain of Pylades,   15
          Host of Orestes of Laconia:

str. 2   Orestes, whom, when the murderer's blade
          Had slain his father, his nurse Arsinoë
          Saved from the dread hand and the grievous guile
          Of Clytemnestra; when the maid Cassandra
          Daughter of Dardan Priam, felt the edge
              Of the bright sword of bronze;
              When with the soul of Agamemnon,   20
              To the dark shores of Acheron
                  That ruthless woman's will

ant. 2   Had sent her hasting down. Whence came this?
          Maybe was it Iphigeneia, done to death
          Far from her home beside Euripus' banks,
          Sparked that harsh-handed rage within her soul?
          Or in thraldom to her paramour's bed, her nightly   25
              Adulterous joy beguiled her?
              A sin that is most sorely loathed
              By new-wed brides, that can never
                  Be hid away, the prey

ep. 2   Of strangers' chatter, while the tongues of neighbours
              Take joy in tales of evil.
          For wealth earns ever an equal toll of envy,
          But a man of humble lot may boast unheard.   30
          Thus he died, that heroic son of Atreus,
          Returned after long years to famed Amyclae;

str. 3   Who destroyed, too, the prophet maid,
          When the city of Troy was burnt in flames
          For Helen's sake, and to their sumptuous homes
          He had wrought ruin. But his son, yet a child,
          Came to old Strophius, to be his guest,   35
              Dwelling beneath Parnassus.
              Then, grown in years, with the god of War

Beside him, he slew his mother, and gave
    Aegisthus to bloody death.

ant. 3   Look, friends, how on a changing path
Where three ways meet, my steps are whirled about,
Though following a straight road heretofore.
Some gale, is it, has carried me off course,   40
Like a sea-going barque? Ah Muse, 'tis yours,
    If you agreed to hire
    Your voice for pay or silver fee,
    To praise now one name, then another,
        Weaving a mingled theme,

ep. 3   Whether singing his father's Pythian crown,
        Or Thrasydaeus' honour;
For the joy and glory of both flame like a fire.   45
In days gone by their racing chariot won
At Olympia's far-famed contest a rich glory,
Bright as the sunlight's gleam, with their swift steeds;

str. 4   Then, entering the lists at Pytho
For stripped runners, their swift feet put to shame
The host of all Hellas. May the gods grant me   50
To love the fair things that their grace bestows,
And strive for that my life's prime can attain.
    In the affairs of cities
    The greatest blessings flow, I deem,
    From the middle stream of men; the lot
        Of tyrants I deplore.

ant. 4   On fine deeds for the common weal
My hopes are set; the doom of jealous envy
Is put to naught, if a man gains the heights   55
And through a peaceful life shuns the fell path
Of pride. His onwards steps will find the verge
    Of death's dark day more gracious,
    Leaving to his beloved kin
    Of all possessions the most blest,
        An honourable name.

ep. 4   This it was spread abroad the wide-sung praise
                Of Iolaus' glory,   60
         And of the might of Castor, and your fame
         O royal Pollux; you twin sons divine,
         Who live today within Therapnae's dwellings,
         Tomorrow in the halls of high Olympus.

Notes

1–2 Semele ... Ino: daughters of Cadmus and Harmonia, victims of tragic deaths who were subsequently immortalized, Semele as a goddess on Olympus, Ino as the sea-nymph Leucothea.

4. Melia: the mother by Apollo of Ismenus, of whom nothing is known but that the Ismenion shrine and the River Ismenus at Thebes bore his name.

Pytho: named not only because the victory is Pythian but because it is the chief centre of Apollo worship; the justice of the oracle points towards the role of the oracle in the myth of Orestes, though this is not explicitly stated in the ode.

14. a third victor's crown: this includes his father's Olympic victories, mentioned at lines 46–8.

15. domain of Pylades: Pylades, the son of Strophius of Phocis (in which Delphi lies), befriended Orestes when he fled into exile after the murder of his father Agamemnon by Clytemnestra. The epithet provides the transition to the myth of Orestes and Clytemnestra.

16. Orestes of Laconia: this implies the location of the home of Agamemnon and Clytemnestra at Amyclae near Sparta; Aeschylus places it in Argos, and Homer in Mycenae. Stesichorus (frag. 216, *PMG*) and Simonides (frag. 44) place it in Laconia.

17. Arsinoë: in Stesichorus' version of the story the nurse is called Laodamia, in Aeschylus' Kilissa.

Cassandra: the maiden prophetess, daughter of King Priam of Troy, brought home as a prisoner by Agamemnon at the end of the Trojan War, and murdered with him by Clytemnestra: see Aeschylus' *Agamemnon*.

21. Acheron: the river of the Underworld.

22. Iphigeneia: daughter of Agamemnon and Clytemnestra. When setting out from Greece to start the war against Troy, the Greek forces under Agamemnon were held up by contrary winds at Aulis. Agamemnon was persuaded by the prophet Calchas that a favourable wind could only be secured if the gods were propitiated by the sacrifice of Agamemnon's daughter Iphigeneia; this was done.

Euripus: the channel separating Euboea from the Attic mainland, where Aulis stands.

28–30. strangers' chatter: cf. Aeschylus, *Agamemnon* 449–51, 'the people's voice is heavy with anger. . . .'

32. Amyclae: see note on line 16.

33. Helen: wife of Menelaus king of Sparta and brother of Agamemnon. Her abduction by Paris to Troy was the cause of the Trojan War.

35. Strophius: the father of Pylades. He married the sister of Agamemnon. The nurse brought Orestes to him after the murder of Agamemnon. (Cf. Aeschylus, *Choephori*.)

38. Look, friends: the form of the break-off is not uncommon: cf. P 10.51–4, N 3.26–8. The story, though relevant to Apollo, is not exactly an appropriate exemplum for the young victor, and Pindar makes a mild joke of his 'digression' from the purpose of praise.

Where three ways meet: a reference to the fact that Pindar has three victories to celebrate in this ode.

41. Ah Muse . . .: I prefer to translate: 'Muse, if you have agreed to hire your voice for a fee, you must dart hither and thither, other ways than for Pythonicus and Thrasydaeus . . .'; i.e. he is under an obligation (he claims) to put other material in his ode besides praise of his patron. For the reference to the fee, see I 2.6; Callimachus, frag. 222.

46. their racing chariot: Pindar seems to attribute all three victories jointly to Thrasydaeus and his father, though the order of events matches the order in which the victors are named.

50. May the gods grant me . . .: Pindar's praise of an aristocratic form of government in preference to that of tyrants has been thought to refer to his experiences of the Sicilian tyrants and to imply a date of 474 for this ode; but it seems rather to refer to the wicked behaviour of the tyrannical Aegisthus and Clytemnestra; respectable aristocrats like

Thrasydaeus and Pythonicus are unlikely to go in for matricide. Furthermore, they will be less exposed to envy than an autocrat.

D. C. Young, *Three Odes of Pindar*, pp. 9–19, convincingly demonstrates that this is a common lyric topos: it 'is not a personal defense against charges of specific tyrannies and oligarchies . . .; it is a general statement, in no way personal to Pindar, cast in a traditional poetic *topos* and intended to reflect and thus to praise the victor's way of life.' Parallels he cites include Archilochus frag. 22, Diehl, Anacreon 8 (*PMG* 361) and especially Simonides 71 (*PMG* 584): 'what mortal life, what tyranny, can be enjoyable without pleasure? Without that, even the gods' eternity is not to be envied'; and Euripides, *Hippolytus* 1013–20, where Hippolytus asserts that athletic victory, followed by repute in the polis, means more to him than autocratic rule (tyranny).

The 'blessings' of line 53 are a verbal echo of the 'wealth' of line 29 which characterizes the Aegisthus household and which is one of Aeschylus' explanations for its doom (*Agamemnon* 471, 832–3).

55. fell path of pride: an Aeschylean note. The word for pride, *hybris*, a leitmotif of the *Oresteia*, elsewhere means 'violence' in Pindar.

61–2. Castor . . . Pollux: their myth is told in N 10.49–90. The immortal Polydeuces (Pollux in Latin) chose to forfeit half his immortality in order to share both death and life, alternately under the earth and on Olympus, with his mortal brother Castor. They are mentioned here, presumably, as athlete heroes, and perhaps also because of the Spartan location of the main myth.

For Midas of Acragas
Winner of the Aulos-Playing Contest (490)

This victory – the only non-athletic victory celebrated in Pindar's odes – was won at the same Pythian festival as that of Xenocrates, celebrated in Pythian 6. That ode, as has been noted, was written largely as a tribute to the friendship which had sprung up between Pindar and Xenocrates' son Thrasybulus, who as his father's charioteer won that victory for him. It seems probable that Midas was a musician in the service of Xenocrates or his brother Theron at Acragas, and came to Delphi as a follower of Thrasybulus. Very possibly Thrasybulus commissioned this ode from Pindar on his behalf. The scholiasts tell us that Midas also won a competition at the Panathenaea in Athens.

The aulos, Midas' instrument, though conventionally translated 'flute' was in fact a double-reed instrument resembling more the modern oboe. The instruments were often played in pairs. No translation is entirely satisfactory: 'shawm', though accurate, is scarcely more intelligible than the Greek name, while 'pipe' is too indeterminate. I prefer to keep the term 'aulos', though Conway's translation uses 'flute'.

After an invocation addressed to the city of Acragas, the ode begins to focus on Midas, and celebrates his art by introducing the myth of Perseus and Medusa, at whose death Athena invented the aulos to imitate the shrieks of the dying Gorgon's sisters. The ode concludes with a typical Pindaric warning of the uncertainty of human fortunes.

The story of Perseus and of the invention of the aulos was well known to his audience, so that Pindar is not constrained to produce a linear narrative, but alludes to the key episodes, as a way of gradually deepening the texture of his evocation of the central scene. The following résumé of the story will help the reader to understand the references in the ode.

Danaë was the only child of Acrisius, king of Argos, who was warned by an oracle that he would be killed by his grandson. In

order to safeguard Danaë from male attentions Acrisius locked
her up in a tower. Zeus, however, contrived an entry by turning
himself into a shower of gold, and his union with Danaë resulted
in the birth of Perseus. Acrisius, not daring to commit the
sacrilege of shedding his daughter's blood, had Danaë and the
infant Perseus enclosed in a wooden chest and pushed out to
sea. A fisherman of the Aegean island of Seriphos found them
and brought them safely to land. They then became the captives
of Polydectes, king of Seriphos, who treated them as slaves.
Later, intending to marry Danaë, Polydectes pretended that his
bride was to be the famous Hippodamia, daughter of Oenomaus, king of Elis (her story is told in O 1). He called upon the
chieftains of the island to give him wedding presents. Perseus,
now grown to manhood, resolved to bring back as his present
the head of Medusa, which turned to stone anyone who looked
at it. He was helped by Athena, who gave him a burnished
shield with which to see the reflection of Medusa without
looking at her. He needed also winged sandals, a wallet in which
to carry Medusa's head, and a helmet to make him invisible.
The whereabouts of these was known only to the three Grey
Sisters, 'the grim offspring of Phorcus', who had only one tooth
and one eye, shared between them. Perseus stole their eye as it
was passed fron the hand of one to another, and refused to
return it to them until they told him where he could find these
three things. They did so, and thus armed Perseus completed his
task, and returning to Seriphos with Medusa's head, turned
Polydectes and the islanders to stone.

str. 1   I pray you, lover of splendour,
                    Seat of Persephone, fairest of all
                Cities of men, high-built upon your hill above
            The stream of Acragas, and her rich banks of pasture,
                O queen, grant of your gentle heart to accept
                This crown of Pytho, Midas' glory, and give him   5
                Goodwill of the immortals and of men;
                    Welcome him too that he surpassed
                        All Hellas in the art
                    That long ago Pallas Athene invented,
                        Weaving in music's rich refrain
                    The ghoulish dirge of the fierce-hearted Gorgons.

str. 2   This in their anguished struggle
    From those dread maidens' lips was heard streaming, 10
And from those writhing serpent heads untouchable,
When Perseus o'er the third of those fell sisters launched
    His cry of triumph, and brought fatal doom
    To Seriphos by the sea – doom for that isle
    And for her people. Yes, for he had made blind
      The grim offspring of Phorcus, and bitter
        The wedding-gift he brought
    To Polydectes, thus to end his mother's
      Long slavery and enforced wedlock –   15
    That son of Danaë, who raped the head

str. 3   Of the fair-cheeked Medusa;
    He who, men tell, was from a flowing stream
Of gold begotten. But when the goddess maid delivered
From these labours this man she loved, then she contrived
    The manifold melodies of the flute, to make
    In music's notes an image of the shrill
    Lamenting cries, strung from Euryale's   20
      Ravening jaws. A goddess found,
        But finding, gave the strain
    To mortal men to hold, naming it the tune
      Of many heads, a glorious grace
    For the great contests where the peoples gather.

str. 4   Often its clear call rings   25
    From the light bronze, and from the reeds which grow
Beside the Graces' city, home of lovely dances,
Where the nymph, daughter of Kephissus, has her precinct;
    Faithful their witness to the dancers' feet.
Now if a mortal man wins happy fortune
Not without toil shall this be seen: a god may
    Bring it to pass – today, maybe –
      Yes, but the will of fate   30
None can escape. Soon shall there come an hour
    To strike beyond all expectation,
And give one boon past hope, withhold another.

Notes

1. **lover of splendour:** the same phrase is used by Bacchylides (18.60) of Athens.

2. **Seat of Persephone:** the goddess Persephone, daughter of Demeter the goddess of fertility, was the object of special worship by the Greeks of Sicily (Cicero spoke of Sicily as 'entirely consecrated to Ceres and Libera', i.e. Demeter and Persephone); and Acragas, one of the largest cities of Sicily, is therefore spoken of as her seat. Zeus was said to have appointed Persephone to be the tutelary goddess of the island (see N 1.14). Legend located her seizure by Hades at Enna in the centre of the island, though it was also attributed to the spring Cyane at Syracuse. The museum at Agrigento contains a rich collection of votive terracottas of Demeter, indicating the prominence of this Underworld cult there.

7. **the Gorgons:** three sisters, Stheno, Euryale and Medusa. Athena turned them into the three Gorgons, monsters with snakes in place of hair, out of envy or spite at the seduction of the beautiful Medusa by Poseidon. Anyone who looked at the head of Medusa was immediately turned into stone.

16. **fair-cheeked Medusa:** Medusa is always portrayed as pretty in Attic vase-paintings (from 440 onwards), showing the beauty that she had before Athena's punishment. Pindar's reference here is the earliest in art or literature to the 'fair Medusa' (see J. D. Beazley, 'The Rosi Krater', *JHS* 67 [1949]: 1–19). Archaic art – notably the pediment of the temple of Artemis on Corfu and the metope from the sixth-century Temple C at Selinus in Sicily – shows Medusa in the form of the grinning Gorgon head with a diminutive body, at the moment of her beheading by Perseus.

19. **the goddess maid:** Athena.

18. **this man she loved:** Perseus.

20 **Euryale:** the one sister is mentioned to stand for both.

21. **an image of the ... cries:** the sound of the aulos will have been similar not so much to the oboe as to its more strident folk-instrument cousins, the modern Greek clarino or Turkish zurna.

24. **a glorious grace:** the 'many-headed tune' was a standard virtuoso piece. According to Plutarch (*de musica* 7) it was invented by the Phrygian musician Olympos (c. 700) or his pupil Crates. It seems likely

that Midas actually played this tune for his winning performance, as the scholiasts suggest.

25. bronze ... reeds: The aulos was composed of a tube, often of bronze, though it could also be of bone, ivory or wood, with a double-reed mouthpiece. The bore of the aulos could be straight or conical. See M. L. West, *Ancient Greek Music* (Oxford 1992), pp. 81–109.

26. the Graces' city: Orchomenos, near Thebes. For their worship there cf. O 14.

28. Not without toil: the phrase is more appropriate for an effortful athletic victory than for a musical performance.

32. past hope: the scholiasts explain these words by a story that Midas' reed broke in mid-performance, but he nonetheless continued playing and won the prize. An epigram in the *Greek Anthology* (6.54; by Paul the Silentiary) shows that such things could happen, and could be the subject of poems; but it is not easy to find this allusion in Pindar's words, and the closing lines seem rather to sound a generalized warning note, or perhaps to offer a consolation for some other victory not achieved.

For Chromius of Aetna
Winner of the Chariot Race (476?)

Chromius was the brother-in-law of Hieron, the tyrant (ruler) of Syracuse and Gela, the most powerful of the group of rulers of the Greek city-states of Sicily and South Italy. In the year 476 Hieron transferred the population of Catana to Syracuse and refounded Catana under its new name of Aetna. He appointed Chromius to be its governor.

The opening lines of strophe 2 indicate that Pindar was present as director of the chorus (or possibly as performer of the ode). The poet speaks of Chromius as a man with whom he was personally acquainted. It is therefore probable that the ode was written during Pindar's visit to Sicily in 476/5.

The ode seems to have been performed before the house of Chromius on Ortygia, an island converted by the construction of a causeway into a peninsula of the city of Syracuse. The mention, in the opening lines of the ode, of Alpheus and the goddess Artemis derives from the legend attached to the fountain Arethusa on Ortygia. One version of the legend tells how the young huntsman Alpheus was enamoured of the nymph Arethusa; but she, wishing to escape him, fled overseas from the Peloponnese to Ortygia. Alpheus was turned by the gods into a river, the largest river of the Peloponnese, which flows past Olympia. Alpheus then continued his pursuit under the sea to Ortygia where his waters were turned into the fountain Arethusa. Another version of the story is that it was Artemis whom Alpheus vainly pursued. This version is connected with the cult of Artemis established on Ortygia by early Greek colonists from Elis.

The connection of the myth with the subject of the ode has been a puzzle to commentators ancient and modern, who have searched for dynastic connections between Chromius and Heracles, or posited special instructions from the victor to the author. The plainest counsel of desperation was that of Chrysippus, who said that Heracles was an appropriate topic for a Nemean

victory because of his killing the Nemean lion – even though
there is not one word about the lion in this ode! The explanation
of the myth is quite general: Heracles is one of Pindar's
touchstones of excellence, and his first deed is a splendid omen
for future success which Chromius may also expect to enjoy. A
more specific application is suggested by P. W. Rose, 'The Myth
of Pindar's First Nemean: Sportsmen, Poetry and Paideia', *HSCP*
78 (1974): 145–75: what has begun well will continue well, is
the moral.

str. 1   O revered ground where Alpheus
       Stayed his pursuit, and Artemis found rest,
          Ortygia,
       Let thy name, branch of glorious Syracuse
       And sister of Delos, prelude my song,
       Whose words shall ring sweet to the ear, in praise   5
       Of race-horses swift-footed as the wind,
          And in honour of Zeus of Aetna.
       For Chromius' chariot and Nemea's contest
       Charge me to yoke to his victorious deeds
          My melody of triumph.

ant. 1   This the gods founded and inspired
       And the supreme valour of the man I praise.
          For in success
       Breeds the full height of fame, and Poetry   10
       Loves above all to tell of the great games.
       Spread then of glory's fragrance a full measure
       To grace this isle, which Zeus, lord of Olympus,
          Gave to Persephone, and ruled
       Nodding his flowing locks, that Sicily
       Bear on her soil a dower of harvest riches
          First of all fruitful earth,

ep. 1   And her proud crown of glorious citadels.   15
       Bestowed upon her too the son of Cronos
          A people of proud horsemen,
          Wooers of war and bronze-clad might,
       Crowned too not seldom with the shining fronds
       Of the Olympiad olive. Many a glory
          In truth my arrows' flight shall compass.

str. 2   Now stand I at the courtyard gate,
           Singing my lays, where dwells a generous host;   20
                Friendly the feast
           Laid for my welcome, and her thronging guests
           Know well these halls of hospitable fame.
           And if the smoke of envy's blame arise,
           Good friends has he to douse the fire at source.
                Many the diverse arts of men;
           Each to his kind, and let him follow straight   25
           The paths appointed, striving with the skill
                That nature's gift endowed him.

ant. 2   For strength of arm plies to its goal
           In deed and act; the mind nurtures her harvest
                Of wise counsels –
           Whoso the gift inherits to foresee
           Things yet to come. Son of Agesidamus,
           Both one and the other in your talents lie.   30
           I love not to keep hidden in my house
                Wealthy treasure, but to take joy
           Of that I have, and amongst friends be known
           Of liberal repute. Like hopes to these,
                In this our life of toil,

ep. 2   Every man shares. For me, my eager thought
           Clings, on the high peaks of his valorous deeds,
                To Heracles, and bids me
                Unfold the ancient tale, how he
           This son of Zeus – sped from his mother's womb   35
           To the bright light of day with his twin brother –
                From childbirth pangs barely was free

str. 3   When Hera from her golden throne,
           Failed not to mark him, wrapped in swaddling robes
                Of saffron hue,
           And the gods' queen with anger in her heart
           Sent serpents speeding. Through the open doors   40
           O'er the wide floor came they to the chamber's depth,
           Thirsting to fold upon the babes new-born
                Their pointed fangs and gaping jaws.
           But Heracles, raising upright his head,

Stood to defy them, and then first knew he
  The taste of battle's trial.

ant. 3   One to each hand he seized – those hands
Invincible – the necks of the two snakes,   45
    And hanging there
Throttled within his grip, the flying minutes
Strained from these monsters' forms their breath of life.
And a dire terror struck the hearts of all
The maidservants allotted to the task
    Of tending to Alcmene's bed.
But she herself leapt from her couch, unrobed,   50
And ran barefoot, with no thought but to fend
    The fierce beasts from their prey.

ep. 3   And the Cadmean chiefs in their bronze armour
Came quickly thronging and Amphitryon
    His unsheathed sword in hand,
    Torment of fear piercing his heart;
Grief in his own house spells for every man
A bitter load, but for another's sorrow
    The heart soon knows relief from care.

str. 4   And he stood there, a mingled play   55
Of fear, wonder and gladness in his heart.
    For well he saw
The miracle of his son's spirit and strength,
And that the messengers' report stood now
Reversed by the immortals' will. He summoned
The peerless prophet of the most high Zeus,   60
    His neighbour, the seer of true vision,
Tiresias; who then declared to him
And all the gathered host, what chance of fortunes
    Heracles should encounter;

ant. 4   Of monsters merciless how many
On the dry land, how many on the sea
    He should destroy;
And of mankind, whom bent upon the path   65
Of pride and treachery he should consign
To an accursed death. This too he told:

When that the gods join battle with the Giants
  On Phlegra's plain, then shall his bow
Speed forth a gale of shafts to quell their might,
And the fair glory of their gleaming locks
  Lie sullied in the dust.

ep. 4 And he in peace for all time shall enjoy,
    In the home of the blessed, leisure unbroken,   70
      A recompense most choice
    For his great deeds of toil; and winning
  The lovely Hebe for his bride, and sharing
  His marriage feast beside Zeus, son of Cronos,
    Shall live to grace his august law.

Notes

1. **Alpheus:** The River Alpheus of Elis, which was thought to flow under the sea and emerge in the spring Arethusa.

2. **and Artemis found rest:** the phrase should be translated 'cradle of Artemis'. Artemis and her twin Apollo were born on the island of Delos, another name for which was Ortygia, 'quail island', because of the numerous quails found there, which were sacred to Artemis. Pindar builds on the coincidence of names to make Syracuse a holy place of Artemis. He emphasizes the link by calling Ortygia 'sister of Delos'.

6. **Zeus of Aetna:** the chief religious cult in Sicily was that of Zeus of Mt Etna, the volcano from which the newly founded town took its name.

10. **success:** victory in the Games.

14. **Persephone:** the queen of the Underworld, and daughter of Demeter, goddess of fertility. She was supposed to have been seized by Hades and carried off to the Underworld at Enna in Sicily, or at the spring Cyane in Syracuse. (Cf. P 12.2.)

17. **Olympiad olive:** the prize at Olympia was a wreath of wild olive.

18. **In truth my arrows' flight shall compass:** literally, 'hitting the mark without falsehood'. Pindar's aim is to praise accurately, neither too little nor yet too much.

19. **Now stand I:** Pindar composed this ode during his visit to Sicily in

476/5. The poem is envisaged as the representative of the poet, present at the celebration. One should not forget that the poem is actually performed by a chorus of twelve or more performers, dancing as they sing the poet's words. (Some scholars have argued for solo performance of certain odes, of which this could be one.)

24. the smoke of envy's blame: praise incites envy among the less fortunate, so Pindar emphasizes the ability of honest friends to counteract slanders.

29. Son of Agesidamus: Chromius.

31. Wealthy treasure: the just use of wealth is a way to be loved both in life and after death. Literal-minded critics (Wilamowitz) have taken this remark as a reproof to Chromius for meanness; but as often advice constitutes praise, the addressee being envisaged as a practitioner of the recommended behaviour. For a similar passage see P 11.54-8.

33. Heracles: the ancient commentators complained of the irrelevance of the myth of Heracles to Chromius' situation. But Heracles is always a touchstone of excellence for Pindar. The story fulfils the need for praise that Pindar has just asserted and puts the human victor in a context of mythical resonance. The myth in effect encapsulates the entire career of Heracles from his first labour, in infancy, to his eventual assumption to Olympus, and represents the theme of rest and fulfilment earned by early trials.

This passage is the earliest known account of this story, which may have been a Theban folktale. Pindar tells it also in Pa. 20. It was popular on Attic vases and appears also on Theban coins of the period 479-31.

The story is told in a more straightforward linear fashion than is common in Pindar. Note how the subject of the narrative changes from clause to clause: Hera, the snakes, Heracles, the flying minutes, the maidservants, Alcmene, the Cadmean chiefs, Amphitryon.

36. his twin brother: Iphicles. Alcmene, wife of Amphitryon king of Thebes, was visited by Zeus (who extended one night to the length of three to enjoy his pleasure with her), and in due course gave birth to twins, one of whom was of divine parentage (Heracles) and the other human (Iphicles). Amphitryon, as is usual in this common mythic story pattern, regards both as his own.

38. Hera: the queen of the gods, wife of Zeus, who had it in for Heracles as the offspring of Zeus' amour with Alcmene.

51. Cadmean: Theban. The legendary Cadmus was the founder of Thebes.

61. Tiresias: the legendary prophet of Thebes, well known from the stories of Oedipus, Pentheus and other Theban legends.

65. and of mankind, whom . . . : Pindar's Greek seems to refer to a specific human enemy, but it is hard to say to whom he is referring. His human enemies included Alcyoneus, Busiris and Antaeus, though the first and third might also count as Giants, which would spoil the triple pattern of beasts, men and giants in the prophecy.

67. Phlegra's plain: A volcanic region near Cumae in southern Italy. In 475/4 Hieron of Syracuse defeated the Carthaginians near Cumae (an event alluded to in P 1.15–20 and 69–75), but that is after the most likely date of N 1. The allusion does not demand to be linked to a historical event.

70. In the home of the blessed: on the death of Heracles he was awarded a place among the immortals on Mt Olympus. The goddess of youth and beauty, Hebe, daughter of Hera, became his wife.

great deeds of toil: Pindar never mentions all twelve of the Labours of Heracles, which were canonized in art by the metopes of the Temple of Zeus at Olympia, built between about 470 and 450. He concentrates on the Peloponnesian labours and the Gigantomachy.

For Timodemus of Acharnae
Winner of the Pankration (485?)

Timodemus was a member of the Athenian deme (district) of Acharnae. According to the scholiast, his father had been settled as a cleruch in the island of Salamis, and Timodemus had been brought up there. There is no independent evidence for this assertion, which is clearly an inference from the mention of Salamis in the ode. The ode makes plain that the association of the Timodemids with Acharnae went back many years.

The family had been successful athletes for generations, winning victories at the Pythian, Isthmian and Nemean Games as well as in local Athenian ones. This Nemean victory was Timodemus' first.

The ode was probably sung at Athens on the winner's return home, probably in a procession, for which its metrical construction, a series of identical strophes, makes it suitable.

There is no evidence for the date of the ode, except for the rather risky assumption that, because it mentions Salamis without referring to the Battle of Salamis of 480, it must be earlier than that date.

The pankration was a violent form of wrestling in which most things were permitted, including upright and ground wrestling, striking, twisting the opponent's limbs, dislocating his feet and breaking his fingers; however, gouging the eyes was (theoretically) forbidden, and biting and kicking were scorned.

str. 1   Like to those woven strains of song,
       Wherein the Homerid bards are wont to offer
       Invocation to Zeus, here too I praise
         One who has his foundation laid
       Of victory's honour in the sacred games,
         First in the precinct, famed in song,
           Of Zeus of Nemea.   5

str. 2   If too, propitious destiny,
       Guiding him in his fathers' path, has granted

That he shall be the glory of great Athens,
   Well may it prove, not once or twice
Timonous' son shall cull the fairest flowers
   At the Isthmus, and in the games
      Of Pytho too. For near   10

str. 3   The Pleiades, those mountain maids,
   Needs must Orion follow close behind.
And Salamis, need I tell, can nurse a man
   Of warrior breed. Hector in Troy
Heard Ajax challenge, and for you, Timodemus,
   The stern Pankration's proof of valour
      Raises high your renown.   15

str. 4   For men of noble name, Acharnae
   Down the long years is known; and in the games
The Timodemid clan has supreme honour.
   First by Parnassus lordly height
In four contests their athletes won the prize,
   Then in the vales of noble Pelops
      Eight times the men of Corinth   20

str. 5   Crowned them ere now: seven at Nemea
   Where Zeus presides, in their own city more
Than man may count. To Zeus then, countrymen,
   Sound your triumphant hymn, to honour
Timodemus as he rides home to fame.
   Strike up, and let your voices ring
      Rich melodies of song.   25

Notes

1. **woven strains of song**: the Greek word for woven is *rhapton*, from which the word rhapsode, a reciter, derives.

2. **the Homerid bards**: literally 'sons of Homer', a guild of reciters of Homer, particularly associated with Chios. The term could describe professional reciters anywhere.

10. **Timonous' son**: Timodemus.

11. The Pleiades: the daughters of the giant Atlas, who held the sky aloft, and became Mount Atlas, in northwest Africa.

12. Needs must Orion follow: the point is that as the major constellation of Orion is always just behind the indistinct Pleiades, so a victory at a superior contest may be expected to follow that at Nemea. Like a rhapsode, the victor has begun from Zeus (of Nemea) – a prelude to the major business of his career.

13. Salamis: Pindar needs an Athenian locale with an association with a major hero, and Salamis is the nearest available; there are no heroes of Acharnae! Salamis is the home of one of Pindar's favourite heroes, Ajax, one of the leading warriors of the Trojan War.

19. by Parnassus: at Delphi, home of the Pythian Games.

20. in the vales of noble Pelops: i.e. in the Peloponnese, where both Nemea and Isthmia were located. The phrase may indicate that the Timodemids are coming ever closer to the games of Pelops himself, the Olympic contest, at which they have evidently never yet won a victory.

20. the men of Corinth: the Corinthians were in charge of the Isthmian Games, which took place in Corinthian territory.

For Aristocleidas of Aegina
Winner of the Pankration (c. 475)

There is no external evidence for the date of the ode, and nothing
is known of Aristocleidas (the correct Dorian spelling) beyond
what may be gleaned from the poem itself. He seems not to have
come from a prominent athletic victory, as greater attention is
devoted to praise of Aegina than to the victor and his family; and
it appears from lines 70 ff. that he may have been older than
most athletes. The emphasis on the achievements of the Aeginetan heroes Peleus, Telamon and Achilles being won without
help from anybody may reflect this characteristic of Aristocleidas,
who has only his own inborn talent (cf. line 40) and no family
tradition to back him up. Stylistic considerations suggest a date
around 475, soon after the great Sicilian odes.

The elements of the poem are the normal ones, though great
skill is shown in combining them rather than simply aligning
them in an archaic paratactic fashion. The central myth is
arranged as a tricolon crescendo – Heracles/Peleus and Telamon/
Achilles.

str. 1 Muse whom I worship, mother of my spirit,
  I beg thee come, this festal month of Nemea,
  To the Dorian island, thronged with many a guest,
   To Aegina come.
  For by the water of Asopus waits
  Young manhood's choir, triumphant architects
   Of songs of revel,
   Longing to hear thy voice.   5
   One venture thirsts for this,
  And one for that. An athlete's victories crave
   Song above all,
  Fit servitor of his crowns and valorous deeds.

ant. 1 Of song grant, of my skill, full measure. Strike,
  O daughter of the lord of cloud-capped heaven, 10

Chords to his honour; mine to wed them with
    The youthful voices
And with the lyre. A joyful task have I
To praise this land, where dwelt the Myrmidons
    In days gone by.
    Now to their meeting-place
    Long cherished in old story,
Aristocleidas, by thy favour proved,   15
    Brings no disgrace,
Whose strength endured the challenge, and failed not

ep. 1   The Pankration's forceful round. Balm for your hurts
And healing for weary limbs your victor's crown
        Brings to you now
    In the deep valley of Nemea.
     Have you fair looks, and deeds,
Son of Aristophanes, fashioned in beauty's form?   20
And have you scaled valour's high peaks? No further
Tempt then the uneasy task, beyond the pillars
Of Heracles to sail the uncharted sea,

str. 2   Those famous marks the hero-god set up
To bound the sailor's voyage. And he slew
Huge monsters in the deep, and he traced out
    The shoals and eddies,
And journeying to the farthest goal destined   25
For safe return, made plain the ends of earth.
    O heart of mine
    To what far foreign headland
    Lead you my sail astray?
Aeacus and his race are my ship's burthen
    The word attesting,
The flower of truth, which bids 'Praise noble men';

ant. 2   And strangers' cargo brings a man small profit.   30
Search nearer home. There you have fitting glory,
Rich theme for song. For in great deeds of daring
    Long years ago
Peleus rejoiced, who cut the giant spear,
Whose single hand unaided took Iolcus;
    And Thetis too

The ocean maid, he held   35
   Struggling in his strong grasp.
And Telamon, that man of mighty strength,
   Staunch friend-in-arms
With Iolaus, felled Laomedon.

ep. 2   When too the bronze-bowed Amazons to encounter
         Iolaus led him, their man-devouring dread
               Could never dull
            The sharp blade of his soul. By worth
               Of inborn talent a man   40
         Wins rich repute. Whose art is but instructed,
         An obscure feather-brain he, now here aspiring
         Now there, and steps with no sure foot, essaying
         A thousand valorous deeds to no avail.

str. 3   Fair-haired Achilles dwelling in Philyra's halls,
         While yet a child made mighty deeds his play;
         Many a time his hand brandished the short
               Tipped javelin,
         Like to the wind in speed, and with wild lions   45
         He fought, and dealt them death. Boars too he slew,
               Whose panting frames,
            The first in his sixth year
            And then through all his days –
         He brought to the Centaur, Cronos' son. Astonished
               The divine eyes
         Of Artemis and bold Athene saw him   50

ant. 3   Slay without help of hound or artful net
         The stag his fleet foot mastered. This tale too
         Of men of old have I. Wise-hearted Chiron
               Nursed the great Jason
         Under his roof of stone, and to Asclepius
         Taught the soft-fingered skills of medicine's lore.   55
               For Nereus' daughter
            Glorious in her fruit,
            He set the marriage feast,
         And reared her peerless son, and taught him all
               The crafts of battle,
         Stirring his eager soul to high endeavour.

ep. 3   Till that the winds of the high sea should send him
         To Troy, to meet the Lycian lances ringing   60
                 Their shrill war-cry,
             And Phrygian and Dardanian foes;
                 And with the Ethiops' spears
         In close combat, fronting them hand-to-hand,
         He pledged his heart, their chieftain, great Memnon
         Fiery cousin to Helenus, should travel
         His homeward road no more. Far-flung the light

str. 4   That shines thenceforth for the sons of Aeacus.
         Zeus, thine their blood and in thy honour the contest   65
         For which the voice of youth this hymn is chanting,
                 Proclaiming joy
         To the land that bred them. For Aristocleidas' crown
         Ring out a cheer, for on the page of glory
                 His brave exploits
             Have writ this island's name,
                 And her revered College   70
         Of priests of Pytho. Now by proof of deed
                 Is the issue plain
         Where a man shall reveal his gifts excelling,

ant. 4   A boy amongst young boys, man amongst men,
         Elder with eld, each in each tripart age
         Of this our life. Yet, to four virtues heir,
                 Our mortal span
         This too enjoins, to hold the moment's task   75
         Steadfast in mind. In these you have your share.
                 Friend, fare you well;
             I send you now this gift
                 Of milk and honey blended,
         And the cream of the mixing crowns the bowl,
                 A draught of song
         Borne on the breath of flutes of Aeolis,

ep. 4   Though it comes late. Yet of all birds on wing   80
         Swift is the eagle, from the deep sky afar
                 Spying his mark,
             Lo, suddenly hath he seized, swooping,
                 His tawny-dappled prey.

But chattering daws have a lowly range.
In your honour then, if high-throned Clio wills,
For your proud spirit of conquest, from Nemea
From Megara and Epidaurus the light has shone.

Notes

1 **Muse**: she reappears in the final lines of the ode, identified as Clio. In later times the Muses were assigned to particular genres, and Clio was the Muse of history; but in the archaic period they are not so differentiated. Invocation of a Muse is rare in Pindar though common in Bacchylides. The muse as mother of poets is referred to by Hesiod (*Theogony* 94ff.), Homeric Hymn 25.2ff; cf. P 4.176.

2. **festal month of Nemea**: Panemos (June/July); the festival, like others (O 3.20, 10.76–8) took place at the full moon, in this case in mid Panemos (late June).

3. **Dorian island**: Aegina.

4. **Asopus**: a river in Aegina, mentioned in the Etymologicum Magnum as the site of a contest called Amphiphorites. Confusion was caused in earlier commentators by the assumption that the Asopus in Boeotia is meant.

10. **daughter of the lord of cloud-capped heaven**: Mnemosyne (Memory) is the daughter of Zeus (Pa. 7b.15ff.), and the Muses are her daughters. The Greek is difficult but probably means 'Muse, you who are his daughter, begin a hymn of glory to the lord of cloud-capped heaven.' This address to Zeus is picked up at the conclusion of the myth at line 65.

12. **the lyre**: the *lyra* is an instrument essentially the same as the phorminx; both are to be distinguished from the box-lyre or kithara, as well as from the long-armed barbitos used by Sappho. The sound box is a bowl not a box, and was often made from a tortoise-shell.

13. **Myrmidons**: the earliest inhabitants of Aegina. To supply Aegina with a people, Zeus turned ants (*myrmekes*) into human beings (Hesiod, frag. 205, MW). The Myrmidons who accompany Achilles to the Trojan War are the people of Phthia from where he came.

18. **your victor's crown**: strictly, Pindar says 'the song of victory', i.e.

N 3. The idea that song is a cure for the pains of competition is a common one: N 4.1–3, N 8.49–50, I 8.1–3.

20. Son of Aristophanes: Aristocleidas.

21. pillars of Heracles: Mount Atlas and the Rock of Gibraltar on either side of the straits. These were built, according to tradition (Diodorus Siculus 4.18.4) to celebrate his campaigns in Libya; or the passage was cut by the hero:

> Since he wished to leave upon the ocean a monument which would be held in everlasting remembrance, he built out both the promontories, they say, to a great distance; consequently, whereas before that time great space had stood between them, he now narrowed the passage, in order that by making it shallow and narrow he might prevent the great sea-monsters from passing out of the ocean into the inner sea, and that at the same time the fame of their builder might be held in everlasting remembrance by reason of the magnitude of the structures. Some authorities, however, say just the opposite, namely that the two continents were originally joined and that he cut a passage between them, and that by opening the passage he brought it about that the ocean was mingled with our sea.
>
> (Diodorus Siculus 4.18.5)

23. Huge monsters in the deep: what did Heracles actually do? The specific reference is uncertain. The same statement is made at I 3/ 4.73–5; cf. *Odyssey* 12.259.

24–5. The shoals and eddies: probably a reference to the Syrtes, the shoals and shallows off the north coast of Africa.

26. O heart of mine ...: the sea metaphor continues in Pindar's 'apology' for wandering from the point; but it is important to mention Heracles as a touchstone of supreme achievement. The return to the Aeginetan heroes puts them on a plane equivalent to the greatest of the heroes.

28. Aeacus and his race: Aeacus was the legendary first king of Aegina, and the great heroes next mentioned are his descendants.

33. the giant spear: usually, Peleus is said to have been given this spear as a wedding present. Here, the emphasis is on the fact that he obtained it *unaided*.

34. Iolcus: usually Peleus is said to have taken Iolcus (in eastern Thessaly, modern Volos) in company with Jason. Here, he carries out the task *unaided*.

35. Thetis: the immortal sea-nymph, promised by Zeus to Peleus as his bride. Thetis, unwilling, turned herself into fire and various kinds of wild beast, but Peleus held on to her until she surrendered, and the marriage took place, attended by all the gods. Thetis became the mother of Achilles.

37. Telamon: Peleus' brother. The usual legend had it that Heracles accompanied Telamon to overthrow Troy in the generation before the Trojan War, and killed its king, Laomedon, in revenge for his failure to pay the agreed reward for Heracles' help in destroying a dragon. Cf. N 4.25ff., I 5.35, I 6.27; and cf. Euripides, *Trojan Women* 799ff. Pindar omits the name of Heracles here, and replaces him with his charioteer Iolaus, to sharpen the glory of Telamon.

38. Amazons: here again the usual legend held that Heracles accompanied Telamon to fight the Amazons, in order to carry out one of his twelve labours, the bringing back of the girdle of Hippolyta, the queen of the Amazons.

40. inborn talent: this necessary quality for athletic success is exemplified in Achilles, whose myth occupies exactly one triad of the ode. The narrative is highly pictorial, and is constructed in a kind of spiral ring form. The scenes of Achilles with Chiron, and the death of Memnon, were both represented on the throne of Apollo at Amyclae, a repository of mythic iconography: Paus. 3.18.12.

43. Philyra: the mother of Chiron the Centaur (cf. P 3.1).

While yet a child: Achilles, like Siegfried, shows his prowess at an early age. The whole passage may perhaps be drawn from a lost hexameter poem by Hesiod, *The Precepts of Chiron*.

48 the Centaur: Chiron immortal and benevolent figure, lived in his cave in the forests of Mt Pelion. Unlike the other centaurs, wild creatures, he was the giver of the arts of civilization, including medicine, and his pupils included Jason and Asclepius, the god of medicine.

57. Nereus' daughter: Thetis, whose 'fruit' was Achilles.

the marriage feast: of Peleus and Thetis, arranged by Chiron on Mt Pelion; it was attended by all the gods.

60. Lycian lances: in Pindar's Greek it is the Lycians, not the lances, which utter the war-cry. Lycia is in southwestern Asia Minor. Phrygia is further north. The Dardanians are the people of Troy.

62. Ethiops: the Ethiopians under Memnon, son of the Dawn, were allies of the Trojans. Ethiopians are usually envisaged as black men, but their leader Memnon is portrayed on vases as white, and wearing Persian costume. Memnon was killed by Achilles: the story was in the epic *Aethiopis*.

63. Helenus: a seer, son of Priam. Memnon's father Tithonus was Priam's brother.

64. the mention of Memnon is the climax of the narrative which leads back to Aegina; cf. N 6. 48–50.

65. Zeus: the prayer to Zeus echoes the address to him by his daughter at line 10.

thine their blood: Aeacus was the son of Zeus by Oenone who gave her name to the island later called Aegina.

in thy honour: the Nemean Games were dedicated to Zeus.

70. College of priests: there was at Aegina a college (Thearion) and order of priests of Pytho (Delphi) for the worship of Apollo. Like the archons of Athens they provided emissaries to the oracle of Apollo when required. Probably Aristocleidas was a member of this college.

72. A boy among ... boys: one must compete with equals. The three ages should not be matched somehow with the four virtues; all virtues are necessary in each age. That there are four virtues is a commonplace of Greek thought, and Aeschylus, *Seven against Thebes*, line 610 lists them succinctly: 'the temperate, just, noble and pious man'; but the list is not always the same. Simonides (*PMG* 542) praises the 'foursquare man'. Aristocleidas has perhaps passed from the age of athletic competition to that in which a man would function as a priest. There is a nice parallel to the passage in Thomas Browne, *Christian Morals*, section 8: 'Confound not the distinctions of thy life which Nature hath divided: that is, youth, adolescence, manhood and old age, nor in those divided periods, wherein thou art in a manner four, conceive thyself but one. Let every division be happy in its proper virtues, nor one vice run through all.'

76. I send you now: the concluding 'sphragis' or 'seal' on the poem,

which brings the poet into relation with his addressee. The metaphor
of the poem as a drink recurs at O 7.1ff., cf. I 6.74. Milk and honey
was commonly used as an offering for the dead and a drink for the
sick; here the implications are of something both wholesome and sweet.

79. flutes of Aeolis: correctly, pipes; cf. on P 12. The Aeolian mode was
regarded as suitable for use at symposia (Athenaeus 14.624e); it seems
that N 3 is a party poem.

80. Though it comes late: is this an apology for late delivery of the
ode? Rather, the phrase should be taken to mean that the *praise*,
though delayed right to the end of the poem, has finally arrived (C. A.
P. Ruck, *Hermes* 100 [1972]: 153–8).

the eagle: the eagle is introduced as a simile for the swooping down of
praise; its primary reference is to the victor, who soars alone while
unsuccessful contestants and backbiters chatter down below (the jack-
daws). Other commentators have taken the eagle as a symbol of the
poet and the daws for his poetic rivals: but see my 'The Theban Eagle',
with, now, I. L. Pfeijffer, 'The Image of the Eagle in Pindar and Bacchylides', *Classical Philology* 89 (1994): 305–17.

84. Megara: there were several festivals at Megara; the one probably
referred to is the Alkathoia (cf. N 5.45ff.). **Epidaurus:** the Asclepieia
(Paus. 2.26.7). Aristocleides has won victories at both.

For Timasarchus of Aegina
Winner of the Wrestling Match (473?)

Timasarchus was a member of the Theandrid family, several of whose members are mentioned in the course of the ode. The content of the ode contains the usual features, though the myth – again relating to the deeds of Peleus and Telamon – is more allusively told than in Nemean 5 or Isthmian 6. This may suggest that Nemean 4 is later than those odes. Another possible argument regarding the date concerns the mention of the trainer Melesias in line 93, who also features as trainer in Olympian 8, dated to 460 BC. A trainer might have a long career but if Melesias is the father of Thucydides the politician his *floruit* is likely to have been around 470. Hostilities between Athens and Aegina were acute after 466 so the absence of any discomfiture about Melesias' role may suggest a date before then. The mention of Teucer as king of Cyprus in line 46 is perhaps more likely to have been made after Cyprus came under Greek rule as a result of Spartan conquest in 478. Any date between 478 and 466 would be entirely plausible.

The heading of the ode indicates that Timasarchus won the (adult) wrestling, but the mention of his trainer and his father would be more usual in an ode for a boy victor.

The reference in lines 33ff. to 'plots' against Pindar should not be taken as alluding to particular political difficulties or to the jealousy of Pindar's critics, but as a particularly baroque form of the conventional topoi of the impediments to praise.

The ode is written in strophic form and not in triads, so may have been intended for processional performance.

str. 1   For toils that fall to man's accomplishment
        Best of all doctors is a cheerful heart.
           But the wise daughters of the Muse
           Bring too their healing balm, the soft
              Embrace of song.
        Nor can the warmth of water soothe more surely

The body's pain, than will the praise 5
Of high desert tuned to the lyre. For words
Live longer down the years than deeds,
If that a man may with the Graces' favour
Haply bring forth the heart's deep mood
To live upon the tongue. May it be mine

str. 2   Such prelude to my songs of praise to render,
Honouring Zeus, Cronos' son, and Nemea,
And Timasarchus' wrestling-bout; 10
And may the race of Aeacus
Give it acclaim,
Whose high-towered stronghold like a beacon stands
For the just dues of every guest.
Could but Timocritus, your father, still
Know the sun's warmth and healing rays,
How many a note would he have plucked, linking 15
His lively lyre with this my song,
To praise the victor and his chain of crowns

str. 3   Won at Cleonae's contest, and from Athens,
City of noble name and sunlit splendour,
And Thebes ringed with her seven gates,
Where by Amphitryon's glorious tomb, 20
With willing hands
The men of Cadmus' line crowned him with flowers,
For Aegina's sake. For as a friend
Received by friends he found a generous welcome,
Though in a city not his own,
In that rich house, the hall of Heracles.
It was that hero who of yore,
Allied with Telamon's great might, laid low

str. 4   The walls of Troy, and slew the Meropes 25
And that great man of war, giant of terror,
Alkyoneus; yet not before
With rocks his only weapon, he felled
Twelve four-horsed chariots,
And the men who bestrode them twice the number,
Proud horsemen all. Untried were he 30
In battle's storm, who could not understand

What lies within this brief-told tale.
Deeds done, he only who has dared them knows
    What cost the doing. Long is the story,
To tell the whole my Music's rule forbids

str. 5   And Time pressing apace. For with a spell,
A love-charm, the new moon draws on my heart   35
    To grace her festival with song.
    How then: what though the deep sea's tide
        Hold thee waist-high,
Strain, O my soul, against its fell intent;
    Our ship all eyes shall see, riding
In the broad light of day, victorious
    Over the foe, safely to shore.
Another man with envy in his eye –
    Vainly his empty thought rolls round
To fall in darkness to the unheeding soil.   40

str. 6   For me, whatever share of excellence
The throne of Fate endowed, I know full well
    That Time, although his foot be slow,
    Shall bring it to the end ordained.
        Sweet lyre of mine,
Strike up then, and forthwith, to weave the song,
    In strains of Lydian harmony,   45
Dear to Oenone's heart and to Cyprus,
    Where Teucer, son of Telamon,
Rules afar off: and Salamis Ajax holds
    His patrimony; and Achilles
That sunlit island in the Euxine sea.

str. 7   Thetis rules Phthia; Neoptolemus   50
In far-flung Epirus, where soaring headlands
    And pasturing folds fall proudly down
From high Dodona's range, to meet
        The Ionian wave;
And Peleus' warring arm beset Iolcus
    By Pelion's height, and gave the city
To be the servant of the Haimones,
    When he had foiled Acastus' bride   55
Hippolyta and her treacherous guile. Then sought

Pelias' son, stealing his sword
The blade of Daedalus' magic, to contrive

str. 8 His death by ambush; saved by Chiron's hand,
 The fate destined by Zeus he made his own: 60
  Devouring flames, and the sharp claws
  Of fearless lions, and tearing teeth
   Safely endured,
 His Nereid bride he won from her high seat, 65
  And saw, round him enthroned, the gods
 Of sky and sea proffer their gifts, foretelling
  The kingdom he and his race should rule.
 Westwards beyond Gadeira none may pass:
  About, my ship: to Europe's mainland 70
 Turn once again your sail; of Aeacus' sons

str. 9 All the full tale I may not here unfold.
 But for Theandrus' line am I come, ready
  With songs to herald the contests
  Where strong young limbs enrich their pride;
   The songs I pledged
 For Olympia, for the Isthmus and Nemea, 75
  From whence, their worth by trial proved,
 They homeward came bearing the fruits of glory,
  Their victors' crowns. Thus it befalls,
 Your father's clan has honour, Timasarchus,
  – So the word runs – high above all
 In victory's hymns of triumph. Do you bid me

str. 10 For Callicles your mother's brother, too, 80
 A pillar build whiter than Parian marble?
  Gold in the smelter's hand throws forth
  Its clearest gleam, but song praising
   His noble deeds
 Marks out a man to be the peer of kings.
  So may the music of my tongue
 Sound in the ear of Callicles, telling
  By Acheron where he dwells, how once 85
 The contest of the Wielder of the Trident,
  God of the sounding seas, proclaimed him
 Victor, and crowned him with Corinthian parsley.

str. 11 His praise your father's father Euphanes
         Was glad, my son, to sing in years gone by.   90
             But to each his own age-fellow;
             And that which his own eyes have seen,
                 A man may hope
         In telling it to win the highest prize.
             So – if Melesias' praise he sings,
         His words will strive, matching the wrestler's limbs,
             To weave their rhythmic harmony,
         Songs that shall never to the dust be thrown,
         Of kindly sooth to brave endeavour,   95
             But to rebellious strength a stern taskmaster.

Notes

4. the warmth of water: the bath of the wanderer is a conventional
symbol of safe homecoming: see H. Fränkel, *Wege und Formen
frühgriechischen Denkens*, pp. 97ff. At Alcaeus frag. 45, LP, maidens
'wash and soothe' the traveller.

6. words live longer: cf. I 7.17–19, B 9.82–7. The sentiment that opens
N 5, concerning the further reach of poetry than of statues, is not
dissimilar.

11. the race of Aeacus: the legendary first king of Aegina and ancestor
of the Aeginetans.

12. high-towered stronghold: for Aegina's reputation for just dealing,
cf. O 8.22

13. Timocritus: the dead father of the victor is referred to, as often.

15. How many a note: the Greek suggests that Timocritus would often
have played the ode over to himself, as a solo.

17. Cleonae's contest: Nemea was close to the small town of Cleonae,
which provided the administrators and judges of the Games until the
privilege was usurped by Argos in 460.

18. sunlit splendour: *lipara*, literally, 'shining Athens'. Cf. Pindar, frag.
76 and note. The late antique rhetorician Menander (345.2) notes that
one can praise a land as 'dry and waterless' or as '*lipara* and well-
watered'. If 'shining' for Pindar meant moist and fertile, it is a very

inappropriate epithet for Athens. The literally 'shining' buildings of the Acropolis were not built until after the likely date of this ode.

20. Amphitryon: a legendary king of Thebes, husband of Alcmene the mother of Heracles by Zeus. The scholiast tells us that the Iolaeia are the Games referred to here. These were probably celebrated in the gymnasium of Iolaus near the Proetid gate of Thebes (Paus. 9.23.1), but the house of Amphitryon was by the Electran gate (Paus. 9.11.1–7). The tomb of Amphitryon is mentioned in Paus. 1.41.1 but its location is not stated.

24. hall of Heracles: Heracles' temple stood by the Electran gate.

25. with Telamon: the campaign of Heracles and Telamon against Troy is portrayed on the pediment of the temple of Aphaia on Aegina (cf. N 3.37).

26. the Meropes: inhabitants of the island of Cos, defeated by Heracles.

27. Alkyoneus: in the battle of the Gods and Giants at Phlegra, Heracles played a decisive part in the defeat of the latter. See I 6.32–5 and notes. One of the stones thrown by Alkyoneus was pointed out near the Isthmus, an alternative site of the battle. These three adventures of Heracles are all mentioned together by Hesiod, *Catalogue of Women*, frag. 43a61–5; the source may be Pisander's *Heracleia*.

32. Deeds done: the implication is that Timasarchus had a hard struggle to win his bout. For the sentiment cf. Sophocles frag. 223b, Radt.

33. Long is the story ...: This long and elaborate break-off formula merges the metaphor of the poem as ship with that of the wrestling-match. The passage should not be interpreted as a defence of Pindar against 'critics', but as an elaboration of the rule that forbids him carrying on the catalogue of Aeacid heroes to excessive length (Bundy, p. 3 n. 11). The ship of poetry is held in a wrestler's grip by the sea, but 'rides safely to shore' – a Greek expression (*katabainein*) which means both 'to come to land' and 'to enter the wrestling ring'. Meanwhile, the hypothetical critics of the victor see their calumnies crash to the ground like a defeated wrestler (see Lefkowitz, *First-Person Fictions*, p. 167). Pindar refuses to be deflected from the (attractive) task of praising Timasarchus: A. M. Miller, 'N 4.33–43 and the defense of digressive leisure', *Classical Journal* 78 (1982/3): 202–20.

35. a love-charm: literally an 'iynx' or wryneck: the bird was spread-eagled on a wheel and spun round as a common piece of love-magic: see Theocritus 2.17 with Gow's note.

the new moon: the Aeginetan festival at which the ode was to be sung took place at the new moon. The Nemean festival took place at mid month, i.e. full moon, in the month Delphinios (N 5.44). Perhaps the expression should simply be taken to mean 'festival, holiday' (Peter Von der Mühll, *Mus. Helv.* 14 [1967]: 128–30).

45. Lydian harmony: the ode is written in the solemn Lydian mode.

46. Oenone: the mother by Zeus of Aeacus; she gave her name to the island which was later called Aegina.

Cyprus: this island had come under Greek rule with the Spartan conquest of 478. This may have a bearing on its mention here.

48. Salamis: Telamon, after leaving Aegina (see N 5), settled in Salamis and his son Ajax became its ruler in due course.

49. That sunlit island: the island of Leuke in the Black Sea off the mouth of the Danube. There was a cult and temple of Achilles and Helen here, perhaps established by Aeginetan sailors. For a story about the island see Philostratus, *Heroicus*.

51. Phthia: a city of central Thessaly where Peleus found a home after leaving Aegina; it thus became home to Thetis after her marriage to Peleus.

Neoptolemus: son of Achilles. After his return from the Trojan War he went to Epirus in northwest Greece, but soon met his death at Delphi. (See N 7.) His family remained rulers of Epirus.

53. Dodona: southwest of the modern town of Ioannina; there was a temple and oracle of Zeus here.

54–6. Peleus' warring arm: the story is also alluded to in N 5.26ff. When Acastus, the king of Iolcus, abandoned Peleus to the beasts on Mt Pelion, he concealed his invincible sword; but Chiron rescued him and restored his sword, after which Peleus stormed Iolcus and killed Acastus' treacherous wife Hippolyta; the city became the property of the local Haemones of Thessaly. Peleus went on to celebrate his marriage with Thetis.

59. The blade of Daedalus' magic: see note on N 5.26, Hesiod, *Catalogue*, frag. 209. Daedalus is not elsewhere credited as maker of the knife, and it may be better instead to read, with Didymus, the adjective *daidaloi*, beautifully crafted.

61. The fate destined by Zeus: that he should become the husband of Thetis (cf. N 3.35 and note).

69. Gadeira: modern Cadiz, just outside the Pillars of Heracles. This was the limit of sailing for Mediterranean sailors, and it is the limit of Pindar's mythological excursus too; the ship metaphor returns in this second break-off (cf. lines 36–8).

73. Theandrus: an ancestor of Timasarchus. Nothing else is known of him or the other members of this family.

75. Olympia: members of the family had won victories at the Olympian and Isthmian as well as the Nemean Games.

80. A pillar ... whiter than Parian marble: a i.e. a grave-marker. The comparison of poetic celebration to a stele recalls the opening of N 5. Callicles is no longer alive. The family relationships are as follows:

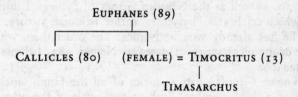

EUPHANES (89)

CALLICLES (80)   (FEMALE) = TIMOCRITUS (13)

TIMASARCHUS

86. the Wielder of the Trident: Poseidon, to whom the Isthmian Games were dedicated.

88. parsley: the victor's prize at the Isthmian Games was a wreath of wild parsley.

93. Melesias: the trainer from Athens, possibly the father of the politician Thucydides. Cf. O 8.54. This tribute to him makes free use in the Greek of the terminology of the wrestling ring.

For Pytheas of Aegina
Winner of the Youth's Pankration (probably 487)

Pytheas was the elder brother of Phylacidas, whose victories are celebrated in Isthmians 5 and 6. Bacchylides' Ode 13 was composed for this same victory of Pytheas. Pytheas acted as trainer to Phylacidas (Isthmian 5.59). The evidence of these odes enables us to advance some tentative arguments about their dating.

The strongest piece of evidence is that Isthmian 5 mentions the recent Battle of Salamis (480) but not that of Plataea (479), suggesting that it was composed before the latter event. It must then have been composed to celebrate the Isthmia of 480. It refers to two Isthmian victories of Phylacidas and one Nemean, as well as the Nemean victory of Pytheas. Isthmian 6 (7), which celebrates Phylacidas' earlier Isthmian victory, states that he has already won at Nemea. The order then, with the most economical series of dates, is Nemea 483, Isthmia 482, Isthmia 480.

Isthmian 6 (6off.) lists victories of all the family, including those of a third member, Euthymenes, uncle of the other two. They include a third Nemean victory and two (or more) Nemean. The minimum time required for such a series of victories is April 486 to July 483, as follows: Isthmia 486, Nemea 485, Isthmia 484, Nemea 483. Nemean 5 precedes all these because it refers to none of them; the only victories of Euthymenes alluded to are in local games. It must therefore be seen as, at latest, a celebration of the Nemea of July 487. The data can most simply be accommodated in the following schema:

unspecified date: two Aeginetan victories of Euthymenes;
  487: Nemean victory of Pytheas (N 5, B 13 celebrate; cf.
    I 6.3 – their first success);
  486: Isthmian victory of Euthymenes (I 6.61);
  485: Nemean victory of Phylacidas (or 483, but not 481 if it

is the earlier Nemean victory referred to in I 6; however,
this is probably Pytheas';
484: Isthmian victory of Euthymenes (I 6.61);
482: Isthmian victory of Phylacidas (I 6 celebrates);
480: Isthmian victory of Phylacidas (I 5 celebrates).

If the failure to mention Plataea in Isthmian 5 is deemed
irrelevant (see introduction to Isthmian 5), the series can be
dated two years later, but it cannot be dated earlier. (Pytheas'
victory of 487 could hypothetically be earlier, but not much
earlier, as the boy of that ode is brother of a boy-winner of 480,
and boyhood lasts from seven to fourteen.)

The family relationships can then be reconstructed as follows,
allowing thirty years for each generation:

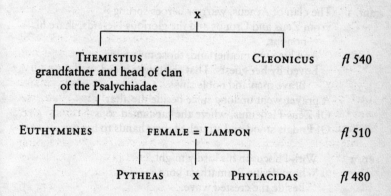

How can we accommodate the Aeginetan Lampon son of
Pytheas mentioned by Herodotus 9.78.1 as active in 479 BC? I
suggest that Pytheas was another brother of Euthymenes; his
son Lampon would then be active in the same generation as our
Pytheas and Phylacidas.

On the dating see A. Severyns, *Bacchylide* (Liège–Paris 1933),
pp. 42ff.; J. H. Finley, 'Pindar and the Persian Invasion', *HSCP*
pp. 63 (1958): 121–2.

The mention of the Athenian trainer Menander at line 48 is
sometimes considered a problem for a dating during a period of
hostilities between Aegina and Athens which lasted from 488 to
480 (though Herodotus calls the war 'undeclared': 5.81); but

the international aristocracy may have had considerable freedom
of movement during wartime: there is no need to see anything
apologetic in his mention here, or in Bacchylides 13 (contra M.
Woloch, 'Athenian Trainers in the Odes of Pindar and Bacchylides', *Classical World* 56 [1963]: 102–4).

str. 1   No sculptor I, to carve an image standing
        Idle upon its step. But upon every craft and sail
          Speed, lovely song, from Aegina
          To tell abroad that Lampon's son,
            Broad-shouldered Pytheas,
        Has won at Nemea the Pankratiast crown,
        Though not yet on his cheek is seen the dower   5
        Of rich-flown summer, mother of the vine-bloom.

ant. 1   The clan of Aeacus, warrior heroes sprung
        From Zeus and Cronos and the glorious Nereids, share his
              honour,
          And his own motherland, those meadows
          Loved by her guests. That she might breed
            Brave men and noble ships
        A prayer went up long since beside the altar
        Of Zeus Hellenius, where the far-famed sons   10
        Of Endais stood and stretched their hands to heaven,

ep. 1   With Phocus in his lordly might,
          Whom divine Psamatheia bore
            Beside the crested wave.
          Of a dread act, a deed maybe
        Unrightly dared, my heart forebodes to tell,
        Wherefore these warriors left this famous isle,   15
        What fate of heaven drove them from Oenone.
          Be still my tongue: here profits not
        To tell the whole truth with clear face unveiled.
        Often is man's best wisdom to be silent.

str. 2   But if of fortune's wealth my praise is due
        Of strength of hand or armoured war, rake a long landing-
                              pit 20
          Straightway for me; my limbs can muster
          A nimble spring; even o'er the main

Eagles can wing their way.
Yet for these men the Muses' peerless choir
Glad welcome sang on Pelion, and with them
Apollo's seven-stringed lyre and golden quill

ant. 2 Led many a lovely strain. To Zeus a prelude, 25
Then sang they first divine Thetis, and Peleus, whom with
guile
Fair-faced Hippolyta, Cretheus' daughter,
Sought to ensnare, as helpmate duping
Magnetes' chief, Acastus
Her husband, with deceit-embroidered counsel,
And false-wrought tales, that Peleus made to force her 30
There in her marriage bed. False tale indeed!

ep. 2 For it was she conjured and begged him
With many a full-hearted prayer.
Her reckless words but chafed
His wrath, and he fearing the Father,
Protector of the law of host and guest,
Straightway denied her. Then from heaven beholding
The king of the high gods, cloud-gathering Zeus, 35
With nodding brow forthwith ordained
A sea-nymph of the golden-spindled Nereids
His bride should be, and to accept this kinship,

str. 3 'Listed Poseidon's favour, who from Aigae
Not seldom journeys to the far-famed Dorian Isthmus.
There
The flute's high note and joyful throngs,
With bold contests for strength of limb,
Receive him as their god.
His inborn fate decrees each man's achievement. 40
For you, Euthymenes, at Aegina
The goddess victory opened her embrace

ant. 3 And touched your ears with fine-wrought melody.
Now as you, Pytheas, tread your uncle's steps, his honours
grace you
And every kinsman of your stock.
Nemea and Aegina's own month,

The feast loved of Apollo,
Brought you to fame; youth's challenge you o'erthrew   45
At home and in the glade by Nisus' hill,
And glad am I that every city strives

ep. 3   For noble ends. Yet mark, Menander
Gave you success, happy respite
    From toil – fitly from Athens,
True craftsman of athletic skill.
Comes now Themistius in your path of praise?   50
Hence chill reserve; sing out full-throated, hoist
Your sail to the mast's topyard, cry him for valour
    Twice crowned at Epidaurus, boxer
Pankratiast, and at Aeacus' city gate
Wreathed with fresh flowers, gift of the fair-haired Graces.

Notes

1. No sculptor I . . .: Pindar alludes to the high reputation of the
Aeginetan school of sculpture (Pliny, *Natural History*, 34.9–10), which
was already established with the creation of the pediments of the
Temple of Aphaia between 500 and 480; the great sculptors Callon
and Onatas reached their acme during the first half of the fifth century.

The sentiment that poetry can outreach sculpture in space, here,
recurs in Simonides' poem to Cleobulus of Lindos (*PMG* 581), where
it is temporal reach that is in question.

2. every craft and sail: the passage has sometimes been used to argue
that there was a sea-trading aristocracy in Aegina. The island was
indeed noted for trade; but there is no reason to suppose that it was
carried on by aristocrats, who in antiquity habitually drew all their
wealth from land. We need not see Pytheas' family as traders.

7. Cronos: father of Zeus, the father of Aeacus, legendary first king of
Aegina.

Nereids: the sea-nymphs, daughters of Nereus. One of them Thetis
became the wife of Aeacus' son Peleus and mother of Achilles.

10. Zeus Hellenius: his temple on the highest peak of Aegina is covered
by the modern chapel of Agios Asomatos. It used to be thought that
the temple of Aphaia was this shrine, until A. Furtwängler discovered
its true identification in 1901.

12. sons of Endais: Telamon and Peleus, sons of Aeacus by his wife Endais, the daughter of Sciron. She is mentioned also by Bacchylides in his ode for this victory, 13.94; perhaps the Psalychiadae had a special devotion to her.

Phocus: 'Seal', the son of Aeacus by Psamatheia ('Sandy'), a sea-nymph. His half-brothers Telamon and Peleus killed him while throwing the discus. For this the two brothers had to leave Aegina, Telamon going to Salamis and Peleus to Thessaly. Phocus' grave stood beside the Aiaceion (Paus. 2.29.6), which is referred to by Pindar at line 53.

Pindar's language here avoids staining the name of the heroes with too much detail about the heinous act, and the expression of embarrassment is used as a break-off to turn to a new stage of the ode: cf. O 9.35, O 13.91, frag. 180.

16. Oenone: the original name of the island of Aegina. Oenone was the mother of Aegina by Zeus.

19–20. landing-pit: a metaphor from the long jump, which in ancient Greece was a standing jump, in which the jumper was assisted by weights held in the hands which he swung to lengthen the leap.

21. Eagles: if the eagle is a metaphor only of the poet, the idea of the bird performing a long jump is grotesque. As often, the eagle acts as a glide from poet to celebrand: the heroes' fame flies over land and sea.

23. the Muses' ... choir: the Muses, singing at the wedding of Peleus and Thetis on Mt Pelion in Thessaly, sang the story of his earlier trials, which culminated in the wedding (line 36): a neat piece of ring composition.

26. Hippolyta: Peleus, having killed Eurytion in the hunt for the Calydonian boar, was purified by Acastus, king of the Magnetes of Thessaly. Acastus' wife Hippolyta (daughter of Jason and granddaughter of Cretheus) fell in love with Peleus and when he rejected her advances accused him of rape. Acastus therefore exposed the hero to beasts on Mt Pelion; he was saved by the Centaur Chiron (or by Hermes): Hesiod frag. 209 MW. Peleus then cut Hippolyta in half and marched an army between the slices (Apollodorus) – an episode which Pindar rejects at N 3.34.

33. the Father: Zeus, protector of guests.

36. golden-spindled: a common epithet of the Nereids. Perhaps their spindles were envisaged as the whirling spray of the sea-waves. Gold is a common designator of divinity.

37. this kinship: the wife of Poseidon was Amphitrite, also a Nereid, so that Peleus on his marriage to Thetis would become the brother-in-law of Poseidon. The transition to the Isthmian Games, of which Poseidon was patron, is very neat. Pindar is suggesting that an Isthmian victory may soon be in Pytheas' grasp: in fact it was his younger brother Phylacidas who won the Isthmian victories (I 5 and 6).

Aigae: the mythical home of Poseidon, in Achaea.

41. Euthymenes: Pytheas' maternal uncle (see introduction). A better reading in the Greek gives him two victories in Aeginetan games. The games on Aegina were the Delphinia and the Hydrophoria (P 8.64ff.).

44. Aegina's own month: the month Delphinios, in which the contests took place.

46. Nisus' hill: a hill near Megara, where Pytheas had won a victory in the local games, the Alkathoia.

48. Menander: Pytheas' trainer, also celebrated in B 13.192. He is described as 'fitly from Athens' because Theseus was credited as the inventor of wrestling (Paus. 1.39.3, etc.). Melesias, who was training Aeginetan athletes twenty years later, was also from Athens.

50. Themistius: Pytheas' grandfather and clan chief, who had won victories in the Asclepieia at Epidaurus.

53. Aeacus' city gate: more accurately, 'in the vestibule of Aeacus', i.e. at his sanctuary on the island; cf. note on line 12, Phocus.

For Alcimidas of Aegina
Winner of the Boys' Wrestling Match (465?)

Alcimidas belonged to one of the leading families of Aegina, the
Bassid clan. This victory, as Pindar says (line 58) is the twenty-
fifth victory won by members of the family at one or other of
the Panhellenic Games. These successes took place in alternate
generations, which prompts Pindar to the conceit that the
intervening generations are like the fields left fallow to regain
their strength; imagery of vegetation and fertility is all-pervasive
in this ode, and it is in this context of overarching Nature that
human strength and weakness, success and failure, are set. The
resonance of the nature-imagery reduces the need for an elaborate myth to give depth to the victor's achievement, and the
mythic section is correspondingly short.

There is no external evidence for the date of the ode, but it is
probably earlier than the outbreak of war between Athens and
Aegina, resulting in the conquest of Aegina in 457/6, since the
Athenian trainer Melesias is mentioned (line 65) without
embarrassment.

str. 1   The race of men and of the gods is one.
      For from one mother have we both
         The life we breathe.
     And yet the whole discrete endowment
       Of power sets us apart;
   For man is naught, but the bronze vault of heaven
   Remains for ever a throne immutable.
     Nevertheless some likeness still
   May we with the immortals claim, whether   5
   Of mind's nobility or body's grace,
       Though knowing not to what goal
   Has destiny, by day or through the right,
     Marked out for us to run.

ant. 1   Here too Alcimidas gives ready proof
      Of natural heritage resembling

                    The harvest fields,
               Which changing year by year, today
                    From their broad acres yield
          Abundant livelihood for man, tomorrow   10
          They take their ease and strength again recapture.
               For from Nemea's lovely games
          Here has come home a boy, bred to the contest,
          Who trod the destined way ordained of Zeus,
                    And has revealed himself
          Now, in the struggle of the wrestlers' ring,
                    A huntsman well requited.

ep. 1   Thus followed he the road   15
          Where trod his grandfather Praxidamas,
                    True scion of this stock;
          For he, victorious in Olympia's field,
          First to the clan of Aeacus brought home
                    The wreath that Alpheus' banks bestow:
                    And five times crowned at Isthmus' games
                         And at Nemea thrice,   20
          The faded memory of Socleides' name,
          First of the sons of Agesimachus,
                    He brought once more to honour.

str. 2   For the three others, athletes crowned, of all
               Who have tasted the toils of contest,
                    Won to the heights
               Of brave renown. Thus with heaven's aid
                    No other house they proved   25
          In all the folded vales of broad Hellas
          Has in its treasures more crowns laid away
               For victory in the boxer's ring.
          Bold boast: I doubt not, like an archer's arrow
          It hits the mark full-square. For this great clan, then,
                    Come, Muse, strike up, and breathe
          A gale of noble praise. For those who see
                    The light of day no more

ant. 2   It is by song and on the tongues of men   30
               Their noble deeds live down the years.
                    And no short measure

Of fine deeds has the Bassid clan:
　　Their race is old in story,
Their ships ride home the burthen of their praise,
And to the ploughmen of the Muses' meadow
　　Rich store they can provide, for song
To honour proud achievement. Came there not
In holy Pytho once to victory,
　　His hands bound in the thongs,   35
A man of the same blood, who won the favour
　　Of the children of Leto,

ep. 2　　　Goddess of the gold spindle?
Callias his name, and by Castalia's fountain
　　As evening fell, his glory
Flamed with the Graces' song. And by the bridge
That spans the restless sea, Creontidas   40
　　Found honour, in Poseidon's precinct,
　　At the feast of the neighbouring people,
　　　Where bulls are sacrificed,
Their two-year ritual. The lion's herb, too,
By the primeval hills of shady Phlious
　　Graced his victorious brow.

str. 3　Wide are the roads from every side, that lead   45
　　The voice of chronicle to adorn
　　　This island's fame.
　　For by their deeds of valour proved
　　　The sons of Aeacus
Raised high their destined glory, and o'er land
And far across the sea flies forth their name.
　　Even to the Ethiopian race,
When mighty Memnon came not home again,   50
Their fame took wing; for dire strife fell upon them
　　When great Achilles stepped
Down from his chariot to the ground, and slew
　　The son of shining Dawn,

ant. 3　With his fell-pointed spear. In these great deeds
　　The bards of old found for their songs
　　　A broad highway;
　　And I, too, at the self-same call

Follow my art's resource.
Yet, as they tell of ships that ride the storm,   55
That wave which each moment threatens most nearly
   The straining hull, breeds in all hearts
The sharpest breath of fear. Now I right gladly
Bending my shoulder to a twofold burden,
      Come as a messenger
To sing, Alcimidas, your proud success,   60
      The five-and-twentieth now

ep. 3   Earned by your famous race,
At the contests which men entitle sacred.
      And two more prizes still,
The wreaths of victory at Olympia,
In the precinct of Zeus, the son of Cronos,
      The chance fall of the lot denied
      To you and Polytimidas.
         Now to the dolphin's speed
Through the sea-foam, Melesias let me liken,   65
Skilful master of hands and supple strength,
      A most wise charioteer.

Notes

1. **The race of men and of the gods is one:** the translation is much disputed, and an alternative is 'there is one race of men and one of gods'; but the fact that both men and gods have one mother assures us that Conway's translation is correct.

2. **one mother:** Gaia, the Earth. Cf. Homeric Hymn 30, to Ge (Gaia).

7. **to what goal:** the Greek should rather be translated 'along what course'. Life is a road along which men ignorantly stumble. No goal is in view.

9. **resembling the harvest fields:** the alternation of fallow and cultivated land is characteristic of the world of nature; so the alternation of successful generations in Alcimidas' family is an indication that they live according to 'Nature'. (Nature is often synonymous with breeding in Pindar.)

15. **Praxidamas:** The genealogy is as follows:

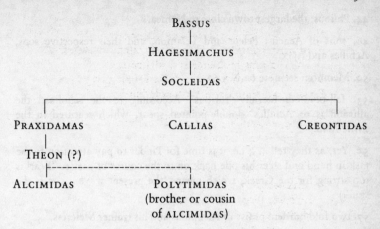

BASSUS
|
HAGESIMACHUS
|
SOCLEIDAS

PRAXIDAMAS   CALLIAS   CREONTIDAS
|
THEON (?)

ALCIMIDAS   POLYTIMIDAS
                     (brother or cousin
                     of ALCIMIDAS)

The argument of these lines is that Hagesimachus' glory as a victor was almost forgotten in the subsequent generation because Socleidas was no athlete; however, the success of Praxidamas and his two brothers revived the memory of the family's prowess. Socleidas is the greatest of Hagesimachus' sons because he fathered three victors. Praxidamas' son, the father of Alcimidas, who according to a dubious statement by the scholiast may have been called Theon, is not mentioned in the ode because he was likewise no athlete. In line 23 'three others', 'others' is not in the Greek; the reference is to Praxidamas, Callias and Creontidas (lines 36, 40).

31. the Bassid clan: We now learn that the family claimed descent from one Bassus.

36. Callias: Alcimidas' great-uncle, winner of a Pythian victory. Castalia is the sacred spring of Delphi.

40. Creontidas: Alcimidas' other great-uncle, winner of a victory at the Isthmus (of Corinth).

two-year ritual: the Isthmian and Nemean Games took place every two years, the Olympian and Pythian every four.

42. The lion's herb: the reference is to the Lion of Nemea and to the parsley from which the Nemean victor's crown was made. The word translated 'herb' means 'pasture'. The idea of the Lion grazing peacefully on parsley is a rather comic one; but the expression reinforces the pattern of plant imagery that pervades the poem.

44. Phlious: the largest town close to Nemea.

46. sons of Aeacus: Peleus and Telamon, and their respective sons, Achilles and Ajax.

50. Memnon: see note on N 3.62.

53. fell-pointed: literally 'furious'. According to the scholiast, the allusion is to Achilles' double-pointed spear, which featured in the *Little Iliad*.

55. Yet, as they tell . . . : i.e. it is time for Pindar to pay attention to the task in hand and steer his ode back on to the course of praise. ('Fear' is too strong for the Greek, which means 'the present wave . . . stirs the soul'.)

57. two fold burden: praise of Alcimidas and his trainer Melesias.

63. chance fall of the lot: this obscure passage is best explained by the assumption of the introduction of a bye-round on this occasion. If there was an uneven number of contestants for the wrestling, one of them drew a bye and stood aside for a round, a process known as *ephedreia* ('sitting aside'). When he re-entered the contest, he would be fighting an opponent already tired from his previous round. The procedure is described in Lucian, *Hermotimus* 40. Here, then, Alcimidas and Polytimidas must both have failed to draw the bye, and thus fought an extra round; their fresher opponent(s) won.

Polytimidas: probably brother or cousin of Alcimidas.

65. Melesias: the scholiast on N 4.93 says that Melesias was an Athenian; he may then be the same as the Melesias known as the father of Thucydides (not the historian but the political opponent of Pericles). He is also mentioned in O 8.54, and was clearly a leading trainer of athletes in Aegina.

67. charioteer: metaphorically speaking, i.e. as trainer.

For Sogenes of Aegina
Winner of the Boys' Pentathlon (485?)

This is the only Nemean ode for which a date is given by the scholiasts; unfortunately they give two (547 and 527), both manifestly impossible as they fall before Pindar's birth. Numbers cannot be emended, so this evidence fails us. The myth in Nemean 7 appears to be a recasting of that in Paean 6, and it has been thought possible to deduce that the Nemean falls not long after the paean. However, the only evidence for the paean's date is a reference in lines 123–5 to Aegina as 'ruling amidst the Dorian sea', a description which would be inappropriate after the Battle of Salamis. So the paean might be c. 490, the Nemean c. 485.

The ancient scholars Aristodemus and Aristarchus stated that in this ode Pindar was defending himself against a charge of slanderous treatment of the myth of Neoptolemus in a paean. With the publication of the papyrus of the paeans in 1908, it became evident that Paean 6 was what they had in mind. In the paean (for Apollo) the myth is given an Apolline, and therefore pro-Trojan slant; in the Nemean, for an Aeginetan, the favour is due rather to Neoptolemus with his Aeginetan descent.

Neoptolemus, the son of Achilles, in the mythical tradition was generally regarded as the first great war-criminal: at the Sack of Troy, he killed King Priam even though the latter had taken refuge at the altar of Zeus; and he hurled the young child Astyanax from the city walls. Apollo's vengeance was to ensure his death when he visited Delphi, in a quarrel over the division of the sacrificial meats. Despite this, Neoptolemus became a protecting hero at Delphi and was regarded as responsible for the good conduct of sacrifices: his cult was maintained there by the Aenianes, from the region of Dodona in Neoptolemus' legendary kingdom of Molossia (Strabo 9.5.22; Heliodorus, *Aethiopica* 3.10.1; see in general L. Woodbury, 'Neoptolemus at Delphi: Pindar N 7.30ff.' [*Phoenix* 33 (1979): 95–123]). In Paean 6 Pindar gives the hostile tradition while in the Nemean he concentrates on the role of Neoptolemus as a protector of the sanctuary.

Pindar often told myths on two occasions with different emphases, and the question arises as to whether the differences here are so great, and the tone of apology so apparent, that the one must be seen as an apology for the other. Few questions in Pindar have attracted more discussion: for summaries of the case see H. Lloyd-Jones, 'Modern Interpretation of Pindar', *JHS* 93 (1973): 109–37; G. Most, *The Measures of Praise: Structure and Function in Pindar's Second Pythian and Seventh Nemean Odes* (Göttingen 1985). In my opinion Pindar is not so much recanting his earlier treatment as offering a justification for telling an old myth in a different way (as he does in, for example, Olympian 1 where he invents new details to flatter the hero). The theme of his poem is the poet's duty to give true, genuine honour to his subjects – a task in which Homer failed in his exaggerated praise of Odysseus, while Pindar hopes to succeed in it in the case of Neoptolemus whom tradition has unfairly reviled.

Only the recurrence of this topic at the very end (lines 102–5), when the Neoptolemus section appeared completed, gives an impression of anxiety over his treatment of the subject. It is very possible that Aeginetans had been offended by the narrative of the paean; but, except for these last four lines, everything in the poem could make sense to a listener who had never heard the paean or cared about Aeginetan sensitivities.

Many passages in the ode are obscure and difficult to interpret, which has increased the impression among scholars that Pindar is in a state of embarrassment; but there may be other explanations for this obscurity, such as our own ignorance and the uncertainty of the text at crucial places.

str. 1 Goddess of childbirth, Eleithuia,
    Maid to the throne of the deep-thinking Fates,
    Child of all-powerful Hera, hear my song.
     For without thee should we see neither
     The light of day, nor know the kindly dark,
     Nor win the gift of Hebe, thy sister,
      The glorious limbs of Youth.
    Yet is the life we breathe not given to all   5
     For a like end. Destiny's bar

Yokes one man to this venture, one to that.
    But with thy favour now
Sogenes, listed on the roll of valour,
Thearion's son, with the Pentathlete victors
    Rises to glory on my song.

ant. 1   For his city is one of music-lovers,
The sons of Aeacus, bred to the clash of spears;   10
And glad are they to embrace a spirit, that shares
    Their love of contest. If success
Crowns a man's venture, sweeter then than honey
The theme he pours into the Muses' stream.
    But lacking songs to praise them,
The mightiest feats of valour can but find
    A sorry grave of deep darkness.
But for fine deeds a mirror to establish,
    One way alone we know,
If Memory's shining diadem will grant   15
Recompense for their labours, in the glory
    Of music on the tongues of men.

ep. 1   Wise men are they
    Who know the tempest that shall blow
      The third day hence,
Whom thirst for profit shall not bring to grief.
Yet rich and poor alike travel the road
    That leads at last to death.
    Yet I am fain to think   20
That by the sweet charm of great Homer's word
    Odysseus wins a larger fame
    Than his proved deeds would grant him.

str. 2   Through false tales and the skilled magic
Of wingéd words, a majesty enfolds him.
The poet's art by his fables deceives us
    And leads the mind astray. For blind
Of heart are all the most of men. Never,
Had they but been minded to know the truth,   25
    Never would mighty Ajax,
In anger's travail for the arms denied him,
    Have plunged his sharp sword through his breast:

Ajax, the mightiest warrior in battle
    Of all, save but Achilles,
Whom on their war-ships, to bring back his bride
To fair-haired Menelaus, the swift breath
    Of straight-flown Zephyrus escorted

ant. 2   To Ilos' city. Yet forget not,   30
Death's wave comes to all men, falling on him
Who recked not of it, and alike on him
    Who had some foretaste of it. But honour,
Honour is theirs, who win richly from heaven
        Storied renown, so to secure a name
        Deathless even in the grave.
So was it when came to the great centre-stone
    Of earth's broad breast Neoptolemus,   35
And lies in Pytho's soil – he who laid low
    Priam's city, stern struggle
Where too the Danai laboured. Sailing thence
He failed of Skyros, and far-wandering brought
    His scattered sails to Ephyra.

ep. 2   Then was his kingdom
        For a brief time Molossia;
            But since that day
His race has held that honoured throne. But he   40
Departed straight to the god's temple, bringing
        The chief spoils of Troy's city
        As offerings to Apollo.
There, o'er the meats of sacrifice, a quarrel
    Broke with a man who chanced to meet him,
        And with a knife-blade slew him.

str. 3   Heavy the grief of those who guard
The rights of Delphi's guests. Yet he fulfilled
The lot of destiny; for it was decreed
    That in that ancient precinct, one
Of Aeacus' mighty race should lie forever,   45
Beside the strong-walled house of the great god,
        To dwell, guardian of right
Over the pomps and ceremonies of heroes
    With their rich sacrifice. To pay

His name and fame full justice, shall suffice
　　Three words: where he presides
O'er brave exploits, no false witness could be
A son of thine, Aegina, and of Zeus.
　　Boldly I this for him proclaim:　　　　　　　　　50

ant. 3　　The splendour of their valorous deeds
Born of that house's heritage, gives him
A royal path to glory's record. Yet
　　As all know well, pleasant is rest
In every work of man; there can be surfeit
Even of honey and the lovely flower
　　　Of Aphrodite's joys.
By our inborn talent find we each one
　　The different path of life we tread,
One here, one there. But what can never be　　　　55
　　Is that one man should win
A life entire of blessings. I know no man
To whom Fate gave this lot abidingly.
　　But you, Thearion, she grants

ep. 3　　　　No grudging share
　　Of happiness, courage to dare
　　　Deeds of high mettle,
And lessens not your heart's good understanding.　　60
I am your guest. From dark slander shall I
　　Defend you, as a friend
　　Brings to a friend a draught
Of purest water, to your true renown
　　Giving due praise. For men of worth
　　　This is the fit reward.

str. 4　　Should an Achaean from his home
Above the Ionian sea, be near me now, no　　　　65
Blame shall he voice. In his land, in my title
　　Of Proxenos I have full trust;
On my own folk I look with serene eyes,
Moderate in all I do, guarding my steps
　　From every violent act.
And may my days to come follow a like
　　Path of goodwill. Who knows me well

Shall say if shafts of slander on my tongue
   Come with their jarring note.
Son of the house of Euxenos, Sogenes,   70
Ne'er, as an athlete whose foot faults the line,
   Launching his bronze-tipped javelin,

ant. 4   Have I so cast a sharp-flung word.
To you I swear it, who from the wrestlers' ring,
Its struggle and sweat, and from the sun's hot ray
   Kept your strong limbs and shoulders free.
If it were toil, greater the joy thereafter.
But this: to pay grace to the victor's honour,
    If, borne on wings aloft   75
I called a cry too shrill, no churlish heart
   Is mine, not to subscribe it fully.
Weaving of wreaths is a light task: strike up:
   The Muse makes gifts of gold
And of white ivory together mingled,
And, gleaming like the lily's flower, can steal
   The clear spray from the deep sea's wave.

ep. 4   Bear Zeus in mind
   Chanting your notes of song widespread   80
     For Nemea's honour;
And peace be in your hearts. For it is fitting
That on this soil voices of gentle measure
    Should celebrate in song
    The almighty King of gods.
For it was he, so runs the tale, begot
   Great Aeacus to be his son
    Within a mortal womb,

str. 5   And to be ruler of his country   85
Of splendid name, and to you, Heracles,
To be a kind and loyal host, and brother.
   For of all gifts exchanged of man
No greater taste of joy should we adjudge,
Than if a neighbour shall befriend a neighbour
    With steadfast loyalty.
If too a god allow us such relation,
   With you, great conqueror of the giants,   90

In friendship's tie so bonded, Sogenes
    Would deem his life well-blessed,
With tender spirit cherishing his father,
To hold in sacred trust the well-found homestead
    By his forebears bequeathed to him.

ant. 5   For he lives in your holy precinct,
As if beneath a four-horsed chariot yoke,
Binding on this hand and on that, the house
    Wherein he dwells. O blessèd one,
Your task it can well be to win for him
Propitious grace from Hera's husband, and   95
    The grey-eyed goddess maid.
Not seldom is it in your power to grant
    To mortal souls, strength to withstand
The toils that baffle them. May you for these,
    Father and son, accord
A life of steadfast strength, that fortune's blessing
Cleave to them both, in youth and sunlit age.
    And may their children's children ever   100

ep. 5   Preserve these honours,
    And achieve fortune happier still
       In years to come.
But shall my heart never admit that I
With words none can redeem smirched Neoptolemus.
    Yet to repeat the same
       Saying three times or more,
Argues a wit helpless and weak, as one   105
    Who to his babes mumbles the tale
       'Corinth the son of Zeus'.

Notes

1. **Eleithuia:** the goddess of childbirth. The scholiasts tell us, on the basis of a now lost epigram of Simonides (frag. 166, Bgk) that Thearion was blessed with a son only late in life, so that the blessing was the greater. The name Sogenes may be interpreted as 'saviour of the clan'. This would shed light on the passage at lines 98–101 with its reference to youth and old age, and grandchildren; and if the reference to the

delights of love at line 53 has any special significance, perhaps the boy was even now considering marriage.

4. Hebe: the goddess of youth and beauty.

12ff.: lacking songs: the need of success to be celebrated in song if it is to endure, is a commonplace in Pindar; in this ode it becomes a dominant theme.

17. Wise men: in general, and in this context especially patrons, who know that the future brings oblivion unless song is given. There follows an example of a song which gave too much honour to Odysseus – by which the stupid were fooled (lines 23–4).

25. Had they but been minded to know the truth: we expect some phrase like 'they would not have believed Homer'; instead we have '(the Greeks) would not have believed Odysseus (and so awarded him the arms of Achilles instead of to Ajax)'. After the death of Achilles at Troy the Greeks decided to give his golden armour to the warrior adjudged to have fought most gallantly. Ajax expected to receive this award, but the persuasive power of Odysseus induced the Greeks to award it to himself. Ajax thereupon killed himself in shame: see Sophocles' *Ajax*. Ajax was of course an Aeginetan hero and Pindar naturally prefers to honour him than the 'sophistic' Odysseus, whose words, like Grace in O 1.30–3, can make the false seem true.

29. Zephyrus: the West Wind.

30. Ilos' city: Ilium, the ancient name of Troy.

Death's wave: the power of memory to overcome death picks up the assertions of lines 12–16; Pindar has shown how death can be overcome by false, bad poetry; now he must show how poetry can set right injustice.

33. So was it: one of the most difficult textual cruces in Pindar. Conway translates *emolen*, he came. The scholiasts read *emolon*, I came or they came. The accentuation of *boathoon* (a form of a root meaning 'help', not translated at all by Conway) may vary and give different senses. The punctuation is also uncertain, and a stop may be put before 'in the grave'. Translate: (a) some of the Helpers, now dead, came to the great centre-stone of earth's broad breast [i.e. Delphi] ... (described as 'plain nonsense' by Wilamowitz, but supported recently by Woodbury); (b) he (i.e. Neoptolemus) came as a helper to the great centre-stone ... (Conway's interpretation); (c) I came (or 'have come') as a helper to the great centre-stone . . . Lloyd-Jones chooses (c) and takes it as a reference to Pindar's visit to Delphi to perform the Paean; but 'I came' is used elsewhere in Pindar to refer to the coming of the poet to the occasion of the present ode, and it may be possible to take this as a reference to Pindar coming metaphorically to Delphi in the course of this ode. The meaning then is 'I have come to help a hero's reputation: and here is the myth of Neoptolemus to show how.'

37. Skyros: an island in the Aegean which was the home of Neoptolemus in his youth until he was summoned by the Greeks to take part in the Trojan War after the death of his father Achilles. In the sixth Paean Pindar tells us that Neoptolemus was fated never to see his mother again or return home, and that Apollo swore that he should die at Delphi. The hostility of Apollo is entirely omitted from the seventh Nemean.

Ephyra: a city in Epirus, the northwestern region of Greece, opposite Corfu.

38. Molossia: the region of Epirus, named after Molossus the son of Neoptolemus and Andromache, whom Neoptolemus brought as a captive from Troy. The legendary kingdom of Molossia included the coast and Dodona, and was more extensive than the fifth-century Molossian kingdom, which was inhabited by non-Greeks. The region around Dodona was inhabited in Pindar's time by the Aenianes, who honoured the memory of Neoptolemus and maintained his cult honours at Delphi.

42. with a knife-blade: the accidental death of Neoptolemus was attributed by Pherecydes, our earliest source besides Pindar, to a man named Machaireus, which means 'he of the sacrificial knife'. In the paean, Apollo's agency in the hero's death is emphasized; not so here.

45. should lie forever: Neoptolemus' tomb was in the sanctuary of Apollo at Delphi: Paus. 10.24.6. Although the common legendary tradition had it that Neoptolemus had come to pillage the temples, his death redeemed him and gave him a hero's powers. His cult was maintained by the Aenianes of the region around Dodona (Strabo 9.5.22, Heliodorus, *Aethiopica* 3.10.1), and his function was to maintain good order in the sacrificial rituals (at which he had been so unfortunately let down).

49. no false witness: Conway's translation is unlikely. Neoptolemus could hardly be the witness in the case to give justice to himself. Prefer:

'No false witness stands over the deeds of the offspring of Zeus and you, Aegina.' The witness may be Apollo, or – in the context of the discussion of poetic honesty – it may be Pindar himself.

52. pleasant is rest: the phrase is a common 'break-off' motif, used to abandon one topic and move on to the next.

54. inborn talent: again a common epinician topic: cf. B 10.35–8. The uncertainty of fortune's gifts are mentioned as a foil to the coming praise of Thearion, the victor's father, who acted as Pindar's host in Aegina and seems perhaps to have had a formal role of proxenos, with a duty of entertaining honoured guests in the island.

57. Fate: one or other of the Fates commonly accompany Eleithuia at births (e.g. Pa. 12.17, I 6 .17), so that this reference recalls the opening line of the ode.

61. your guest: as in line 65, Pindar emphasizes his guest-relationship with Thearion. The scholiast states that this refers to a Theoxenia, a guest-banquet of the gods, being held in Aegina, at which Pindar was present. There is no way of knowing what evidence he had for this statement.

From dark slander: there is no way of knowing what slanders were being directed at Thearion, but the phrase emphasizes the poet's duty of praise.

64. an Achaean: this seems to refer to a descendant of Neoptolemus in his home in Epirus by the Ionian sea – or possibly to Neoptolemus himself. It seems a little unlikely that anyone from Epirus would be present on Aegina for this occasion.

65. my title of Proxenos: a proxenos was something like a consul, and had the responsibility of looking after the interests of foreigners in his own city. It seems faintly improbable that Pindar was a proxenos of the Epirotes in Thebes, and it may be better to take this with what follows: 'trusting in my title of proxeny I have full trust among my own folk', here referring to 'his' fellow-citizens of Aegina. These are hard lines to understand.

70–4. To you I swear it: Conway's translation is not correct. Translate: 'I swear that I did not step up to the mark and hurl my swift tongue like a bronze-cheeked javelin in such a way as to send neck and strength out of the wrestling ring before the limbs were touched by the blazing sun.' But what does it mean? Pindar denies having made a losing throw which would have prevented his going on to the next and last contest in the pentathlon, the wrestling. Pindar often alludes to the event in question and uses it as a metaphor for his own poetry (cf. P 1.42–5). Was there perhaps some dispute as to whether Sogenes had stepped over the mark as he threw the javelin? Pindar asserts that his praise at least is perfectly positioned.

74. If it were toil . . .: a consolation to Sogenes for the effort now rewarded by victory. Farnell remarks feelingly: 'a sentence that the boy could at last understand'.

76. not to subscribe it fully: I cannot understand Conway's translation. The word translated 'subscribe' means 'pay': Pindar promises to pay his debt of praise – an easy job, as he goes on to say.

85. his country: the MSS have 'my country'. Pindar regards Aegina as his own land by virtue of his guest-relationship with Thearion. So the Aeginetan hero Aeacus is envisaged as having been the host of the Theban hero Heracles, an otherwise unknown connection. The guest then leads to the introduction of Heracles who has a role to play in celebrating any athletic victory.

90. great conqueror of the giants: cf. N 4.27 on Heracles' assistance to the gods in their battle with the Giants.

93. As if beneath a four-horsed chariot yoke: the house in which Sogenes lived apparently (so the scholiasts say), was between two shrines of Heracles, which Pindar compares to the double yoke of a four-horsed chariot.

95. Hera's husband: Zeus.

grey-eyed goddess maid: Athena.

102. But shall my heart never admit: this return to the theme of Neoptolemus is very remarkable and does suggest that it has become a bone of contention with some unknown critics. However, the expression may be a litotes of a type common in Pindar: 'not savaging' is used to mean 'praising'; cf. the strong expressions at P 4.99 'not staining with lies', P 9.80, 'not dishonouring him' i.e. 'honouring him'. See A. Köhnken, 'Gebrauch und Funktion der Litotes bei Pindar', *Glotta* 54 (1976): 62–7.

103. words none can redeem: a better translation may be 'words which cannot be changed'. Pindar will then be asserting his right to alter his myths to suit his occasions, rather than parrot them the same way every time.

105. Corinth the son of Zeus: a proverbial expression for mindless repetition.

For Deinis of Aegina
Winner of the Foot Race (459?)

It appears from the opening lines of the ode that Deinis (the Doric form of the name is to be preferred to the Attic Deinias), the victor, was a young man in his prime. His father Megas, who was no longer alive, had also been a Nemean victor.

However, the description of the two men's victories at lines 16 and 47ff. makes it uncertain exactly what victories each achieved. Line 16 states that Deinis was victorious 'twice'; lines 47ff. offer celebration of the success of, literally, 'twice two feet'. These lines, taken together, could mean five different things. (1) Each won one victory, in the stadion race. So the scholiast (inscr.) states. Line 16 refers to the pair together, and 47ff. to the fact that the two men between them had four feet (or two victories, each won with a pair of feet). (2) Deinis won one victory in the diaulos (double stadion race). So the scholiast on line 26 (16) states. (3) Deinis won two victories in the stadion. (4) Deinis won two victories (or one diaulodromos) and Megas won one. This was Dissen's argument, but the even number of line 48 does not fit this pattern. (5) Each won two victories; so that 'two feet' in line 48 means 'two people's feet'. I find the last of these the most natural explanation of the repeated play on the number two, and a corollary would be that there is no need to see the event as a double race. Deinis and Megas each won two victories in the foot race.

Curiously, the ancient scholar Didymus remarks that neither Deinis nor Megas was included in the Nemean victor lists to which he had access.

The myth, which concerns the dispute between Ajax and Odysseus for the arms of Achilles, a theme treated also in N 8, has been seen by some commentators as alluding to political tension between Athens and Aegina in the period beginning 460 (or, alternatively, by different commentators, about 490). It is hard to see why, and there is no reliable way of dating the ode.

str. 1   O sovereign Youth, herald of Aphrodite
              And her sweet passions born of heaven,
          Whose wing lights on the eyes of youth and maid,
              And whose constraining hands
          On one with kindly touch, but on another
              All too ungently fall –
          Happy is he who in his every act
          Fails not the moment due, and can prevail
              The noblest loves to master.   5

ant. 1   Such loves were shepherd to the bridal bed
              Of Zeus and Aegina, to bring them
          The Cyprian goddess' gifts. And there was born
              A son, king of Oenone,
          Peerless in counsel and in might of hand.
              Many, and oft, would plead
          His audience, for the flower of warrior pride
          Dwelling in lands nearby, were glad unbidden
              His sovereign laws to obey,   10

ep. 1   Those who in Athens' rock-built city marshalled
              The people's host, and the great line
              Of Pelops' sons, rulers in Sparta.
                  A suppliant now come I,
          To embrace the knees of Aeacus, long revered,
          Bringing for his dear city, and for these
          His citizens, a Lydian circlet, richly   15
          With fluted notes embroidered, glory's prize
              For Deinis and his father Megas,
                  Victorious in the foot race
              Twice on Nemea's field. True is it,
          Good fortune founded with the help of heaven,
          Lasts for mankind far longer down the years.

str. 2   Such was it loaded Kinyras with riches
              In sea-girt Cyprus long ago.
          Look, on feet lightly-poised I stand, to take
              New breath before I speak.
          Story is vast in range: new ways to find   20
              And test upon the touchstone,
          Here danger lies: words are rich food for envy,

Who lays her hand ever upon the noble,
    Striving not with lesser men.

ant. 2   She it was devoured the son of Telamon,
        His body pierced with his own sword.
    A dauntless heart having no able tongue,
        Howsoe'er fierce the battle,
    Lies hid, forgotten; but the highest prize
        For shifty craft lies spread.   25
    The Danaans' secret votes courted Odysseus,
    But Ajax, cheated of the golden arms,
        Wrestled with bloody death.

ep. 2   Unlike indeed, those other wounds they struck
        And cleft the hot flesh of the foe,
        Beneath their fence of serried spears   30
            Bearing the brunt of war;
    Whether beside Achilles newly slain,
    Or whatsoever toll of ills filled full
    Those crowded days of death. Yet even of old
    Treachery's tongue, breeder of hate, was known,
        Close companied with tales of guile,
        False-hearted to the core,
        She sows the evil seed of blame,
    Violates true merit's lustre, and exalts
    The worthless man's unsavoury repute.

str. 3   Such thoughts, great Zeus, never may it be mine   35
        To foster, but of life to tread
    The simple paths, and dying leave my children
        No ill-engendered fame.
    Gold is for some their prayer, for some wide acres;
        My trust shall be to dwell
    Beloved of friends, till earth shall shroud my limbs,
    Praising where praise is due, on evil-doers
        Sowing widespread rebuke.

ant. 3   Midst poets and just minds true excellence   40
        Reaches full height, as trees refreshed
    By fruitful showers spread to the moistening air.
        For many a diverse cause

A man needs friends: under the toils of contest
Most need of all; and joy
Seeks too to see clearly before her eyes
The sign of trust. To bring your spirit, Megas,
To earth again, lies not

ep. 3   Within my power, and useless is the end   45
Of idle hopes. But for your race
And for the Chariades to build
A mighty pillar of the Muse,
This task I can, to honour those swift feet
That won the double prize, twice glorious;
And glad am I if I may utter praise
To match the act; for by songs and their charm
A man can draw the pains of toil
Even from weary limbs.   50
Yes, hymns of revelry were known
Long years ago, e'er yet the strife arose
Betwixt Adrastus and the sons of Cadmus.

Notes

1. O sovereign Youth: the goddess Hora, seasonableness, is an emblem
of sexual attractiveness. One should not therefore deduce that Pindar
was in love with the victor. Attractiveness is an appropriate topic of
praise for a young man. See Peter von der Mühll, 'Persönliche Verliebtheit des Dichters?' Mus. Helv. 21 (1964): 198ff.; S. Instone, 'Love and
Sex in Pindar', BICS 37 (1990): 30–42. It is notable that the invocation
does not lead to an actual prayer.

6. loves: the erotes are portrayed in art of the sixth century and in
Pindar's time as slim young men; it is only in hellenistic times that they
become putti. See also Pindar, frag. 122.4; B frag. 9.73.

Zeus and Aegina: for the story see also Pa. 6.134–7, I 8.21ff.

7. Cyprian goddess: Aphrodite.

a son: Aeacus.

10. Athens ... Sparta: Pindar might be here evoking the past greatness
of Aegina, when the cities that were in the mid fifth century the two
greatest in Greece, came to pay homage to Aegina. There might be an

allusion to the historical embassies of Athens and Sparta to Aegina in 498 or 480 (Herodotus 5.80, 8.64; cf. 8.123). Of course the inhabitants of Sparta were not, strictly speaking in mythic chronology, descendants of Pelops in Aeacus' time. The occasion referred to is the drought which affected Greece, which Aeacus ended by his prayers to Zeus: see N 5.10ff. and notes.

15. **Lydian circlet:** a kind of headscarf often given to victorious athletes. Lydian is a byword for luxury, and also the name of the mode in which the ode's music was written. In frag. 179 Pindar again refers to an ode as a woven headband.

16. **Victorious in the foot race twice:** see the introduction to the ode.

17. **founded with the help of heaven:** a standard topic in Pindar: cf. N 6.24 and note.

Kinyras: a legendary king of Cyprus and a byword for wealth and good fortune. Cf. P 2.15 and note.

19. **feet lightly-poised:** Pindar's metaphors for his poetic activity often reflect the event in which his addressee was successful, and function as an introduction to the act of praise.

20. **new ways to find:** Pindar is enthusiastic about telling old myths in new ways: O 1.13, N 7.33 with note. Here he speaks of the danger of new praise – an indication that the myth can function specifically *as* praise.

21. **food for envy:** cf. P 2.55ff. B 3.68 for the food metaphor.

23. **son of Telamon:** the myth is told also in N 7 of how Ajax, defeated in the judgment over the arms of Achilles, which his mother Thetis had promised to whoever had done most for her son, and which the Greeks awarded to Odysseus for his plausible speeches, committed suicide. The story was told in the epic *Aethiopis* and *Little Iliad*, and the former of these included a voting scene as described here. This vote was also the subject of Aeschylus' play, *The Judgment of Arms*, in which Odysseus won by deceit. The voting was rigged according to Sophocles, *Ajax* 1135. The scene was also a popular one in vase-painting. W. W. Lloyd (*Pindar and Aeschylus: Aegina and Athens* [London 1862]) argued that there is an allusion to the rigged voting which elected Themistocles the best general after Salamis in 480 (Herodotus 8.123), and that the ode is an attack on Athenian rhetorical dishonesty, but the parallel does not seem sufficiently close to present itself as inescapable or even necessary.

26. Odysseus: on the common theme of Odysseus as a trickster, see W. B. Stanford, *The Ulysses Theme* (London 1963), pp. 81–117.

35. Such thoughts: after exemplifying the danger inherent in praise and the envious guile that can destroy a reputation, Pindar makes a new start at just praise for his addressee; the prayer for his own avoidance of envy can be taken as applying to the victor also.

40. true excellence reaches full height: cf. frag. 227, 'deeds rise and shine', B 3.88ff. There is also a suggestion that excellence is a product of nature, of the good stock from which it springs, as in the elaborate tree metaphor of N 11.37ff.

43. A man needs friends: *sc.* to display his success; and his father, who could do this so well, is dead: so the ode will have to undertake the task.

44. Megas: Deinis' dead father. The mention of dead relatives is frequent in the odes: cf. O 14, I 7.24–5, O 8.77ff., P 5.90ff., N 4.85ff.

46. Chariades: the correct form is Chariadae.

47. pillar of the Muse: rather a (grave)stone.

swift feet: see introduction.

50. by songs and their charm: the idea of the ode as a recompense and cure for pains is combined with the old idea that wounds can be cured by incantations, en-chant-ments.

51. Adrastus . . . : the expedition of the Seven against Thebes, here taken as representing very ancient times.

For Chromius of Aetna
Winner of the Chariot Race (474?)

This ode and the two which follow were not written to celebrate victories in the Nemean Games. Because the Nemeans were the last of the four books of epinicians in ancient editions, these three odes were tacked on to the end. This ode was written for a victory in the Sicyonian Pythia, with which the ode's myth is concerned. It is monostrophic, i.e. not written in triads like most epinicia, and one should perhaps envisage a different kind of performance from the usual choric dance.

Chromius is the Sicilian general celebrated in Nemean 1, who was made governor of the city of Aetna after its foundation shortly before 476. This ode seems to belong just after the other, perhaps 474 or a little later. Line 44 indicates that Chromius was a man of mature years at this time. Of course chariot-racing did not require the contestant to be young and athletic, but only to pay for a chariot and driver.

str. 1   Let us now as Apollo bids, O Muses,
           From Sicyon lead our chant of triumph
           To Aetna, the new-founded city,
           And Chromius' house of happy fortune,
   Whose doors, flung wide, brim over with the stream of guests.
           For him, then, play aloud
           The sweet notes of your praise,
        For mounted in his victor's chariot
        He gives the signal for the song, in honour
           Of Leto and her twin children,
        Who keep their joint watch over rocky Pytho.   5

str. 2   There is a saying on the lips of men
           That no deed nobly done should lie
           Hidden in silence 'neath the ground,
           Whose fit reward is divine song,
   Proud poetry's praise. Then let the sounding lyre ring out,

And the flute's note, to honour
     The greatest of all contests
Of horsemen's skill, which for Apollo's glory
Adrastus founded by Asopus' stream;
     These shall my song now call to mind,
And crown that hero with illustrious honour.   10

str. 3   He the enthronéd king then of that land
               Made known his city's name and fame,
               With his new festivals, and contests
               For strength of limb and richly-carved
          Chariots, sped on their rival course. For he had fled
               From bold Amphiaraus
               And bitter civil strife,
          Driven far from his father's halls, and far
          From Argos city; and Talaus' sons were kings
               No more, enforced by war's fell fury.
          For men of power tread down the older right.   15

str. 4   But when in marriage to this son of Oikleus
               They gave, as for a pledge of faith,
               Eriphyle, who was to prove
               Her husband's slayer, they became
          The greatest captains of the fair-haired Danai.
               And on a time they led
               Their soldier host against
          Seven-gated Thebes – a road that won no sign
          Of happy omen, but the lightning flash
               Of Zeus bade not their hot-head madness
          Lead forth from home, but to renounce their march. 20

str. 5   But to a fated end clearly revealed
               The host sped forth upon its way,
               Clad in their brazen mail and trappings
               Of horsemen's gear. But their fond hopes
          Of sweet return were sundered on Ismenus' banks,
               And their young limbs fed fat,
               With smoke white-billowing,
          Seven burning pyres; but for Amphiaraus
          Zeus with his thunderbolt's consuming might

Cleft open the deep-breasted earth,
And hid him from man's sight, horses and all,   25

str. 6   E'er that the spear of Periclymenus
        Should pierce his back, and that in shame
        His warrior heart should meet its end.
        For even the children of the gods
  Take flight in terrors sprung from heaven. – O son of Cronos,
          If it can be, would that
          This test of warrior worth,
        This trial for life or death, against the host
        Of the Phoenician spears, I might delay
         For many a day. Great father Zeus,
        I beg thee grant the sons of Aetna's city   30

str. 7   Long share of wisdom's rule, and that this people
        May be full partners in the glories
        Their city shall reveal. For here,
        Be sure, are men who love full well
  A horseman's skill, and hearts that reck not of possessions,
          Hard to believe. For Honour,
          Who brings men high renown,
        By hope of gain in secret is perverted.
        Had you been shield-bearer to Chromius, battling
         On foot, on horse or on the sea,
        You would have judged, facing the conflict's din,   35

str. 8   That under stress of war it was that goddess,
        Honour, that bred within his heart
        The warrior mettle to fend off
        The havoc of Mars. Few men there are
  Who have the strength of hand, or heart, to devise plans
          To turn the cloud of bloodshed,
          Threatening their very door,
        Onto the ranks of their dread enemies.
        Hector's renown found its full flower, they say,
         Beside Scamander's stream, and here
        Near to Helorus' steeply-riven banks,   40

str. 9   Whose name men call the ford of goddess Rhea,
        There shone forth a like gleam of glory

To light Agesidamus' son,
In his first years of young manhood;
And many another day of his deeds could I tell
Braved on the dusty land
Or on the neighbouring sea.
But from the dangers which beset our youth,
If rightly met, comes to our elder years
An age of peace. Then let him know
That heaven has given him blessings beyond count.   45

str. 10   For if, together with possessions rich,
A man wins glorious renown,
Achievement has no higher peak
For mortal footsteps to attain.
Peace and the banquet like each other passing well;
And victory flowers anew
In the sweet chant of song;
While by the wine-bowl can the singer's voice
Be more courageous yet. Then let the draught
Be poured and mixed, that sweet and rich
Proclaimer of the songs of revelry.   50

str. 11   And let the strong child of the vine be served
In silver goblets, which his steeds
For Chromius won, and which with wreaths
Woven as Apollo's rite demands,
They brought from holy Sicyon. Father Zeus, I pray thee,
May the song that I sing
To praise this deed of valour,
Be by the Graces blest, and may our voices
More than all others, honour his victory.
For that I set my arrow's aim,
As near as may be to the Muses' mark.   55

Notes

1. as Apollo bids: Better, 'Let us process from Apollo's [sanctuary] at Sicyon'. The ode seems written for a procession rather than a dance.

9. Adrastus founded: the games dedicated to Apollo at Sicyon were in legend founded by Adrastus of Argos, who also founded the Nemean

Games. They were originally known as the Adrasteia, but in the early sixth century the tyrant Cleisthenes of Sicyon rededicated them to Apollo as a gesture against possible Argive domination of his city; he suppressed the cult of Adrastus in Sicyon altogether. See Herodotus 5.67; Richard Stoneman, 'Pindar and the Mythological Tradition', *Philologus* 125 (1981): 44–63. Pindar derived the story from the epic *Thebais*: his style of narrative here is notably linear, appropriate perhaps for a less familiar myth.

Asopus: apparently a river near Sicyon.

13. Amphiaraus: usurped the throne of Argos from Adrastus, who retired temporarily to Sicyon.

14. Talaus: father of Adrastus.

16. Oikleus: better, Oikles, father of Amphiaraus.

Eriphyle: the sister of Adrastus. By her marriage to Amphiaraus, the quarrel between the two was made up. She became responsible for the death of Amphiaraus because, when he was hesitating to join the expedition of the Seven against Thebes, having foreseen through his prophetic powers that it would meet with disaster, Eriphyle persuaded him to join, having been suborned by Polynices, one of the Seven, who was the son of Oedipus and had been exiled from Thebes by his brother Eteocles.

19. no sign of happy omen: cf. *Iliad* 4.381, possibly deriving from the *Thebais*.

22. Ismenus: a river near Thebes: see Paus. 9.9.1, which quotes a passage of the *Thebais*.

24. seven . . . pyres: There was a place at Thebes called the Seven Pyres, usually regarded as the graves of the children of Niobe. Seven is in fact the wrong number for the graves of the Seven against Thebes, since Adrastus got away and Amphiaraus was swallowed by the earth and re-emerged at Oropus in Attica. Adrastus may be seen as extra to the seven (Paus. 10.10.3) but the arithmetic still does not work.

26. Periclymenus: one of the defenders of Thebes.

27. even the children of the gods: Amphiaraus was not the son of a god, so his flight is the more excusable. For the phrase cf. Euripides, *Alcestis* 989ff., 'even the sons of gods can die'.

28. Phoenician spears: there had been a peace treaty with Carthage since the battle of Himera in 480. It is unclear what 'this trial' is meant to be, and perhaps it is an imaginary threat; but Chromius, a more successful general than the Seven against Thebes, will be able to outface it.

33. Hard to believe: a note of warning or advice not to be avaricious, which functions as praise of Chromius for his open-handedness.

39. Scamander: the river at Troy.

40. Helorus: a river in Sicily where about 492 Hippocrates, tyrant of Gela, defeated the Syracusans. His sons Gelon and Hieron, and Chromius their friend, assisted at the battle. Chromius must have been a young man at this time (like Hector). The subsequent struggles between the Sicilian city-states, and possibly the naval defeat of the Etruscans at Cumae in 474 (if the ode was written after this date) are reflected in the extensive praise of Chromius in the rest of the ode.

44. our elder years: a similar sentiment about peaceful old age after trials occurs at I 6.10–13.

50. let the draught be poured: the procession ends and the banquet can begin.

51. silver goblets: the prizes of victory in the Sicyonian Pythia.

53. holy Sicyon: holy because at the beginning of the world the respective honours of gods and mortals were allocated here: Hesiod, *Theogony* 35ff. (cf. Callimachus frag. 119).

55. the Muses' mark: the Muses close the poem as they opened it. The poem's aim is achieved.

For Theaius of Argos
Winner of the Wrestling Match (after 464)

This ode, though it includes mention of a Nemean victory among the many victories of Theaius, is not a Nemean ode as its specific occasion is a victory won at Argos. Like Nemeans 9 and 11, it is one of three attached as an appendix to the end of the four books of Pindar's epinicians which in ancient editions included the Nemeans after the Isthmians, not before, as in modern editions. As Pindar's only ode for an Argive, it includes an extensive catalogue of the legends of Argos, reminding one of the admonition said to have been made to Pindar by the poetess Corinna, that 'You should sow with the hand, not with the sack' (Plutarch, *Glory of Athens* 4).

A curious detail is that bronze is mentioned in every triad of the ode, perhaps bringing an echo of the Age of Heroes to the poem. Argos was famed for bronze and metalwork generally.

The ode was performed at the Heraea, the festival of Hera, the patron goddess of Argos, probably at the Heraeum, whose remains overlook the plain of Argos a few miles north of the city.

There is no external evidence for the date of the ode. If the 'city of Proitos' referred to in lines 39–42 is (as it should be) Tiryns, there must be some point in drawing attention to the fact that Theaius' mother's family came from there and saying that Theaius should not be ashamed of it. Presumably his mother's side was the only one which had been successful in athletic contests. Now Tiryns was captured by Argos in 465/4 or thereabouts, so that after 464 there would be some reason for an Argive to be embarrassed about Tirynthian ancestry. There appears also to have been an earlier synoecism of the Tirynthians, who were virtually enslaved by Argos (Herodotus 6.83, Aristotle, *Politics* 1303a6), perhaps in 494 (Paus. 2.25.7, 8.27.1); if Theaius' mother had been one of the subjugated Tirynthians and had married a free Aergive, Theaius would have had class anxieties as well as interstate rivalry to worry about.

However, the synoecism may have taken place only in the 460s. Stylistic reasons suggest a later rather than earlier date in Pindar's career. The Heraea were celebrated in the uneven years BC in Panemos (= June); the Panathenaea, which Pindar refers to as recent (33ff) were held in year three of every Olympiad in Hecatombaeon (July/August); so Pindar refers to the Panathenaea of ten months before and the Olympic Games fourteen months ahead. The Heraea victory will have been won in 468, 464 or 460. I favour 464. See further W. G. Forrest, 'Themistocles and Argos', CQ 10 (1960): 223ff., and my D. Phil. thesis, 'A Commentary on Six Nemean Odes of Pindar' (Oxford 1977), pp. 532–4.

str. 1   Of Danaus' city, and his fifty daughters
        On their resplendent thrones, sing, O ye Graces.
           Of Argos sing, the home of Hera,
           Abode worthy a god. This city's name
             A thousand deeds of her bold sons
               Light with the flame of valour.
        Long is the tale of Perseus and the Gorgon
        Medusa: many the cities that the hands
           Of Epaphus founded   5
        In Egypt: nor does Hypermnestra fail
        Of glory, who alone of all, kept hid
             Her sword within its sheath.

ant. 1   To Diomede a god's immortal power
        The grey-eyed goddess gave, fair-haired Athene;
           And once in Thebes the earth, sundered
        By lightning bolts of Zeus, engulfed the seer
           Son of Oikleus, storm-cloud of war.
             Adorned with beauty's tresses,
        Her women of old brought Argos fame, and Zeus   10
        Paying court to Alcmene and to Danaë,
             Gave proof of this.
        And for Lynceus and for Adrastus' father
        She set within their hearts the fruit of wisdom
             Linked with unswerving right.

ep. 1   She bred that warrior soul
           Amphitryon, whose race received the god

Of strength supreme, when in bronze arms he slew
  The Teleboai; for great Zeus   15
  Taking his likeness, brought the seed
Of Heracles the dauntless to his chamber;
   Who now upon Olympus dwelling,
    Has to his wedded wife,
Beside her mother, guardian of marriage, Hebe
    Fairest of all the goddesses.

str. 2   My tongue lacks time the long tale to unfold
Of noble deeds sprung from that sacred land
   Of Argos, and harsh the penalty   20
For wearying men's ears. Yet come, strike up
   The lyre's melodious chords, and let
    Your inward vision scan
The wrestlers' ring. The games and their bronze prize
To the Sacrifice of Oxen call the people,
     To honour Hera,
And the contest's decision. Twice victor there,
Oulias' son, Theaius, may forget
    The toils he braved so well.

ant. 2   Once, too, he overcame the host of Hellas   25
At Pytho, and by happy fortune won
   Crowns at the Isthmus and Nemea;
Three victories for the Muses' plough to till,
   Won beside Ocean's gates, and three
    Within the sacred field
Where king Adrastus set the games. Ah, Zeus,
His thought may dream dreams though his tongue be silent;
     With thee, great Father,
Lies every issue, but well tried in toil,   30
And with a brave heart in his breast, he begs
    No favour undeserved.

ep. 2   Clear are the words I sing
To Zeus, and whosoever braves the struggle
For the supreme prize at the greatest games –
   That highest glory held by Pisa,
   The games founded by Heracles.
Yet twice, at Athens' feasts, sweet revels rang

As for a prelude, when Theaius   35
   The fruitful olive's oil
In richly figured urns, fresh from the kiln,
   Brought home to Hera's lordly people.

str. 3   Comes to you too, by favour of the Graces
And of the sons of Tyndareus, no less,
   The glory of the contests won
By that renownéd race, your mother's kin.
   Had I the blood of Thrasycles   40
      And Antias within me,
Proud should I be to hold my head on high
Before the eyes of Argos. Many a crown
   Has Proetus' city,
Famed for its heroes, won – four victories
At Corinth in the Isthmus vale, and four
   Won from Cleonae's judges.

ant. 3   From Sicyon too, loaded with silver cups
To grace their wine, and from Pellene's city
   They homeward came, mantled with robes
Of woven wool. But for the numberless
   Prizes of bronze, that lengthy count   45
      No leisure were enough
For me to tell: for Cleitor and Tegea
And the Achaeans' lofty citadels,
      Lycaeon too
On the race-course of Zeus, set them on high,
Endowed with strength of arm or speed of foot
   To gain their victories.

ep. 3   Since Pamphaes gave welcome
Within his house to Castor and to Pollux,   50
No wonder if his kin inherit inborn
   The talent of the athlete's prowess.
   For the two brothers, at the games
Of Sparta's wide-built city, joint patrons
   With Hermes and with Heracles,
      The presidency share.
And due regard have they for men of justice.
   Truly the gods are faithful friends.

str. 4 Now, each alternate day they change their dwelling,   55
One day beside Zeus, their belovéd father;
  Then in the valley of Therapnae
Within the earth's deep folds, these brothers share
  Their common destiny; for so,
    Rather than be for ever
A god and dwell in heaven, Pollux chose
For both this twofold life, when Castor fell,
    Laid low in combat.
For Idas, in hot anger for the cattle   60
Stolen from him, with his bronze-pointed spear
    Dealt him a grievous wound;

ant. 4 When Lynceus, who of all mankind possessed
The sharpest eye, as he kept widespread watch
  From Mount Taygetus, had spied him
Sitting within an oak tree's hollow trunk.
  And the two sons of Aphareus
    Came upon racing feet
Straightway, and swiftly planned and wrought upon
                                                      him 65
Their sinful deed. But from the hands of Zeus
      Dire chastisement
Fell on them too; for straight came Leda's son
In hot pursuit, till by their father's grave
    They stood and turned to face him.

ep. 4   Then seizing from the tomb
A polished stone, ornament to the dead,
They hurled it at Pollux, but could not crush him
  Or stay his course; but springing on them
  He drove his swift bronze javelin
In Lynceus' flank. And Zeus upon Idas   70
  Launched his fire-wrought consuming bolt,
    And the two burned together,
Friendless, upon one pyre. Hard is it for men
  To strive against a mightier power.

str. 5 Then swiftly ran the son of Tyndareus
Back to his warrior brother, and he found him
  Still living, but within his throat

Death's rattle sounded. Then with hot tears streaming   75
    And bitter groans, he cried aloud:
        'O Father, son of Cronos,
What release shall there be from sorrows? Grant
That I too with my brother here may die,
    Great king, I beg thee.
For glory is departed from a man
Robbed of his friends, and under stress of toils
    Few mortals will abide

ant. 5   Faithful companions to share in the labour.'
He ended, and Zeus came and stood before him
    And spoke these words: 'Thou art my son;   80
But after in thy mother's womb was set
    The mortal seed of this thy brother,
        Sprung from her hero husband.
But see then, none the less this choice I give thee:
If freed from death and the harsh years of age,
        It is thy will
To dwell beside my throne upon Olympus,
Companion to Athene and to Ares,
        God of the shadowing spear,

ep. 5   This choice is thine to take.   85
But if, in thy heart's travail for thy brother,
Thou art in mind to share all things alike
    With him, then half thy days shalt thou
    Beneath the earth draw breath, and half
Within the golden citadels of heaven.'
    He spoke, and Pollux had no thought
        But for the single choice;
And Zeus made free the eye, and then the voice   90
    Of Castor of the brazen circlet.

Notes

1. This extensive catalogue of heroes is paralleled at I 7, and frag. 29ff.; such overindulgence is commoner in odes for cities where Pindar had few commissions. Pindar may be describing a collection of dedicatory statues of the heroes at the temple of Hera; cf. his reference at line 19 to 'all that the sacred precinct of Argos contains', where Conway

mistranslates 'precinct' as 'land'. The relevant genealogies are as follows:

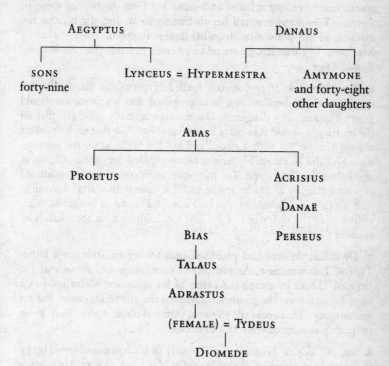

AEGYPTUS ——— **DANAUS**

SONS forty-nine | **LYNCEUS = HYPERMESTRA** | **AMYMONE** and forty-eight other daughters

ABAS

PROETUS | **ACRISIUS**

DANAË

PERSEUS

BIAS

TALAUS

ADRASTUS

(FEMALE) = **TYDEUS**

DIOMEDE

Danaus: expelled from Egypt by his brother Aegyptus, Danaus came to Argos where he supplanted Aghenor as king. He is the eponym of the Danaoi, one of the divisions of the Bronze Age Greeks.

2. O ye Graces: there were statues of the Graces in the temple of Hera at Argos: Paus. 2.17.3.

3. home of Hera: the chief goddess of Argos, whose sanctuary at the Heraion dates from the seventh century. At *Iliad* 4.51ff. Argos, Sparta and Mycenae are listed as her three favourite cities: cf. Callimachus, frag. 55.

4. Perseus: for the legend of Perseus, king of Argos, see P 10, P 12. He is a special hero of Argos: I 5.33. The killing of the Gorgon is a popular theme in archaic art.

5. **Epaphus:** an ancestor of Danaus. He was the son of Zeus and Io, a priestess of Hera at Argos. Zeus made love to Io, and in jealousy Hera transformed her into a heifer and drove her from Argos. She came to Egypt, where Zeus restored her to human form, and she became the mother of Epaphus who founded many Egyptian cities including Memphis. Io's wanderings are told by herself in Aeschylus' *Prometheus Bound* 839ff.

6. **Hypermnestra:** more correctly spelled Hypermestra. To resolve his quarrel with his brother, Aegyptus proposed that his fifty sons should marry Danaus' fifty daughters. Danaus treacherously arranged that all the marriages should take place on the same day, but that each daughter should arm herself with a sword and kill her husband on the wedding night. All did so except Hypermnestra who spared her husband Lynceus and helped him to escape. The forty-nine murderesses were condemned to spend eternity in Hades trying to fill a sieve with water. According to P 9.112ff. the daughters also had a second round of husbands, who, oblivious of the ill-fortune of the first lot, competed for their hands by running a foot race.

7. **Diomede:** Athena had promised immortality to Diomede's father Tydeus, but withdrew the gift after Tydeus disgraced himself at the siege of Thebes by eating the brains of his opponent Melanippus in a fit of berserk fury; the goddess transferred the gift to Diomede. For his immortality, cf. Ibycus *PMG* 294, Attic skolion *PMG* 894; he is frequently associated with Athena in cult.

8. **Son of Oikleus:** Amphiaraus. The story of his being swallowed up by the earth at the siege of Thebes is told at N 9.24–5, O 6.14. He is made an Argive at Hesiod, frags. 25.34–6, but his cult was at Oropus.

11. **Alcmene:** the mother by Zeus of Heracles. Her husband Amphitryon was an Argive who had migrated to Thebes.

Danaë: her father Acrisius, having been warned by an oracle that he would meet his death at the hands of a son of Danaë, shut her up in a bronze tower. But Zeus changed himself into a shower of gold in order to visit her, and their son Perseus was born. On returning to Argos after killing the Gorgon Medusa, Perseus accidentally killed his grandfather with a discus which he was hurling during the Games held in his honour.

12. **Lynceus:** husband of Hypermestra. According to one version of the myth he returned to Argos and killed Danaus, becoming king of Argos himself.

Adrastus' father: Talaus, another king of Argos. Adrastus was the leader of the Seven against Thebes. Talaus and Lynceus were celebrated as 'just kings' (H. Lloyd-Jones, *Justice of Zeus*, p. 50), and their tombs stood side by side in the market-place at Argos.

fruit of wisdom: cf. the phrase used of Rhadamanthys, P 2.74.

13. the god of strength supreme: Heracles. Cf. I 7.5.

15. The Teleboai: also known as the Taphioi, they inhabited the Echinades islands (now Meganisi). It was while Amphitryon was fighting them that Zeus visited Alcmene.

18. Hebe: the goddess of youth and beauty, daughter of Zeus and Hera, whom Heracles married on his eventual admission to Olympus. Hera was regarded as a protectress of marriage.

19. sacred land: correctly, 'sacred precinct'. Pindar may be describing a series of dedications in the sanctuary.

21. strike up: Pindar addresses himself, or his lyre: cf. O 1.4 and 17; O 9.11–14; N 4.36; B frag. 20b.

22. bronze prize: the prize at the Argive Hecatombaea or Heraea (instituted, according to legend, by Lynceus) was a bronze shield. The 'Argive shield' was the standard hoplite shield, and Argos may have had a monopoly on their manufacture. The Hecatombaea were celebrated in the uneven years BC, in Panemos (= June) in a stadium on the Larisa hill (Paus. 2.24.2, Burkert, pp. 162ff.).

27. Ocean's gates: the Isthmus of Corinth.

28. the sacred field: the Nemean Games, founded by Adrastus during the expedition of the Seven against Thebes.

29. Ah, Zeus: Pindar means that Theaius is hoping for the highest of all athletic distinctions, a victory at the Olympic Games (held at Pisa: cf. note on O 10.35ff.), whose presiding deity was Zeus. A Panathenaic vase (J. D. Beazley, *Attic Black Figure Vase-Painters* [Oxford 1956], 414.2) shows two boxers flanked by an official and a figure labelled Olympias, the personification of the Olympic Games. This can only mean that a victor in the boxing at the Panathenaea stood a good chance of winning at Olympia two years later; the vase is in effect a prayer, like these words of Pindar.

35. olive's oil: the prize at the Panathenaea consisted of a quantity of olive oil, presented in amphoras; according to the event, the number of amphoras ranged from six to sixty.

38. sons of Tyndareus: Tyndareus was king of Sparta and husband of Leda, who was seduced by Zeus in the form of a swan and bore twin sons, Castor (a mortal) and Polydeuces (the Latin form is Pollux), who was immortal. She also bore Helen and Clytemnestra, the wives of the brothers Menelaus and Agamemnon respectively. Castor and Polydeuces are commonly known as the Dioscuri (sons of Zeus). Their assistance to Theasius is in virtue of their character as athlete heroes. They shared a temple with the Graces at Sparta (Paus. 3.14.6).

39–40. Thrasycles, Antias: ancestors of Theaius' mother.

41. Proetus' city: Tiryns. Proetus was the brother of Acrisius king of Argos. It appears that Theaius' mother was of Tirynthian ancestry. Tiryns was conquered by Argos in 465/4. For the possible bearing of this on the date see the introduction to the ode.

42. Cleonae: a town near Nemea which provided the local administration of the Games and the twelve judges, until its conquest by Argos probably in the 460s. The line could imply that the judges no longer come from Cleonae.

43. Sicyon: the Adrasteia (I 3.44) or Pythia (the scholiast here). The former were transferred to Dionysus by the tyrant Cleisthenes (600–570) as an anti-Argive move. (See R. Stoneman, *Philologus* 125 [1981]: 45–6.) The prizes were silver wine cups (cf. N 9.51).

44. Pellene: the Games were called either the Hermaea (Photius) or the Heraea (Suda); the former is more probable, cf. Paus. 7.27.1. But there were other Games also: Paus. 7.27.14. The prizes of woollen cloaks are mentioned by Pindar also at O 9.98, O 13.109, O 7.86.

47. Cleitor: the Koriasia (cf. Paus. 5.2.37, a Cleitorian dedication). **Tegea:** the Aleaea, dedicated to Athena Alea.

Achaeans' lofty citadels: for the bronze hydriai given as prizes here, see D. M. Robinson, 'New Greek Bronze Vases. A commentary on Pindar', *American Journal of Archaeology* 46 (1942): 172–97: they had female heads for handles (Callimachus, frag. 122).

48. Lycaeon: held by the sanctuary of Pan according to Paus. 8.38.4–5; the prize was of bronze armour (scholiast on O 7.153).

49. Pamphaes gave welcome: a return of the hospitality theme also exampled by Hypermestra (line 6). Pamphaes, an ancestor of Theaius, was said to have entertained the two gods in his house. This probably refers to the festival of the Theoxenia, 'entertainment of the gods', when banquets were held at which the gods were deemed to be guests. Such festivals were common and held for many gods but the Dioscuri were particularly popular recipients: cf. I 2.39. A famous story about Simonides (frag. 510, PMG) tells us how he was saved by the Dioscuri who came to dinner and called him away from it just before the building collapsed, killing all within. See in general A. D. Nock, 'The Cult of Heroes', Harvard Theological Review 37 (1944), 141ff.; Selected Essays (1972), 576ff., especially 152–5 = 585–8. F. Deneken, De Theoxeniis (dissertation, Berlin 1881), p. 33, suggests that these festivals are often connected with the origin of a clan. Often the priestship was hereditary. In this connection it is interesting that the name Pamphaes is found on an inscription from the Heraion of 105 BC (Wilamowitz, p. 526, n. 1); perhaps a descendant of this man.

52. joint patrons: there were statues of the Dioscuri at the racecourse in Sparta (Paus. 3.14.7), and a statue of Heracles at the gymnasium. Hermes is regularly an overseer of games but we do not know of an appropriate statue of him at Sparta.

54. the gods are faithful friends: the motif of hospitality and loyalty becomes more pronounced. The Dioscuri (by whom oaths were often sworn: Plutarch, On Brotherly Love) were introduced at line 38 in the context of the prayer for an Olympic victory; this aphorism is tantamount to a promise that the gods will deliver the victory Theaius wants. The myth which follows demonstrates the unusual capacity of these twin gods for loyalty.

55. Now, each alternate day: the two brothers, one divine and one mortal, could not bear to be parted by death, and Polydeuces chose instead to share his immortality with Castor and to be dead with him for half of eternity, alive the other half. The tradition that one is divine, one mortal, comes from the epic Cypria: Hesiod frag. 24 calls them both sons of Zeus, while in the Iliad 3.236–44 there is no hint of divine parentage and both are lying dead under the earth in Therapnae. The opening of the myth introduces the conclusion, and the narrative then loops back to the opening of the story, which is told in a limpid linear form in Greek of exceptional beauty.

56. Therapnae: southeast of Sparta on the left bank of the River

Eurotas; the sanctuary of Helen and Menelaus has been excavated here, on a hill with a spectacular view across the plain towards Mt Taygetus.

60. Idas: the strongest of all men (*Iliad* 9.558). Idas and Lynceus (not the husband of Hypermestra) were sons of Aphareus. There are several explanations of the quarrel. (1) They quarrelled with the Dioscuri over the division of a herd of stolen cattle. A metope on the Sicyonian treasury at Delphi shows the four (though one is broken away) leading off the cattle together. (Cf. Apollodorus 3.2.2.) The Cypria has two occasions of a quarrel between the two pairs, first (2) over the rape of the daughters of Leucippus (brother of Aphareus) by the Dioscuri, and secondly (3) over the theft of cattle by the Dioscuri from the Apharids. Pindar makes no mention of the discreditable story of the rape, and his imprecise phrase 'in anger somehow about the cattle' indicates a refusal to choose between the two alternative versions. Conway's 'stolen' is not in the Greek.

61. Mount Taygetus: the large mountain to the west of Sparta.

62. within an oak tree's hollow trunk: the Cypria (frag. 15 Bernabé) says that both brothers were hiding in the hollow tree, and it is possible that Pindar's Greek should be emended here to say the same. Lynceus' sight was so sharp (lynx-eyed) that he could see them even in the tree. Pausanias (4.2.7) absurdly says that it was Lynceus who was inside the tree, gazing over the countryside.

66. Leda's son: Pollux.

67. seizing from the tomb a polished stone: the sacrilegious aspect of the Apharids' deed is emphasized. Aphareus' tomb stood in the market-place at Sparta (Paus. 3.11.11).

68. could not crush him: as son of Zeus, Pollux is invulnerable.

72. Hard is it . . . : cf. O 10.39ff.

73. son of Tyndareus: i.e. Pollux, actually the son of Zeus.

78. Faithful companions: the last sounding of the loyalty theme.

79. stood before him: cf. O 13.67, O 1.75, for this epiphany of the god.

90. of the brazen circlet: the traditional epithet of Castor – and the last sounding of the leitmotif of bronze in the ode.

For Aristagoras of Tenedos
Prytanis (?446 or later)

This ode does not celebrate an athletic victory but was written for the inauguration of Aristagoras as prytanis, that is, president or chief magistrate of the governing body of the Aegean island of Tenedos. This ceremony included a religious festival and a banquet, as we see from the first antistrophe.

The ode also refers to Aristagoras as an athlete who had won many victories at local games. This is probably the reason for its inclusion by ancient scholars in the book of Nemean odes. Its structure is less complex than that of the full-scale epinicians.

The name of Aristagoras' father is variously given in the MSS as Hagesilas (Conway writes Agesilas) or Arcesilas. If he was the son of Hagesilas, he was thus the elder brother of that Theoxenus of Tenedos for whom Pindar composed the love poem frag. 123, and in whose arms (still young) he is alleged to have died. If these were the same man, the poem might be supposed to date from late in Pindar's career, perhaps 446 or later; the melancholy tone of the ode, like that of P 8, would be in harmony with this. However, the metrical values of Hagesilas and Arcesilas are not the same, and the former reading seems impossible. The similarity of names in Pindar's only two odes for Tenedians remains curious. There is no external evidence for the date.

str. 1   Daughter of Rhea, guardian of parliaments,
        Hestia, sister of all-highest Zeus,
           And of Hera who shares his throne,
        Welcome with goodwill to your sacred hall
        Aristagoras, and his fellows with goodwill,
           Beneath your glorious sceptre.
        For they in honouring you keep watch and ward
        On Tenedos island and secure her weal.   5

ant. 1   First of all other gods they worship you
        With many a gift of wine and many a victim,

And the lyre sounds for you, and song.
And at their well-spread tables, never bare,
The rites of Zeus, the hospitable father,
    Receive their due. And now
May Aristagoras enjoy, with glory
And an untroubled heart, his twelve-month rule.   10

ep. 1   Of such a man I happy deem
      Firstly Agesilas his father,
Then his own proud-built body, and heritage
  Of dauntless courage. But let him
Who enjoys wealth, and beauty beyond others,
And in the athlete's field has shown his strength,
Remember that this body's fine array   15
    Is mortal, and that at the last
      The earth will be his vesture.

str. 2   But now his citizens with words of honour
Must praise him, and with song sweeter than honey
    Make his name rich. For in the contests
Of neighbouring cities, Aristagoras
And his renownéd clan have won the crown
    At sixteen victories;   20
A glorious toll, gained in the Wrestlers' ring
And the Pankration's great-hearted struggle.

ant. 2   Too fearful for his youthful years, his parents
Forbade him try his strength on Pytho's field,
    Or in Olympia's contest. Yet
By the god of True Speech, I am of mind
That by Castalia and the tree-clad hill   25
    Of Cronos, had he ventured,
His homeward way had been more richly honoured
Than of all those who strove to meet his challenge,

ep. 2   Had he but kept the fourth-year feast
      Of Heracles, its revel and song,
And with a gleaming wreath bound up his hair.
    But in this life one shall we find
Whom vain and empty-headed boasts will rob   30
Of his success; another, his own strength

Too much mistrusting, sees his hand held back
   From the rewards which are his due,
     By a too fearful heart.

str. 3   Yet was it easy to forecast in him
   Peisander's blood from ancient Sparta, who
     Came with Orestes from Amyclae,
   And hither led the Aeolian bronze-clad host;   35
   And from his mother's stock from Melanippus,
     Descends the ancient line
   That once was blended by Ismenus' stream.
   For valour's heritage from years of old

ant. 3   Now to this generation, now to that
   Alternately gives to the race its vigour.
     As the dark furrow may not yield
   Its fruit unceasingly, nor will the tree
   Through all the passing years give of its flower   40
     The same sweet-scented wealth,
   But waits the changing time, so too, for men,
   Our mortal destiny shares the same law.

ep. 3   But to mankind is given of Zeus
     No sign of clear import; and yet
   Do we on our proud-hearted schemes embark,
     And many a deed we meditate,   45
   Our limbs bound fast to hopes untamed, foreknowing
   Never what may betide. But we must seek
   Only for modest gain: from those desires
     Which cannot be attained, there springs
      The sharpest of all madness.

Notes

1. **Hestia:** the guardian goddess of the hearth and home, and in this instance the presiding deity of the city hall. She is also invoked by Bacchylides in his Ode 14B.

8–9. **tables, never bare:** The Prytaneion was where official guests of the city were entertained, and there were usually certain individuals who had been given the right to dine there in perpetuity. (Socrates in his

Apology 36de jestingly proposed that his punishment for allegedly 'corrupting the young' with philosophy should be, instead of execution, free dinners for life in the Prytaneion of Athens.)

11. Agesilas: the correct Dorian form is Hagesilas. However, most MSS have Arcesilas, as do the scholiasts, and this is required by the metre; Wilamowitz (following MS B) proposed the restoration of Hagesilas here, the name of the father of Theoxenus, Pindar's other Tenedian addressee (frag. 123).

16. earth ... his vesture: a common turn of phrase. *Iliad* 3.57 refers to the 'cloak of stone', while this phrase recurs in Aeschylus, *Agamemnon* 872, Alcaeus frag. 129.17: in this latter passage, as perhaps here, it is prompted by the thought of the evanescence of youthful beauty.

20. sixteen victories: the locations are not specified.

27. feast of Heracles: the Olympic Games.

33. Peisander: a legendary figure from whom Aristagoras traced his descent.

34. Orestes from Amyclae: in one version of the legend Orestes, son of Agamemnon, is a native of Amyclae like Agamemnon's brother Menelaus.

35. led the ... bronze-clad host: this refers to the colonization of Tenedos at an early date by Aeolians from the mainland. The more usual tradition held that the colonists were led by Penthilos, the son of Orestes.

37. Melanippus: an ancient Theban hero.

Ismenus' stream: the river of Thebes.

37–42. Now to this generation ... : this theme of the alternation of active and fallow generations appears also at N 6.15ff., where the agricultural metaphor is more fully worked out.

42. mortal: the word, repeated from line 15, tolls like a bell through the ode.

45–6. foreknowing never ... : literally 'our limbs are bound by immodest hopes, and the streams of foreknowledge lie far off.' Cf. O 7.44 on the 'modesty of foresight'. These lines make a very gloomy end to a celebratory poem, and emphasize the topic of missed opportunities that appeared in antistrophe 2.

48. **desires:** the Greek word usually has erotic connotations (cf. N 8. 1–5), and one wonders whether Pindar is thinking of some hopeless love of his own for Aristagoras as well as his brother.

For Herodotus of Thebes
Winner of the Chariot Race (458?)

The unusual opening of this ode provides some indication of a possible date, which is not known with certainty. Pindar had been commissioned by the inhabitants of Carthaea on the island of Ceos to write for them a paean for Delian Apollo; this has come down to us as Paean 4. In the opening section of Isthmian 1 Pindar addresses a request to the island of Delos to be forgiven if in virtue of his loyalty to Thebes he gives precedence to the composition of this ode for his Theban compatriot Herodotus. He promises at the same time not to neglect the task he owes to the islanders of Ceos.

Carthaea was the native city of the well-known poet Simonides, an older man than Pindar, and possibly his rival. It is unlikely that the citizens of Carthaea would have asked Pindar to write the paean for them until after the death of Simonides in 468. A later date for the victory of Herodotus, and this ode, can thus be regarded as virtually certain.

Ten years afterwards, in 458, Thebes and Sparta were on the point of entering into the alliance which found them in 457 fighting side by side against the Athenian army at Tanagra. It seems very probable that the lengthy passage from lines 17–30, in which Pindar links together the praises of Castor and Iolaus, who were traditional heroes respectively of Sparta and Thebes, is an echo of the political situation of 458. If so, that year would be the date of the victory of Herodotus and of this ode. The Isthmian Games were held in April or May, and if the ode was composed in the early summer it gives additional point to the hopes expressed in line 65 for a victory at the Pythian Games, which were due to be held in August of the same year. (The next Olympic Games, for which Pindar also expresses hopes, were due to be held in 456.)

Herodotus' father Asopodorus (34ff.) may be the man who commanded the Theban cavalry at Plataea in 479 (Herodotus 9.69). After the defeat of the Persians, the Greeks meted out severe punishment to Thebes, which had taken the Persian side. This would provide a natural context for the exile to Orchomenus which the scholiast tells us was inflicted on Asopodorus. After this metaphorical wreck of his fortunes, the return of good 'weather' twenty years later would be something to rejoice at.

str. 1   City beloved, my mother,
         Thebes of the golden shield, my debt to you
         Shall I set higher than all other need
         That would my leisure steal. O rocky Delos,
         Be not then wroth with me, who to your service
            Have given my heart in pledge.
           Is there a loyalty more dear
         Than good men treasure for their parents' love?   5
         Grant me my plea, isle of Apollo, and I
         To honour Phoebus of the flowing hair,

ant. 1   Shall with heaven's help not fail
         To seal with song my dues to beauty's grace,
         For both these vows, stirring the dancer's footstep
         Both 'midst the sailor folk of sea-girt Ceos,
         And on the ridge that bars the ocean's tide,
            The Isthmus' rising plain.
           For to the men of Cadmus' line   10
         Six crowns she gave of victory at her contests,
         Triumphant glory for their fathers' city,
         Where once Alcmene bore that dauntless son,

ep. 1   To whom long since the fierce hounds of Geryon
           Yielded in trembling terror.
    But I now for Herodotus would fashion,
    And for his four-horsed chariot, this meed
         Of praise, and that brave talent,
    Which with no other hand beside him plied   15
    His horses' reins, would marry to the strain
        Of Castor or of Iolaus;
    For they of all heroes of Thebes and Sparta
    Were born the greatest in their mastery
        Of the chariot-driver's skill.

str. 2   And in unnumbered contests
            They strove with rival athletes in the Games,
            And decked their home with many a prize, with tripods
            And bowls and drinking-cups of gold. Rich was   20
            Their taste of glory from their victors' crowns,
                And clearly can be seen
              The light of their brave excellence,
            Whether in the one-stade course for stripped runners,
            Or in the race for full-armed fighting men,
            That echoed with the thunder of their shields;

ant. 2   Or when with strong young hands
            They launched the pointed javelin, or hurled
            The discus with its heavy weight of stone.   25
            For the Pentathlon was not then devised,
            But each of the five contests then was given
                Its own appointed right.
              From these full many a time these heroes,
            With many a garland braided on their hair,
            Were hailed as victors near the springs of Dirke
            And in the land beside Eurotas' stream,

ep. 2   That son of Iphicles born of the race   30
                That sprang from the Sown Men,
            And the son of Tyndareus, who 'midst the Achaeans
            Dwelt in Therapnae's height above the plain.
                To those heroes, farewell.
            Now as I cast the mantle of my song
            Upon Poseidon and the sacred Isthmus
                And on the lake shores of Onchestus,
            I shall amidst my victor's honours praise
            The glorious fortune of Asopodorus
                His father, and the fields

str. 3   Of his ancestral homestead   35
            Near to Orchomenus, where he found harbour,
            When, as if shipwrecked in the unmeasured deep,
            He struggled to withstand the bitter chill
            Of dire misfortune's blows. Now once again
                The fate that gave his race
              Their heritage of happiness

From days of old, grants him a sunlit sky.   40
But he whose heart has known of pain and labour,
Has learnt to see with the clear eyes of wisdom.

ant. 3   If ever a man strives
With all his soul's endeavour, sparing himself
Neither expense nor labour to attain
True excellence, then must we give to those
Who have achieved the goal, a proud tribute
        Of lordly praise, and shun
    All thoughts of envious jealousy.
To a poet's mind the gift is slight, to speak   45
A kind word for unnumbered toils, and build
For all to share a monument of beauty.

ep. 3   Dues for work done are prized by all, one this
            One that, to each his choice,
Whether he be shepherd, ploughman, or fowler,
Or from the deep-sea's harvest fills his table;
        Yet the chief aim of each,
To ward his belly from pernicious hunger.
But he who wins the rich delight of fame   50
    In the Games or in the ranks of war,
Receives that welcome, most exalted prize,
The widespread praise of citizens and strangers
        Flowering upon their tongue.

str. 4   Now must we raise our voices,
Making requital of his favours given,
To praise the son of Cronos, the earth-shaker,
Our neighbour and the chariots' good protector,
And guardian of the flying horses' course.
        And must we too proclaim
    Your sons, Amphitryon, and praise   55
The vale of Minyas, and Demeter's precinct
Of glorious name Eleusis, and Euboea,
Each city where the curved race-course is set.

ant. 4   You too, Protesilas,
I would invoke, and praise your holy shrine
In Phylake, built by Achaean men.

Yet to tell all the glories that were given
By Hermes, lord of contests, to your steeds,   60
   For this, Herodotus,
  The measured moments of my song
Have all too brief a span. And yet indeed
Often enough deeds that no lips have praised
Earn for reward a larger share of joy.

ep. 4   May the sweet-voiced Pierides raise high
     Your name on wings of glory;   65
And once again your hand be strung with garlands
From Pytho's vale, and with those wreaths most choice
   Of Alpheus and the field
Of great Olympia, to bring new honour
To seven-gated Thebes. Now should a man
  Store hidden wealth within his halls,
And upon others fall with mocking laughter,
Little thinks he his soul shall fare to Hades
     With not a shred of glory.

Notes

3. O rocky Delos: the island of Delos, birthplace of Apollo and home to one of his most important cults. Pindar had been commissioned to compose a paean for the people of Ceos for performance at Delos, which he had put off to compose the present ode. See introduction.

she gave: i.e. the Isthmus. To emphasize the close relation between Thebes and the Isthmus, Pindar recalls six victories won by Thebans at the Isthmian Games.

12. that dauntless son: Heracles, the greatest hero of Thebes.

13. the fierce hounds of Geryon: one of the Twelve Labours of Heracles was to bring back to Greece from Spain the cattle of the monster Geryon, which were guarded by the two-headed dog Orthrus. The story is also the subject of Pindar's second dithyramb (see notes there) and was treated in the poem of which frag. 169 is preserved.

16. Of Castor or of Iolaus: Castor and his twin brother Polydeuces (sons of Tyndareus or of Zeus) were noted athletes (see N 10.49ff. and notes), and Iolaus, the son of Iphicles the brother of Heracles, was the charioteer of Heracles. Together they are appropriate epinician heroes.

Their linkage here seems further to suggest the perhaps recent alliance
of Thebes and Sparta. The Kastoreion is the name of a kind of war
dance, but is used here and at P 2.69 as a metonymy for 'epinician'.

25. discus ... of stone: see note on O 10.72.

30. the Sown Men: see note on I 7.10.

31. Therapnae: a city on a plateau overlooking the left bank of the
Eurotas, where there was a shrine of the Dioscuri (Castor and Polydeuces) and their sister Helen. (See N 10.56.)

33. Onchestus: a city by Lake Copais, on the northern boundary of
Boeotia and not far from Orchomenus, which appears from the
following strophe to have been the ancestral home of Asopodorus.

36. as if shipwrecked: not to be taken literally, as do some of the
scholiasts, and Farnell. The metaphor for exile recurs at P 4.291; cf.
O 12.

52. the earth-shaker: Poseidon, patron of the Isthmian Games. He is
described here as 'our neighbour' because he had cult at Onchestus.

55. your sons, Amphitryon: Heracles and Amphitryon's grandson
Iolaus. The Heracleia and the Iolaeia were two important Theban
festivals. These and the following festivals were all places where
Herodotus had won victories.

56. The vale of Minyas: Orchomenus, where the Games were the
Minyeia, named after the mythical King Minyas.

57. Eleusis: the city west of Athens where the Mysteries of Demeter
were celebrated.

Euboea: the name of the relevant festival here is not known.

59. Protesilas: Protesilaus (the Attic form) was the first Greek to leap
ashore at Troy (*Iliad* 2.702) and was killed instantly. He came from the
Thessalian city of Phylake, and there was a shrine for him there. See
Philostratus, *Heroicus* 2.3; Burkert, p. 244.

62. all too brief a span: a standard form of break-off; cf. frag. 180;
B 3.94ff.

65. Pytho's vale: the prayer for a victory at a greater festival is a
common component of praise: see Bundy, pp. 77ff.

67. should a man store hidden wealth: the warning against miserliness is a common form of praise of open-handedness (cf. N 9.46, O 10. 86–93); generosity is a protection against the oblivion of the grave. The downbeat conclusion of the praise is rather surprising.

For Xenocrates of Acragas
Winner of the Chariot Race (470?)

Xenocrates was the brother of Theron, ruler of Acragas in Sicily, and the Isthmian victory here celebrated is mentioned in Pindar's second Olympian ode, written for Theron's victory at Olympia in 476. It must therefore have been won before that date, perhaps at the Isthmia of April/May 476. Xenocrates had also won a Pythian chariot victory in 490. However, the official epinician odes for both these victories were commissioned from Simonides, and have not survived. Pindar nevertheless wrote Pythian 6 to celebrate the earlier victory. Both odes are in fact addressed to Thrasybulus, the son of Xenocrates, who is said to have been the charioteer in the Pythian victory and who apparently formed a warm friendship with Pindar.

It is clear from lines 35ff., where Pindar speaks of Xenocrates in the past tense, that he is now dead. The final epode may reflect the troubled times in Acragas following the death of Theron in 472 when a democratic government was installed. The ode should probably be dated soon after 472.

The elaborate disquisition on payment for choral compositions which opens the ode has been a puzzle to commentators. Some have taken it as an ostentatious request for a fee, perhaps one long outstanding since the odes of 490. Others have seen it as a dig at Simonides, who according to tradition was the first poet to accept fees for his work and who was thus regarded as avaricious. (Pindar might thus be preening himself on having made a free gift of Pythian 6.) It seems more in keeping with the epinician purpose of praise to interpret the passage as a form of thanks for past payments and confidence in continuing generosity: in effect praise of the client's wealth. The ability of the client to pay enables him to maintain status even in an age when poetry is part of a commercial transaction. See L. Woodbury, 'Pindar and the Mercenary Muse', *TAPA* 99 (1968): 527–42; and Introduction, pp. xviii, xxxvi, on the problematic relation of paid poetry to honest praise.

str. 1   In days gone by poets who mounted, Thrasybulus,
        The chariot of the golden-crested Muses,
        Saluting them with the proud-sounding lyre,
        Would lightly launch their songs sweeter than honey
        In praise of youth, wherever beauty's form,
        Robbing rich summer of her fairest wealth,
        Made suit to dreams of high-throned Aphrodite.   5

ant. 1   For then the Muse had not yet bowed to love of gain,
        Or made herself a hireling journeyman;
        Nor in the market clad in masks of silver
        Did honey-tongued Terpsichore barter
        Her gentle-voiced and sweetly-sung refrains.
        But now she bids us pander to that word
        The Argive spoke, too sadly near to truth: 10

ep. 1   'Money, money makes man' said he
        By goods and friends alike deserted. No,
        For you, friend, have a wise heart. Not unknown
        This Isthmian chariot victory that I sing,
        Which to Xenocrates Poseidon granted,
        And sent to him to bind upon his brow   15
          The crown of Dorian parsley,

str. 2   Honouring thus a master of the chariot's grace,
        The glory of the Acragantine people.
        And in Krisa the god of endless power
        Apollo saw him, and bestowed there too
        The light of fame upon him. And he won
        The glorious favours of the Erechtheid people
        In radiant Athens, where no fault could mar   20

ant. 2   The hand that steered the car and primed the horses' speed,
        Bearing on every rein at the just moment –
        Nicomachus, whom the heralds of the season
        From Elis, the truce-bearers of great Zeus
        Knew well, remembering his friendly service.
        And with glad words of welcome they received him,   25
        When golden Victory nursed him on her bosom

ep. 2   In their own land, the land they name
           The precinct of Olympian Zeus. Of honours
           That cannot die Aenesidamus' sons
           Were there made free. For indeed, Thrasybulus,
           No stranger is the palace of your sires
           To the lovely refrains of victory's revel   30
                Or to sweet songs of triumph.

str. 3   For no cliff-track or steep road need he climb, who brings
           The honours of the maids of Helicon
           To dwell with famous men. Now let me launch
           A far-thrown javelin, to match its flight   35
           With the rich charm beyond all other men
           That graced the temper of Xenocrates.
           The greetings of his citizens acclaimed him

ant. 3   A man revered; the racing steeds bred in his stable
           Honour his care for Panhellenic rite;
           And to all banquets of the gods he gave
           A zealous welcome; for his guests no breath
           Of storm could force his hospitable sail   40
           To slacken, but his voyage plied to Phasis
           In summer, and in winter to the Nile.

ep. 3   Then, though the hopes of jealous envy
           Spread mischief through the minds of men, let not
           Your tongue cease to proclaim your father's honour,
           Or these songs in his praise; I made them not   45
           To lie in idle silence. Take, then, and render
           This message, Nicasippus, to my friend
                Whose love I hold in honour.

Notes

8. clad in masks of silver: because paid for in silver, the ode is 'silvered'.
Commentators have referred to the practice of dancers in modern
Greece sticking silver coins to their faces after dancing, or have thought
it a reference to glamorous adornments for the slave market. The
scholiasts quote a line of Anacreon (*PMG* 384): 'silver Persuasion did
not at that time shine out', which seems to be making the same point
as Pindar, that in the past poetry was not composed for a fee.

10. **The Argive:** a man named Aristodemus, whose saying, here quoted, became proverbial. It continues, in full: 'no poor man ever becomes distinguished or honourable'.

14. **Poseidon:** patron of the Isthmian Games.

16. **parsley:** the prize at the Isthmian Games was a crown of wild parsley.

19. **Erechtheid:** Erechtheus was an early king of Athens, and was worshipped with Athena Polias at the Erechtheum on the Acropolis.

22. **Nicomachus:** the charioteer in Xenocrates' victory at the Athenian Games.

the heralds of the season: the territory of Elis sent out heralds to all the Greek states every four years, before the festival, to announce a sacred truce.

24. **friendly service:** we do not know what service Nicomachus rendered to the heralds.

28. **Aenesidamus' sons:** Theron and Xenocrates.

41–2. **Phasis ... the Nile:** Phasis at the eastern end of the Black Sea was considered the farthest point to which Greek sailors could take their ships in summer, and the Egyptian ports on the Nile the farthest possible in winter. The phrase became a commonplace to denote the utmost achievement in any undertaking.

47. **Nicasippus:** evidently the messenger who took the ode to Thrasybulus in Sicily.

For Melissus of Thebes

Winner of the Chariot Race [at Nemea] and the Pankration
[at the Isthmus] (477?)

It is uncertain whether these two poems are actually two poems
or a single one. Both are in the same metre, as no two other
poems of Pindar are. One of the two ancient manuscripts shows
them as one poem, the other as two. In favour of their being
two poems is the fact that the praises of Melissus are repeated
in both parts; and that the scholiasts treat them as two, even
though they classed both as Isthmians where one is for a
Nemean victory. There is also a technical metrical argument,
namely that in the odes in general certain syllables which may
by position be either long or short are always treated as short in
the first triad of the ode; however, in this poem certain such
syllables occur which are treated as short only in the second and
later triads.

Isthmian 4 could certainly stand as a complete poem by itself
and lacks none of the necessary elements of the epinician
programme. Isthmian 3, though short and with a very abrupt
ending, could perhaps also stand alone. An attractive suggestion
of Conway's was that Isthmian 3 was composed as a new
introduction for a re-performance of Isthmian 4 to incorporate
celebration of a new victory with the chariot. Privitera suggested
that Isthmian 4, like Isthmian 3, was written for a chariot
victory, since chariots are mentioned prominently at line 46 (all
references are to the continuous line-numbering of the two
odes). But the conclusion is inescapable that this ode celebrates
a victory in the pankration, in the light of lines 62 and 67ff. It
seems to me possible that Melissus had entered for the chariot
race as well as the pankration, and that lines 46ff. are by way of
consolation for a failure to win the chariot race, even though he
was successful in the pankration. There would then be good
reason to re-use the ode for a successful entry into the chariot-
racing at the Nemean Games, presumably three months later in
the same year. The cost to the victor would also be less than

commissioning a full new ode; and we may presume that Pindar forgot his own metrical rule in writing the new prelude. But these are matters of speculation, and there is not the evidence to solve the problem with certainty.

Melissus belonged to the clan of the Cleonymidae, a wealthy and distinguished Theban family. Both odes refer to the family's distinction in former years, but indicate that they had suffered some eclipse of their reputation. Isthmian 4 suggests that Melissus' victory has restored some of the lustre lost since the death of four family members in battle.

This battle may give a clue to the date of the ode. It was probably the Battle of Plataea of 479, in which the Theban army, fighting on the side of the Persians, suffered severe losses. If so, the victory celebrated in Isthmian 4 may have been won at the Isthmian Games of April/May 478 or 476, and the Nemean victory of Isthmian 3 at the next following Nemean Games of July 477 or 475. Maehler prefers the later date of 474/3. The reference in line 80 to the 'new-built ring of altars' near the Electran Gate may indicate that they had been destroyed during the siege of Thebes by the Greek forces under Pausanias, which followed immediately after the Battle of Plataea, and they were no doubt rebuilt without delay for the annual festival of the Heracleia. But again, these are matters of speculation.

str. 1 If any man has won good fortune's prize
  Or in the famous Games or in the achievement
  Of a rich store of wealth, yet holds his spirit
   Free from insatiate pride,
  He well deserves that in his ears should ring
  The praises of his townsmen. For from thee,
  Great Zeus, only may mortal souls be given
  Worth of true excellence; and happy fortune   5
   More full and lasting lives with men
  Of reverent mind, but for rebellious hearts
  No such fair flower dwells with them all their days.

ant. 1 Now to pay grace to glorious deeds our song
  Must praise a valiant man, and in triumphant
  Revel raise him on high with generous honours.
   Not for one contest only
  But for two triumphs may Melissus now

Refresh his heart with the sweet taste of joy;   10
For in the lowland valleys of the Isthmus
He won the victor's garlands, and within
    The hollow glen that bears the name
Of the deep-chested lion, his chariot,
Victorious on the race-course, gave to Thebes

ep. 1   The glory of the herald's proclamation.
To the prowess of his kin he brings no shame;
            You know indeed
The old-time glory of Cleonymus   15
        Won on the chariot's course;
        And of his mother's line
The sons of Labdacus begrudged no wealth
Or labour spent amidst the four-horsed teams.
        But through the rolling years
    The age of man sees many a change;
        Only the children of the gods
        Are free from wounding blows.

(I.4) str. 1   A thousand ways, thanks to the gods' goodwill
Open on every side widespread before me.
For you Melissus, at the Isthmian Games   20
        Have for my craft made clear
An easy pathway for my song to render
The glorious valour of your kinsmen's race –
That flowering spirit which with the aid of heaven
Ever endows the sons of Cleonymus
    Throughout their mortal span. And yet   (5)
Now this way, that way lights on all mankind
The changing gale that drives them on their course.

ant. 1   They then at Thebes are spoken of with honour   25
From years of old, known as ambassadors
Of neighbouring peoples, men who had no share
        In loud-voiced insolence.
And of all testimonies that the air
May carry to man's ears, of the unmatched fame
Of those who live or those who are no more,   (10)
Of this they harvest all the fairest fruit.
        Their proud valour is of a temper

To reach from their own homestead to the pillars
Of Heracles, that bound the ends of earth.   30

ep. 1   Beyond that mark a further excellence
         Let no man strive to attain. They became too
                 Breeders of horse,
         And with Ares, the god of arms, found favour.   (15)
                 And yet in one brief day
                 The harsh snow-storm of war
         Bereft their happy hearth of four brave men.   35
         But now for them the dark of wintry months
                 Is fled away, as though
             The varied earth's embroidery
             Put forth again her purple hues
                 And blossoms rosy-red,

str. 2   As was ordained of heaven. And he who dwells –
         The god who shakes the earth – beside Onchestus,
         And by the bridge that spans the ocean's wave   (20)
                 Before the walls of Corinth,
         Granting now to their race this song most fair,
         Brings from her bed again the praise they won   40
         For deeds of glory in the days of old.
         For she lay fallen in the arms of sleep.
             Now, wakening once more, her beauty
         Shines forth in gleaming splendour like the star
         Of Dawn, beyond all other lights of heaven.

ant. 2   In the lands of Athens too their fame was known,   (25)
         Proclaimed as victors in the chariot's course;
         And in Adrastus' games at Sicyon's city,
                 Like garlands from the bards
                                                               45
         Of those far days crowned them with leaves of glory;
         Nor from the peoples' feasts, the Panagyries,
         Did they withhold their chariots' curving grace;
         And in contest with all the hosts of Hellas,
             On horse and chariot they rejoiced
         To spend their wealth. Who does not put to proof
         His worth, remains forgotten and unsung.   (30)

ep. 2   Yet even for those who strive, fortune maybe
         Conceals her light, ere yet their steps attain
                 The furthest goal;   50
         For her gifts render both of good and ill.
                 And often does the craft
                 Of lesser souls outstrip
         And bring to naught the strength of better men.   (35)
         Full well you know how in the far-spent night
                 The blood-stained might of Ajax
             Pierced through with his own sword, brought shame
             To the sons of Hellas, all who journeyed
                 Unto the land of Troy.

str. 3   Yet has great Homer set his name in honour   55
         Through all mankind, and on his poet's staff
         Has raised aloft his every deed of valour,
                 In words inspired of heaven
         To charm the soul of all posterity.
         For this it is gives to the path of song   (40)
         Immortal life, if on the poet's tongue
         Fair praise is fairly set. And far and wide
                 Over the fruitful earth and o'er
         The spreading sea, the fame of noble deeds
         Sends forth a ray whose light shall live for ever.   60

ant. 3   May it be mine to win the Muses' favour,
         When for Melissus too that light is kindled   (45)
         By this my burning torch of song – a worthy
                 Garland to crown the brow
         Of a pankratiast victor, one who springs
         From Telesiades' stock. For in his heart
         Is bred the daring of loud-roaring lions   65
         In the brunt of battle, in craft a very fox,
             Who lies prone and with spreading feet
         Stays off the eagle's swoop. Needs must a man
         Devise all means to break the foeman's power.

ep. 3   For it was not his fortune to inherit
         The stature of Orion. Slight his frame
                 To look upon,   (50)
         But with his wrestling strength to take a throw,

Heavy indeed the fall.
And long since, as we know,
To the house of Antaeus there came a hero   70
From Thebes of Cadmus, race, to Libya's corn-lands,
   Small in his body's height   (55)
   But of a soul indomitable,
   Bringing a wrestler's grip to stay him
   Who crowned with skulls of strangers

str. 4   Poseidon's holy shrine. That hero it was,
Alcmene's mighty son, who came at last
To high Olympus; he who, searching out
   All the far lands of earth
And rock-walled stretches of the foaming seas,
Tempered the rough straits for the seamen's sails.   75
Now at the side of Zeus the Aegis-bearer
He dwells, enjoying happiness most fair,
   Of the immortal gods a friend
Held in high honour, lord of golden halls,
Husband of Hebe, son-in-law to Hera.   (60)

ant. 4   For him then, we his fellow citizens
Above Electra's gates make ready now
His feast, and on the new-built ring of altars   80
   Burn sacrifice, to honour
Those eight dead warriors of brazen mail –
The sons whom Megara, Creon's daughter, bore him.
And to their glory rises high the flame
Beneath the setting sun's beshrouded rays,
   Mounting aloft an endless stream   (65)
Through the long hours of night, of singeing smoke
In billowing clouds to chafe the vault of heaven.

ep. 4   And on the second morning comes the day   85
Appointed for the yearly Games, where strength
      Strips for the test.
There with the myrtle garlands gleaming white
      Upon his brow, my hero   (70)
      Showed himself twice a victor,
And as a boy long since a third he won,
Reliant on the wisdom of the skilled

> Pilot who steered his helm.
> With Orseas then my song of triumph
> Shall link his name, and shed upon them   90
> Its joyful shower of glory.

Notes

7. our song must praise: for song as the reward of deeds cf. N 7.15, O 7.15, P 2.13, I 8.3–4, etc.

9. two triumphs: the pankration victory at the Isthmus and now the chariot victory at Nemea.

11. the name of the deep-chested lion: i.e. the Nemean Games, held near the cave of the Lion destroyed by Heracles.

15. Cleonymus: an ancestor of Melissus.

17. Labdacus: an early king of Thebes, grandfather of Oedipus.

18. age ... sees many a change: if this is the end of the ode it is very downbeat; but there are similar downbeat endings in other odes, e.g. O 7.94. However, the gnome would act very neatly as a transition to the praise beginning at line 19ff.

children of the gods: the children of the gods are not normally considered as invulnerable: cf. O 10.15, N 9.27. But the contrast with 'man' perhaps suggests that the phrase is really a periphrasis for 'gods'.

19. A thousand ways: the phrase is used to open an ode by Bacchylides (19), but can also appear in mid-ode (B 5.31, 9.47).

23. The changing gale: another way of expressing the same idea as in line 18, 'the rolling years'.

26. ambassadors: Greek *proxenos*. Proxenoi were natives of one city appointed to represent the interests of another city.

30. pillars of Heracles: the straits of Gibraltar, used proverbially to indicate the extreme of human achievement.

34. in one brief day: possibly a reference to the Battle of Plataea (479); cf. introduction. For the metaphor of the snow-storm of war cf. I 5.50.

37. The god who shakes the earth: Poseidon, god of the sea and of subterranean powers, and patron of the Isthmian Games. One of his reputed homes was at Onchestus by Lake Copais in Boeotia.

of Athens: presumably at the Panathenaea.

44. Adrastus' games: the Sicyonian Pythia: cf. N 9.9 and note.

46. Panagyries: Conway's translation emphasizes the connection with the modern *paniyiri*, or fête.

48. forgotten and unsung: the standard view, cf. O 9.103, etc.

53. Ajax: for the story of Ajax's failure to win the arms of Achilles, and his subsequent suicide, cf. N 7.20–30, N 8.21–34. But whereas in those odes Pindar emphasizes the deceit involved in depriving Ajax of the prize, here the emphasis is on Homer's praise of the hero. Is Pindar consoling Melissus for missing a prize in the chariot race, and offering to overlay the disgrace with praise, like Homer?

56. poet's staff: the *rhabdos* carried by the rhapsode or reciter.

64. lions: cf. O 11.19ff. for the metaphor of the lion to represent inborn excellence.

65. with spreading feet: E. N. Gardiner, *JHS* 2 (1906): 20–1, suggested that this may be a reference to the throw known as *hyptiasmos*, resembling the stomach-throw of judo.

70. Antaeus: a giant of Libya, who killed all strangers and placed their skulls on the roof of a temple of Poseidon. He derived his strength from contact with the ground. Heracles overcame him by lifting him off the ground until his strength drained out of him.

Small in his body's height: Heracles is normally regarded as a big powerful man; this unusual description is designed to flatter Melissus, who was plainly on the small side.

73. Olympus: after his death Heracles was given immortality and a home with the gods.

79. Electra's gates: one of the Seven Gates of Thebes. See Paus. 9.11.1–4 on the topography. The Heracleia were celebrated just outside the gates in a stadium and wrestling ground dedicated to Heracles. The festival consisted of a night feast, followed on the second day by athletics. It continued to be held into the Roman period.

80. new-built ring of altars: perhaps new-built because they had been destroyed in the siege of Thebes following the Battle of Plataea in 479.

81. eight dead warriors: the cult of the sons of Heracles was located

here. Pindar tactfully refrains from mentioning the fact that, according
to the myth, these offspring had been killed by Heracles himself in a fit
of madness: see Euripides' *Heracles*. Very probably the myth had its
origin as an explanation of the existence of the cult at the graves.

90. Orseas: Melissus' trainer. Usually the trainer is mentioned where
the victor is still a boy, but that is not stated in this ode.

For Phylakidas of Aegina
Winner of the Pankration (480 or 478)

Phylakidas was the younger brother of Pytheas, whose earlier victory as an adolescent at the Nemean Games is celebrated in Nemean 5. Another, earlier, victory of Phylakidas is celebrated in Isthmian 6. For the family and the dating of this series of odes see the introduction to Nemean 5. Pytheas had probably been the trainer of Phylakidas for this event.

The Battle of Salamis, referred to at line 49 of this ode, took place in about September 480. The Isthmian Games took place in April/May of the same year, so that the ode would have been completed at least five months after the victory. Modern scholars think of the battles of Salamis and of Plataea (479) as a pair, and expect that if Pindar mentions one he would mention the other. However, Plataea is irrelevant to his purpose here, and as it was also a defeat for Thebes it is not something he cares to dwell on; so it would be possible to date the whole series of odes two years later, and this one in 478.

The ode does not contain a full myth, but general praise of the heroes of the line of Aeacus.

str. 1   Mother of the sun, Theia, goddess of many names,
      Thanks to thee men ascribe to gold a strength exceeding
         All other powers that are.
       For ships that sail the seas in rivalry
         And racing chariot steeds   5
         For thy honour, O queen,
       Rise to the height of wondrous deeds amidst
         The whirling wheels of struggle.

ant. 1   And in the contests of the Games, he reaps that prize
      Of glory that all hearts desire, whose strength of arm
         Or speed of foot has won   10
       Many a crown to bind upon his brow.
         But the gods' will is judge

Of man's prowess. Two blessings
Only can nurse the dearest gift of life
Amidst good fortune's flower,

ep. 1   If a man knows success and hears his glory
Proclaimed abroad.
Seek not to become Zeus. The best is yours
If the hand of fate grants to you these fair things;   15
For mortals mortal gifts are fitting.
For you, Phylakidas, twice has the Isthmus
Laid to your name the deathless flower of valour,
And at Nemea too, both you
And Pytheas won the crown
Of the Pankration. But my heart desires
No taste of song lacking the praise
Of the sons of Aeacus. For I am come   20
With the Graces' gift in hand for Lampon's sons

str. 2   To this city of righteous law. Her feet have trod
The clear high-road of deeds inspired of the gods' will;
Then grudge not the proud praise
Fit for a draught of song her toils to honour.   25
Her great heroes of battle
Too, have won fame. Their glory
The rich-wrought harmonies of lyre and flute
Proclaim through the long years

ant. 2   Of countless time. To the resource of poet's skill
By grace of Zeus was given a task by Oineus' sons,
Those mighty warriors worshipped
With flaming offerings by Aetolian men,   30
And in Thebes Iolaus,
The charioteer, has honour,
Perseus in Argos, Pollux and Castor's spear
Beside Eurotas' stream;

ep. 2   But in Oenone Aeacus and his sons'
Great-hearted courage   35
Is fitly praised; not without battle, twice
They ravaged the city of Troy, with Heracles
Leading them in the first assault,

And then with Atreus' sons. Now let me drive
My chariot far aloft. Tell me, who slew
   Cycnus, who slew the mighty Hector,
     And brought death to that dauntless
Commander of the Ethiopian host,   40
   Clad in his arms of bronze, Memnon?
Who with his spear wounded the noble warrior
Telephus, by the banks of Caicus?

str. 3   Even these for whom my voice proclaims their land of birth
Aegina's glorious isle; her walls high-built of old,
     A tower that valorous venture   45
      Would well despair to climb. Many a song
       My tongue could launch swift-spun
       To honour them. Yes, now
      Could Salamis embattled, Ajax' city
       Tell of their sailors' might,

ant. 3   Who saved her in the deadly tempest sent of Zeus,
When slaughter fell like hail upon a countless host.   50
     Yet, let proud boasts be stilled
      'Neath the waters of silence. Zeus it is
       Bestows both good and ill,
       Zeus who is lord of all.
      But for the joy of songs of triumph, sweet
       As honey to the ear,

ep. 3   Such honours long. Let him contest the struggle   55
       Who has learnt well
Of Cleonicus' race their athletes' valour;
The long toil of brave souls has not lain buried
   In blind darkness, unseen of men;
Nor has the cost that fell to them destroyed
Their zealous hope. Pytheas too I praise,
    Supreme master of movement, teaching
      Phylakidas the path   60
Of true-spent blows, skilled with his hands, in spirit
   A stern contestant. Bring for him
The crown, and bring the fillet of fine wool
And send forth upon wings this new-made song.

Notes

1. **Theia:** this deity is not often mentioned in Greek literature. As mother of the Sun, Moon and Dawn, she is the giver of luminosity (Hesiod, *Theogony* 371–4). Brightness is the predominant attribute of victory.

3. **gold:** the reference in this and the following lines seems to be to competition in trireme and chariot races for golden prizes rather than to commerce. The ships and chariots are the first terms of a priamel culminating in the contests of men; for the form, compare Sappho's Ode 195 LP with its crescendo of horsemen, infantry and ships, culminating in 'the one one loves'.

11. **the gods' will:** the idea recurs at lines 52ff.; and the two blessings of line 12 are also recalled in line 54. The warning of line 14, to avoid excessive pride, is repeated at line 51; and the crown first mentioned in line 8 reappears at line 62. The final vaunt at the end of the poem closely recalls the terms Pindar lays down for praise of achievement in this passage.

17. **twice has the Isthmus:** in 482 and 480 (or two years later).

18. **And at Nemea:** in 487 (Pytheas) and 485 (Phylakidas) – or two years later.

22. **city of righteous law:** Aegina had a high reputation for just dealing, especially in trade: cf. O 8.23 (of 480). The same praise is given to Corinth (O 13), Locri (O 9) and Aetna (N 9).

26. **Her great heroes:** the following catalogue of heroes has as its climax the achievement of the Battle of Salamis.

30. **flaming offerings:** the only reference in literature to the cult of Meleager, one of the sons of Oineus (the other was Tydeus). Offerings with fire were normally reserved for gods.

33. **Perseus:** for his myth see P 10, P 12.

Castor's spear: a kind of kenning meaning 'the spearman Castor'. See N 10 for the myth of Castor.

34. **Oenone:** i.e. Aegina. The pediments of the temple of Aphaia on Aegina portrayed the two expeditions of the heroes against Troy: the west pediment, of 500, portrayed the later (Homeric) campaign, while the east pediment, of 490, portrayed the earlier attack in which Heracles

took part. This was prompted by the action of King Laomedon of Troy, who failed to keep his promise to Heracles to reward him for killing a monster which was plaguing the land. Heracles in company with Telamon, one of the sons of Aeacus, took Troy and killed Laomedon.

39–40. Cycnus, Hector, Memnon: all killed by Achilles. Cycnus was king of Colonae, near Troy, and an ally of Troy in the Trojan War. On his death he was turned into a swan. For Hector and Memnon, see Glossary.

41. Telephus: king of Mysia in Asia Minor, wounded by Achilles when the Greek army landed in Mysia on its way to Troy. The Caicus is a river of Mysia.

49. Salamis ... Ajax' city: because he was the son of Telamon of Aegina, subsequently king of Salamis. The Aeginetan contribution was of decisive importance at the Battle of Salamis: Herodotus 8.93.1. As it began, 'Prayers were offered to all the gods; and Telamon and Ajax were invoked at once from Salamis while a ship was sent to Aegina to fetch Aeacus himself and the other Aeacids' (Herodotus 8.64).

52. Zeus ... bestows: at *Iliad* 24.527ff. Zeus is said to have two jars from which he doles out good and evil to men.

55. Cleonicus: perhaps the great-uncle of Phylakidas: see introduction to N 5.

59. Pytheas: Phylakidas' elder brother, and his trainer; it is now seven years since his own Nemean victory.

62. The crown: the culmination of the praise promised at line 8 of this finely symmetrical ode.

For Phylakidas of Aegina
Winner of the Pankration (probably 482)

This is one of three odes for victories won by the sons of
Lampon; the other two are Nemean 5 and Isthmian 5. For the
date of this ode, most probably 482, see the discussion in the
introduction to Nemean 5.

The ode pays tribute not only to Phylakidas but to other
members of his family to Lampon his father (praised at some
length towards the end of the ode), to Pytheas his elder brother
and to Euthymenes his maternal uncle. For a family so clearly
ambitious for athletic distinction it is not surprising that Pindar
includes the wish in strophe 1 that they may gain the crowning
success of an Olympic victory.

As in other Aeginetan odes, the glories of the Aeacid clan are
given a prominent place, and the myth tells the story of the
prophecy Heracles made to Telamon the son of Aeacus concerning the birth of his son Ajax.

str. 1   As when a feast is joined of men in merry revel,
        Now do we mix a second bowl of song
          The Muses' gift to honour Lampon's clan,
        Famed on the athletes' field. They at Nemea first
        In thy honour, great Zeus, attained the crowning flower;
            And now again, by grace
        Of the lord of Isthmus and the fifty daughters   5
        Of Nereus, is the youngest of their sons
          Phylakidas named a victor.
        May it be ours to offer yet a third
        To Zeus the Saviour at Olympia,
        And shower upon the isle of Aegina
          The honeyed music of our songs.

ant. 1   For if a man rejoicing in expense and labour   10
        Achieves great deeds founded of divine will,
        And by the gods' grace there is planted for him

The lovely flower of fame, then in the furthest reaches
Of happy fortune is his anchor cast already
  And the gods give him honour.
That such proud-hearted spirit may reward him,
Ere yet his eyes look on the path of death   15
  Or the white hairs of age,
Is the prayer of Cleonicus' son; and
To high-throned Clotho and her sister Fates
Add this my plea, that they may look with favour
  On this dear wish of my good friend.

ep. 1   And for you, Aeacus' sons, riding your gleaming
Chariots, the poet's task I see most clear before me,
  As I set foot upon this isle, to shower   20
  My songs of praise upon you.
For your fair deeds a thousand roads are cut
  A hundred foot in span, stretching
Unhindered whether beyond the distant springs of Nile
  Or through the Hyperborean lands.
No city is there of such alien mind
  Or witless speech, that does not hear
  The fame of the great hero Peleus,   25
That happy man wed to a goddess maid,

str. 2   Or of Ajax or mighty Telamon his father,
  Whom once across the sea Alcmene's son
  Led forth, an eager ally in the pride
Of brazen-armoured war, with men of Tiryns to Troy,
That city of many a hero's toil, to bring revenge
    For his false treachery   30
  Upon Laomedon. And Pergamon
He captured, and with Telamon laid low
    The race of Meropes,
And on that shepherd in stature like a mountain,
Alkyoneus, meeting with him at Phlegra,
Heracles spared not of his strength to loose
  The sounding music of his bowstring.

ant. 2   But when he came to call the son of Aeacus   35
  To join him in that famous voyage, he found him
  At the banquet table seated with all his men.

And as he stood there with the lion's skin upon him –
That warrior of the mighty spear, Amphitryon's son –
     The chieftain Telamon   40
    Called to him to pour forth the first libation
    Of nectar, and he handed him the wine-cup
      Rough with its figured gold.
    And Heracles lifted his hands to heaven,
    Those hands invincible, and spoke these words:
    'If ever thou hast given, great father Zeus,
     A kindly ear unto my vows

ep. 2   Now do I beg thee, now with solemn prayer
To grant that a brave son be born of Eriboea   45
    To this hero, to be our host and friend
      By the award of fate.
    And may his body's frame be no less hardy
    Than this wild creature's skin that rides
Upon my shoulder now – the beast I slew long since,
     First of my labours, in Nemea.
    And may his soul be of a like valour.'
     So he spoke and the god sent down
     The king of birds, a mighty eagle;
    And his heart thrilled within him with sweet joy.   50

str. 3   And he proclaimed these words as with a prophet's tongue:
     'The son for whom you pray, lo, Telamon,
    He shall be born to you. And from this eagle
Seen by our eyes, so let his name be made Ajax
The man of might, a most dread warrior to the peoples
     Amidst the toils of war.'
    He spoke, and on the word straightway was seated.   55
    Too long for me all their great deeds to tell.
     For I have come, my Muse,
    Steward of revels for Phylakidas,
    For Pytheas and Euthymenes, and after
    The mode of Argive men, so shall my praise
     Even in words most brief be spoken.

ant. 3   For thrice at the Isthmus the Pankration's crown they
                                won,   60
     And others from Nemea's leafy vale,

These famous young sons and their mother's brother.
Precious indeed this share of song they have endowed
To the clear light of day; the dewdrops of the Graces
    They shower in gleaming beauty
On the Psaluchid clan, Themistius' house   65
Raising to great renown, and this city
    Their home, beloved of heaven.
Lampon to all he does brings the resource
Of practised care, this word of Hesiod
Holding in high honour, and to his sons
    Declares it and its worth commends,

ep. 3   Bringing a glory shared by all his city.
Well-loved for kindly deeds to strangers, moderate is   70
    The path his mind pursues, and modest measure
       Governs his acts, nor does
His tongue outrun his thoughts: amidst athletes
    A man whose worth you well might say
Prevails as over all earth's rocks the Naxian whetstone,
    That conquers bronze. For him shall I
Pour forth a draught of Dirke's holy water,
    The spring which the deep-bosomed maids
    Of golden-robed Mnemosyne   75
Made flow beside the well-walled gates of Cadmus.

Notes

2. **a second bowl of song:** the first was Nemean 5, for Phylakidas' elder brother Pytheas.

5. **the lord of Isthmus:** Poseidon, presiding deity of the Isthmian Games.

6. **fifty daughters of Nereus:** the Nereids or sea-nymphs.

youngest of their sons: we know nothing of the brothers of Phylakidas other than Pytheas.

7. **Zeus the Saviour:** according to ancient commentators, it was the practice at banquets to offer three libations: the first to Zeus, the second to Earth and the Heroes, and the third to Zeus the Saviour. Here Pindar allots the second, as a mark of honour for Lampon's race and Phylakidas, to Poseidon and the Nereids, and combines the third with a prayer for an Olympic success for the family.

16. Cleonicus' son: Lampon the father of Phylakidas. He looks forward to taking pride in an Olympic victory by one of his family.

17. Clotho: one of the three Fates.

20. As I set foot upon this isle: Pindar is envisaged as present in his ode, and may in fact have been so in person.

to shower my songs: the metaphor recurs at line 64, 'the dewdrops of the Graces'.

23. springs of Nile ... Hyperborean lands: traditionally regarded as the most southerly and northerly parts of the earth.

28. Tiryns: the traditional birthplace and home of Heracles was Thebes, but according to one legend he was brought up at Tiryns, the city near Argos once ruled by his ancestor Perseus. This would account for his being accompanied by men of Tiryns on his expedition to Troy.

Troy: The two expeditions to Troy, by Heracles and Telamon and the more famous one in the next generation by Agamemnon, Menelaus and Achilles, were the subject of the pediments of the temple of Aphaia on Aegina. The second expedition was represented on the earlier, west pediment (c. 500) while the first was represented on the east pediment (c. 490). Images of these heroes were constantly present to the people of Aegina.

30. Laomedon: king of Troy, father of Priam. For the story of his treachery see note on I 5.36.

31. Pergamon: the name for the citadel of Troy is Homeric (*Iliad* 5.446 etc.).

31-2 Meropes: while returning from Troy, Heracles and Telamon landed on the Aegean island of Cos, home of the Meropes, who attacked them. The two heroes defeated them and killed their king, Eurypylus. See *Iliad* 14.255, 15.28.

33. Alkyoneus: a giant who stole the cattle of the Sun from Erytheia, and was killed by Heracles, either at Phlegra in Chalcidice (or the Phlegra near Naples) during the battle of the Gods and Giants (the version Pindar follows here) or at the Isthmus of Corinth. Pindar is here following the epic *Heracleia* of Pisander.

35. But when he came to call: Pindar loops his narrative back to the beginning of the expedition.

36. found him at the banquet: there is a word missing in the Greek text of this line. Peter von der Mühll (*Mus. Helv.* 14 [1957]: 128–30) suggested 'at the marriage feast' of Telamon. Cf. Apollodorus 3.161ff.

37. the lion's skin: Heracles is traditionally represented in art and literature as wearing the skin of a lion, usually interpreted as that of the Nemean lion which he killed as one of his early labours.

40. first libation: recalls the libation of line 1. Is it implied that Phylakidas' victory is as great as the heroes'?
  The scene is highly pictorial, and one may wonder whether it was represented in painting or sculpture in the Aiakeion on Aegina; however, no such scene is mentioned by Pausanias in his description (9.29).

45. Eriboea: wife of Telamon.

53. Ajax: Pindar derives this name, in Greek spelt Aias, from the Greek word for eagle, *aietos*.

58. The mode of Argive men: the brevity of speech of people from Argos was proverbial, like the laconic utterances of the Laconians.

60–1. thrice . . .: for the details see the introduction to N 5.

65. Themistius: the grandfather of Phylakidas.

67. this word of Hesiod: *Works and Days* 412, 'taking pains helps the work'.

70. kindly deeds to strangers: the family's hospitality is also praised at N 5.8.

73. the Naxian whetstone: emery, a stone worked from a remote period in the island of Naxos.

74. Dirke's holy water: the Theban river. The metaphor also recalls the 'second bowl of song' of the beginning of the ode.

75. Mnemosyne: Memory, mother of the Muses by Zeus.

For Strepsiades of Thebes
Winner of the Pankration (454?)

This ode celebrates not only the victor Strepsiades but his maternal uncle of the same name, who fell in battle defending Thebes. According to the scholiast, the elder Strepsiades died 'in the Peloponnesian War'. It has been suggested that this might refer to preliminary skirmishes in the conflict of Athens and Sparta. A reference to the battle mentioned by Herodotus 5.77–81, which took place in 510, seems too early. (Pindar would have been only sixteen.) A preferred date has been the battle of Oenophyta of 457/6, when Thebes was defeated by Athens. But there is no reason to suppose that Thebes was actually defeated in the battle in which Strepsiades died ('the hail of blood' in line 27 could equally well have been a victorious clash – the parallels from Tyrtaeus 9.20–2, etc., strongly suggest this – and the reference to the return of 'clear skies' in line 38 rather suggests a positive outcome too), so that this conjecture is unsupported. If a reference to the Battle of Oenophyta is accepted, then the prayer for a Pythian victory may look forward to the coming Pythian Games later in the same summer, in which case the ode would be dated to 454. For a decisive dismissal of these arguments for dating, see D. C. Young, *Pindar Isthmian 7: Myth and Exemplum*, Mnemosyne Supplement 15 (1971).

The ode contains no myth, and the lengthy list of Theban myths at the beginning recalls Corinna's supposed advice to the poet to 'sow with the hand, not the sack'. The generalized treatment of Strepsiades the elder's heroic death (no details of the battle) gives him the exemplary value of a mythic narrative.

str. 1   Blest city of Thebes, whence of the ancient glories
        Known of your land, springs to your heart
        The greatest joy? Was it maybe
      When Dionysus of the flowing locks
      You brought to the light of day, beside the throne   5

And clashing cymbals of Demeter? Or
    When in the deep of night
You welcomed as a golden shower of snow
    The mightiest of the gods,

ant. 1   When by Amphitryon's palace doors appearing
      He bedded with his bride, to give her
        The seed of Heracles? Or was it
    The fame Tiresias' wise counsel won?
    Or glorious Iolaus the skilled horseman?
    Or the unwearied spears of the Sown Men?   10
      Or when from the turmoil
    Of pealing battle-cries you sent Adrastus
      Home to Argos, the city

ep. 1   Of horse, of countless followers bereft?
    Or when you gave the Dorian colony
        Of Lacedaemon's men
    Strength to stand up in courage, when Aegeus' sons,   15
    Born of your stock, captured Amyclae,
    As Pytho's prophet had ordained?
    Yes, but the glory of old time
      Sleeps, and the minds of men
        Remember not,

str. 2   Unless it be that blended in rich streams
      Of sounding song, the poet's wisdom
      Brings to their ear its perfect flower.
    Sound then for Strepsiades too the sweet-sung   20
    Revel of triumph, who wears the Isthmian crown
    Of the Pankration; his strength a marvel
      To see, beauty adorns
    His limbs, and to his body's grace he brings
      No lesser share of valour.

ant. 2   The Muses violet-tressed nurse high the flame
      Of his renown, and of this flower
      He has made free his mother's brother
    Who shares his name, to whom bronze-armoured Ares   25
    Brought death. But for the brave is laid in store
    The recompense of honour. Let him know well

Whoever in this dark
Storm-cloud fends off from his belovéd land
The blood-stained hail of war,

ep. 2   And brings destruction to the enemy's host,
Such a man shall exalt his city's race
To the utmost of glory,
Both while he lives and when he is no more.   30
And you, son of Diodotus,
In prowess rivalling the might
Of Meleager and of Hector
And Amphiaraus, you
Breathed forth the spirit

str. 3   Of your fair-flowering prime, fronting the line   35
Of battle, where brave-hearted men
Bore up on the last slender hope
The strife of war. Bitter the grief they suffered,
Not to be told. But now has the great god,
Holder of earth, granted me summer skies
After the winter's cold.
Songs will I sing, with wreaths my brow adorning,
And may no jealous envy

ant. 3   Of heaven mar whatever taste of joy   40
Delights each passing day, granting
My onward steps to tread a path
Carefree, to old age and the appointed end.
For all alike we come to death, albeit
With varied fate; whose eyes would peer aloft
To distant realms, too small
Is he to reach the bronze-floored throne of heaven.
Pegasus winging high

ep. 3   Threw down to earth his lord Bellerophon,   45
Who thought to reach the abodes of heaven, and share
The company of Zeus.
Sweets gained unrightly await an end most bitter.
But for us, Loxias, we pray thee,
God of the golden-flowing hair,
Grant us in thy contest also,

To win the gleaming flower   50
Of Pytho's crown.

Notes

5. Dionysus: born to Semele at Thebes: see O 2.25ff., and the narrative at the opening of Euripides' *Bacchae*.

clashing cymbals: used by Demeter in her search for her daughter Koré (Aristophanes, *Acharnians* 708) There is probably no reference to the ritual clashing of cymbals as in the rites of Cybele, sometimes identified with Demeter. The rites of Demeter Thesmophoros were celebrated on the Cadmeia in Thebes.

shower of snow: usually, Zeus is envisaged as coming to Alcmene in the form of her husband Amphitryon. The detail of the golden shower is borrowed from the story of Danaë.

10. the Sown Men: warriors who sprang up from the teeth of a dragon, sown in the soil by Cadmus, and became ancestors of the Thebans (cf. I 1.30).

12. the Dorian colony: Dorian rule in Sparta was not firmly established in legendary times until they had defeated the people of neighbouring Amyclae. To do this they were advised by the Delphic oracle to get help from the descendants of Aegeus (king of Athens and father of Theseus). One branch of this clan had settled in Thebes (Pindar belonged to it), and with their help the Spartans took Amyclae and established their supremacy. According to the scholiast, the Aegeid leader on this occasion was Timomachus, who was reputed to have reorganized the Spartan army. (See further note on P 5.73–81.)

16. glory ... sleeps: interpreted by Farnell as a reference to Spartan abandonment of Thebes after the Battle of Oenophyta; but there is no need to see a specific reference in this gnomic statement.

27. blood-stained hail: the metaphor recurs at I 5.51.

Diodotus: the victor's father.

32. Meleager: a legendary hero of Calydon in Aetolia, who took part in the Argonautic expedition and was the hero of the legend of the Calydonian boar-hunt.

Hector, Amphiaraus: Amphiaraus was actually fighting against Thebes, but this is not part of the comparison.

35. fronting the line: a topos of praise for the dead; cf. Tyrtaeus 6–7.1, 21, 30, etc., and the inscription on the Anavyssos kouros. These references are offered by D. C. Young, op. cit. in the introduction to the ode.

36. Bitter the grief they suffered: better to translate 'I suffered'. This is not a reference, as some commentators have supposed, to Pindar's sorrow at a Theban defeat, but a topos of mourning for Strepsiades.

38. summer skies: i.e. political peace. It picks up the hail-metaphor of line 27: cf. I 4.15–19 for the progression. The 'great god' is Poseidon, tutelary deity of the Isthmian Games.

41. My onward steps: according to the scholiast, the victor speaks here. He had observed, clumsily, the way in which poet and victor blend into one at the climax of praise. The envy of the gods may be feared because Strepsiades lives while his uncle is dead. The warning not to over-reach is a foil to the prayer for a Pythian victory. For the topos of continuing prosperity, cf. I 6.12–14, N 8.35–9: the interest is not in (imminent) death but in the maintenance of a manner of life over a long period (D. C. Young). (Cf. Tyrtaeus 9.37–42.)

44–45. Pegasus, Bellerophon: for the story of Bellerophon see O 13.63ff. and introduction to that ode.

For Cleandrus of Aegina
Winner of the Pankration (478)

As the opening strophe makes clear, this ode celebrates victories
won by Cleandrus at both the Isthmian and the Nemean Games.
The Nemean victory was probably won in the summer of the
previous year, and the Nemean is the more recent. The reference
to recent sorrows alludes to the Persian invasion of 480/79, in
which Thebes took the Persian side while Aegina was foremost
among the opponents of Persia – a situation calling for especial
tact in the composition of the ode. The ode may be dated to the
Isthmian Games of 478.

The myth pays particular attention to the connections of Thebes
and Aegina. The statement in line 100 that the gods turned away
the threat to Greece is a compliment to the Aeginetans, who are
seen as able to sway even the gods. The point is reinforced by the
myth, where Aeacus is influential even on the gods (lines 23–5)
and Achilles earns laments even from the gods (line 57).

str. 1   Bring for Cleandrus in his pride of youthful years
      A recompense of glory for his toils. Young men
      Come, to his father Telesarchus take your way,
         And by his gleaming doors
      Raise up on high your songs of triumph, the reward
      Of victory at the Isthmus; and Nemea too
        Saw him prevailing in the contests' prize.
          For his honour
      I too, though heavy grief weighs on my heart,   5
      Am bidden to invoke the glorious Muse.
      From great sorrow released let us not languish
   Bereft of victors' crowns, nor brood upon our woes.
      Let us have done with ills that know no cure,
      And send abroad a sweet taste of delight
         Even after pain: for now
      The stone of Tantalus, hung o'er our heads,   10
        Some god has set aside, that evil

str. 2   Hellas' brave heart could not endure. But now for me
           The fear that is gone on its way has made an end
           To a cruel load of care. Best is it in all things
                 To set the task in hand
           Clearly before our eyes: treacherous the years that hang
           Over our mortal span, twisting the path of life.
               Yet even for this, healing is given to men,
                   If but in freedom   15
               They put their trust. Brave hope then must we cherish,
               And a man nursed in seven-gated Thebes
               To Aegina must offer the first flower
           Of Beauty's grace; for both were of one father born
               The youngest daughters of Asopus' river;
               And sovereign Zeus looked upon them with favour.
                   One of these did he set
               By Dirke's lovely waters, to be queen   20
                   Of this city of charioteers,

str. 3   But you he carried to Oenopia's isle and wedded.
           And there you bore to the loud-roaring god of thunder
           Aeacus, a son divine, noblest of mortal men,
                 Who gave even to the gods
           Decision of their strife. Foremost in valour were
           His godlike sons and their sons' sons, who took delight 25
               In battle, and to front the ringing medley
                   Of brazen arms;
               Wise too were they and reason ruled their hearts.
               These virtues even the gods, in council gathered,
               Remembered well, when for marriage with Thetis
           There arose strife 'twixt Zeus and glorious Poseidon
               When each of the two gods would have her be
               His lovely bride, for passion filled their hearts.
                   But for them did the wisdom   30
               Of the immortal gods not grant this union
                   Should come to pass, when to their ears

str. 4   Came the prophetic oracle. For in their midst
           Wise-counselled Themis told that it was ruled of fate
           That the sea-goddess should bring forth a son, of strength
                 Mightier than his father,
           Whose hand should launch a shaft more powerful than the
                                                                    bolt

Of thunder or the fearsome trident, if she wed   35
  With Zeus or with his brothers. 'Cease,' said she,
    'From this design,
  But with a mortal let her bed be blessed,
  And let her see her son dying in war –
  Like Ares shall he be in strength of arm
And in fleetness of foot like to the lightning flash.
  If my word you would hear, grant that her marriage
  Be for an honour given of heaven to Peleus,
    The son of Aeacus,
  Who, so they tell, is of all men most righteous,
    Dwelling upon Iolcus' plain.   40

str. 5 'And to the immortal cave of Chiron let your bidding
Speedily take its way, nor let the ballot-leaves
Of strife be set amidst us twice by Nereus' daughter.
    But on the full-moon's eve
  Let her for this hero unloose the lovely girdle   45
  Of her pure maidenhood.' Such words the goddess spoke
    To the children of Cronos; and they nodded
      Giving assent
    With their immortal brows. Nor was the fruit
    Of these words cast away. For the two gods,
    So the tale runs, joined in their honours given
To the wedding of maid Thetis, and the tongues of poets
  Have made known the young valour of Achilles
  To those who knew it not. For it was he
    In vine-clad Mysia
  Made the blood flow, and scattered o'er the plain
    The darkened gore of Telephus.   50

str. 6 For Atreus' sons he built a bridge for their return,
And freed Helen, and with his spear cut the great sinews
Of Troy asunder, those heroes who, as he plied
    The task of murderous battle
Sought to withstand him on the plain, proud-hearted
                     Memnon
That man of might, and Hector and warriors many
                     another 55
  Noble and brave. For these Achilles' hand
    Pointed the way

Down to Persephone's abode, that prince
Of Aeacus' sons, bringing to Aegina
And his own stock the height of fame. Nor even
In death was he of songs forsaken, but the maids
Of Helicon stood by his pyre and grave,
And poured o'er him their dirge in chorus. Thus
Even the immortals ruled
That to a brave man, though he be no more,   60
The songs of goddesses be given.

str. 7   Now too that word holds, and the Muses' chariot
Speeds forth to praise the memory of Nicocles
Of boxing fame. Honour him then who in the vale
Of Isthmus won the crown
Of Dorian parsley. Like to those resistless hands
Of old, he too conquered long since and put to rout   65
The men who dwelt nearby; and to his glory
Brings no disfame
This son of his proud uncle's race. Go then,
Let one of his own age bring to Cleandrus,
For his pankration victory, to bind
Upon his brow, the lovely myrtle's crown; for he
In the games of Alcathous won success,
And young men welcomed him at Epidaurus.
Now must brave souls resound
His praise, who in no corner-hole has hidden   70
His youth, untried of noble deeds.

Notes

2. his gleaming doors: indicating the wealth of Telesarchus.

6. great sorrow: the defeat of the Persian invaders under Xerxes at
Salamis 480 and Plataea 479; Thebes took the Persian side, and was
afterwards severely punished by the Greek allies led by Pausanias, the
Spartan king.

10. The stone of Tantalus: Tantalus was tortured in the Underworld
by a stone balanced eternally over his head, about to fall. See O 1.36
and note. The reference is to the threat of Persian defeat of Hellas,
which the gods have removed as a result in part of Aeginetan bravery.
The myths echo the theme of Aeginetan influence over the gods.

16. To Aegina: Thebes and Aegina were allied in friendship by hostility to Athens, and Pindar's affection for Aegina is the subject of many of his odes.

17. daughters of Asopus' river: Thebe and Aegina. Asopus is the largest river in Boeotia, and also the name of a spring on Aegina.

21. But you: i.e. the nymph Aegina.

Oenopia: another name for Aegina, also known as Oenone.

23–5: even to the gods: Aeacus was usually considered to be the judge of the dead in the Underworld. The reference here is rather to the following story of the marriage of Peleus and Thetis; Aeacus influenced divine affairs by providing a husband for Thetis to defuse the strife of Zeus and Poseidon.

27. Thetis: this is Pindar's fullest and most straightforward narrative of the marriage of Peleus, son of Aeacus, to the sea-nymph Thetis; see also N 4, N 5. The narrative may be derived from the part of Hesiod's *Catalogue of Women* concerning Aegina.

33. her son: Achilles.

40. Iolcus: the modern Volos in eastern Thessaly. Peleus left Aegina his birthplace (N 5.15 and note) and settled in Iolcus.

41. the . . . cave of Chiron: where the wedding was celebrated.

42. ballot-leaves of strife: Conway, in common with many editors, takes the reference to leaves as implying the use of leaves for voting, as was later done at Syracuse. But this custom is not known in Pindar's time. 'Leaves of strife' seems rather to be a metaphorical expression, as the 'leaves of Ocean' are springs in frag. 326; cf. the 'leaves of song' at I 4.27. Strife would occur twice because the birth of a son to Zeus or Poseidon would bring renewed quarrelling on top of the present dispute.

44. full-moon's eve: the full moon falls at mid month (O 3.19) and is a lucky day for marriage.

47. the two gods: the text is disputed, and Conway translates a conjecture by Triclinius, *anakte*. Peter Von der Mühll (*Mus. Helv.* 22 [1965]: 49–52) suggested that the MS text, *anakta*, could give the following sense: 'For the lord [*sc.* Peleus], so the tale runs, also gave honour to the wedding . . .' But at line 33 *anax* is used to refer to

Achilles, and I incline to see Achilles as the subject here: 'even Achilles approved the wedding of Thetis'; the baroque idea that he gave approval to the marriage of his own parents does fit better with the grammatical run of the rest of the sentence, of which Achilles is the subject. Pindar may be being deliberately ambiguous.

49. vine-clad Mysia: a district in Asia Minor, where the Greek forces landed on their way to Troy. Telephus, the king of Mysia, was wounded by Achilles after tripping over a vine, and his wound was incurable except by scrapings from Achilles' own sword. The event is shown, in now very damaged form, on the frieze of the great altar of Pergamum; see also Lycophron 1245–9. (Cf. O 9.70–9, I 4.41.)

54. Memnon: cf. N 3.63 and note.

56. songs ... the maids of Helicon: in a piece of ring-composition, the songs recalls those of line 47 which introduce Achilles. The mourning of the Muses for Achilles is described by Homer, *Odyssey* 24.60, and was also in the *Aethiopis*. The Boeotian name for the Muses, whose home was on Mt Helicon, is chosen because Pindar is writing as a Theban for an Aeginetan. Even the gods (and even those of Thebes) give honour to the Aeginetan heroes; cf. lines 10 and 23–5.

61. Nicocles: a cousin of Cleandrus, who, it appears, had won a victory in the Isthmian Games but was no longer alive.

65. those resistless hands: of Achilles.

This son: Cleandrus.

67. the games of Alcathous: the local games of Megara.

68. Epidaurus: Cleandrus had also been successful in the local games of Epidaurus.

For an Aeginetan

This short fragment is all that is left at the end of the manuscript of the Isthmian odes. It is possible that frags. 4, 150 and 190 belong to the same poem. (Only frag. 150 is translated in this book.) The praises of Aegina repeat topics frequently alluded to in other odes; the dolphin in line 7 is a common symbol of excellence: see Richard Stoneman, 'The Ideal Courtier: Pindar and Hieron in Pythian 2', *CQ* 34 (1984): 43–9.

> Famous the tale of Aeacus
> famous is Aegina renowned for ships;
> by the favours of the gods
> the Dorian people of Hyllus and Aegimius
> came and founded it.
>
> Under their dispensation
> they do not overstep the customs or laws
> of strangers; in their virtue they are like
> dolphins of the sea, and skilled stewards
> of the Muses and of athletic contests.

Notes

Aegimius: the father of Pamphylus and Dymas; he gave one third of his land to the descendants of Heracles' son Hyllus, and the three heroes gave their names to the Dorian tribes Pamphyloi, Dymanes and Hylleis.

PAEANS

For the Thebans at the Ismenion

This paean was composed for the festival of the Daphnephoria, held in spring; a kind of maypole, hung with 365 garlands and topped with metal spheres to represent the heavenly bodies, was the focal point of the procession. According to Proclus (*ap.* Photius, *Bibliotheca* 321) the Daphnephoria was a festival held every nine years, in the inclusive Greek reckoning (a 'Great Year'), but Pausanias (9.10.4) implies that it was annual, since the daphnephoros (bay-bearer), a boy with both parents still living, was appointed as priest of Ismenian Apollo for a single year. A painting by Lord Leighton is a vivid imaginative reconstruction of the event.

Only the last ten lines of the poem survive.

> Before reaching the painful [threshold] of old age
> a man should shade his soul
> with cheerfulness, free of anger
> in due measure
> and see to the resources of his house.
>
> ié ié, now the year that brings all to fulfilment   5
> and the Seasons, daughters of Themis,
> have come to the horse-driving city of Thebes
> to bring a banquet for Apollo, lover of garlands.
> May he crown the people
> with flowers of wise government.   10

Notes

1. **threshold of old age:** the phrase occurs also at Mimnermus 1.5, West.

6. **Seasons:** as daughters of the goddess of Right, also Hesiod, *Theogony* 901.

For the Men of Abdera

Abdera was a Greek colony on the Thracian coast. In legend it was founded by Heracles at the grave of his lover Abderus; it may previously have been a Phoenician settlement, as the name seems to be Semitic. Historically, it was settled in 654 or 652 by Greeks from Clazomenae; they were driven out, and later the Teans, driven from their home by the Persian general Harpagus in 545, resettled the site (Herodotus 1.168). At a later date some of the Tean settlers in Abdera returned to Teos and refounded it (Strabo 14.1.30). Abdera came under Persian rule by 514 and was freed after the defeat of the Persians at Eion in 475, after which it became one of the largest contributors to the Delian League.

These historical details have a bearing on the understanding of the allusions in line 29: see the note there. They do not help much with dating the ode, though if the 'last war' of line 105 refers to the expulsion of the Persians, the poem could belong after 478 (and probably after Pindar's return from his Sicilian visit of 476); but this could equally be a reference to a local conflict.

The paean was performed by a chorus of citizens of Abdera, who speak in their own person; the occasion is unknown. It is remarkable that the poem contains a historical narrative rather than a myth. A few passages are missing in the papyrus, but both the beginning and end of the poem are present.

> Son of the Naiad Thronia and of Poseidon
> Abderus of the bronze breastplate,
> from you I shall begin this paean
> for an Ionian people
> [approaching] Apollo Derenius and Aphrodite   5
> [6–23]
> I dwell in this Thracian land
> rich in vines and fruit.   25
> Let not mighty Time

falter in its steady and beneficent advance.
I am a young city:
yet I bore my mother's mother
shattered by the fire of war.   30
If any man goes to help his friends
by savage opposition to his enemies
the effort expended at the right moment
brings tranquillity.
Ié ié Paian ié ié; Paian
desert me never.

. . . mighty strength of men makes the highest wall . . .   37
. . .
. . . race of Poseidon   40
. . .
. . . what is dedicated to good counsel and respect   50
always blossoms in gentle weather.
May god grant the one; but the
envy which thinks evil   55
departs from those who are long dead;
a man must render to his parents
a glorious reputation.
They gained by war
a land full of gifts   60
and laid the foundations of their prosperity
beyond Mount Athos:
for they drove out the spear-bearing Paiones
from their divine nurse.
Heavy doom fell upon them:
but as they endured, the god helped them to success.
One who has done something noble
blazes with good report:
so the brightest light came upon them
as they fought the enemy before Mount Melamphyllos. 70
Ié ié Paian ié ié; Paian
desert me never.

'But the light-armed troops will clash
with a numerous army
as they come to the river.'
It was the first day of the month:

the crimson-footed maiden, kindly Hecate,
announced what would transpire ...   79
[80–95]
The dances summon you to sacred Delos   96
and the shining-armed Delphian maidens
who regularly dance their soft measures
around the high Parnassian rocks
sing their melody with sweet voice.
[Grant] me ... grace, Abderus,
and forward your horse-delighting people
by your strength in their last war.   105
Ié ié Paian, ié ié; Paian
desert me never.

Notes

1. **Thronia:** a nymph of Western Locri: Hesiod frag. 137, MW; *FGrH* 40F1.

2. **Abderus:** usually regarded as a son of Hermes (Hellanicus *FGrH* F105; Apollodorus 2.97).

5. **Derenius:** there was a district of Abdera named Derenus: Lycophron, *Alexandra* 440.

26. **mighty Time:** similar sentiments at O 8.9 and N 7.64.

28. **a young city:** the refoundation by the Teans took place in 543, while most colonies had been founded in the sixth century or even earlier.

29. **I bore my mother's mother:** this extraordinary statement has called forth much discussion. The view of G. L. Huxley, accepted by S. Radt in his commentary on the passage, is pretty certainly correct: the men of Abdera speak as 'I', their mother is Abdera and Abdera's mother is Teos; the Abderitans 'bore' their grandmother Teos in the sense that they refounded the city after its abandonment under Persian aggression and destruction by fire in the Ionian revolt of 499. The alternative view that the grandmother is Athens – supported by Wilamowitz and used to support an argument for the dating of the ode soon after the Persian sack of Athens – has nothing to recommend it.

37. **the highest wall:** cf. frag. 213, where walls are said to be better than treachery.

51. gentle weather: the political metaphor is common in Pindar; cf. frag. 109 and many passages in the epinicia.

62. beyond Mount Athos: an extravagant claim, perhaps meaning no more than 'beyond' (west of) the River Strymon. One would expect the Paiones to be located further northwest than this.

73. But the light-armed troops . . . : the oracle of Hecate is speaking, as is explained just below.

77. crimson-footed: used at O 6.94 of Demeter.

96. you: Apollo.

97. maidens: cf. Pa. 6.15ff. on the maiden-choruses of Delphi.

105. last war: probably a local conflict.

PAEAN 4

For the Ceans at Delos (after 458?)

This paean is referred to by Pindar himself in the opening lines of Isthmian 1, where he says that he has interrupted work on it to compose the epinician for one of his Theban compatriots. The date of the paean thus depends on the date assigned to Isthmian 1. It is likely that Pindar would not have been asked to compose an ode for Ceos while their native poet, Simonides, was still active, and therefore that it should be dated after his death in 458. The theme of the ode is love of one's own country, and is illustrated through some otherwise little-known Cean legends. Early rulers of Ceos are detailed, who had been offered rule in other lands but preferred to remain on their native soil, exemplifying a characteristic piece of Pindaric wisdom, not to seek after what is afar off.

> The short-backed breast of earth   14
> [?I would not] exchange for Babylon . . .

> Though I dwell on a rock   21
> I am famous among the Hellenes
> for achievement in the Games,
> and I am known for my abundance in the Muses.
> Even if my soil furnishes
> the life-giving gift of Dionysus,
> the cure of helplessness,
> still I am without horses and unsuited for pasture of cattle.
> Yet Melampus himself did not wish
> to leave his native land and rule in Argos,
> abandoning his gift of prophecy.   30
> Ié ié o ié Paian.

> The native city . . .
> and a man loves his kin:
> only the foolish long for what is remote.

I admire the saying of lord Euxantius   35
who refused the Cretans' invitation
to be their king,
and hold a one-seventh share
in the hundred cities of Pasiphae.
He explained to them a portent:
'I tremble at the war of Zeus   40
and at the loud-roaring Earth-shaker.
Once upon a time they,
with their thunderbolt and trident,
sent the land and all its people
to Tartarus, leaving only
my mother and the whole of her house unharmed.   45
Then shall I, for the temptation of wealth,
reject entirely the statutes of the blessed ones
to obtain a great possession elsewhere?
Fear would prevent me.
Oh my heart, forget the cypresses,   50
forget the pasture by Mount Ida . . .'

Ié ié, o ié Paian.   62

Notes

24. abundance in the Muses: a reference to the poets Simonides and his nephew Bacchylides, who came from Ceos.

28. Melampus: for the story of the prophet who was invited to rule in Argos, see Herodotus 9.34. According to the *Odyssey* (15.225–47) his home was at Pylos.

34. long for what is remote: a common Pindaric sentiment.

35. Euxantius: this piece of Cean folklore is referred to also by Bacchylides, Ode 1, and in later recondite sources including Ovid's *Ibis* and Nonnus' *Dionysiaca*, as well as Apollodorus 3.1.1. Euxantius was the son of Minos, king of Crete, and Dexithea; thus he had a title to the Cretan throne.

39. hundred cities: canonical since Homer: *Iliad* 2.649. Pasiphae was the daughter of King Minos.

44. sent ... to Tartarus: the Telchines were the original inhabitants of Ceos: Dexithea was a Telchin. Zeus punished them for impiety by destruction – by a tidal wave according to Pliny, *Natural History* 2.206. Only Dexithea and another woman, Makelo, were spared. Callimachus, frag. 75.68ff., says that this was because they had shown hospitality to the gods. Excavations on Ceos have revealed a Bronze Age temple destroyed by an earthquake.

For the Athenians at Delos

Nothing can be said about the date or occasion of this ode. Wilamowitz surmised that it was performed by a chorus of Euboeans, because of the myth in lines 36ff.; but there is no particular reason why they should be interested in Delos, and it is better to assume performance by Athenians as the heading in the papyrus indicates. Only the end of the ode is preserved; line 37 marks the beginning of the seventh strophe.

> Ié Delian Apollo.   19

> ... they took Euboea and settled there.   36

> Ié ié Delian Apollo:
> they colonized the scattered islands,
> rich in sheep,
> and they held illustrious Delos: 40
> Golden-haired Apollo gave them
> the body of Asteria to dwell in

> Ié ié Delian Apollo.
> There, children of Leto,
> receive me your servant   45
> with kindly mien
> as I pour out the honey-voiced cry
> of the glorious paean.

Notes

36. they took ...: Who did? A scholiast preserved at line 45 says that this refers to the Athenian colonists of Euboea, Pandorus and Aeclus. The former was traditionally the founder of Chalcis, the latter of Eretria, and a third, Kothos, was the founder of Cerinthus. See also

Pseudo-Scymnus 571–6; the colonization was attributed to the period before the Trojan War: Strabo 10.1.8.

38. scattered islands: the Sporades, namely Scyros Peparethus and Sciathus, which lie north of Euboea.

42. Asteria: another name of Delos. Asteria was a sister of Leto who fled from Zeus' attentions and was transformed into an island: Pa. 7b.42–9. Later Leto gave birth to the twins Apollo and Artemis there. Asteria is also used as a name of Delos by Callimachus, Hymn 4.36–40. Cf. Σ Lycophron, *Alexandra* 401.

For the Delphians at Pytho

The ode was composed for performance at the Theoxenia (60), at which the god was host at a banquet. The Theoxenia was attended by embassies from all over Greece and had the function of praying for fertility for the land. Pindar and his descendants were entitled to a share in the sacrifice, as were those who offered the largest leek (*porreezwiebel*) to Leto (Polemo, *ap*. Athenaeus 9.372c).

The ode has been variously dated. Wilamowitz suggested that it may have been performed at the same Pythian festival as Pythian 6, which also begins with an invocation of Aphrodite and the Graces, who are not conjoined elsewhere in Pindar's poetry. If so, the ode would belong to 490. Lines 123–5 could perhaps not have been written after the Battle of Salamis. However, if Pindar already held the proedria at Delphi one should maybe envisage a later date when he was more advanced in years.

The major conundrum posed by this poem is its relation to the Seventh Nemean (which can also not be securely dated). It has been supposed since the scholiasts that Nemean 7 was written to rectify the account of the story of Neoptolemus given in one of the paeans; and when the paeans were rediscovered in 1908 this was identified as the poem in question. The issue is discussed in the introduction to Nemean 7: the different manners of telling the myth in the two poems reflect the different purposes and audiences of the performances. The paean is composed in honour of the god Apollo, who in legend was pro-Trojan, while the Nemean honours the Aeginetans, whose heroic ancestors had fought against Troy. Truth is for Pindar an ethical concept (Schadewaldt, *Der Aufbau des pindarischen Epinikion* [Tübingen 1966]). Perhaps it is better to see the issue in terms of rhetorical practice: the story is told to suit the purpose.

The papyrus is damaged, but both beginning and end of the poem are preserved.

By Olympian Zeus I pray you,
Glorious Pytho, famous for oracles,
receive me, the singing spokesman of the Pierides,
in this holy season,
with Aphrodite and the Graces.
Hearing the din of Castalia
deprived of the chorus of men
beside the bronze gates of the spring,
I have come to give aid to your clansmen
and to support my own privileges.   10
With a loving heart,
like a child obeying his dear mother,
I have come to the grove of Apollo – nurse of garlands and
    festivities –
where the daughters of the Delphians,
chanting for the son of Leto,
dance by the shady navel stone of earth,
beating the ground with swift feet . . .
[19–49]

How did the [strife] of the immortals begin?   50
The gods can persuade the wise of these things,
but mortals cannot discover them.
But you, Muses – for you know all things
(you share this dignity with the dark Cloudfather
and with Mnemosyne) –
hear me now:
my tongue longs to [pour] the sweetest distillation of
    honey
as I come to the broad lists of Loxias,
the guest-festival of the gods.   60

The sacrifice is for all of glorious Greece
for which the Delphian people prayed
[for deliverance from] famine . . .
[66–78]

wearing the mortal body of archer Paris,
the god   80
at once effected a delay to the capture of Troy:
he shackled with rough slaughter

the violent son of the blue-haired sea-nymph Thetis,
the trusty bulwark of the Achaeans,
who had often hurled his implacable strength
against white-armed Hera
and against Polias.
By his great efforts
he had taken Dardania, if Apollo had not prevented it.   90
But Zeus, seated among golden clouds
on the peak of Mount Olympus –
watchman of the gods –
had not the temerity to dissolve the decision of Fate:
for the sake of high-tressed Helen
great Pergamon was to be annihilated
in a blaze of dazzling fire.
When they had placed in the wailing grave
the mighty corpse of the son of Peleus,
messengers went over the waves of the sea   100
to fetch strong Neoptolemus from Scyros,
and he destroyed the city of Ilium.
But he did not see his dear mother again,
nor his father's horses in the fields of the Myrmidons,
when he raised up their bronze-helmed army.
He came close to the Molossian land of Tomaros,
evading neither the winds   110
nor the Archer of the broad quiver.
The god swore, because he had
slain aged Priam as he sprang to the hearth-altar,
that he should not return to his happy home,
nor reach old age;
but as he fought with the servants
over the high honours
at the sacred precinct by the broad navel of earth,
one killed him.   120
Ié iéte, lads, march to the measure of the paean.

Famous island, ruling amidst the Dorian sea,
bright star of Hellenian Zeus,
we shall not lay you to rest unfed with paeans:
you shall receive the roar of the songs, and tell
where you obtained the spirit of naval command   130
and the virtue of justice to strangers.

He who disposes all things –
the broad-faced son of Cronos –
endowed you with this blessing,
and by the waters of Asopus
once seized the deep-breasted maiden Aegina
from her home.
Then golden tresses of the air
concealed in shadows the spine of your land
so that the immortal marriage-bed ...   140
[141–70]
bronze-delighting ...
angry ...
the numerous flames of ..., and of voices
to cover the limitless achievements
of the sons of Aeacus. You love
your ancestral city ...
and you shade your happy people ...
with garlands of blooming health.
Accept, O Paean ...
the celebration of the lawful Muses.   180

Notes

10. to support my own privileges: this presumably refers to Pindar's privilege of proedria at the Theoxenia: Paus. 9.23.2. Plutarch, *De Sera Numinis Vindicta* 13; Libanius, *Oration* 20, 2.

51. the wise: i.e. poets, distinguished from ordinary 'mortals'.

53. you know all things: *Iliad* 2.484ff.; Hesiod, *Theogony* 26–8, where the Muses claim to be able to tell both false and true.

61. guest-festival of the gods: the literal meaning of Theoxenia.

62. for all of glorious Greece: the Theoxenia celebrated the role of the Delphian people's prayers in saving Greece from famine on some unknown occasion, just as the prayers of Aeacus had once saved Greece from drought: N 5.10.

66–78. The argument in the missing section must have run 'Apollo helps men in need. So he helped Troy by delaying its capture.'

90. Dardania: the land of Troy.

94. had not the temerity ...: Zeus is not free to overthrow Fate: see *Iliad* 16.439–43 where Hera upbraids him for wishing to save Sarpedon in despite of Fate. However, the distinction of Fate and the Will of Zeus is not always clear; at *Iliad* 24.527ff. Zeus allots to Achilles the death which is fated for him. See in general H. Lloyd-Jones, *The Justice of Zeus* (Berkeley 1971), p. 5 and passim.

102. Neoptolemus: the son of Achilles; it was fated that Troy could not fall without his intervention (and that of Philoctetes: cf. P 1.54). Neoptolemus became the exemplar of the war-criminal for the Greeks, when during the final sack of Troy he murdered King Priam as he clung to an altar for sanctuary, and hurled the young child Astyanax from the walls. For these crimes Apollo ensured his failure to return home, and eventual death: see further the notes on N 7.

107. Myrmidons: the people ruled by Achilles in Phthiotis. They were so called because they were supposed to be descended from the men created from ants after the depopulation of the world through the drought to which Aeacus' prayers put an end.

109. Tomaros: the itinerary is that described in N 7 also: see notes there. The point is that Neoptolemus did not reach either Scyros or Phthia, his native homes.

111. the Archer: Apollo.

113. because he had slain aged Priam: this idea is first found in Pindar; cf. the later treatments in Virgil, *Aeneid* 2.535ff., Tryphiodorus, *Capture of Troy* 640ff.

120. one killed him: cf. N 7.42, where the reference to a knife (*machaira*) alludes to the name of the murderer, Machaireus ('Butcher').

124. bright star of Hellenian Zeus: the island of Aegina. Delos is described as a star in frag. 33d.5ff. The description of Aegina as 'ruling amidst the Dorian sea' might have been difficult to carry off after the Battle of Salamis.

132. He who disposes all things: a similar phrase is used of Zeus by Pindar at I 5.52. For the idea, cf. the passage of the *Iliad*, 24.527ff., which describes the two jars in which Zeus keeps all good and bad fortune for men.

135. Asopus: a river on Aegina: cf. N 3.4 and note. The tale of Zeus and Aegina is also told at N 8.6ff., I 8.21ff.

137. golden tresses of the air: cf. the occasion on which mist covers Mt Ida as Zeus and Hera make love, *Iliad* 14.350ff.

141–70. This passage may have contained the legend of Aeacus' prayer to save Greece from drought.

. . . to Delos

This poem, which tells part of the legend of Delos, is undateable
and the identity of those who commissioned it cannot be
discovered.

Only the opening is preserved, in part. The first section is an
interesting document of Pindar's 'theory of poetry', in which he
rejects the authority of Homer (cf. Nemean 7.21) in favour of
the true inspiration which he claims to receive from the Muses.

> Apollo! . . .
> [1–9]
> sing hymns   10
> going not along the trodden path of Homer
> but with different horses
> . . . winged chariot . . .
> . . . Muse . . .
> I pray to Mnemosyne   15
> the fine-robed daughter of Heaven,
> and to her daughters,
> to give me facility.
> The minds of men are blind
> when anyone hunts out the deep road of truth
> without the daughters of Helicon.   20
> But they have given to me
> this immortal task
> [23–41]
>
> . . . why should I believe?
> The daughter of Coeus,
> disdaining the love of Zeus . . .
> I am afraid to say what is incredible: . . .   45
> hurled into the sea she became a shining rock,
> and the sailors of old call her Ortygia.
> She drifted hither and thither on the Aegean:

then the powerful one fell in love with her   50
and had union with her
and she brought forth a race of archers . . .

Notes

12. **with different horses:** the sentiment recalls the injunction to 'praise an old wine but a new song' (O 9.48, with note), so that novelty seems to be valued for its own sake as well as because it contradicts Homer. For the metaphor of the path of song, cf. N 6.53, P 4.247.

20. **without the daughters of Helicon:** the superior knowledge of poets who are instructed by the Muses is also emphasized at Pa. 6.51.

44. **daughter of Coeus:** Asteria, the sister of Leto. Cf. Pa. 5.42. Hesiod, *Theogony* 409, mentions that their mother was Phoebe of Ceos.

48. **Ortygia:** another name for Delos. One version of the legend said that Asteria turned into a quail as she jumped: the Greek for 'quail' is *ortyx*, and this was the origin of the name (Apollodorus 1.21). The drifting of the island is mentioned also in frag. 33c–d, cf. Callimachus, *Hymn* 4.36–8.

PAEAN 8

[For the Delphians] at Pytho?

The date and occasion of this poem are not known. Snell supposed that it might have been commissioned by the Athenians because of the unusual reference (in a Delphic context) to Athena as 'Pallas' (line 82); but it seems more likely that it was for a Delphian chorus, as it celebrates a Delphic myth, namely the series of legendary temples that preceded the historical temple of Apollo.

According to this legend, which is first found in this poem and may even have been invented by Pindar, there was a series of temples at Delphi. The full account is given by Pausanias 10.5.9. The first temple was built of laurel branches brought from Tempe. The discovery of remains of a mid-eighth-century temple of laurel branches at Eretria suggests that such a building is perfectly feasible. The second was, 'according to the Delphians', made by bees out of wax and feathers. This clearly could not have been a real place of worship, but bees are important in the legends of Delphi, and their flight could be observed for oracular purposes (Homeric Hymn to Hermes 552–66, cf. Hymn to Apollo 513–64). Bee-names characterize the priests of Delphi, and at P 4.60–1 Pindar calls the priestess at Delphi 'the Delphic bee'. The third temple, of bronze, was built by Hephaestus (as described here) and the fourth by the heroes Trophonius and Agamedes. For a stimulating treatment of the whole legend see C. Sourvinou-Inwood, CQ 29 (1979): 231–51.

Several features of this poem – the laurel branches, the connection with Tempe, the involvement of Pallas – are recalled in Aristonous' Hymn to Apollo (Diehl, *Anthologia Lyrica Graeca* [1949] 6.134).

Only the opening part of the poem is (poorly) preserved.

... Renowned prophets of Apollo   13
I [have come] over land and Ocean ...

Themis . . .
[16–62]

. . . temple. A strong wind   63
brought [. . .] to the Hyperboreans.
Muses, what was its design,
built by the skilled hands of Hephaestus and Athena?
Bronze were the walls,
bronze the pillars that supported it,
and six golden enchantresses   70
sang above the acroterion.
But the children of Cronos
opened the earth with a thunderbolt
and concealed that most holy of all creations,
in anger at the sweet singing,
because visitors pined away,
far from their parents and wives,
hanging their hearts on that honey-minded voice.
. . . destroyed men with its virginal . . .   80
. . . a masterpiece of imperishable . . .
Pallas placed in it . . .
with a voice . . .
what is and what was heretofore . . .
Mnemosyne . . .
told them all . . .
[86ff.]

A scholion preserved in the papyrus indicates what was in the
conclusion of the poem:
    'The god gave an oracle to Erginus [the father of Trophonius
and Agamedes]:

> Erginus, son of Clymenus son of Presbonius,
> You have come to seek a family, but now
> Place a new tip on the old plough.

Pindar says that the god gave him this response when he wanted
to father children.'
    Further notes by the scholiast refer to the story of Erginus'
war against Thebes, which is told by Apollodorus 2.4.11:
Clymenus, king of the Minyans, was wounded by a Theban at
Onchestus, and his son Erginus avenged him by making war on

Thebes. He made a treaty and sent heralds for the tribute; but Heracles met them on the way and mutilated them by cutting off their ears and noses, which he sent back to Erginus as the Theban 'tribute'. Erginus then marched on Thebes but was defeated. Apart from references to Onchestus, the death of Clymenus, war on Thebes, and the mutilation of the hostages by Heracles, it is not clear exactly how Pindar told the story, but it looks as if Apollodorus followed this poem quite closely.

Notes

13. **Renowned prophets of Apollo:** this may in fact be the opening line of the paean: the fragment preserved in *POxy* 3822 frag. seems to have a symbol indicating the end of a poem immediately before this line: see I. Rutherford, *ZPE* 86 (1991): 5.

15. **Themis:** possibly a reference to the peaceable take-over of Delphi by the sisters Themis, Earth and Phoibe, with Apollo; which was represented on the east pediment of the Alcmaeonid temple at Delphi, c. 550–500.

68. **Bronze were the walls:** Pausanias (10.5.11) remarks that there is nothing implausible in these lines, since the temple of Athena of the Brazen House at Sparta also had bronze walls.

70–1. **enchantresses:** their work seems also to have been mentioned in line 62 where part of the word for 'wryneck' is preserved. Wrynecks were used in magical rites. Philostratus, *Life of Apollonius* 6.11, in a discussion of the oracle of Delphi, informs us 'from one of them [the temples] it is said that golden figures of the wryneck were hung up which possessed in a manner the charm of the Sirens'. The enchantresses are indeed like Homer's Sirens (*Odyssey* 12.39–43) who lure travellers away from their homes for ever with their sweet singing.

82. **Pallas placed in it:** these lines describe the institution of the Pythia at Delphi, with her ability to tell the past and present (and presumably the future also). The name Pallas, normally an Athenian epithet for Athena, recurs also in Aristonous' *Hymn to Apollo* (see introduction, above), where she leads Apollo to Pytho.

86ff. The poem went on to treat of the fourth temple, built by the brothers Trophonius and Agamedes, sons respectively of the mortal Erginus and the god Apollo. The story according to Pausanias (9.37.3)

was that they built the temple and treasury, but left a secret entrance
by which they could go in and steal the treasures. The owner of the
treasury, Hyreus, set a trap for the thieves. Agamedes was caught in it,
whereupon Trophonius cut off his head to prevent identification of the
thief which would implicate him. The earth then split open and
swallowed Trophonius; he became an oracular hero in his own right,
at Lebadeia. There is no knowing whether this part of the myth was
told in the paean, and it is perhaps unlikely as it is so discreditable to
the heroes.

Scholion. a new tip on the old plough: a proverbial expression for an
old man taking a new young wife.

The date and occasion of this ode are unknown. The subject of
the preserved fragment is Hecuba's prophetic dream of the birth
of her son Paris (Alexander), as described by the prophetess
Cassandra. It is uncertain whether the poem should in fact be
classified as a paean (I. Rutherford, *Eos* [1991]).

> [Alexander] hastening   10
> [her] divine heart cried out with a terrible wail,
> and prophesied in this fashion:
> 'O Zeus . . . of broad vision . . .
> accomplish the fated suffering . . .
> since Hecuba [told] the Dardanians
> how [in a dream] she saw herself
> pregnant with this man.
> She seems to give birth to a Hundred-Hander,
> bearer of fire,
> and all Ilion was torn to the ground.
> She told the prodigy of her dream . . .
> foreknowledge . . .   25
> . . .'

Notes

21. Hundred-Hander: the 300-handed giants were Briareus, Gyes and
Cottus, children of Sky and Earth.

22. all Ilion: the birth of Paris began the chain of events which led to
the Trojan War. A similar argument is put forward by Helen in
Euripides' *Trojan Women* 919–22. The earliest source seems to be the
epic *Cypria*, frag. 11 Bernabé, and the image of the torch recurs in
Euripides, *Andromache* 293–8, and other writers.

PAEAN 9

For the Thebans at the Ismenion

This ode composed in response to an eclipse of the sun became a famous anthology piece in antiquity, so that large portions of it are preserved in the literary tradition as well as in the papyrus. It is quoted at length by the Roman historian, Dionysius of Halicarnassus in his life of Demosthenes (line 7), and the first ten lines also by Philo, *On Providence* 2.97. There is a striking translation by Thomas Love Peacock, 'Pindar on the Eclipse of the Sun' (1806), which begins 'All-enlight'ning, all-beholding, / All-transcending star of day! / Why, thy sacred orb enfolding, / Why does darkness veil thy ray?'

There are two eclipses in Pindar's lifetime which come into question: that of 17 February 478 and that of 30 April 463. The latter is perhaps the more likely.

Ray of the Sun, distant in vision,
Mother of the eyes,
What have you in mind,
concealing yourself, brightest of stars,
in the daytime?
Why have you made powerless
the strength of men and the paths of wisdom,
by hastening down the tracks of darkness?   5
Are you driving on to a different course?
By Zeus I pray you, driver of swift horses,
turn this universal portent to harmlessness
and blessing for the Thebans . . .   10
[11–13]
Do you bring some sign of war
or blight of crops,
or an excess of snow, or raging civic discord   15
or a flood of the sea over the earth
or the heat of summer drenched in fierce rain?
Will you overwhelm the earth with flood   20

and create a new race of men from the beginning?
I bewail nothing that I shall suffer in common with all . . .
[22–33]
by divine . . . I was ordained
to assemble a grand chorus
close to the immortal bed of Melia
to honour you with the meditations of my heart.
I pray you, archer-god,
as I dedicate the oracle by the Muses' art . . .   40
when Melia, the daughter of Ocean,
united with you, Pythius,
and brought to birth Teneros, the wide in strength,
the unexcelled spokesman of what is right.
To him, long-haired Father,   45
you entrusted the people of Cadmus
in the city of Zeathus,
because of his wisdom and courage.
Yes, and the sea-dwelling Lord of the Trident
honoured him above all men
and drew together the ground of the Euripus.   49
. . .

Notes

35. **Melia:** a river-nymph of Thebes; a spring was named after her and she had a cult in the temple of Apollo Ismenius at Thebes.

38. **archer-god:** the poet is now addressing Apollo, who was closely identified with the sun, instead of the 'Ray of the Sun'.

41. **Teneros:** one of two sons of Melia by Apollo; the other was Ismenius. Both had the gift of prophecy. Cf. P 11.46 and scholiast, Pa. 7.45.

45. **long-haired Father:** i.e. Apollo, regularly portrayed with long hair.

46. **Zeathus:** an alternative spelling of Zethus, who with his brother Amphion built the walls of Thebes.

49. **Euripus:** the narrow strait between Attica and Euboea. The point of this allusion cannot be determined.

PAEAN 12

For the Naxians, to Delos

Line 5 suggests that a Naxian chorus is involved, but the identity of the festival cannot be conjectured. The myth told is of the birth of Apollo and Artemis to Leto on Delos.

. . . the nine Muses . . .	2
. . . plucks the flowers of such song	4
[there] often comes from Naxos	
a sacrifice of sheep with shining fat,	
mixed with the Graces, by the hill of Cynthus,	
where, they say, Zeus,	
the gatherer of dark clouds and lord of the bright	
thunderbolt	
took his seat on the crags to wait in foreknowledge	10
while the gentle-hearted daughter of Coeus	
was released from her sweet labour;	
the sun blazed in full splendour	
as the twin children entered the bright light of day,	15
and Eleithyia and Lachesis poured from their mouths	
a great cry . . .	
. . .	

Notes

8. **Cynthus:** Mt Cynthus is the hill which dominates the little island of Delos.

11. **daughter of Coeus:** Leto. In Pa. 5 and 7b the same expression denotes her sister, Asteria.

12. **sweet labour:** the same expression is used of birth-pangs at O 6.43.

17. **Eleithyia and Lachesis:** Lachesis is one of the Fates, and Eleithyia is the goddess of birth (see also O 7.64, N 7.1).

Unidentified occasion. This poem and the next may actually be *prosodia* (processional poems) for heroes (I. Rutherford, *ZPE* 92 (1992): 59–72.

> . . . rewards of glory.   31
> The tuneful Muse, at the conclusion
> [of the festival]
> sings a song of pleasant words . . .
> and will recall even one who dwells   35
> far from the festival of the heroine.
> When gold is tested, the conclusion . . .
> and of swift thought . . .
> when it is set up with wisdom . . .   40

Note

The incomplete line 40 was the last line of the poem.

PAEAN 15

For the Aeginetans, to Aeacus

Possibly, like the preceding poem, a prosodion. The ritual involved may be a Theoxenia or divine banquet, as described by the scholiasts on Nemean 7.86. One should envisage a procession perhaps from the Aiakeion in the town of Aegina to Mt Panhellenion, a five-mile journey. See I. Rutherford, ZPE 92 (1992): 59–72.

> On this joyful day
> the immortal mares of Poseidon
> carry Aeac[us],
> and aged Nereus follows.
> The Father, the son of Cronos . . .
> turning his eye [with] his hand
> to the ambrosial table of the gods
> where nectar is poured out to drink . . .
> comes to the year . . .
> last. . . .

For the Argives, to Electryon

Like Paeans 14 and 15, this is probably not a paean, as was seen by the first editor, Lobel. The tantalizing scraps belong to a narration of the theft of the cattle of Electryon, king of Mycenae, and the murder of his sons, by the Teleboae or Taphioi who dwelt on the Echinades islands (the pirates of line 9). See Apollodorus 2.54.

> In the holy shrine of the sons of Tyndareus
> a cultivated grove
> offers to a poet material for song
> . . . blazes through the city
> . . . brightness of hymns . . . unwearying
> . . . around Dardania
> . . . as once in Thebes
> . . . when the pirates
> . . . secretly by night . . .

Occasion unknown. The fragments come from a narrative of the
infant Heracles' exploit of strangling the snakes sent by Hera to
kill him. The story is told in a rather similar way in Nemean 1.

. . . Alcides . . .	4
. . . hissing . . .	6
when the snakes, sent from a god . . .	8
through the doors . . .	
. . . against the baby of heavenly Zeus	
. . . and he raised his head against them	10
. . . with his hand threw the embroidered swaddling	
clothes from his limbs	
and revealed his nature	
. . . light flashed from his eyes.	
[Alcmene] unclad, from the bed of birth	
. . . screamed out in fear.	15
The Cephallenian maids all, seized by fear,	
rushed from the house of Amphitryon . . .	

Notes

4. Alcides: i.e. Heracles.

19. Cephallenian maids: a scholiast makes clear their identity. Amphitryon, Heracles' mortal father, had just been campaigning against the
Teleboae, who dwelt in the Echinades islands close to Cephallenia.

The poem invokes Hera, but there is not much left of it.

> Ié ié queen of the Olympians,   3
> bride of the best of husbands
> [5–8]
> this holy spring,
> strength of Achelous   10
> Iéié queen of the Olympians,
> bride of the best of husbands.
> Sweet . . . will be
> eternal . . .
> procession for the city   15
> sailors . . .
> [17–18]
> Ié ié queen of the Olympians
> bride of the best of husbands
> . . .

DITHYRAMBS

The Descent of Heracles *or* Cerberus;
for the Thebans (after 470)

Dithyrambs, unlike other choral lyrics, generally had titles in this resembling that other genre, tragedy, which was also dedicated to Dionysus. The title, taken with the fact that fragment 81 is in the same metre, suggests that that fragment occurred somewhere in this poem, the length of which is unknown. Other preserved dithyrambs, e.g. those of Bacchylides, range from thirty to 130 lines.

This poem is a vivid evocation of the atmosphere of the festival of Dionysus, in which the gods themselves are imagined as taking part, as they do also in the Epidaurian hymn to the Mother of the Gods, *PMG* 935.

> In former times the long-stretched chant of the dithyramb
>   wound along
> And the false 's' sounded from the mouths of men,
> . . . spread out . . .
> knowing   5
> how the sons of Uranus
> celebrate the rites of Bromius
> in the halls by the sceptre of Zeus.
> The whirling of the drums begins
> beside the holy Great Mother,
> and the castanets clatter   10
> while the feast is lit by bright pine-torches.
> The loud shrieking of the Naiads is roused,
> their wailing and whooping as their necks arch back
> in the wild clamour.
> The mighty thunderbolt, breathing fire,   15
> twirls in the midst, and the spear of the Earth-shaker,
> while the mighty shield of Pallas
> rumbles with the hissing of its thousand snakes.
> Artemis the shepherdess strides swiftly through,   20
> yoking the tribe of lions in Bacchic frenzy . . .

and . . . is soothed by the dances and the herds of beasts.
The Muse made me the supreme herald   25
of wise words for Hellas of the lovely dances
and I pray to chariot-loving Thebes
where, legend tells, Cadmus in the wisdom of his heart
took Harmony to wife. He heard the voice of Zeus
and bore a race glorious among mortals . . .   30

[frag. 81]
I praise you, Geryon,
in comparison with him,
but I keep quiet about
what does not please Zeus.

Notes

2. **the false 's':** the poet Lasus of Hermione, born c. 548–5, wrote a
dithyramb in which the letter 's' was not used at all. However, Pindar
seems to be contrasting his practice with that of all his predecessors,
but the point is obscure. The letter here named is the Dorian san, which
perhaps had a more hissing sound than sigma.

7. **sons of Uranus:** this commonly refers to the Olympian gods, though
it can be used of the Titans also: Hesiod, *Theogony* 502; Pindar P 3.4.

8. **whirling of the drums:** the action is often represented on vase-
paintings: the drum is something like a tambourine, but without the
little cymbals, and is played by drumming with the fingers while
whirling it around the player's head.

8. **Great Mother:** the Phrygian goddess Cybele. Her lion-chariot was
represented on the north frieze of the Siphnian treasury at Delphi (525).
She is often associated with the rites of Dionysus: Euripides, *Bacchae*
72–82.

10. **castanets clatter:** the same music-making is described in a fragment
from the *Semele* of the tragic poet Diogenes of Athens (*Tragicorum
Graecorum Fragmenta*, ed. A. Nauck [1889], 45F1): 'Yet I hear the
Asian women of Cybele, with their hair-bands, making a roar with the
whirling of the drums and the clashing of the bronze cymbals from
hand to hand.'

29. **Cadmus . . . Harmony:** the founder of Thebes married Harmonia,

daughter of Ares and Aphrodite. The story is told in full in Nonnus' *Dionysiaca* 4. Roberto Calasso, *The Marriage of Cadmus and Harmony* (London 1993), Chapter 12, can be heartily recommended for its evocation of the legendary world of Greece.

frag. 81. Geryon: a king of Erytheia (Cadiz). It was one of Heracles' labours to steal his cattle. Pindar expresses similar doubt about the morality of Heracles' action in frag. 169: see the notes there.

DITHYRAMB: frag. 75

To the Athenians

Pindar won an Athenian victory in the contest for dithyrambs in 497/6, at the age of twenty-one, according to the papyrus *Life* (*POxy* 2438.9–10). But if this, his second such victory (line 8) is it, the first must have been in his extreme youth. It seems more probable that this poem is a later one. The reference to the 'highly-adorned market-place' in line 5 has been connected by commentators with the embellishment of the Athenian agora by Conon in 470–61; but the connection is a risky one.

> Hither to the dance, Olympians!
> Pour on it your grace O gods,
> as you visit the navel-stone
> smoking with many sheep
> in holy Athens,
> and its famous and highly-adorned market-place.   5
> Take your share of the violet-crowns
> and the songs gathered in springtime,
> and behold me marching with the brightness of Zeus
> for the second time
> to the ivy-crowned god
> Bromius, whom mortals call the Loud Roarer   10
> when they dance for the birth of their forefathers
> and the women of Cadmus' family.
> I the clear prophet shall not omit
> how, when the chamber of the purple-clad Seasons is opened,

the nectarous plants bring on the sweet-scented spring.   15
Then on the immortal earth the lovely leafage
of violets swells up, roses are mingled with tresses,
voices echo to the sound of pipes,
and the dancers celebrate Semele of the circling tiara.

[frag. 83]

They used to talk of the Boeotian swine.

Notes

6. violet-crowns: wreaths of violets worn for the spring festival. Cf.
frag. 76.

10. Bromius: Dionysus.

frag. 83. The proverb 'Boeotian swine' is quoted by the scholiast on
O 6.152; Boeotians were a byword for stupidity in neighbouring Attica.

DITHYRAMB: frags. 76–7

To the Athenians

The historical background to this poem is the Athenian naval
victory over the Persians at Artemisium, as indicated by Plutarch, who quotes frag. 77. It could be even later, after the
Battle of Eion (475), for example.

O glorious Athens,
shining, violet-crowned,
celebrated in song,
bulwark of Hellas,
city of the gods . . .

when the sons of Athens
established the shining foundation of freedom

Note

shining: a famous line, much mocked by Aristophanes (*Knights* 1329, *Acharnians* 637, *Clouds* 299). In *Acharnians* he writes 'though meeter, I ween, for an oily sardine, than for our noble city the praise is' (cf. N 4.18).

DITHYRAMB: frag. 78

Occasion unknown; perhaps for a festival in armour.

War-whoop, daughter of battle,
hear the prelude of swords,
while the men performed
for the city
the sacrificial slaughter.

PROSODION: frag. 89a

[To Artemis?]

What is finer,
in beginning a song or in ending one,
than to celebrate deep-bosomed Leto
and the driver of swift horses?

PARTHENEIA
(Maiden Songs)

PARTHENEION I (frag. 94A = 104C)

Partheneia (maiden songs) are written for choruses of girls, and are commonly associated with the initiation rites of girls reaching puberty. This one is for one of the girls of the house of Aioladas – probably a granddaughter, as in Partheneion 2. The lines preserved are a classic statement of Pindar's 'theory of poetry', that only achievement and its proper celebration can win immortal fame.

> ... that I should become a prophet,   5
> servant of the gods;
> the honours of mortals are diverse;
> envy hangs over every man
> for his virtues,
> but he who has nothing –
> his head is hidden in black silence.
> I would pray the sons of Cronus
> in friendship
> to grant happiness to Aioladas and his family
> for a long time: for the days of men are immortal,
> though their bodies die.
> Whoever is not deprived by harsh necessity
> of a house with children,
> lives a life that escapes unholy trouble;
> but before the birth ...

Notes

16. a house with children: similar sentiments at O 10.86ff.

PARTHENEION 2 (frag. 94B = 104D)

Daphnephorikon for the Thebans
at the Ismenion. For Agasicles.

The daphnephoria was a Theban festival in honour of Apollo.
(Cf. Paean 1 and introductory note.)

The family relations of the persons mentioned in this poem
are probably as follows (for an alternative view, in which
Damaena is the daughter of Pagondas, the dancer herself, see L.
Lehnus, 'Pindaro: il dafneforico per Agasicle', *Bulletin of the
Institute of Classical Studies* 31 (1984): 61–92).

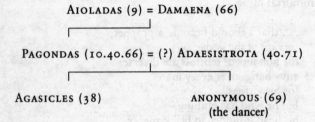

AIOLADAS (9) = DAMAENA (66)

PAGONDAS (10.40.66) = (?) ADAESISTROTA (40.71)

AGASICLES (38)   ANONYMOUS (69)
                                   (the dancer)

The poem is spoken in the person of the unnamed sister of
Agasicles.

The father of Pindar was said by the ancient *Lives* to be called
Pagondas, but this may be mere speculation based on this poem.
The name is not uncommon at Thebes. One Pagondas was
general at the Battle of Delium in 424, and clearly cannot have
been Pindar's father; he might have had a son of twelve as early
as 450, but this would still be a late poem of Pindar, if the same
Pagondas is in question. Frag. 94c is also from a partheneion
alleged to be written for members of Pindar's own family.

> . . . for Loxias the foreknowing   3
> is coming to bring his immortal grace
> to Thebes.
> Dressed in my robe swiftly
> and bearing in my tender hands
> the bright branches of laurel

I will sing the dwelling of Aioladas
and of his son Pagondas,   10
adorning my maidenly head with garlands,
and I will imitate in my song   15
the siren chant to pipes of lotus reed

which silences the brisk blasts of Zephyrus
when in the fierce weather of winter
Boreas makes shiver . . . the waves of the sea . . .
[20–30]
Many things that have gone before . . .
adorned with words, and some . . .
Zeus knows, but I must keep
my mind on maidenly matters
and speak such with my tongue.   35
No beneficial song must I forget
for any man or woman
whose children I am intent on.
I have come to the dance as a trusty witness
for Agasicles and for his noble parents   40
in the matter of the proxeny:
for they were honoured, of old and now,
by the dwellers round about
for their renowned victories with swift horses,   45
both those on the shores of famous Onchestus,
and those . . . the temple of Itonia . . .
their manes were adorned with garlands
and at Pisa
[50–9]
seven-gated Thebes.   60

Then . . . jealous anger
at the wise mind of these men
brought vicious, unrelenting discord,
but they loved the trusty paths of justice.
Son of Damaena, lead me now,
stepping on with well-omened foot:
your first daughter will gladly follow you,
treading the path of the lovely-leaved laurel
closely with her sandals,
she whom Andaesistrota cared for . . .

Notes

7. bright branches of laurel: a reference to the re-censing of the temple with fresh bay.

13–15. imitate ... the siren chant: cf. Alcman, frag. 1, 96–7, 'she is not more tuneful than the Sirens – for they are gods – but ...'

19. makes shiver ... the waves of the sea: G. Most (*ZPE* 64 [1986]: 33–8) argues that the text here is corrupt and the word translated as 'sea' should be read as 'Pan', a god who sometimes stirs up the waves.

41. proxeny: Agasicles' family had had the duty of entertaining foreign visitors to Thebes.

45. victories: one Pagondas had won a chariot victory at Olympia in 682, as we know from Paus. 5.8.7. He was probably an ancestor of this family.

46. Onchestus: a town on Lake Copais.

47. Itonia: a name of Athena in Thessaly.

61. jealous anger: the historical reference cannot be recovered.

66. Son of Damaena: Pagondas, as closest relative of the 'boy with both parents alive', bears the *kopo* ('maypole') in the procession.

71. Andaesistrota: here taken as the girl's mother. She could also be the mistress of an 'academy' like that of Sappho on Lesbos, at which young girls were prepared for adulthood.

FRAGMENT 94C

Daphnephorikon for the Thebans at the Ismenion

A passage of the papyrus *Life* of Pindar (*POxy* 2438.24ff.) tells us:

> He married Megacleia, daughter of Lysitheus and Calline, and had a son Daiphantus, for whom he also wrote a daphnephorikon;

and two daughters, Protomache and Eumetis: he mentions them
in the ode which begins

> The leader of the Muses, Apollo,
> calls me to dance.
> . . .
> lead your servant, glorious Leto . . .

SELECTED
FRAGMENTS

Hymns

Fragments 29–35 For the Thebans, to Zeus

The fragments attributed to this hymn are quoted in several separate works and were first associated by August Boeckh because they share the same metre in several details. The ode exhibits an abundance of mythological details, and it is not easy to see how the different narratives may have been combined. The evocation of the island of Delos as a star for the gods, to whom earth is as distant as our heaven, is a remarkable imaginative *tour-de-force*.

Fragment 29

Shall we sing of Ismenus
or Melia of the golden distaff
or Cadmus, or the sacred progeny of the Sown Men
or Theba with her dark diadem
or the might of Heracles that dares all things
or the joyful honours of Dionysus
or the marriage of white-armed Harmony?

Fragment 30

[the Muses sing]
first how the Fates
brought heavenly Themis of the wise counsel
on golden horses from the springs of Ocean
to the awesome stair that marks the shining way to Olympus,
to be the original wife of Zeus the Saviour:
she gave birth to the Seasons with golden diadems,
who never forget to bring forth brilliant fruit.

Fragment 32

[Cadmus heard Apollo] demonstrating the correct paths of music

Fragment 33

Lord Time, who holds sway over all the blessed ones

Fragment 33a

[a very damaged passage refers to Heracles' fight against the Meropes of Cos]

Fragment 33b

in due time Apollo was born

Fragment 33c

Hail, daughter of the sea, established by the gods,
favourite sprig of the children of shining-tressed Leto,
unmoved wonder of the broad earth, whom mortals call
Delos, but the blessed ones on Olympus
call the far-seen star of the dark blue earth

Fragment 33d

Formerly she was borne about on the waves
by the blasts of all the winds;
but when the daughter of Coeus, grasped by the pains of labour,
set foot on her, at once
four tall columns, shod in adamant,
sprang up from the roots of earth
and held the rock on their brows
so that the mother could look on her offspring in bliss.

Fragment 34

[Zeus] who gave birth to blond Athena when struck by the sacred axe

Fragment 35

[the Titans] released from their chains by your hands, lord

Notes

29. Ismenus: a son of Apollo, a seer, to whom the Ismenion at Thebes was dedicated.

Melia: a Theban nymph: cf. P 11.4, hyporcheme frag. 29.1, Pa. 7.4, 9.35 and 43.

Sown Men: who sprang from the dragon's teeth sown by Cadmus after killing the dragon that guarded the site of Thebes. They became the ancestors of the Theban race.

33a. Meropes: cf. N 4.26, I 6.31 and notes.

33d. daughter of Coeus: Leto.

34. Athena: Zeus swallowed his wife Metis (Intelligence) and then became pregnant in his head with Athena, goddess of wisdom. Hephaestus released her by splitting Zeus' head open with an axe. The scene was depicted on the east pediment of the Parthenon.

35. Titans: see note on P 4.291.

Fragment 43 From an unidentified hymn

[Amphiaraus speaks to his son Amphilochus:]

My son, make your mind like the flesh of the sea-creature that clings to the rocks, when you travel through the cities; give easy assent to present company, think otherwise at other times.

Note

The advice of adaptability to present company is a commonplace of archaic aristocratic and sympotic poetry; see for example Theognis, 215–18.

Fragments 95–9 Hymn to Pan

The opening of this hymn is quoted by the scholiast on Pythian 3.78 where Pindar speaks of his duty to pray to the Great

Mother. Pan is the goat-horned, goat-legged god of the countryside, inducer of panic but also on occasion a helper. A rape
could euphemistically be called a 'panic marriage'. The parentage of Pan presented by Pindar is mentioned by a scholiast
on Virgil (= frag. 100): Pindar makes him son of Apollo
and Penelope, born on Mt Lycaion. This is unusual; he is
normally son of Hermes and Penelope, though other variants
are found.

Another address to Pan was recently discovered in *POxy*
2624: M. van der Weiden has argued (*ZPE* 64 [1986]: 15–32),
that this may also be by Pindar. A more likely possibility is
Simonides.

> Pan, lord of Arcadia
> guardian of holy fanes . . .
> attendant of the Great Mother,
> darling and delight of the Lady Graces . . .
> Blessed one, whom the Olympians
> call the ubiquitous hound
> of the Great Goddess . . .
> you sing your honeyed songs aloud . . .
> most accomplished dancer

Fragment 104 Daphnephorikon for Galaxion in Boeotia

'The inhabitants of Galaxion recognized the epiphany of the
god Apollo by the abundance – over-abundance – of milk';
Plutarch (*Pythian Oracle* 29, p. 409a) goes on to quote these
lines:

> Rich milk
> gushed out from all the flocks
> like purest water from a spring.
> They ran to fill their pitchers.
> No wine-skin or amphora was left in their houses,
> and the wooden pails and the jars were all filled.

Hyporchemes

The term 'hyporcheme' is a broad category, meaning simply
'song accompanied by dance'. Athenaeus (*Deipnosophists*
14.30) states that it can apply to many types of song. An

epinician would be a type of hyporcheme. However, the term is often used more specifically to refer to a kind of war-dance, a genre often associated with Crete (cf. the end of frag. 107ab). It must be remembered that the classification of Pindar's odes, and the classes into which they were divided, were the work of the Alexandrian editors and do not reflect Pindar's own definitions.

Fragments 105 to Hieron

This fragment is quoted by the scholiast on Pythian 2.69, explaining that this hyporcheme is the Kastoreion (usually, a type of war-dance) referred to. The reference in the second passage is without context.

> Hear what I say,
> eponymous father of sacred rites,
> founder of Aetna.

> He who does not have a house on a wagon
> is a wanderer among the peoples of the Scythians
> and is without honour.

Fragment 106

This fragment is quoted by a scholiast on Aristophanes' *Peace* 73. It is a fine example of priamel.

> The Laconian hound of Taygetus
> is the fastest creature for the hunt;
> Goats of Syros are best for milking.
> Armour from Argos, war-chariots from Thebes –
> but for a well-made racing chariot look in
> Sicily of the glistening fruit.

Fragment 107ab

This fragment, quoted by Plutarch in his *Symposiac Questions*, has also been attributed to Simonides. Pelasgia and Dotis are both in Thessaly, as is Molossia, mentioned at the end. Perhaps the piece was written for a Thessalian patron. Hounds from Laconia, where Amyclae is, were particularly prized.

Imitate the Pelasgian horse
or the dog of Amyclae
when you wind out with your agile foot
the pursuit of the twisting melody
as if you were hunting to death
the horned deer
across the flowery plains of Dotis:
it twists its head around on its neck . . .
every path . . .

I know how to stir the light dancing of feet:
they call the tuning Cretan, the instrument Molossian.

Note

tuning Cretan: the strings of the lyre could be tuned to different relative pitches in order to play in different 'modes'. Several Dorian modes were thought of as having a Cretan origin, as well as the 'cretic' rhythm, resembling the 5/8 time of much modern Balkan folk music. But this fragment is not especially cretic in its rhythm. The hyporcheme was thought of as a Cretan genre.

Fragment 108ab

When a god shows the beginning
in any matter, the path is straight
to seize achievement:
and the conclusion is glorious.

God can
raise up incorruptible light in black night
or cover the pure radiance of day
in storm-clouds of darkness.

Note

For the thought, cf. P 9.67–8 on the speed with which gods achieve their ends.

Fragment 109

Another of Stobaeus' selections; the words are addressed to the Thebans during the Persian War. The sentiment recalls that expressed feelingly in Pythian 8 (for Aegina): see the discussion there of the political significance of Tranquillity.

> Let someone bring the community of the citizens into clear day
> by seeking out the bright light of noble-hearted Tranquillity,
> and take quarrelsome civil discord out of our hearts
> for it is a bringer of poverty
> and a poor nurse of children.

Fragment 110

Quoted by the anthologist Stobaeus who made a voluminous collection of pithy quotations.

> War is sweet to those who have no experience of it,
> but the experienced man trembles exceedingly at heart
> on its approach.

Fragment 111

A rather corrupt passage quoted in a grammarian; it describes Heracles' fight with Antaeus, the Libyan giant whose strength was derived from the earth, so that Heracles vanquished him by lifting him from the ground until his strength drained out. The last line recalls the description of Heracles' fight with Geryon, frag. 169.24. Several further lines have been recovered on a papyrus but few complete words can be identified.

> . . . drank up [sweat?] mixed with blood
> and inflicted many wounds. Brandishing his rough club,
> at last he raised him and struck it against his mighty ribs,
> cracking his bones.

Encomia

Fragment 119 To Theron of Acragas

Quoted by a scholiast on Olympian 2.22 and 38, perhaps deriving from the Sicilian historian Timaeus.

> [The ancestors of Theron hailed from Thebes, tracing their descent
>   from Cadmus]
> and they settled in Rhodes . . .
> leaving there, they now dwell around this high city,

offering innumerable gifts to the gods;
a cloud of eternal wealth accompanies them.

Fragments 120–1 To Alexander, the son of Amyntas

This is Alexander I, king of Macedon c. 495–50; he helped the Greeks in the Persian War, and was admitted to compete at the Olympic Games, a privilege reserved for those of Hellenic blood. He invited Pindar to his court to enhance its Hellenic aspirations.

> Sharer of a name with the happy sons of Dardanus,
> bold son of Amyntas . . .
> one must praise the noble . . .
> with lovely songs.
> This alone touches a man to immortal honours,
> but a good deed hidden in silence dies.

Notes

Sharer of a name: Alexander is the normal designation of the Trojan prince Paris, son of Priam.

This alone: the sentiment is very characteristic of Pindar's philosophy of praise. The eccentric grammar of the word 'touch' is that of the Greek also.

Fragment 122 To Xenophon of Corinth

Athenaeus, who quotes these lines as part of his long disquisition on courtesans (13.21–71), explains the occasion of the poem:

> Xenophon the Corinthian, when going to Olympia to the games, vowed that, if he were victorious, he would bring Aphrodite some courtesans. And Pindar at first wrote a panegyric on him [i.e. Olympian 13] but afterwards he composed a scolium [a drinking song] on him, which was sung at the sacrificial feasts; in the exordium of which he turns at once to the courtesans who joined in the sacrifice to Aphrodite, in the presence of Xenophon, while he was sacrificing to the goddess of himself.

Athenaeus goes on to quote the following passages of the song.
Athenaeus also explains (Chapter 32): 'It is an ancient custom

at Corinth (as Chamaeleon of Heraclea relates, in his treatise on Pindar) whenever the city addresses any supplication to Aphrodite about any important matter, to employ as many courtesans as possible to join in the supplication.' Temple prostitution was also not unknown in other parts of the Greek world.

> Most hospitable young ladies
> servants of seduction in wealthy Corinth,
> who kindle the yellow tears of pale incense
> and often fly in your thoughts
> to heavenly Aphrodite,
> mother of loves,
> You have the privilege, my dears,
> without need of long speeches
> of plucking the fruit of the tender season
> in beds of tenderness.
> All things are fine when compulsion . . .

> But I wonder what the lords of the Isthmus
> will say of me, making my winding song
> share its opening with women whom many men share?
> We test gold with the pure lodestone . . .

> Lady of Cyprus,
> it is to your sanctuary
> that Xenophon has come,
> shining with glory
> and accompanied by a herd of a hundred young ladies.

Fragment 123 To Theoxenus of Tenedos

The erotic tone of this poem, which is complete, led ancient followers of the biographical fallacy to the view that Pindar was personally in love with Theoxenus. The story became current, possibly on the authority of Chamaeleon, that Pindar died in Theoxenus' arms in the theatre at Argos. Scepticism about the involvement of Pindar's personal feelings in this poem is expressed by Peter Von der Mühll, 'Persönliche Verliebtheit des Dichters?' (*Mus. Helv.* 21 [1964]: 168–72). One should perhaps consider an approach resembling that which has lately become commoner to the poems of Sappho, and see such expressions of erotic admiration as part of an institutional setting, perhaps even part of a beauty contest of the kind we know to have taken place in some parts of the Greek world, or at least as social poetry for festive occasions, over the wine.

The Agesilas mentioned in the last line, Theoxenus' father, is a Tenedian like the man named in Nemean 11.11, where one MS has Agesilas, but the others have Arcesilas, which is required by the metre. The coincidence is curious, but it is scarcely possible that both are the same man.

> In youth
> One should pluck the fruits of love in season;
> and anyone who sees the shafts of light flashing from
> Theoxenus' eyes
> and does not swell up with desire,
> has a dark heart, forged of steel or adamant
> in a cold fire.
> He is dishonoured by Aphrodite of the curling eyelashes:
> either he devotes all his energy to getting money
> or he has a woman's temper and is easily deflected in any direction.
> For myself, her influence makes me
> soft as the wax of holy bees,
> when I see a shapely youth.
> Persuasion and Grace
> have taken up residence
> with the son of Agesilas in Tenedos.

Note

Persuasion and Grace: both are aspects of falling in love and commonly linked together: compare Ibycus 7 (*PMG* 288) where both are associated with Aphrodite.

Fragment 124ab To Thrasybulus of Acragas

Thrasybulus is the brother and successor of Hieron, who ruled from 467–66, when he was overthrown. This fragment is quoted by Athenaeus in a chapter on cups (11.60). The reference suggests that Attic cups were considered special; but is the reference to a black-figure terracotta cup or a chased metal one? The reference to the poem as a gift resembles Pythian 2.68, Nemean 3.76–80, and other examples.

Thrasybulus, I send you an after-dinner gift –
this load of sweet song. Let it be
both a pleasure to the dinner-guests
and a spur to the fruits of Dionysus and the cups of Athens.
When the sorrows of travail have departed from the breasts of men,
and we steer together on a sea of wealth
to a deceitful shore,
he who was penniless becomes rich, while the wealthy . . .

their minds subdued by the arrows of the vine . . .

Fragments 124d–26 To Hieron

to play the lyre . . .
(mind and voice dulled with wine . . .)

which Terpander of Lesbos invented
and struck the antiphonal strings with his high plectrum
in the feasts of the Lydians . . .

joy in life . . .
a life of delight is best for men.

Note

Terpander: a poet who worked in Sparta in the mid seventh century. Doubt attaches to the genuineness of the surviving fragments. His home island of Lesbos lies close to the Asia Minor mainland where the kingdom of Lydia was; Sappho also mentions Lydian luxuries, and there was clearly a good deal of cultural interchange across the water.

Fragment 127

Quoted by Athenaeus (13.76) in a chapter of similar admonitions to temperance in love.

One should both love
and yield to love in season;
do not, my soul, pursue a chase
beyond the number of your years.

Fragment 128

Quoted by Athenaeus (10.30) as part of his discourse on drinking practice. Cottabos was a game in which the drinker had to flick the last dregs in his cup at a target.

> The Graces who attend
> Aphrodite and her loves
> when I drink with Cheimarus
> and throw my cottabos for the son of Agathon

Laments

Fragment 128c

> The seasonable paeans are the maidservants of the children
> of Leto with the golden spindle;
> the . . . go searching for Dionysus,
> blooming in his wreath of ivy;
> and the . . . for the departed.
> One sings out the echoing Linus-song, 'Ai Linon',
> another the hymeneal which Fate receives
> when newly-weds first touch;
> another the Ialemus when strength is sapped by the darts of disease.
> The son of Oeagrus, Orpheus of the golden sword . . .

Notes

Ai Linon: the Linos song is a song sung at the vintage but also a lament for the dying of the vegetation. Linos became personified as a son of Urania (Hesiod frag. 305 MW) and he had a shrine and cult on Mt Helicon: Paus. 9.29.3.

Ialemus: the personification of the funeral dirge, a son of Apollo and Calliope.

Orpheus: son of Oeagrus and one of the Muses, perhaps Calliope. A Thracian, he is the musician *par excellence* of mythology. His descent to Hades to reclaim his wife Eurydice is the subject of Virgil, *Georgics* 4; he was later torn apart by Bacchants as he lamented his failure and his head, still singing, was borne away down the River Strymon.

Fragments 129–31a

This fragment and the next two, which are of great importance for the understanding of Pindar's religion and Greek ideas of reincarnation and life after death, should be read in conjunction with Olympian 2.56–80 and the notes there. Fragment 129 describes the life of the Blessed in the Elysian Fields.

> The strength of the sun shines on them below
> while here it is night,
> their city is surrounded by meadows of red roses
> and shady incense-trees . . . ,
> loaded with fruit trees.
> Some enjoy themselves with horses and athletic sports,
> others in games of draughts or playing the lyre:
> every blessing is in bloom for them.
> Sweet scents spread across the land,
> incense is mixed with shining fire . . .
> All are blessed, through the rites that free from pain.
>
> [but for the damned]
> the sluggish rivers of gloomy night belch limitless darkness.

Fragment 131b

> The body of every man
> follows in the train of all-powerful death,
> but an image of the living is left behind:
> that alone is from god.
> It sleeps when the limbs are busy,
> but during sleep it shows in numerous dreams
> the coming judgment that shares out pleasure and pain.

Note

an image of the living: a good example is the ghost of Patroclus which appears to Achilles in the *Iliad* 23.65ff.

Fragment 133

The fragment comes from Plato's *Meno* 81b, where it is quoted as part of Plato's discussion of reincarnation and inborn knowledge. Empedocles' theories about reincarnation (frags 146–7, H. Diels and W. Kranz, *Die Fragmente der Vorsokratiker* [Berlin 1903–10]), have points of contact with the ideas expressed here. Cf. Olympian 2. 56–80 and notes.

> Those to whom Persephone shows the penance of ancient sorrow,
> their souls she returns to the sunlight above
> in the ninth year. They become
> illustrious kings
> and men distinguished for high strength and wisdom;
> and for the rest of time they are known among men
> as pure heroes.

Fragment 137 To Hippocrates of Athens

> Happy is he who has seen these things
> before he goes below the earth:
> he knows the end of life,
> and he knows the god-given beginning.

Note

Compare the riddling apophthegm of Alcmaeon of Croton, 'men die because they cannot join the end to the beginning' (frag. 2DK). The initiate knows how to ensure that he remembers his earthly life when he enters the Underworld, and will not drink the water of forgetfulness; thus he can ensure an improved lot on reincarnation.

The remaining fragments cannot be attributed to particular books of odes.

Fragment 140a For the Parians? (Hyporcheme?)

This remarkably obscure fragment is a good example of the way scholarship may be left groping in front of a tattered piece of papyrus. It evidently tells of some part of the saga of Heracles, probably his journey to Troy and the Land of the Amazons with Telamon. (Some scraps of a story about Heracles and the Amazon foundation of Ephesus are preserved in frags 173–6.)

The burden of the present passage is the foundation of a temple for Apollo on Paros, and this is likely to be a local legend, so that it is anybody's guess how Pindar might have narrated it. Wilamowitz suggested that the enemies Heracles faces might be the sons of Minos, whom he encountered on Paros (Apollodorus 2.5.9); another possibility might be King Diomede with his man-eating mares (told in the previous chapter of Apollodorus, 2.5.8).

> They foresaw fate . . .
> Heracles. On the sea
> . . . coming in a ship . . .
> mightiest of all . . .
> soul . . .
> angry at the insolence of the king who murders strangers
> . . . he obeyed the lord of Delos
> and ceased his wicked work.
> . . . the voice of your renowned, shrill-throated trumpets, Far-Archer.
> Remember that in the vales of holy Paros
> he established an altar to the Lord
> and one to father Cronius as he crossed the Isthmus,
> when the heralds began the news
> of the death doom on Laomedon.
> For it had been said of old . . .
> came to his kinsmen . . .

Fragment 140b [Hyporcheme? Possibly for Locri Epizephyrii?]

This is the beginning of a poem. It concerns an Ionian poet of Locri Epizephyrii in south Italy, very probably (as Wilamowitz saw) Xenocritus, who lived in the early seventh century. This poet provides a foil to discussion of Pindar's own talents, evoked in the lovely metaphor that concludes the fragment.

The small hill Zephyrion is the one which gave the city its name. The Ausonian Sea is more properly called the Sicilian Sea.

> Ion – . . .
> song and harmony
> he devised for the pipes,
> and one of the Locrians, those
> who [live] by the white crested hill of Zephyrion
> . . . across the Ausonian Sea
> . . . like a wagon . . .
> harnessed for Apollo and . . .

I . . . singing a little . . .
tending my slow-tongued cry am roused up
like the dolphin of the sea
whom the lovely melody of pipes
stirs in the waveless sea.

Fragment 140c

[the Tyndarids] soften the violent onslaught of the sea and the swift
blasts of the wind.

Note

The Dioscuri have the role of protecting sailors, in which they were
envisaged as appearing in the form of St Elmo's Fire.

Fragment 140d

What is God? Everything.

Fragment 141

God, who creates all things for men
and nurtures artistry in the singer.

Fragment 143

[The gods]

They know no sickness nor old age,
they are free of pains:
they have escaped
the loud-resounding crossing of Acheron.

Fragment 146

Quoted in a scholiast on Homer, who provides the paraphrases
in parentheses.

(Athena) sitting closely on the right hand of her father
. . . the fire breathing thunderbolt . . .
(she gives her orders to the gods)

Fragment 148

Dancer, lord of brightness, Apollo of the broad quiver.

Fragment 150

Quoted by Eustathius in his commentary on the *Iliad*. The *Iliad* opens with an invocation of the Muse who is to sing; the poet passes on her utterance.

Prophecy, Muse, and I will be your mouthpiece.

Fragment 155

What shall I do to please you,
Son of Cronus, strong in thunder,
and what to please the Muses
and to be cared for by Good Cheer –
this I ask of you.

Fragment 156

Silenus the violent,
leader of the dance,
whom Mount Malea nursed,
husband of the Naiad.

Note

Silenus: the leader of the satyrs and regular companion of Dionysus, a drunken old man with goatish elements.

Fragment 159

Time is the best redeemer of just men.

Fragment 160

Even their friends betray the dead.

Fragment 166

Quoted by Athenaeus (11.51) in a chapter on drinking horns. The reference is to the wedding of Pirithous, son of Ixion, at which a fight broke out between the Lapiths and their guests, the centaurs. The quelling of the fight by Apollo is portrayed on the pediment of the Temple of Zeus at Olympia.

> When the Centaurs shared out
> the man-taming blows of fragrant wine,
> they pushed the white milk violently off the tables
> with their hands, and, drunk with the contents of silver-mounted
> > horns,
> they wandered around in a trance . . .

Fragment 168

Philostratus (*Imagines* 2.24) cites Pindar for a story that 'when Heracles came to the hut of Coronus he ate a whole ox for dinner, so that not even the bones were left over'. Athenaeus (10.1) quotes the following verses. Coronus was a king of the Lapiths against whom Heracles fought on Aegimius' behalf.

> They garlanded two hot carcasses of oxen for the embers, and roasted them in the fire. Then I [heard] the voice of the flesh and the deep groan of the bones. There was plenty of time to divide them . . .

Fragment 169a

The opening lines of this poem have long been known from their quotation in Plato's *Gorgias* (484b), where Callicles uses them to justify his doctrine that 'might is right', the stronger have the right to rule the weaker. It has been long agreed that Plato (or Callicles) is misrepresenting Pindar, who, whatever he meant in these lines, cannot have meant this. Many discussions have been devoted to the problem, and a good summary with bibliography is that of H. Lloyd-Jones, 'Pindar Fr. 169', *Harvard Studies in Classical Philology* 76 (1972): 45–56 = *Greek Epic Lyric and Tragedy: Academic Papers* (Oxford 1990), pp. 154–65.

Two key words, *nomos* (custom) and *dikaion* (making just)

require interpretation to make sense of Pindar's thought here. In summary, I take the view that *nomos* means 'whatever is accepted as the order of things, as a norm'; and that *dikaion* means 'making just' in the sense that whatever attitude one might normally take to an act, acceptance of it as a norm can make it right. That is, Heracles is a great hero and a touchstone of excellence; so whatever he does, even if it looks like criminal behaviour, must be accepted as just in the order of the universe. (Lloyd-Jones would add that it is just because it is the will of Zeus.) This is a profound expression of a religious sensibility radically different from the Christian.

The moral is drawn from an account of Heracles' theft of the cattle of Geryon, the three-headed son of the nymph Callirhoe and Chrysaor, the son of the Gorgon Medusa. Heracles killed Geryon's herdsman Eurytion and brought the cattle back to Eurystheus (son of Sthenelus of line 44) as one of his labours. This story had earlier been treated by Stesichorus (early sixth century) in his *Geryoneis*, the extensive fragments of which were first published in the 1970s. Stesichorus treated Geryon, despite his monstrous form, with the empathy due to a Homeric hero, to Heracles' disadvantage. This treatment was certainly known to Pindar, who occasionally echoes it, and this prompts his rehandling of the moral of the tale. The epic poet Pisander, in an unknown context, referred to Heracles as 'most just of murderers' (frag. 10 Bernabé), which seems to state the same paradox as Pindar's words.

> Custom is lord of all things,
> of mortals and immortals.
> He leads them, making just what is most violent
> with a superior hand. Witness
> the deeds of Heracles: 5
> he drove the cattle of Geryon
> to the Cyclopean portal of Eurystheus
> without reward or wage
> . . . the mares of Diomede
> . . . the ruler of the Cicones   10
> by Lake Bistonis
> . . . the mighty son of bronze-corsleted Enyalios
> . . .
> not in insolence but in virtue.   15

[It is better] to die when [property] is stolen
than to behave wickedly.
Entering the great [hall]
[secretly] by night, he [found] his way,   20
seized a light and made his way to the stone mangers,
threw [in the groom] . . .
the horses [tore him apart]
in his madness. At once
there resounded the din
of bones being ground.   25
Straightaway he [broke] the woven bronze chain
which ran through the stalls of the beasts
and struck them with his club as they chewed,
one on a leg, one on an arm,   30
a third with her teeth sunk in the severed head.
. . .
announced the woeful news
the fierce tyrant   35
shoeless from his ornate bed
[37–40]
there came on the son [of Ares]
[a labour] of Heracles
in addition, [the twelfth]
by the orders of Hera: the son of Sthenelus
ordered him to go alone   45
without an army.
And Iolaus, remaining at Seven-Gated Thebes,
building a tomb for Amphitryon
. . . on the mound
[sacrificed beasts] with fine horns   50
. . . the people of [Cadmus] willingly
. . .

Notes

7. **Eurystheus:** the king of Mycenae at whose orders Heracles performed
his twelve labours.

9. **Diomede:** a king of the Cicones in Thrace who fed strangers to his
man-eating mares.

16–17. **better to die:** the sentiment echoes a phrase in Stesichorus'

Geryoneis, S11.20–1 *SLG*: 'now is it better for me to suffer what is fated . . . and shame . . .'

Fragment 172

The youth of the godlike Peleus
shone with ten thousand achievements:
first on the plain of Troy with the son of Alcmena,
and when they went after the girdle of the Amazon,
and when he sailed on the famous voyage of Jason
and captured Medea in her Colchian home.

Fragment 180

This passage is plainly a break-off formula akin to that at Nemean 5.16–18, for example.

Do not break open to everyone words which are not advantageous.
Sometimes the ways of silence are best.
Words which assert themselves are a spur to conflict.

Fragment 182

This passage, which is quoted by Aristides, is said by him to refer to Eriphyle. It probably relates to her acceptance of the bribe to persuade her husband Amphiaraus to go to war. As a result of this wrong decision (wits blinded by *ate*), her sons later murdered her in revenge for their father's death.

Alas, how the mind of ephemeral men can be deceived, in its
   ignorance.

Fragment 194 To the Thebans

The golden sandal clatters to the holy songs:
hey, let us build a dazzling structure,
an utterance of stories . . .

(the nectar of my song)
will exalt Thebes, renowned though she is,
still higher in the paths of gods and men.

Fragment 198a

Famous Thebes brought me up
to be neither a stranger
nor unskilled in the Muses.

Fragment 198b

... the ambrosial water, lovely as honey, that flows from the
beautiful spring Tilphossa.

Note

Tilphossa: a spring at Thebes.

Fragment 199

This passage is quoted by Plutarch in his *Life of Lycurgus of
Sparta*.

[Sparta] where the councils of the elders
and the platoons of the young men excel,
as well as dancing, the Muse and Splendour.

Fragment 201

This passage is quoted by Strabo, *Geography* 17.1.19, where he
explains that the people of Mendes worship Pan and the goat.

Egyptian Mendes, on the sea cliffs
at the furthest branch of the Nile, where
the rock-climbing goats copulate with women . . .

Fragment 203

[Scythians] who show indifference
to a dead horse lying in the open, and mock it,
but secretly strip the skin off its head and feet
with crooked teeth.

Fragment 205

Lady Truth,
origin of all excellence,
do not strike my composition
against rough falsehood.

Note

Cf. O 10.4–6.

Fragment 213

Whether the mortal race of men
should scale a wall with justice
or by the use of crooked deceits,
I am in two minds to declare for certain.

Fragment 214 On a Just Man

Sweet Hope, nurse of old age
accompanies him and nurses his heart:
she most unremittingly directs the wayward minds of mortals.

Fragment 215 [For the Thebans?]

Different people have different customs,
and each man praises his own kind of justice.
Do not despise my rustic birth.
I can . . . my country with the Muses' comb
like the blond hair of a girl . . .

Fragment 220

[on table fare]
nothing need be despised, nor changed,
of the things which the gleaming earth
and the waves of the sea bring forth.

Fragment 221

> Some take pleasure in the prizes and garlands
> of storm-footed horses,
> others in treasure-chambers full of gold;
> yet others enjoy embarking on the waves of the sea
> in a swift ship.

Fragment 222

Quoted by the scholiast on Pythian 4.230 to explain why the Golden Fleece is called immortal.

> Gold is the child of Zeus.
> Moths and weevils cannot devour it.

Fragment 224

> A man whom the gods love is equal to a god.

Fragment 225

Quoted by the scholiast on Olympian 2.24.

> When god sends a joy to man,
> he first strikes at his black heart.

Fragment 226

This phrase, quoted by Aristides (*Oration* 51.5) seems a remarkable anticipation of Socrates' doctrine that no one does evil willingly.

> No one comes on evil of his own free will.

Fragment 227

> The interests of the young
> pursued with dedication
> lead to glory; their deeds in time
> shine on high.

Fragment 234

A horse in the harness,
an ox at the plough.
A dolphin speeds most swiftly next to a ship,
and he who wills death to a boar
must find a courageous hound.

Fragment 346 [Dithyramb: 'The Descent of Heracles' or 'Cerberus']

This very damaged fragment, first published among the *Oxy-rhynchus Papyri* in 1967, is an important addition to our knowledge of Pindar's treatment of the legends of Heracles. It concerns his initiation at Eleusis before his descent to the Underworld to bring back Cerberus, and his meeting there with Meleager. (Compare the account in Apollodorus 2.5.12.) Pindar may have derived his narrative from an epic model; however, there is clear influence of some passages of the narrative on Virgil's description of Aeneas' arrival in the Underworld in *Aeneid* 6.309–14, and it is an intriguing possibility that Virgil had been reading Pindar himself when he wrote these lines. An authoritative treatment of the fragment is H. Lloyd-Jones, 'Heracles at Eleusis', *Maia* 19 (1967): 206–29 = *Greek Epic, Lyric and Tragedy: Academic Papers* (Oxford 1990), pp. 167–87.

The wise leader of the opening is probably Eumolpus, the Eleusinian king who initiated Heracles.

Stronger . . .
wise leader . . .
. . .
possessions in season
. . . good laws which make the people joyful . . .
to Eleusis, to Persephone and her mother on her golden throne
he established the rite for the citizens . . .
double . . . saw
. . . to Heracles first
. . . path . . .
husband, the son of Amphitryon
. . .

at once, of the dead [as many as the leaves which
the earth] brings forth and as many as there are [waves] in the
  sea . . .
. . .
the great son of Zeus
. . .
met him
Meleager alone . . .

Notes

as many as the leaves: the supplement is probable in the light of the use
of this simile by Virgil in the corresponding passage. However, Virgil's
second comparison is not with the waves but with migrating seabirds
flocking on the shore.

Meleager: only Meleager and Medusa did not turn away from Heracles
when he entered the Underworld.

GLOSSARY

ACHERON, *river of the Underworld:* N 4.85.

AEACUS, *mother of Aegina and father of Peleus, Telamon; ancestor of Aeacids and of Aeginetans:* N 4.11.

AEGIMIUS, *Dorian king, father of Dyman, Pamphylos and father-in-law of Hyllus – the three ancestors of the Dorian tribes:* I 9.2.

AETNA, *name given to the city founded by Hieron on the site of Catana in 475.*

ADRASTUS, *leader of the Seven against Thebes:* O 6.13.

AJAX, *(1) son of Telamon, regarded as a Salaminian hero; (2) son of Oileus of Locri, appears in the* Iliad *but only once in Pindar:* O 9.112.

ALCMENA, *mother of Heracles.*

ALPHEUS, *river running past Olympia:* O 9.18; *it was thought to run under the sea and re-emerge at Arethusa in Sicily,* N 1.1.

AMPHIARAUS, *an Argive seer, one of the Seven against Thebes.*

AMPHITRYON, *father of Heracles.*

APHRODITE, *goddess of love; also called Cypria.*

APOLLO, *god of music, oracles, and patron of the Pythian Games; son of Leto, sister of Artemis; also called Loxias, Pythius.*

ARES, *god of war.*

ASTERIA, *sister of Leto, transformed into the island of Delos:* Pa. 5.42.

ATHENA, *goddess of wisdom and of Athens; also called Polias, Pallas.*

CADMUS, *legendary founder of Thebes:* N 1.51. *Married Harmonia; their wedding was attended by the gods:* P 3.87, frag. 29.

CASTALIA, *spring at Delphi, often used as metonym for Delphi itself:* O 7.17, O 9.17.

CASTOR, *one of the Dioscuri; his brother is Polydeuces. Castor was regarded as the mortal twin of the pair.*

CHIRON, *wisest of the centaurs, educator of heroes, dwelling in a cave on Mt Pelion.*

CRISA, *or* KRISA, *the nearest town to Delphi.*

DELOS, *an island in the centre of the Aegean, sacred to Apollo (and Artemis), who were born there: Pa. 2.96, frag. 33b.*

DELPHI, *the reputed centre of the world, site of the Pythian Games; also called Crisa, Pytho.*

DIOSCURI, *twin sons of Zeus and Leda; their mortal father was Tyndareus of Sparta.*

DIRKE, *a river at Thebes, near Pindar's home. It runs along the slope of the Cadmeia (modern Plakioussa): O 10.85, I 1.29, I 6.74, I 8.20.*

ELEITHYIA, *goddess of childbirth: O 6.42, N 7.1, and note.*

EUNOMIA, *Lawfulness personified.*

EUROTAS, *river running through Sparta.*

FATES, *Clotho the spinner, Lachesis the allotter and Atropos the inescapable, who allot man's fate at birth: O 1.26, O 7.64, I 6.17, and note Pa. 12.17.*

GRACES, *Charites, three goddesses representing glory and artistic beauty: O 2.50, O.14.4.*

HEBE, *goddess of youth and beauty, married Heracles when he ascended to Olympus: N 10.8, I 3/4.77.*

HECTOR, *son of Priam and chief of the Trojan heroes; killed by Achilles.*

HERACLES, *greatest of the heroes, a model for athletes often referred to as son of Alcmena.*

HILL OF CRONOS, *the conical hill which overlooks the sanctuary at Olympia.*

IOLAUS, *nephew and charioteer of Heracles: P 11.60.*

LETO, *mother of Artemis and Apollo, sister of Asteria: Pa. 5.*

LOXIAS, *a name of Apollo.*

MAENALUS, MT, *a mountain in Arcadia: O 9.59.*

MEMNON, *son of the Dawn; leader of the Ethiopians, allies of Troy in the Trojan War: O 2.83, N 3.62-3, N 6.50.*

MUSES, *goddesses of poetry: Clio, Euterpe, Thalia, Melpomene, Terpsichore, Erato, Urania, Polyhymnia, Calliope. Also called Pierides, from their haunts in northern Greece, and Heliconiadae from Mt Helicon.*

OENONE, *a nymph, an early name of Aegina,* N 8.7.

OLYMPIA, *in the western Peloponnese, site of the Olympic Games; also called Pisa.*

PALLAS, *a name of Athena.*

PARNASSUS, MT, *the mountain on whose slopes Delphi lies:* O 13.106.

PELEUS, *son of Aeacus, born of Telamon; married the sea-nymph Thetis:* N 5.26ff., O 2.77, N 4.54ff.

PELION, MT, *mountain in Thessaly, home of Chiron.*

PIERIDES, *see Muses.*

PISA, *the town where the sanctuary of Olympia was situated.*

POLYDEUCES, *one of the Dioscuri; born immortal, he gave up his immortality to share half-life, half-death with his brother Castor:* N 10.

POSEIDON, *god of the sea, earthquakes. Also called Earthshaker.*

PYTHO, *a name for Delphi:* O 2.37, *etc.*

TAYGETUS, MT, *the mountain lying to the west of Sparta:* P 1.64.

THEMIS, *goddess of lawful Right:* O 8.22, O 13.8.

THERAPNAE, *hill-top site near Sparta, where the Dioscuri were buried:* N 10.56.

TIRESIAS, *a Theban prophet:* N 1.61.

TITANS, *children of Uranus and Gaea, they include Cronos the father of Zeus who overthrew them and imprisoned them:* P 4.291.

TROY, *also called Dardania, Pergama.*

RESPONSES TO PINDAR

As remarked in the Introduction, Pindar's poetry has always been regarded as difficult. Even in antiquity, the commentators were often at a loss to understand allusions; and, as I showed there, this often led to errors in interpretation and indeed to a complete misconception of the nature of his poetry. Not least among the difficulties they found was the correct interpretation of his metre and the line-divisions, and the nature of responsion between strophe and antistrophe, and each succeeding pair of strophe and antistrophe. The colometry of the ancient scholars was only reformed in the nineteenth century, by August Boeckh, who established the line divisions found in our current editions. It is clear that Horace, for one, did not understand the nature of Pindar's metre, in describing his 'profound unmeasurable song' (*Odes* 4.2).

But the 'profound' is as important as the 'unmeasurable'. Pindar was always thought of as a deep poet, perhaps just because of his obscurity, but surely also because the complex of ideas which informs his poetry is in fact an all-encompassing view of man's condition. So technique and outlook were always important to the poets in later times who responded to his work.

The purpose of the brief selection of critical responses which follows is to illustrate the ways in which poets and others understood Pindar, and used him to construct their own writing (he was particularly important to Ronsard in the sixteenth century, to Ben Jonson and many other English poets in the seventeenth and eighteenth centuries, and to the Germans from Gryphius and Klopstock to Goethe and Hölderlin in the eighteenth and nineteenth centuries), as well as how some thinkers rejected his example completely.

Fuller treatment of the themes can be found in the following books:

Robin Harrison, *Hölderlin and Greek Literature* (Oxford 1975).

Carol Maddison, *Apollo and the Nine: A History of the Ode* (London 1960).

Isidore Silver, *The Pindaric Odes of Ronsard* (Paris 1937).

Humphrey Trevelyan, *Goethe and the Greeks* (Cambridge 1941; reissued with introduction by Hugh Lloyd-Jones [Cambridge 1981]).

Penelope B. Wilson, 'The Knowledge and Appreciation of Pindar in the Seventeenth and Eighteenth Centuries', unpublished D. Phil. dissertation (Oxford 1976) – on English poets.

Horace, Ode IV.2, trans. Philip Francis (1742).

> He, who to Pindar's height attempts to rise,
> Like Icarus, with waxen pinions tries
> His pathless way, and from the venturous theme
> Falling shall leave to azure seas his name.
>
> As when a river, swollen by sudden showers,
> O'er its known banks from some steep mountain pours,
> So in profound, unmeasurable song
> The deep-mouth'd Pindar, foaming, pours along.
>
> Well he deserves Apollo's laurel'd crown,
> Whether new words he rolls enraptur'd down
> Impetuous through the Dithyrambic strains;
> Free from all laws, but what himself ordains;
>
> Whether in lofty tone sublime he sings
> The immortal gods, or god-descended kings,
> With death deserv'd who smote the Centaurs dire,
> And quencht the fierce Chimæra's breath of fire;
>
> Or whom th' Olympic palm, celestial prize!
> Victorious crowns, and raises to the skies,
> Wrestler or steed – with honours that outlive
> The mortal fame which thousand statues give;
>
> Or mourns some hapless youth in plaintive lay,
> From his fond, weeping bride, ah! torn away;
> His manners pure, his courage, and his name,
> Snatcht from the grave, he vindicates to fame.
>
> Thus, when the Theban swan attempts the skies,
> A nobler gale of rapture bids him rise;
> But like a bee, which through the breezy groves
> With feeble wing and idle murmurs roves,

Sits on the bloom, and with unceasing toil
From thyme sweet-breathing culls his flowery spoil;
So I, weak bard! round Tibur's lucid spring,
Of humbler strain laborious verses sing.

'Tis thine with deeper hand to strike the lyre,
When Cæsar shall his raptur'd bard inspire,
And crown'd with laurel, well-earn'd meed of war,
Drag the fierce Gaul at his triumphal car;

Than whom the gods ne'er gave, or bounteous Fate,
To human kind a gift more good or great,
Nor from the treasures shall again unfold,
Though time roll backward to his ancient gold.

Be thine the festal days, the city's joys,
The Forum silenc'd from litigious noise,
The public games for Cæsar safe restor'd,
A blessing oft with pious vows implor'd.

Then, if my voice can reach the glorious theme;
Then will I sing, amid the loud acclaim –
'Hail, brightest sun; in Rome's fair annals shine;
Cæsar returns – eternal praise be thine.'

As the procession awful moves along,
Let shouts of triumph fill our joyful song;
Repeated shouts of triumph Rome shall raise,
And to the bounteous gods our altars blaze.

Of thy fair herds twice ten shall grateful bleed,
While I, with pious care, one steerling feed:
Wean'd from the dam, o'er pastures large he roves.
And for my vows his rising youth he proves:

His horns like Luna's bending fires appear,
When the third night she rises to her sphere;
And, yellow all the rest, one spot there glows
Full in his front, and bright as winter snows.

Pierre Ronsard, Ode XI, from Ronsard, *Oeuvres Complètes*
(Paris 1950).

Str. 2   Le bon Poëte endoctriné
          Par le seul naturel bien-né
          Se haste de ravir le prix;
          Mais ces rimeurs qui ont appris
          Avec travail peines et ruses,

A leur honte enfantent des vers
Qui tousjours courent de travers
Outre la carrière des Muses.

Eux comparez à nos chants beaux,
Sont faits semblables aux corbeaux
Qui dessous les feuilles caquettent
Contre deux Aigles, qui aguettent
Aupres du throne de leur Roy,
Le temps de ruer leurs tempestes
Dessus les misérables testes
De ces criards palles d'effroy,

Ant.   Voyans l'Aigle; mais ny les ans,
Ny l'audace des vents nuisans,
Ny la dent des pluies qui mord,
Ne donne aux vers doctes la mort.
Par eux la Parque est devancée,
Ils fuyent l'eternelle nuit,
Tousjours fleurissans par le fruit
Que la Muse ente en leur pensée:
Le temps qui les suit de bien loin,
En est aux peuples le tesmoin.

Mais quoy! la Muse babillarde
L'honneur d'un chacun ne regarde,
Animant ores cestui-ci,
Et ores ces deux-là, car elle,
Des hauts Dieux la fille eternelle,
Ne se valette pas ainsi.

Ep.   L'ayant prise pour ma guide
Avec le chant incognu
De mon luth, je suis venu
Où Loire en flotant se ride
Contre les champs plantureux
De tes ancestres heureux.

R. R. Bolgar, *The Classical Heritage and its Beneficiaries*
(Cambridge 1954), pp. 324–5.

But these elements which Dorat has picked out are precisely those
that Ronsard also imitates. The classical borrowings in the *Odes*,
as analysed by Laumonier, fall into five classes: rhythm, style,
imagery, myth and history, ideas. Those in the first class are

admittedly inconsiderable. French is not a language which depends for its effects on the alternance of long and short syllables, so Ronsard could not follow Dorat and model his lines more or less exactly on the Greek. His debt to the classics in this particular field is therefore of a more subtle kind. What he learnt from Pindar and Horace was the value of rhythmic patterns. He became aware that unity could be combined with variety. How that combination was to be achieved in French, was a matter he had to work out for himself. But the general conception came from his reading.

When we come to consider style and structure we find that the main features of the original Epiniceans are faithfully reproduced. Thus the *Ode au Seigneur de Carnavalet* begins with the usual Pindaric invocation to a deity. Then in true Pindaric fashion, Carnavalet himself, the hero, is abruptly introduced.

> Dirai-je l'expérience
> Que tu as en la science,
> Ou ta main qui sçait l'adresse
> De façonner la jeunesse . . .

Next comes the myth which makes the centrepiece of the poems, and this is followed by a further reference to the hero and by an epode to the Muses which balance as in Pindar the two introductory items. Admittedly, Ronsard does not always follow the Pindaric structure in such meticulous detail. He often omits the invocation or alternatively the myth; for he is on the whole disinclined to permit himself the sharp transitions from one topic to another, which are a necessary accompaniment of Pindar's technique. But even where he does not follow his model entirely he goes some of the way; and he certainly does his best to maintain that elevation of style which is the most notable characteristic of the Greek poet.

Elevation of style depends to a great extent on imagery and the choice of subject-matter; and it is here perhaps that the French stands closest to the Greek. Pindar derived his imagery for the most part from such phenomena of light and movement as entered into his daily experience, from architecture, from the games themselves and from the common life of his day on the land, in the cities and as travellers saw it by road and sea. Laumonier's analysis shows that all these spheres of sensitivity yielded Ronsard a substantial number of images. He succeeded therefore in entering into Pindar's world. And images were not the only key with which he unlocked the doors of the past. Ronsard, like most of his contemporaries, regarded myths as allegories: 'La poésie n'estoit au premier âge qu'un théologie allégorique.' It was an opinion he shared with Dorat. Valuing the classical stories for their content as well as for their plastic beauty, he used them freely, sometimes retaining his model complete as in the tale of Bellerophon which adorns the *Ode au Carnavalet*, sometimes adapting the Greek original to suit his subject, sometimes contenting himself with a mere reference, but always instructing his reader in the intricacies of Greek legend or presupposing a prior knowledge. These odes are meaningless to a man who is not a Humanist.

Images and myths belong to the preconscious levels of the human mind. To them we must add, even in poetry, the formulated concepts of the conscious intellect. In this realm too Ronsard's borrowings were considerable.

The *Odes* are full of sentences which reproduce the gnomic sayings in the Epiniceans. Man is ephemeral, and God alone remains stable; man's fortune is uncertain, now ill, now good; it is a fine thing to reward noble deeds with lasting praise; great deeds are not to be accomplished easily; and so on. All Pindar's common themes are fully represented.

Ben Jonson, Conclusion to 'An Epistle to Sir Edward Sackville', in *Ben Jonson: Complete Poems* (Harmondsworth 1975), pp. 146–7.

> 'Tis by degrees that men arrive at glad
> Profit in aught; each day some little add,
> In time 'twill be a heap; this is not true
> Alone in money, but in manners too.
> Yet we must more than move still, or go on,
> We must accomplish; 'tis the last key-stone
> That makes the arch. The rest that there were put
> Are nothing till that comes to bind and shut.
> Then stands it a triumphal mark! Then men
> Observe the strength, the height, the why, and when,
> It was erected; and still walking under
> Meet some new matter to look up and wonder!
> Such notes are virtuous men! They live as fast
> As they are high; are rooted and will last.
> They need no stilts, nor rise upon their toes,
> As if they would belie their stature; those

Are dwarfs of honour, and have neither weight
Nor fashion; if they chance aspire to height,
'Tis like light canes, that first rise big and brave,
Shoot forth in smooth and comely spaces; have
But few and fair divisions: but being got
Aloft, grow less and straitened; full of knot;
And last, go out in nothing: you that see
Their difference, cannot choose which you will be.
You know (without my flattering you) too much
For me to be your indice. Keep you such,
That I may love your person (as I do)
Without your gift, though I can rate that too,
By thanking thus the courtesy to life,
Which you will bury, but therein, the strife
May grow so great to be example, when
(As their true rule or lesson) either men
Donors or donees to their practice shall
Find you to reckon nothing, me owe all.

Abraham Cowley, Preface to his translation of Olympia 2 (London 1668), pp. 155-6.

If a man should undertake to translate *Pindar* word for word, it would be thought that one *Mad-man* had translated *another*; as may appear, when he that understands not the *Original*, reads the verbal *Traduction* of him into *Latin Prose*, than which nothing seems more *Raving*. And sure, *Rhyme*, without the addition of *Wit*, and the *Spirit* of *Poetry* (*quod nequeo monstrare et sentio tantum*) would but make it ten times more *Distracted* than it is in *Prose*. We must consider in *Pindar* the great difference of time betwixt his age and ours, which changes, as in *Pictures*, at least the *Colours* of *Poetry*, the no less difference betwixt the *Religions* and *Customs* of our *Countrys*, and a thousand particularities of places, persons, and manners, which do but confusedly appear to our *Eyes* at so great a distance. And lastly, (which were enough alone for my purpose) we must consider that our *Ears* are strangers to the *Musick* of his *Numbers*, which sometimes (especially in *Songs* and *Odes*) almost without any thing else, makes an excellent *Poet*; for though the *Grammarians* and *Criticks* have laboured to reduce his *Verses* into regular feet and measures (as they have also those of the *Greek* and *Latine Comedies*) yet in effect they are little better than *Prose* to our Ears. And I would gladly know what applause our best pieces of *English Poesie* could expect from a *Frenchman* or *Italian*, if converted faithfully, and word for word, into *French* or *Italian Prose*. And when we have considered all this, we must needs confess, that after all these losses sustained by *Pindar*, all we can adde to him by our wit or invention (not deserting still his subject) is not like to make him a *Richer man* than he was in his *own Country*. This is in some measure to be applyed to all *Translations*; and the not observing of it, is the cause that all which ever I yet saw, are so much inferiour to our *Originals*. The like happens too in *Pictures*, from the same root of exact *Imitation*; which being a vile and unworthy kind of *Servitude*, is incapable of producing any thing good or noble. I have seen *Originals* both in *Painting* and *Poesie*, much more beautiful than their *natural Objects*; but I never saw a *Copy* better than the *Original*, which indeed cannot be otherwise; for men resolving in no case to shoot *beyond* the *Mark*, it is a thousand to one if they shoot not *short* of it. It does not at all trouble me that the *Grammarians* perhaps will not suffer this libertine way of rendring forreign Authors, to be called *Translation*; for I am not so much enamoured of the *Name Translator*, as not to wish rather to be *Something Better*, though it want yet a *Name*. I speak not so much all this, in defence of my manner of *Translating*, or *Imitating* (or what other Title they please) the two ensuing *Odes* of *Pindar*; for that would not deserve half these words, as by this occasion to rectifie the opinion of divers men upon this matter. The *Psalms* of *David*, (which I believe to have been in their *Original*, to the *Hebrews* of his time, though not to our *Hebrews* of *Buxtorfius*'s making, the most exalted pieces of *Poesie*) are a great example of what I have said; all the *Translators* of which (even Mr *Sands* himself; for in despight of popular errour, I will be bold not to except him) for this very reason, that they have not sought to supply the lost Excellencies of another *Language* with new ones in their own; are so far from doing honour, or at least justice to that *Divine Poet*, that, methinks, they revile him worse than *Shimei*. And *Bucanan* himself (though much the best of them all, and indeed a great Person) comes in my opinion no less short of *David*, than his *Country* does of *Judæa*. Upon this ground, I have in these two *Odes* of *Pindar* taken, left out, and added what I please; nor make it so much my aim to let the Reader know precisely what he spoke, as what was his *way* and *manner* of speaking; which has not been yet (that I know of) introduced into *English*, though it be the noblest and highest kind of writing in Verse; and which might, perhaps, be put into the List of *Pancirol-lus*, among the *lost Inventions* of *Antiquity*. This *Essay* is but to try how it will look in an *English habit*: for which experiment, I have chosen one of his *Olympique*, and another of his *Nemeæan Odes*; which are as followeth.

Joseph Warton, from 'Ode to Mr West on his Translation of Pindar' (1749).

> The fearful, frigid lays of cold and creeping art
>   Nor touch, nor can transport the unfeeling heart;
>   Pindar, our inmost bosom piercing, warms
>   With glory's love, and eager thirst of arms:
>   When Freedom speaks in his majestic strain,
>   The patriot-passions beat in every vein:
>   We long to sit with heroes old,
>   'Mid groves of vegetable gold,
>   Where Cadmus and Achilles dwell,
> And still of daring deeds and dangers tell.
> . . .
>
> In roaring cataracts down Andes' channelled steeps
> Mark how enormous Orellana sweeps!
> Monarch of mighty floods! supremely strong,
> Foaming from cliff to cliff he whirls along,
> Swollen with an hundred hills' collected snows:
> Thence over nameless regions widely flows,
>   Round fragrant isles, and citron-groves,
>   Where still the naked Indian roves,
>   And safely builds his leafy bower,
> From slavery far, and curst Iberian power;
>
> So rapid Pindar flows.

Tennyson, remark reported by F. T. Palgrave (undated): (Hallam Tennyson, *Alfred Lord Tennyson: A Memoir* [London, 1897] II, 499).

Pindar ... a kind of Australian poet; has long tracts of gravel, with immensely large nuggets imbedded.

H. Trevelyan, *Goethe and the Greeks* (Cambridge 1941), pp. 54–5.

More serious than the mistranslation of an occasional sentence in Pindar was his complete misconception of the nature of the Theban's poetry. Here he erred with his age, which loved to see in Pindar a poet who poured out his song in a divine ecstasy without forethought or rules. Herder, it is true, was well aware of the conscious artist in Pindar. But he seems to have assumed that in the lost dithyrambs Pindar allowed himself a wilder style. This genre, he believed, had in the earliest times sprung from the orgiastic celebrations of the god of wine, and even at a later date the poet 'followed no other plan than what the imagination painted ... and the dance demanded'. The speech of these dithyrambs was novel, bold, irregular. It was the poet's right to coin new words, since the language was still poor. 'So too the metre had no rules, just as their dance and the tones of their speech had none; but for that very reason it was the more polymetric, sonorous and varied.' Herder must have talked to Goethe of Pindar during the winter at Strassburg, but either he did not explain his attitude fully, or Goethe did not grasp all that was said to him. For it is plain from *Wandrers Sturmlied* that Pindar was for Goethe the god-intoxicated dithyrambist, despiser of rules and all conventional checks on the stream of inspiration. Not indeed that *Wandrers Sturmlied* should be taken as an imitation of Pindar. Conscious imitation was contrary to all Goethe's principles at this time. But Pindar's example appeared to him to justify the abandonment of all rules of form. Like the old dithyrambist he sang without plan, just as the imagination poured forth its glowing images. At times intensity of feeling made articulate expression almost impossible ('Weh! Weh! Innre Wärme, Seelen-wärme, Mittelpunkt!'). There was no set metre, only a rhythm, which is indeed for its very freedom 'the more polymetric, sonorous and varied'. New-coined words are frequent – 'Feuerflügeln', 'Blumenfüssen', 'Flutschlamm' in four lines – and grammatically impossible constructions also abound – 'Dich, dich strömt mein Lied', 'Glühte deine Seel Gefahren, Pindar, Mut'. How little this has in common with Pindar's highly formalised lyric has often been pointed out, never with more clearness and force than by Wilamowitz-Moellendorf. 'Goethe tried to make himself a picture of the form of this lyric, but he was hardly likely to succeed. In the harsh word-order, that breaks every grammatical rule, he imagined himself to be following Pindar, perhaps also in the rhythms. In fact no greater contrast could exist than that between the lawless style of this unschooled revolutionary and Pindar's rigid technique.'

David Constantine, *Hölderlin* (Oxford 1988), pp. 237–40.

Hölderlin's translation of Pindar during his last months in Homburg is an extraordinary undertaking in several respects. First the sheer labour of it. Some 2,000 lines of translated verse have survived (it is likely that more were done and are missing) and since what we have in the manuscript is, almost certainly, a fair copy, an immense work must have been done before it could be made. And for what? Not for publication. Like so much else done in Homburg the translation of Pindar served Hölderlin in the strict discipline of learning his poetic craft. Long stretches of the translated verse are as inaccessible as the unendingly hypotactic sentences of 'Die Verfahrungsweise des poëtischen Geistes'. Hölderlin translated Pindar literally, word for word. Abraham Cowley, still thought too bold by some, had shied away from such a procedure, asserting:

'If a man should undertake to translate *Pindar* word for word, it would be thought that *one Mad-man* had translated *another*; as may appear, when a person who understands not the *Original*, reads the verbal Traduction of him into *Latin Prose*, than which nothing seems more *Raving*.'

But Hölderlin proceeded word by word, abiding by the Greek order and the division of the lines in the Greek text, and obliging his own language to follow as best it could. In a sense this is only the drastic intensification of an exercise poets often engage in, one which older poetics actually used to enjoin upon them as essential. It was said of Ronsard, for example, that he spent twelve years dealing intensively with the Greeks 'damit er sein Frantzösisches desto besser ausswürgen köndte'. Hölderlin's belief that an apprenticeship 'abroad' was indispensable harks back interestingly to the early stages in the modern literature of Europe when poets beginning to write in their own vernacular still came to it via Greek or Latin. And being German he had also in mind a belief (and perhaps he was proving it) in the sisterhood of his native language and the Greek. At its most modest this took the form of an assertion that Pindar went a lot better into German than into French; but for Hölderlin, willing the resurgence of his country in ideal forms deriving from Greece, the kinship of the languages was a powerfully attractive metaphor. As he worked at the translation, subordinating his own speech wholly to the Greek, he discovered their unalterable differences too; which is every bit as valuable as discovering their similarities.

Hölderlin's Pindar translations are of the greatest intrinsic interest, but here I must restrict myself to indicating their importance as a means to an end. In Homburg Hölderlin was chiefly preoccupied with the mechanics of poetry, he was fascinated by the possibility of calculation in poetry and it looks – to me, at least – as if in translating Pindar literally he was seeking to arrive at poetic language, at his own poetic vernacular, in a mechanical and calculated way. His method as a translator produced long passages of German which are quite unintelligible without the Greek original; others which are embarrassingly difficult or absurd; but others he would certainly have been pleased to call verse of his own. There are moments of miraculous success, when by mechanically adhering to the Greek he achieved a fine poetry in German:

> Sie
> Aber entwürdigend ihn
> In Irren der Sinne
> Eine andere Vermählung begieng, heimlich dem Vater
> Zuvor dem bärtigen getraut dem Apollo
> Und tragend den Saamen des Gottes den reinen.
> Nicht sollte sie kommen zum bräutlichen Tisch,
> Noch zu der Allertönenden Freudengeschrei
> Der Hymenäen.
>
> (v.76–7)

> Des
> Mädchens aber, woher, das Geschlecht
> Du erfragst, o König? das herrschende
> Der du von allem das Ende
> Weist und alle Pfade;
> Und welche die Erde im Frühlinge Blätter
> Ausschikt, und wie viel
> Im Meere und den Flüssen Sand

Von den Wellen und den Stößen der Winde gewälzt wird,
Und was aufkömmt, und was
Einst seyn wird, wohl du siehst.

(v.104)

Hölderlin's interest was primarily linguistic, he wanted to see what German could be made to do; but *en route*, so to speak, he learned a good deal about the workings and the manner and tone of Pindar's poems which he was then able to adopt for his own uses later. I think it worth emphasizing the primacy of the *poetic* over the translational intention. The whole undertaking only makes sense if seen in that light; and then it makes excellent sense. The most obvious characteristic of the translations is their literalness, their slavish cleaving to the letter of the original; nowhere else did Hölderlin subordinate himself to that degree. It is an act almost of self-annihilation under the revered model, under the sacred, nearly irresistible Greek canon. Yet simultaneously, and to the same degree, it is appropriation, self-discovery, self-identification and in the end self-assertion. Because in the end, as I said, it is not Pindar for Pindar's sake, Hölderlin is not a translator at all in any ordinary sense, not one really subordinating himself to an admired original and seeking to introduce it truly and justly into another language. On the contrary, it is Pindar for Hölderlin's sake, a calculated study of him, learning from him, adoption and use of him for his, Hölderlin's, own quite distinct purposes. It might be thought a perilous undertaking, self-subordination to this degree, and perhaps only a poet as disciplined and essentially sure of himself as Hölderlin would dare attempt it.

Ulrich von Wilamowitz-Moelendorff, *Pindaros* (Berlin 1922), p. 463 (translated by Richard Stoneman).

His world is quite strange to us; its customs, its thoughts and desires for us charmless, if not actually objectionable. He himself is no richly endowed spirit. He knows nothing of the power and greatness of his fatherland, nothing of progress in any direction. Neither the exploration of the broad earth nor the solving of the thousand riddles that Nature arouses in and around us, attracts him at all. He has no conception of science; were it to come near him, he would reject it as godless foolishness. All the greatness that our souls depend on is Ionic–Attic; but he will know nothing of its nature; not only Odysseus, but even Homer are antipathetic to him. His art itself is alien to us, no less in what is unique to him than in his traditional style. But yet: he is Pindar, a complete man, and human, and prophet of the Muses. He compels us first to attend to him, and then to love him. The longer one lives with him, the faster one clings to him. I have experienced this; I hope that I have succeeded in showing him in some measure as he was, in making the path to him easier, so that others too may learn to understand him. Then we shall love him and win a loyal companion for our lives: πιστὸν τὸ θεῖον [loyal are the gods].

B. L. Gildersleeve, *Olympian Odes* (New York 1885), pp. xxxvi–viii.

What is the immediate effect of the detailed work of his poems, that detailed work by which he is at first more comprehensible? The detail of Pindar's odes produces, from the very outset of the study, an irresistible effect of opulence and elevation. Opulence is wealth that makes itself felt, that suggests, almost insultingly, a contrast, and that contrast is indigence. It is one half of an aristocrat, elevation being the other, so that in art as in thought, as in politics, as in religion, Pindar is true to his birth and to his order. This opulence, this abundance of resource, shows itself in strength and in splendor, for πλοῦτος is μεγάνωρ, πλοῦτος is εὐρυσθενής. The word splendor and all its synonyms seem to be made for Pindar. He drains dry the Greek vocabulary of words for light and bright, shine and glimmer, glitter and glister, ray and radiance, flame and flare and flash, gleam and glow, burn and blaze. The first Olympian begins with wealth and strength, with flaming fire of gold, and the shining star of the sun. The fame of Hieron is resplendent, and the shoulder of Pelops gleams. No light like the light of the eye, thought the Greek, and the ancestors of Theron were the eye of Sicily, and Adrastos longs for the missing eye of his army. So the midmonth moon in her golden chariot flashed full the eye of evening into the face of Herakles. Wealth is not enough. It must be picked out, set off. It is not the uniform stare of a metallic surface, it must be adorned with the tracery that heightens the value of the background. Pindar delights in elaboration. His *epinikion* itself, as we have seen, combines the two moral elements of the games πόνος δαπάνα τε. His lyre has a various range of notes, his quiver is full of arrows, and at times such is the shower of notes, such the rain of arrows, such the sparkle and flash and flame of the lights, such the sweet din and rumble and roar of the music of earth and the music of heaven, that the poet himself, overcome by the resources of his own art, confesses his defeat, and by one strong impulse of his light feet, swims out of the deluge of glory with which he has flooded the world of song.[1] It requires strength to carry this opulence of splendor, but Pindar's opulence is the opulence of strength as well. He does not carve his bow with curious figures so deeply cut that at the drawing of the string the weapon snaps. His is not a sleepy but a vivid opulence, not a lazy but a swift opulence. Everything lives in his poems, everything is personified. Look at the magical way in which he lights up this great lamp of the architecture of his Odeon in the first Pythian. 'O Golden Lyre, joint heirloom of Apollo and the Muses violet-tressed, thou for whom the step, the dancer's step, listeneth'. 'Obeyeth' seems too faint. We see the foot poised, tremulously listening for the notes of the phorminx, as if it had a hearing of its own. A few verses further down, 'snowy Aitna, nursing the livelong year the biting snow', not '*her* snow', as it has been rendered. It is not hers. It has come down to her from Heaven. It is the child of Zeus, and only rests on her cold bosom, the pillar of the sky. Yet again the couch on which the fettered giant lies goads him and galls him, as if it too had a spite against him, as well as the weight of continent and island that pinches his hairy breast. And so it is everywhere; and while this vividness in some instances is faint to us, because our language uses the same personifications familiarly, we must remember that to the Greek they were new, or, at all events, had not entirely lost their saliency by frequent attrition.

C. M. Bowra, *Pindar* (Oxford 1964), pp. 365–6.

Pindar's poetical genius thrives most abundantly in a characteristically Greek sphere of consciousness. The Greeks, from Homer onwards, were haunted, even obsessed, by a sense of the insecurity and the shadowiness of human life and asserted themselves against it by a prodigious exertion of intellectual and physical powers. On the intellectual side they felt the need for something permanent behind the drifting appearances of things, and in Pindar's own time philosophers were already concerned to find out what Being really is. Though Pindar was not likely to be interested in their speculations, there is something in common between him and Parmenides, who drew a sharp line between knowledge and opinion and claimed that the first dealt with reality and the second with appearance. In his view men who relied on their senses were κωφοὶ ὁμῶς τυφλοί τε, τεθηπότες, ἄκριτα φῦλα (frag. 6.7 D–K), while the only true object of knowledge was οὐλομελές τε καὶ ἀτρεμὲς ἠδ' ἀτέλεστον (frag. 8.4 D–K). To bridge the gulf between these two orders was the task of philosophers, who culminated in Plato, but Pindar, who cared nothing for the problem presented in this way, was deeply conscious of it in another way. He saw an enormous gap between the world of men, which is οὐδέν, and the brazen sky, which is the everlasting home of the gods (N. 6.3–4), and he could not but believe that at times this gap can be crossed, not indeed by men trying to be gods, but by gods shedding some of their strength and brightness upon men. His own poetry is largely concerned with bridging the gulf between the flimsy, disordered, transitory world of common experience and the sublime, celestial world of order and harmony which reveals itself not only in visions of the gods but in flights of imaginative insight, in moments of concentrated power and rapturous delight. This made him acutely aware alike of the shadowy character of things around him and of the flashes of illumination by which they were transfigured and redeemed. His poetry is concerned with the points of intersection between the two states. His belief that man is no more than a shadow in a dream (P8.95–6) was applied to men and women in times of catastrophe by Aeschylus (Ag. 1327), Sophocles (Aj. 124; Ant. 1170; frag. 659.6 P), and Euripides (Med. 1224), but whereas the tragedians use the theme dramatically to indicate the annihilating sense of unreality which comes with disaster and cannot themselves be assumed to hold such a view, Pindar makes it his own, and applies it to those many aspects of the human predicament which are not illumined by a celestial light. He wishes to ensure that, when this light shines, the most shall be made of it, and to create for it his own special kind of order through song, which, as a form of κόσμος (N 6.46; frag. 184 Bo.; 194 Sn.), gives shape and harmony through glory and corresponds with a similar process in the actual facts of success and victory (O 3.13; 8.83; P 2.10; N 3.31).

M. I. Finley, 'Silver Tongue', *Aspects of Antiquity* (London 1968), pp. 45–9.

The one choice Pindar did not have if he was to continue in his profession, was in his patrons. The tyrants of Sicily and of Cyrene in North Africa, the traditional aristocracies of Aegina, of his native Thebes, even of Athens – they and their protégés dominated the sporting events at the games, and it was their world and their values which Pindar celebrated, and obviously shared. His poetry therefore raises, within limits, the question which exercises critics of T. S. Eliot. Can one divorce a great poet from his deeply felt but odious beliefs?

Our difficulty is made more acute by the fact that an older contemporary of Pindar's, Simonides, who died in 468 BC aged nearly ninety, was able to escape total commitment to tyranny and horsy aristocracy. Relatively little of Simonides survives, but that little includes a famous epigram on the dead at Marathon, whereas the sole reference to Marathon in Pindar is as the seat of unimportant local games. Not only did Pindar's native Thebes fail to support the effort to throw back the Persian invasions but Thebans actually fought in the invading army. Sir Maurice notes that the pro-Persian element in Thebes was 'the class to which Pindar himself belonged', but he then tries hard to extricate Pindar from his equivocations on the subject. I do not think it can be done. Nor, when Pindar is impressed with Arcesilas of Cyrene, as a 'king in the heroic manner', does that reflect anything more than a courtier's stance. The poet allows his respect for Arcesilas' position to 'spread to the man who holds it'. That is the essence: whatever Pindar touches – and that means the inherent rightness of rule by kings, tyrants and nobles and the inherent truth of the myth which he knows so well and which he weaves so skilfully into his praises – he accepts without probing or doubting. What has been and has been believed is right.

One must not be misled by Pindar's admonitions of virtue, justice and the rule of law. He means them in their archaic or Spartan connotations, as they were being bandied about by every oligarch against the growing demand for popular government and democratic rule. It has been pointed out that the 'quieter moral virtues' are absent in his ethics. Daring, strength and success are what matter, and behind them the wealth without which none of the requisite activity is possible. There is no glory in defeat, no consolation for the defeated.

And now four times you came down with bodies beneath you,
– You meant them harm –
To whom the Pythian feast has given

No glad homecoming like yours.
They, when they meet their mother,
Have no sweet laughter around them, moving delight.
In back streets, out of their enemies' way,
They cower; for disaster has bitten them.

These were value-judgements still widely shared by Greeks of his day. One could not possibly say of Pindar's contemporaries, as Professor Kermode wrote of Eliot's, that 'it is doubtful whether many have much sympathy now with his views'. Pindar lived at a time of conflict and uncertainty. His athletes were still everyman's heroes, but their class and their class-values were being challenged. Even Aeschylus, who is regularly bracketed with Pindar in modern accounts, worried about the implications of the received myths. Hence the *Oresteia* is a serious, if ultimately unresolved, discussion of an ancient moral dilemma. There are no such discussions in Pindar; there are not even any dilemmas, only successes and failures.

E. L. Bundy, *Studia Pindarica* I (Berkeley 1962), pp. 3–4.

Here then are two examples of convention operating to control form and meaning in choral poetry. For both I have given examples from the two poets of whose work complete specimens survive, in order to suggest that they are not mannerisms of a given poet but conventions protecting the artistic integrity of a community of poets working within well-recognized rules of form and order. I have observed and catalogued a host of these conventions and find that they point uniformly, as far as concerns the Epinikion, to one master principle: there is no passage in Pindar and Bakkhulides that is not in its primary intent enkomiastic – that is, designed to enhance the glory of a particular patron. This conclusion, if it can be substantiated, should provide solid comfort to those who have complained of willful irrelevance in the odes, although I fear that these have, in truth, been more comforted than surprised by the spectacle of a professional admirer of athletes who will not stick to his business. Yet it should be evident that the Epinikion must adhere to those principles that have governed enkomia from Homer to Lincoln's *Gettysburg Address*, so that when Pindar speaks pridefully in the first person this is less likely to be the personal Pindar of Thebes than the

Pindar privileged to praise the worthiest of men.[1] If he protests
that he is truthful, he is not making an ethical statement about his
own person, but quieting murmurs from his audience with the
assurance, 'He is every bit as good as I say he is', or 'My words
shall not fall short of his deeds.'[2] If he seems embarrassed by
irrelevance, or by the poverty of his expression, or by his failure
to do justice, these inadequacies have been rigged as foil for the
greatness of the laudandus.[3]

Unfortunately for those who would prefer a Pindar that makes
sense even in praise of athletes to a Pindar that rises to gorgeous
irrelevance in avoiding his unpromising subject, the enkomiast's
rhetorical poses may take forms that speak to one unschooled in
the conventions with something less than the precision intended.
Thus N 7, a straightforward enkomion, has been canonized by
those who follow one guess reported by the scholia as the poet's
personal apology for offensive references to Neoptolemos in the
ode we now possess fragmentarily as Pa. 6;[4] and similar embar-
rassments have been discovered in P 2.[5]

References

1. Cf. O 1.115ff., I 5.51ff., O 2.91–7, and N 4.41ff. Only misinterpre-
   tation can make personal passages of these. In N 4.41ff., for
   example, the enkomiast, according to the rules of order mentioned
   in lines 33ff., momentarily hesitates to continue the catalogue of
   Aiakid heroes (begun with Telamon in line 25 and concluded with
   Peleus in line 68). These rules and his own desire he thrusts aside in
   lines 36–43, where he contrasts himself with the stinter (φθονερὰ
   δ' ἄλλος ἀνὴρ βλέπων) whose mechanical obedience to rules
   ignores what every discerning person can see: for such heroes as the
   Aiakids you must abandon the rules. Here the way of φυά (natural
   enthusiasm) is preferred to the way of τέχνα (mechanical praise).
   (See pp. 29–32.) After this he begins a new crescendo in lines 43ff.
   and completes his catalogue. Thus what Farnell (*The Works of
   Pindar* [London, 1930] I 179) calls 'an expression of arrogant
   egoism' is in reality rhetorical foil to enhance the glory of the
   Aiakids. The school of interpreters that cons the odes for gossip
   should be further warned that the ἄλλος ἀνήρ of line 39 is a
   type, not an individual poet close to or far from the scene of the
   celebration.
2. Cf. O 4.19f., N 1.18, O 6.89f. (ἀλαθέσιν λόγοις is the full praise

with which the laudator escapes the charge of ἀπαιδευσία or ἀμαθία).

3. Cf. N 7.64–9, 102–5, P 11.38–40 (foil for the introduction of the victor in lines 41–5), and P 10.4 (dismissing lines 1–3 as irrelevant to the praise of Hippokleas).

4. The authors of the scholia had only the odes to aid them, as is suggested by the phrasing of the scholium on line 102, ὁ μὲν Καλλίστρατος ... ὁ δὲ ᾿Αριστόδημος κτλ. My view of this ode will be given in a subsequent study in this series.

5. I believe that this ode, on which I am preparing a monograph, contains nothing personal to Pindar.

Mary Lefkowitz, *The First Person in Pindar* (Oxford 1991) pp. 235–7.

However, the proof that there is no choral 'I' in Pindar's *epinikia* lies not in interpretation of the text alone, but also in the very nature of choral and of epinician poetry. As we have seen, pure choral songs and *epinikia* are composed for different purposes and deal with different types of subject matter, which in each case seem to require a different type of first personal statement, since in choral songs, which deal primarily with local and communal concerns, the chorus speaks throughout, but in *epinikia*, which deal with the universal significance of human excellence, the speaker is always the poet. Each type of first personal statement is thus associated with a particular subject matter, so that the topical, descriptive 'I' of the chorus could not occur in an *epinikion*, any more than the poet's official expressions of *xenia* and statements about his art could occur in choral songs like *Paean* 2. It is very unlikely that Pindar would seek to go against tradition by having the chorus speak in an *epinikion*, in which every other transitional statement refers to himself, especially when such an intrusion would have no meaningful function in the ode. Therefore to allow the chorus to speak in odes like I 7 or P 5 would violate what we have observed to be an otherwise consistent principle, that there is no change of speaker within an *epinikion* or a pure choral song.

To determine the origins of this generic distinction between pure choral and monodic song is beyond the scope of this study, and perhaps of any study, in view of the paucity of evidence available. But on the basis of what we have observed about Pindar's *epinikia* and about choral song in general, it is possible to offer at least a hypothetical explanation of why in an epinician ode only the poet may speak. It may at first seem somewhat paradoxical, at least in Plato's terms that 'the city is the man writ large', that the larger group, the chorus, is confined to the smaller subject. But the chorus of a song like *Paean* 2 or the Theban *Partheneion* is composed of a group of private citizens, who by their very nature cannot speak with the great authority of a poet like Pindar, who has from the Muses skill in song and divine knowledge and memory, who knows from the Muses and from his travels the myths and legends of all Greece, not just of his own community. He alone has the qualifications to speak on a general theme, since, unlike a private citizen, his knowledge is not limited to one local area and he is not restricted by the ordinary man's lack of artistic ability. He alone has the authority to give advice, to express *gnomai* to the subjects of his song, either objectively, as in I 5.14 ('do not seek to become Zeus'), or subjectively, as in P 3.59 ('do not, dear soul, strive for immortal life'). It is perhaps because of this intense concern with himself, as poet and citizen, that Pindar's choral odes seem by comparison much less successful. He has little interest in the local and the temporal; his poetry reaches its greatest heights in personal statements like I 8.1ff., where he puts aside immediate concerns, and turns to eternal values.

On the other hand, the Swallows have no such pretensions in their song; they simply describe themselves and what they are doing. In choral song composed by a professional poet, however, some elements of 'poetic' style are occasionally present; thus Alcman's maidens proclaim the *gnome* 'there is vengeance from the gods' (1.36), the Abderitans of *Paean* 2 utter similar pious statements, and, as we have observed, the praise of the Laurel-bearer's family in Pindar's *Partheneion* is not unlike the praise of the victor's family in an *epinikion*. But the general tone, the subject matter, and the first personal statements of each of these songs are all completely choral in nature. The essential distinctions are always preserved.

In the light of this evidence, it is difficult to explain why *epinikia* were usually performed by choruses, in spite of their subject matter, and in spite of the fact that the poet speaks in his own person throughout. Perhaps the early *epinikia* were purely choral in form, concerned with the celebration and the immediate importance of the victory. But with the growth of humanism in Greece, seen particularly in the invention of monodic *enkomia*, like Ibycus' ode to Polycrates, or Simonides' *skolion* to Scopas about the 'good man', greater international importance was attached to victories in the games. Thus the presence of a professional poet was eventually required at the victory celebrations, a poet who would naturally, like his predecessors the epic *aoidoi*, speak in the first person, and concentrate not on local affairs but on the universal significance of the victory. Clearly such a transformation must have taken place sometime in the sixth century, since Simonides, Bacchylides, and Pindar all treat the *epinikion* as a virtually monodic form.

But Pindar did not, like Bacchylides, rely exclusively on the bardic tradition in his epinician statements. He understood the form so well that he was able to transcend it, developing the imagery implicit in Homeric statements about poetry, and inventing special metaphors of his own. He also drew on the tradition of first personal statements in epic and lyric poetry, where the poet speaks not as a professional but as a private citizen, thus incorporating the personal into the official statements of his odes. To say that choral statements occur in his epinician odes is not only to misunderstand the epinician form, but to do Pindar great injustice as a poet.

Richard Stoneman 'Ploughing a Garland', *Maia* 33 (1981): 125–36 (135–6).

I have already suggested once or twice that Pindar uses his metaphors as if they were dead metaphors, and that this is most evident in the mixed metaphors where it is difficult to suppose that he deliberately intended the resulting incongruities. I think that in a certain sense this is true, but that it is true not in terms of the Greek language as a whole but of the *Kunstsprache* in which Pindar writes. There is too little evidence to decide whether Pindar's style is of his own creating – though the dissimilarity of Bacchylides is remarkable – but we must I think assume that the language of this pre-eminently public poetry was a public language, even if that public was only the circumscribed one of the σοφοί. That is, Pindar's hearers were accustomed to tropes of the kind that Pindar uses, even if not every one was instantly familiar. A close parallel for this kind of awareness in a literary public is provided by the contemporaries of the Metaphysical poets, who, as Rosemond Tuve argues in her book *Elizabethan and Metaphysical Imagery* were attuned to a style of writing, of conceit, of allusion, which to us is often desperately far-fetched and obscure. One example she gives is particularly illuminating.

Thomas Carew wrote

> Nor can your snow, *though* you should take
> Alps into your bosom, slake
> The heat of my enamour'd heart . . .

Tuve stresses the incorrectness of letting modern, romantic, or any other associations of the Alps deflect us from recognition of the function of the image in this passage: 'to define this image by its formal cause is to realise that all we know from it is that Carew picked up somewhere that Alps were large, numerous, and snowy'. She deliberately reduces the case *ad absurdum*, but the essential point stands: the conceit functions as *amplificatio*, drawing attention to an important point. The same applies to more complex metaphysical conceits, where the only difference is that the logical bases of the comparison are multiple instead of single. Carew's readers were trained to recognise the rhetorical purpose of imagery and to savour each point for itself. Pindar's audience too would recognise the succinct heightening of style and attend to the surface associations of the individual words. We need not appeal to the nature of the fifth-century mind, nor to Pindar's symbolic intentions, to explain the style.

More complex is the problem of how his audience *responded* to these images, once given that they understood them. Why is the continual mixture of metaphors not merely slovenly writing? What sort of literary artifice is at work here? The answer, I think, tells us something about the nature and range of possible expression in poetry, and may even increase our respect for Aristotle's understanding of the way some Greek poets wrote.

The distinction made by Jakobson between metaphor and metonymy brings us part of the way to the answer. Pindar's metaphors work on a basis of substitution not combination. They are highly traditional. They offer, generally speaking, no insight into the objects to which Pindar applies them. One might forget their metaphoric quality in a discursive medium like prose.

And yet one is continually brought up short by them. They do not wash over us like the orotundities of rhetoric; they shock us and make us look again at the text before us. In fact, the way they work corresponds to the analysis of the literary process made by the leader of the Prague School of critics, Jan Mukařovsky. A literary tradition is seen as a dialectic between motifs to which readers in a particular period become habituated, so that they lose their force – in the jargon, they are 'automatised' – and those which, by their difference from the language that has become traditional, are 'foregrounded' (the accepted translation of the verb corresponding to the Czech noun *aktualisace*). These 'fore-grounded' motifs can either be motifs that were already in the tradition but of secondary importance, or precisely those that were of first importance and had thereby become thoroughly conventional, 'automatised', but by a distancing of attitude (the most obvious type being parody) are 'de-automatised' and recover their power to catch the reader's attention. This description seems to fit exactly the way Pindar uses his traditional metaphors. 'Garland' for 'victory' is automatised – no one thinks about it – but in conjunction with the quite different metaphor of 'ploughing' it brings us up with a start: the terms are both 'foregrounded', and the mannered quality of the verse is brought to our attention. Both particular instance and general principle are brought to the fore. Very much the same happens in the 'cold fire' passage of frag. 123, where a conventional image of brazing is brought to the fore by the use of the paradox of '*cold* fire'. The foregrounding of a traditional metaphor, it could be argued, gives more force to the statement than would the invention of a new image, since it has behind it not only the shock of inconcinnity, but the depth and satisfactoriness of significance that made it a hackneyed image in the first place.

Mary Lefkowitz, *The Lives of the Greek Poets* (London 1981), pp. 60-2.

In his version of the story of Demeter's epiphany, Aristodemus (*FGrHist* 383F*13) assigned an important role to the ordinary people involved with the great poet: 'Pindar was giving a lesson to Olympichus the flute player when there was a noise and flame on the mountain where they were practising. Pindar thought that he saw a stone statue of the Mother of the gods in front of him, and set up a statue near his house of the Mother of the gods and Pan; the citizens of Thebes sent an inquiry to the Delphic oracle about what had happened, and the oracle confirmed that a shrine be established to the Mother of the gods. The citizens were amazed that Pindar had anticipated the oracle and honoured Pindar equally in the ritual to the goddess' (schol. P 3.137b). In his explanation of Pindar's statement that he did not savage Neoptolemus with ruthless words, Aristodemus has Pindar apologise not to the victor or his father but to the citizens of Aegina (schol. N 7.150a). Callimachus, elaborating on a standard form of epitaph, has the dead Simonides engage the audience directly in the story of the desecration of his grave (frag. 64); Eratosthenes has Hesiod's dog identify his murderers (frag. 19 Powell).

Aristodemus' account may in part be based on Pindar's original hymn. Pindar describes an epiphany of the hero Alcmeon in *Pythian* 8; the *Homeric Hymn to Dionysus* describes how a ship's crew reacts to the god's presence and how the captain establishes his cult. But Aristodemus' story, unlike a hymn (e.g. Pindar frag. 33e) concentrates on human responses more than on the divinity, and the original hymn would not have mentioned the 'equal' honour given by the Thebans to Pindar himself. Since Pausanias gives a different account of the hymn's origin, the hymn itself must have provided no indication of exactly how the poet came to write it: Persephone (not Demeter) appeared to Pindar in a dream; Pindar wrote the song for her after his death; the poet recited it in a dream to an old woman relative, who wrote it down from memory (9.23.2). The location, Pindar's house, may have been suggested by his stating in Pythian 3: 'I will pray to the Mother whom girls sing to at night with Pan beside my door' (77–9).

The anecdote in the *Vita* about Pan singing a song (or Paean) of Pindar also could have been deduced from allusions to the circumstances of performance in the song itself (e.g. in Pindar frag. 107ab), or from a direct request to the god to join in their song. Sappho addresses Aphrodite frequently in her poems (e.g. frags. 1, 2); a third-century biography gives special emphasis to her relationship with the goddess: 'she was in such high favour with the citizens that Callias of Mytilene said in ... Aphrodite' (*SLG* 261, 11–16). Once the deities themselves were thought to intervene only in human incarnation, the direct encounters described by archaic poets could no longer be understood. The scholia do not accept that Pindar in Pythian 8 literally meant that he met Alcmeon; they proposed instead that the chorus was speaking about a local hero shrine, or that he was referring to the hero-cult in Thebes of Alcmeon's father Amphiaraus (schol. *Pythian* 7.78ab). Tzetzes insists in his biography that Hesiod's encounter with the Muses was meant allegorically, or took place in a dream (p. 46 W). So in the anecdotes about Pindar's hymn to Pan the imagined circumstances of performance are more carefully preserved than the poet's words, and the poet's response becomes as important as the god's singing.

Hugh Lloyd-Jones, 'Pindar' in *Greek Epic, Lyric and Tragedy* (Oxford 1990), pp. 65–8.

In the light of these considerations, let us consider the recurrent elements of the epinician ode. First, there is the religious background. Pindar is above all else a religious poet, and much of the failure to understand him has been bound up with the failure to understand the Greek religion that pervades his poetry. That failure has encouraged the Romantic error of taking Pindar's religion for a personal construction of his own. For a believer in the archaic Greek religion, to praise a mortal man was a hazardous enterprise. The gods are immortal, and alone enjoy true happiness; men are the creatures of a day, and are subject to all the misfortunes which the day may bring. The gods govern the universe, understandably enough, in their own interest, and with little regard for that of men; the various creation-myths make men an accidental or a casual element in the scheme of things. The gods in Pindar's poetry are most vividly realized as individual personalities, and something of the same concreteness invests even the personified abstractions which so often figure in his work. But these gods work through real forces in the world, so that to deny their existence would be pointless, since the reality of the forces which they stand for cannot be denied.

No man can be pronounced fortunate till he is dead; at any moment an unforeseen catastrophe may overwhelm the happiest among mankind. But men may enjoy moments of felicity; these are dependent on the favour of the gods, and come most of all to men descended from the unions with mortal women which the gods allowed themselves during the heroic age. Such men's heroic nature makes them capable of becoming rulers, warriors, athletes, or poets. Nature is vitally important, and without natural aptitude education is in vain. But natural gifts by themselves are not enough; hard labour and endurance are required, and the need for them is quite as strongly stressed as that for natural gifts. Not that even the conjunction of natural ability and strenuous effort can command success; in the last resort, all mortal triumph is dependent on the favour of the gods. The gods may grudge success to any mortal; the divine envy which may make them do so is conceived by Pindar not as mere spite, but as a facet of divine justice, whose workings mortals are not always able to perceive.

Any man who praises other men must remain always conscious of the danger of provoking envy, not only divine but human. Envy is a force which any man who strives after any kind of *areta*, excellence, must fight; of this the man who praises others must remain aware. Hesiod, the greatest Boeotian poet before Pindar, had stressed the community between kings and poets, both of whom derive authority from Zeus, kings directly, but poets through Apollo and the Muses [*Theogony* 75–103]. Conscious of his own *areta* as an inspired poet, Pindar has a deep sense of community with the men of action, rulers, warriors, and athletic victors, whom he praises; like them he has to struggle against envy, not simply that of rivals, but that which any man who praises others has to strive to overcome. If the poet can contrive to vanquish envy and to place the victory in its setting in the world of gods as well as men, then the victor's brief moment of felicity can in a limited but real sense be made eternal.

To the modern mind it may seem strange, even ridiculous, that athletes should be coupled with rulers and warriors as bearers of *areta*. That is not how the archaic Greeks saw the matter. A victory in the games, with their strong religious associations, carried vast prestige; athletes endured arduous training of a kind that fitted them for war as well as triumph in the games. The Aeginetans, for whom Pindar wrote more odes of victory than for any other community, won the prize for valour awarded by the Greek army after Salamis; the Sicilian tyrants, whatever modern moralizers may say about their ideology, saved the Greeks of Sicily from the Carthaginians and Etruscans. Again, the conventional references to the customary fee should not lead us to suppose, as ancient comic poets did in jest and later grammarians in all seriousness, that Pindar and Simonides were especially mercenary. [See Lefkowitz, *The Lives of the Greek Poets*.] One proof of the noble man's nobility, according to the poetic convention, was his readiness to spend his money generously in assuring that his fame would live.

Yeats lived at a time when there was no generally accepted picture of the world to serve as background for his poetry, so that he was compelled to construct one for himself out of very disparate materials. Pindar, like Dante, inherited the picture of the world fashioned by the religion of his people. The greatest error of Romantic criticism has been to treat this as though it were a personal philosophy or religion of the poet's own making; we can see that it is common to him and to other writers in the genre, both to the older Simonides, of whom we know little, and to the younger Bacchylides, of whom we possess large parts of fourteen victory odes. If we make allowances for the differences of genre and avoid the pervasive error of reading ideas into ancient tragedy that are not there, we can see that it is not very different from the religious outlook that we find in Aeschylus or Sophocles.

This Romantic misconception has been fostered by the force and clarity of Pindar's many statements in the first person, which give the reader nurtured on Romantic verse the irresistible impression of being in contact with a powerful and independent poetic personality. That is in a sense true; but we shall not appreciate Pindar's poetry correctly unless we are aware of how much he has in common with other writers in the same genre, with Greek archaic poetry in general, and with all believers in archaic Greek religion. Presented by a poet whose imagination has grasped its tragic truth with utter honesty and clarity, the austere world of early Greek religion comes across to us in all its beauty and with all its hardness.

Against this backcloth the poet must place the victory won by his client of the moment. The odes commonly start with an elaborate prelude, ultimately deriving, it would seem, from the invocation of deities with which cult-hymns began. Sometimes the poet invokes a god, but more often a personified abstraction, or the hero or heroine who personifies a place; he may address his own Muse, who is about to perform in honour of the victor; he may start with general reflection or with praise of the victory; or he may describe his ode by means of an elaborate simile, likening it to a cup or bowl ceremonially offered by one man to another or to one of the splendid treasuries which wealthy communities built at the great religious centres to contain their dedications.

Nothing is more indicative of the distorting effect exercised by Romanticism upon Pindaric criticism than the proneness of critics to assume that the mention of the victory and the enumeration of other victories won by the victor and by other members of his family must have been irksome duties which the poet resented and was eager to get out of the way as soon as possible in order to give expression to his personal preoccupations. In fact the victory is the starting-point and epicentre of the entire poem, and the other victories of the family must be mentioned too, since they help to demonstrate that these men possess that nobility of nature which makes effort fruitful and wins the divine favour which alone can bring success. In the hands of an indifferent poet this part of the poem might indeed turn out monotonous, but Pindar displays the greatest virtuosity in the avoidance of this danger. With typical Greek realism he frequently remarks that not all the members even of the greatest athletic families possess equal gifts; talent often skips a generation or so. What counted for the Greeks was victory, and Pindar has no compunction in imagining the discomfiture of the defeated rivals of the winner. Not that the odes dwell at all frequently on the incidents of the games, despite the poet's fondness for athletic metaphors.

The character and history of the victors, their families, and the civic communities they belonged to stimulate the poet to recall history as well as legend; to the Greeks of his time the boundary between the two was vague and almost non-existent. Naturally the part of the poems dealing with the victors takes on a special interest when they are great personages like Arcesilas, king of Cyrene, Hieron, ruler of Syracuse, Theron, ruler of Acragas, and other members of his family. A poetic convention that is as old as Hesiod allows Pindar to address such people as an equal, and to advise them to persist in their noble ways, advice which the audience knows there is no possibility of their neglecting, any more than Britannia might reject the advice of those who in song urge her to rule the waves.

G. Nagy, *Pindar's Homer* (Baltimore 1990), pp. 138–42.

For the athlete the ritual significance of these life-and-death struggles by heroes finds its expression in the occasional lyric poetry of Pindar. In order to introduce this topic, however, I choose a remarkably suggestive passage not from Pindar but from quite elsewhere, namely, the *Alcestis* of Euripides. Offstage, the quintessential hero Herakles has just wrestled with and defeated Thanatos, Death personified; then, on stage, he cryptically refers to this confrontation as an athletic event: ἀθληταῖσιν ἄξιον πόνον 'a worthy exertion [**ponos**] for athletes' (Euripides *Alcestis*

1027). In his speech Herakles does not reveal that he has struggled with Thanatos but prefers to represent his life-and-death ordeal as a wrestling match at a local athletic festival. In the words of Herakles his 'exertion' in the wrestling match with Death was a **ponos** (again *Alcestis* 1027). This and another word for 'exertion', **kamatos**, are programmatically used in the diction of Pindar to designate the hardships of preparing for and engaging in athletic competition. Moreover, both **ponos** and **kamatos** are used by the poet to designate the life-and-death struggles of heroes. As with the word **aethlos** 'contest', with **ponos** and **kamatos** there is a collapsing of the distinction between the myth of the hero's struggle and the ritual of the athlete's competition. Accordingly, 'ordeal' may be more apt a translation than 'exertion' for both **ponos** and **kamatos** since it conveys not only a heroic but also a ritual experience.

This set of poetic words, as used in Pindar's diction, helps us understand more clearly the ritual ideology inherited by Greek athletics. As noted, this ideology reveals diachronic features of two kinds of ritual: (1) initiation into adulthood and (2) compensation for the catastrophe of death. In the first case it is easy to see how the ordeal conveyed by words like **aethlos, ponos**, and **kamatos** is characteristic of initiation. In the second case, however, the connection between a hero's ordeal and the idea of compensating for a primordial death is more difficult to intuit. We must call to mind again the formulation of Karl Meuli: in various societies throughout the world, ritual combat can have the function of compensating for guilt about someone's death. The guilt can be canceled by way of an ordeal that decides the guilty person, in that the guilty person is killed in the ordeal while any innocent person survives. Such an ordeal may take the form of either a life-and-death contest or an attenuated form of competition where 'living' and 'dying' may be stylized as winning and losing, respectively. As I have already proposed, however, the ancient Greek model of such an ordeal reflects a rearrangement in ideology: in contrast with other models where the ordeal instituted to compensate for the guilt of a given person's death requires that one contestant 'die' by losing and thereby be proven guilty while the other contestant or contestants 'live', the Greek model requires that one contestant 'live' by winning. This 'survival' of one person is then pluralized, communalized by the **khoros** 'chorus', on the occasion of the epinician or victory celebration. But the Greek model is still an ordeal, instituted to compensate for the guilt of a given person's death; to engage in the ordeal is to engage in the act of compensation. The ordeal, as part of an initiation, leads to a 'winning' of life, a 'rebirth' that compensates for death. [. . . .]

What I am proposing, then, is that the epinician performance is the final realization, the final constitutive event, of the ritual process of athletics. In Pindar's own words the occasion of an epinician ode, stylized as kōmos '[occasion for a] band of revellers', is a lutron 'compensation' for the kamatoi 'ordeals' of the athlete (λύτρον . . . καμάτων Isthmian 8.2). We had seen earlier that the ordeal of the athlete is a formal lutron 'compensation' for a primordial death (λύτρον συμφορᾶς οἰκτρᾶς 'lutron for the pitiful misfortune' Olympian 7.77). Now we see that the Pindaric victory ode is a formal 'compensation' for the athlete's ordeal. The actual Greek word for 'victory ode', epi-nīkion 'epinician', literally means something like 'that which is in compensation for victory [nīkē]'.

Roberto Calasso, *The Marriage of Cadmus and Harmony* (London and New York 1993), pp. 146–7.

In the thick of the stones, marble, and metal at Delphi, the visitor would think of other ghosts, of the first temples to Apollo, now no more. The first, a hut of laurel branches broken from trees in the valley of Tempe; the second, made of wax and feathers; the third, built in bronze by Hephaestus and Athena. Pindar could still wonder: 'Oh Muses, with what patterns did the able hands of Hephaestus and Athena decorate the temple?' We shall never know, but Pindar thought he could recall fragments of an image: 'Bronze the walls and bronze too rose the columns; golden above the pediment chanted six Enchantresses.' These words were already sounding obscure by the time Pausanias heard them. At most, he supposed, the Enchantresses might have been an 'imitation of Homer's Sirens'. Yet they held the secret to a long story, the story of the origins of possession.

Iynx was a girl sorceress. She made up love potions. Not for herself, but because she wanted love to make the rounds. One day she offered a drink to Zeus. The god drank it, and the first girl he saw was Io, wandering about in the grounds of Hera's sanctuary in Argos. Zeus was possessed by love for Io. And so began history on earth, a history of flight, persecution, metamorphosis. The first victim was the sorceress herself. In revenge, Hera turned her into a bird known as the wryneck, because of the way it twists its neck with a sudden jerking movement. When Jason reached Colchis, he knew that if he wanted to get the Golden Fleece he would have to win over the young sorceress Medea. Aphrodite looked down from heaven and decided to help him. A sorceress can only be overcome by a more potent sorcery. So Aphrodite took the wryneck, the 'delirious, multicolored bird', and fixed it with bonds that could not be untied to a little wheel with four spokes. Now the circular motion of the wheel would forever accompany the jerky twisting of the bird's neck. That small object, that plaything, becomes the mechanism, the artifice of possession. It imposes an obsessive circular motion on the mind, a motion that uproots it from its inertia and hooks it onto the divine wheel, which turns incessantly like the spheres. Even the thoughts of the gods get caught on that wheel.

Jason learned to use Aphrodite's gift. Medea immediately lost all consideration for her parents. The girl's mind was obsessed by desire for a distant country, for a name, Greece, which she confused with Jason's presence. Thus, drawing on her sorcery, her herbs and ointments, Medea saved the Stranger and ruined her own family. It wasn't Apollo or Dionysus, then, lords of possession that they were, who invented the *íynx*, this strange object that is the only visible artifact of possession. Aphrodite, goddess of 'the swiftest arrows', got there first; for erotic possession is the starting point for any possession. What at Delphi is an enigma, for Aphrodite is a plaything. The worshipers at Apollo's temple in Delphi would see small wheels hanging from the ceiling, small wheels with the bodies of birds attached. It was said that those wheels produced a voice, a seductive call. They were the Enchant-resses Pindar spoke of, linking the human mind to the circular motion of the heavens.

FURTHER READING

General studies

Bowra, C. M., *Pindar*, Oxford 1964 (outdated interpretation, but a useful source of information).

Bundy, Elroy L., *Studia Pindarica* Berkeley 1986 (epoch-making study which changed the course of Pindaric criticism).

Carne-Ross, D. S., *Pindar*, New Haven 1985 (lively and enthusiastic introduction).

Heath, Malcolm, 'The Origins of Modern Pindaric Criticism', *JHS* 106 (1986): 85–98.

Köhnken, A., *Die Funktion des Mythos bei Pindar*, Berlin 1971.

Lefkowitz, Mary, *First-Person Fictions: Pindar's Poetic 'I'*, Oxford 1991 (reprinted collection of important papers).

—, *The Victory Ode*, New Jersey 1976.

Lloyd-Jones, Hugh, *Greek Epic, Lyric and Tragedy: Academic Papers*, Oxford 1990 (contains a substantial number of essential papers on Pindar).

Nagy, Gregory, *Pindar's Homer*, Baltimore 1990 (a difficult and uneven, but often highly rewarding study of Pindar in his tradition).

Race, William H., *Style and Rhetoric in Pindar's Odes*, Atlanta 1990.

von der Mühll, Peter, *Ausgewählte Kleine Schriften*, Basel 1976 (contains his important series of notes and articles on Pindar from 1958 to 1968).

Wilamowitz-Moellendorff, Ulrich von, *Pindaros*, Berlin 1922 (still in many ways a classic. No translation).

Young, David C., 'Pindaric Criticism', *The Minnesota Review* 4 (1964): 584–641, reprinted with revisions in W. M. Calder and J. Stern (eds), *Pindaros und Bakchylides*, Darmstadt 1971: 1–95 (fundamental survey of past critical approaches).

—, *Three Odes of Pindar*, Mnemosyne Supplement 9, Leiden 1968 (important for its method, relevant to more than these three odes).

Background and lyric poetry

Burnett, Anne Pippin, *The Art of Bacchylides*, Cambridge, Mass., 1985.

Gentili, Bruno, *Poetry and its Public in Ancient Greece*, Baltimore and London 1988.

Lloyd-Jones, Hugh, *The Justice of Zeus*, Berkeley 1971.

Renault, Mary, *The Praise Singer*, London 1978 (novel about Simonides, evocative of the social world of epinician poetry).

Particular issues

Carey, C. J., 'Three Myths in Pindar', *Eranos* 78 (1981): 143–62

'Pindar's Eighth Nemean Ode', *PCPS (Proceedings of the Cambridge Philological Society)* 22 (1976): 26–42.

Dougherty, C., *The Poetics of Colonization*, Oxford 1994.

Gerber, D. E., 'Pindar and Bacchylides 1934–1987', *Lustrum* 31 (1989): 97–269 and 32 (1990): 9–98 (exhaustive survey of every publication on Pindar and Bacchylides from 1934 to 1987, with brief summaries of most contributions.

——(ed.), *Greek Poetry and Philosophy: Studies ... in honour of Leonard Woodbury*, Chico, California 1984 (contains many useful articles on Pindar).

Heath, Malcolm, and Mary Lefkowitz, 'Epinician Performance', *Classical Philology* 86 (1991): 173–91.

Instone, S. J., 'Pythian 11: Did Pindar Err?', *CQ* 36 (1986): 86–94

Kurke, Leslie, *The Traffic in Praise*, Ithaca and London 1991.

Most, Glenn W., *Measures of Praise*, Göttingen 1985.

Pfeijffer, Ilya L., 'The Image of the Eagle in Pindar and Bacchylides', *Classical Philology* 89 (1994): 305–17.

Steiner, Deborah, *The Crown of Song*, London 1986.

Stoneman, Richard, 'The "Theban Eagle"', *CQ* 1976.

—— 'Ploughing a Garland: Metaphor and Metonymy in Pindar', *Maia* n.s. 2 (1981): 125–37.

—— 'The Ideal Courtier: Pindar and Hieron in Pythian 2', *CQ* 34 (1984): 43–9.

Commentaries

Bona, G., *I Peani*, Rome 1988.

Braswell, B. K., *A Commentary on the Fourth Pythian of Pindar*, Berlin 1988.

Farnell, L. R., *Pindar: A Commentary*, London 1932; repr. 1965.

Gentili, B. et al., *Pindaro: Le Pitiche*, Rome 1995.

Lehnus, Luigi, *Pindaro: Olimpiche*, Milan 1981.

Privitera, A., *Le Istmiche*, Rome 1982.

Radt, S. L., *Pindar's Zweite und Sechste Paian*, Amsterdam 1958.

Rutherford, Ian, *Pindar's Paeans*, Oxford 1997.

Weiden, M. J. van der, *Pindar's Dithyrambs*, Amsterdam 1993.

Willcock, M. M., *Pindar, Victory Odes*, Cambridge 1995 (a selection of seven).

ACKNOWLEDGEMENTS

The editor and publisher wish to thank the following for permission to use copyright material:

Cambridge University Press for material from Humphrey Trevelyan, *Goethe and the Greeks*, 1941; and R. R. Bolgar, *The Classical Heritage and its Beneficiaries*, 1954;

Gerald Duckworth and Company Ltd for material from Mary Lefkowitz, *The lives of the Greek Poets*, 1981;

The Johns Hopkins University Press for material from Gregory Nagy, *Pindar's Homer*. © 1990 The Johns Hopkins University Press;

Oxford University Press for material from David Constantine, *Hölderlin* 1988; Hugh Lloyd-Jones, *Greek Epic, Lyric, and Tragedy*, 1990; C. M. Bowra, *Pindar*, 1964; and Mary Lefkowitz, *First-Person Fictions*, 1991;

Random House UK Ltd on behalf of the Estate of the author for material from M. I. Finley, *Aspects of Antiquity*, Chatto & Windus, 1968;

University of California Press for material from Elroy Bundy, *Studia Pindarica*. © 1962 The Regents of the University of California;

Every effort has been made to trace the copyright holders but if any have been inadvertently overlooked the publishers will be pleased to make the necessary arrangement at the first opportunity.

ANCIENT CLASSICS
IN EVERYMAN

Legends of Alexander the Great
edited by Richard Stoneman
*The fascinating adventures of
a dominant figure in European,
Jewish and Arabic folklore until
the fifteenth century*
£5.99

**Juvenal's Satires with the
Satires of Persius**
JUVENAL AND PERSIUS
*Unique and acute observations
of contemporary Roman society*
£5.99

The Epicurean Philosophers
edited by John Gaskin
*The surviving works and wise say-
ings of Epicurus, with the account
of his natural science in Lucretius'*
On the Nature of the Universe
£5.99

**History of the
Peloponnesian War**
THUCYDIDES
*The war that brought to an
end a golden age of democracy*
£5.99

The Discourses
EPICTETUS
*The teachings of one of the
greatest Stoic philosophers*
£6.99

The Education of Cyrus
XENOPHON
*An absorbing insight into the
culture and politics of Ancient
Greece*
£6.99

The Oresteia
AESCHYLUS
*New translation and edition
which analyses the plays in
performance*
£5.99

Suppliants and Other Dramas
AESCHYLUS
*New translation of Aeschylus'
first three surviving plays and
the earliest dramas of western
civilisation*
£5.99

The Odyssey
HOMER
*A classic translation of one of
the greatest adventures ever told*
£5.99

The Republic
PLATO
*The most important and
enduring of Plato's works*
£5.99

All books are available from your local bookshop or direct from:
Littlehampton Book Services Cash Sales, 14 Eldon Way, Lineside Estate,
Littlehampton, West Sussex BN17 7HE *(prices are subject to change)*

To order any of the books, please enclose a cheque (in sterling) made payable to
Littlehampton Book Services, or phone your order through with credit card details (Access,
Visa or Mastercard) on 01903 721596 (24 hour answering service) stating card number
and expiry date. *(Please add £1.25 for package and postage to the total of your order.)*

In the USA, for further information and a complete catalogue call 1-800-526-2778

SAGAS AND OLD ENGLISH LITERATURE
IN EVERYMAN

Egils Saga
translated by Christine Fell
*A gripping story of Viking exploits
in Iceland, Norway and Britain*
£4.99

Edda
SNORRI STURLUSON
*The first complete English
translation of this important
Icelandic text*
£5.99

Anglo-Saxon Prose
edited by Michael Swanton
*Popular tales of Anglo-Saxon
England, written by kings, scribes
and saints*
£4.99

The Fljotsdale Saga and
The Droplaugarsons
translated by Eleanor Howarth
and Jean Young
*A brilliant portrayal of life and
times in medieval Iceland*
£3.99

Anglo-Saxon Poetry
translated by S. A. J. Bradley
*An anthology of prose translations
covering most of the surviving
poetry of early medieval literature*
£6.99

Fergus of Galloway: Knight of King Arthur
GUILLAME LE CLERC
translated by D. D. R. Owen
*Essential reading for students
of Arthurian romance*
£3.99

Three Arthurian Romances from Medieval France
translated and edited by
Ross G. Arthur
Caradoc, The Knight with the
Sword *and* The Perilous
Graveyard – *poems of the Middle
Ages for modern readers*
£5.99

All books are available from your local bookshop or direct from:
Littlehampton Book Services Cash Sales, 14 Eldon Way, Lineside Estate,
Littlehampton, West Sussex BN17 7HE (*prices are subject to change*)

To order any of the books, please enclose a cheque (in sterling) made payable to
Littlehampton Book Services, or phone your order through with credit card details (Access,
Visa or Mastercard) on 01903 721596 (24 hour answering service) stating card number
and expiry date. (*Please add £1.25 for package and postage to the total of your order.*)

In the USA, for further information and a complete catalogue call 1-800-526-2778

MEDIEVAL LITERATURE
IN EVERYMAN

The Canterbury Tales
GEOFFREY CHAUCER
*The complete medieval text with
translations*
£4.99

The Vision of Piers Plowman
WILLIAM LANGLAND
edited by A. V. C. Schmidt
*The only complete edition of the
B-Text available*
£6.99

**Sir Gawain and the Green
Knight, Pearl, Cleanness,
Patience**
edited by J. J. Anderson
*Four major English medieval
poems in one volume*
£5.99

Arthurian Romances
CHRÉTIEN DE TROYES
translated by D. D. R. Owen
*Classic tales from the father of
Arthurian romance*
£5.99

**Everyman and Medieval
Miracle Plays**
edited by A. C. Cawley
*A fully representative selection
from the major play cycles*
£4.99

Anglo-Saxon Poetry
edited by S. A. J. Bradley
*An anthology of prose translations
covering most of the surviving
poetry of early medieval literature*
£6.99

Six Middle English Romances
edited by Maldwyn Mills
Tales of heroism and piety
£4.99

**Ywain and Gawain,
Sir Percyvell of Gales,
The Anturs of Arther**
edited by Maldwyn Mills
*Three Middle English romances
portraying the adventures of
Gawain*
£5.99

**The Birth of Romance:
An Anthology**
translated by Judith Weiss
*The first-ever English translation
of fascinating Anglo-Norman
romances*
£4.99

The Piers Plowman Tradition
edited by Helen Barr
*Four medieval poems of political
and religious dissent – available
together for the first time*
£5.99

All books are available from your local bookshop or direct from:
Littlehampton Book Services Cash Sales, 14 Eldon Way, Lineside Estate,
Littlehampton, West Sussex BN17 7HE (*prices are subject to change*)

To order any of the books, please enclose a cheque (in sterling) made payable to
Littlehampton Book Services, or phone your order through with credit card details (Access,
Visa or Mastercard) on 01903 721596 (24 hour answering service) stating card number
and expiry date. (*Please add £1.25 for package and postage to the total of your order.*)

In the USA, for further information and a complete catalogue call 1-800-526-2778

DRAMA
IN EVERYMAN

The Oresteia
AESCHYLUS
*New translation of one of the
greatest Greek dramatic trilogies
which analyses the plays in
performance*
£5.99

Everyman and Medieval
Miracle Plays
edited by A. C. Cawley
*A selection of the most popular
medieval plays*
£4.99

Complete Plays and Poems
CHRISTOPHER MARLOWE
*The complete works of this great
Elizabethan in one volume*
£5.99

Restoration Plays
edited by Robert Lawrence
*Five comedies and two tragedies
representing the best of the
Restoration stage*
£7.99

Female Playwrights of the
Restoration: Five Comedies
edited by Paddy Lyons
*Rediscovered literary treasures in
a unique selection*
£5.99

Plays, Prose Writings
and Poems
OSCAR WILDE
*The full force of Wilde's wit
in one volume*
£4.99

A Dolls House/The Lady from
the Sea/The Wild Duck
HENRIK IBSEN
introduced by Fay Weldon
*A popular selection of Ibsen's
major plays*
£4.99

The Beggar's Opera and
Other Eighteenth-Century Plays
JOHN GAY et. al.
Including Goldsmith's She Stoops
To Conquer *and Sheridan's* The
School for Scandal, *this is a volume
which reflects the full scope of the
period's theatre*
£6.99

Female Playwrights of the
Nineteenth Century
edited by Adrienne Scullion
*The full range of female nineteenth-
century dramatic development*
£6.99